The Joan Palevsky Imprint in Classical Literature

In honor of beloved Virgil—

"O degli altri poeti onore e lume . . ."

—Dante, *Inferno*

The publisher gratefully acknowledges

the generous contribution to this book provided by the

Classical Literature Endowment Fund

of the University of California Press Foundation,

which is supported by a major gift from Joan Palevsky.

Rome and the Mysterious Orient

Rome and the Mysterious Orient

THREE PLAYS BY

Plautus

Translated with Introductions and Notes by
Amy Richlin

UNIVERSITY OF CALIFORNIA PRESS
Berkeley   Los Angeles   London

University of California Press, one of the most distinguished
university presses in the United States, enriches lives around the
world by advancing scholarship in the humanities, social sciences, and
natural sciences. Its activities are supported by the UC Press
Foundation and by philanthropic contributions from individuals and
institutions. For more information, visit www.ucpress.edu.

University of California Press
Berkeley and Los Angeles, California

University of California Press, Ltd.
London, England

Library of Congress Cataloging-in-Publication Data

Plautus, Titus Maccius.
Rome and the mysterious Orient : three plays by Plautus / translated with introductions
and notes by Amy Richlin.
p.   cm.
Includes bibliographical references and index.
ISBN 0–520–24274–2 (alk. paper)—ISBN 0–520–24275–0 (pbk. : alk. paper)
1. Plautus, Titus Maccius—Translations into English.   2. Rome—Foreign relations—Drama.
3. East and West—Drama.   4. Imperialism—Drama.   5. Colonies—Drama.
I. Richlin, Amy, 1951–   II. Title.
PA6570.A3R53   2005
872'.01—dc22   2005001618

Manufactured in the United States of America

14   13   12   11   10   09   08   07   06   05

10   9   8   7   6   5   4   3   2   1

Printed on Ecobook 50 containing a minimum 50% post-consumer waste, processed chlorine free.
The balance contains virgin pulp, including 25% Forest Stewardship Council Certified for no old
growth tree cutting, processed either TCF or ECF. The sheet is acid-free and meets the minimum
requirements of ANSI/NISO z39.48–1992 (R 1997) (Permanence of Paper). ⊚

To two great lyricists, Sylvia Richlin and Doris Zuckman

and to Sandra Joshel, marking twenty-five years of comedy

CONTENTS

ILLUSTRATIONS

FIGURES

MAP

ACKNOWLEDGMENTS

In one of my earliest memories, I am crawling rapidly up the aisle of an auditorium in Teaneck, New Jersey, clad in a pair of yellow corduroy overalls, while my mother runs behind me, soon to scoop me up and spend the rest of the concert in the ladies' room. My father, a World War II army vet who had played French horn at the Eastman School, in the cavalry, and in a WPA orchestra, was now playing in the Teaneck Symphony and would soon give up the horn to devote his full attention to being a butcher. On weekends, though, we all used to tool up to Rockland County and hang out with my father's old music-business buddies. Frank and Gardy Baker had just opened up a little theater, the Lyric Theater, and they would put on productions: Alec Wilder, Johnny Barrows, Bill Engvick, Martin Russ. My mother played the comb. This matrix of my formative years goes some way to explain the present volume, I guess. It's too little to say that I'm grateful; those players shine in my memory as if spotlit. I can still hear them laughing, and, for that matter, still use Frank Baker's salad dressing recipe.

Fast forward to the fourth grade. My mother and her friend Doris Zuckman are co-writing the annual Sings for the Teaneck branch of the National Council of Jewish Women, and I'm in trouble with my mean fourth-grade teacher. I've been singing one of their numbers to myself at my desk: (to the tune of "St. James Infirmary Blues") "Oh, I went to my obstetrician, I was trembling in my shoes / Oh, he gave me a quick once over, and then gave me the happy news." Off to the principal; luckily Mr. Graham had a better sense of humor than my teacher.

The professional genesis of this project goes way back, too, and I realize I've been lucky to have been surrounded from the beginning by some of the comic geniuses of twentieth-century Classics. First I want to thank Edward Baxter, wherever he may be, for greeting my first efforts in his Plautus class freshman year with the thunderous ukase "NEVER WRITE OUT A TRANSLATION IN THIS CLASS." This project has taught me the usefulness of writing out a translation, but it was excellent advice at the time; he also made us learn to scan Plautus, which came in handy, too. In graduate school I learned to rewrite under the charming and pitiless scrutiny of Gordon Williams, whose ear for Latin in turn I suppose owes something to his teacher, Eduard Fraenkel; a case of *ego nequior,* I'm afraid, but still a divine ancestry. Jeffrey Henderson, whose low tastes I am proud to share, taught me to read Aristophanes and casually suggested I might see about following his footsteps into obscene humor.

Palmer Bovie, an elegant translator of Plautus, gave me my first job; at Dartmouth (job #2) I was lucky enough to share an office wall with James Tatum, whose Pyramic utterances taught me a great deal then and continue to inspire me. I was there when he was staging his translation of *Bacchides* (see Tatum 1983), and had a peanut-gallery view of how it's done; and simultaneously had the remarkable luck to spend time with Douglass Parker, whose translations of Aristophanes have often dazzled my classrooms. The 1980s also brought me in contact with Holt Parker, bon vivant, wit, champion baker, and leading guru of slave torture humor (see Parker 1989); and with Niall Slater, whose *Plautus in Performance* (1985) opened a vigorous and ongoing discussion of Plautus's metatheatrics. He has since done his best to keep me up to date on his prodigious ongoing work on Plautus, to which I haven't begun to do justice here.

Fast forward again to the summer of 2000, when Nancy Rabinowitz, my long-time feminist comrade-in-arms, talked me into helping her run a seminar for the Faculty Resource Network at New York University, cosponsored, under the auspices of Matthew Santirocco, by the College of Arts and Science and the Center for Ancient Studies. Our topic was "Performing Gender and Sexuality in Ancient Greece and Rome," and this is what first impelled me to write out a translation of *Poenulus.* I want to thank the members of that class, many of them professors of drama, for their encouragement and kindness to someone barging in on their field. Through this seminar I also had the chance to wave the translation at Peter Meineck, Producing Artistic Director of the Aquila Theater Company, who obliged with a reading of the soldier's tirade in act 5 that made me believe the words could really come alive.

As usual, my colleagues at the University of Southern California provided me with a congenial environment for writing as well as with a lot of laughs. To Philip Purchase I owe the lead that first helped me understand the political geography of Plautus: Franco Moretti's *Atlas of the European Novel.* Tom Habinek taught me about Roman oral traditions, Greg Thalmann about slavery. Tony Boyle kindly invited me to talk about Plautine geography at the USC/UCLA Latin Seminar in spring 2004. I would also like to thank Joy Connolly and the Stanford Humanities Center's Mellon Foundation Graduate Research Workshop on Greek and

Roman Performances for an opportunity to work through an earlier stage of the material with them in the spring of 2003.

By the grace of coordinators Marilyn Skinner and Bella Vivante, *Iran Man* had its first production in Tucson at the fourth Feminism and Classics conference in May 2004. Special thanks to them and to the cast—Del Chrol, Toph Marshall, Fred Ahl, Alison Futrell, Mark Damon, Liz Scharffenberger, Tom Talboy, Holly Cohen—for improvements to the script and for showing me how it all works in three dimensions. The November 2004 production at Santa Cruz featured a talented young cast who turned Fat Jack into a drug addict, along with a conference that brought in the sophisticated eye of Michael Evenden, who located Plautus's theater firmly in the context of Roman urban blight. Revision continued through the January 2005 performance at the Boston APA meeting, thanks to the Committee on Ancient and Modern Performance.

My long-suffering family have put up with me during the many times when I could see nothing nearer than Africa. Love and snaps to Linden Grabowski for helping me with vocabulary and attitude.

The final stages of the project were enabled by three people above all. Kate Toll of the University of California Press welcomed the manuscript with enthusiasm, and I wish she had been there to see it through. Mary-Kay Gamel, the queen of ancient drama, not only read the manuscript and provided comments and countless ideas, but directed several productions of the work in progress, including the Tucson, Santa Cruz, and Boston productions of *Iran Man.* She has forgotten more about staging ancient drama than I will ever know, and I bow before her. James Tatum's help and generosity at all stages included sharing with me his own translations in progress of *Persa* and *Poenulus: sine te non.* I am also grateful to have received an okay on the basic principles set out in the introduction, at the eleventh hour and when it was much too late to take it all back, from Sander Goldberg, who really knows Roman comedy.

Speaking of the eleventh hour, the final corrections to the manuscript were made both easier and more pleasant by a happy visit to the University of Cambridge in the spring of 2004, thanks to the kindness of the Faculty of Classics and Newnham College. I would like to express my gratitude to Mary Beard, Helen Morales, Richard Hunter, and Onora O'Neill, Principal of Newnham, for their hospitality. The cover illustration and figures appear by permission of the Syndics of Cambridge University Library, with thanks to Stephen Howe of the Classics Faculty Library for getting me started on the hunt. While at Cambridge I had the opportunity to talk about low humor with one of its leading exponents, Emily

Gowers, whose work on food in comedy (1993) far surpasses what I could do with food here. Aptly, she cooked a delicious dinner for me, which makes me reflect on the high correlation, amongst those I'm thanking, between a sense of humor and an ability to cook.

This book is dedicated to three Muses. To Sandra Joshel, who's stood by me through thick and thin and always manages to make me laugh. To Doris Zuckman, who's still funny, and who, standing amongst the tomato plants, was the first to quote me Bette Davis's immortal line, "Old age ain't for sissies." And to the memory of my mother, Sylvia Richlin, whose slow death accompanied this project, reminding me over and over of the dearness of words and the horror of their loss. *Gentlemen Prefer Blondes* made her laugh for quite a long time, though, also *Mama Makes Up Her Mind* and, appropriately, *Messages from My Father.* Plautus's epitaph would suit her, too:

Since Plautus caught up with death, comedy's grieving,
the stage is empty, for Laughter, Play, and Jokes
and all the countless rhythms weep together.

INTRODUCTION

WHY THIS BOOK

A few years ago, I began to feel an increasing need for materials I could use in teaching about Roman attitudes toward the people they conquered, especially in Africa and the Near East. Since my undergraduate days I've been interested in Roman humor and invective, Roman xenophobia and ethnic stereotyping, and I wanted to teach about Roman attitudes that arguably amount to a kind of racism and are certainly connected with imperialism, and how those attitudes are expressed in comedy and pop culture. Hence *Rome and the Mysterious Orient*. The title takes its form from comedy ("Jeeves and the Impending Doom") and melodrama *(Indiana Jones and the Last Crusade)*, and I hope the translations in this book are funny, but that doesn't mean this book is a joke. The title also deliberately uses an old Orientalist cliché (see Said 1979). My point here is that jokes have a cultural job to do, and I hope this book will help people think about that job and how it gets done.

Between the time when I started and the time of publication, world events have only made such a book more useful. The histories of fighting in (what the West thinks of as) the Near East and of incursions by the West into the East and vice versa are very old, and people need to bear this in mind. I think it is also useful to watch an earlier culture, our ancestor in many ways, process its hatred, fear, curiosity, amusement, fascination, enjoyment, adoption—all this and more—and think about how that tallies, or doesn't, with what goes on now.

But nothing is simple, and I also want this book to raise the possibility that Plautus's plays represent the voice of an underclass talking (partly) to an underclass. That means that what the plays have to say about empire and immigrants and race and language has to be taken in its social and historical context: what was going on in the Mediterranean, who the playwrights were, who the actors were, who was in the audience, who paid for the production. The introductions to the volume and the individual plays, along with the notes, are meant to help answer those questions.

The three plays I picked—*Curculio (Weevil)*, *Persa (Iran Man)*, and *Poenulus (Towelheads)*—have to do with Rome and Greece, Rome and the Balkans, Rome and the Near East, Rome and North Africa. The themes they raise fill other Plautus plays, and you might also want to look at *Captivi (P.O.W.s)*, *Stichus (Lineman)*, and *Trinummus (Three Bucks)*, or . . . But these three make a good start.

WHY TRANSLATE THIS WAY

The translations in this book are full of slang and refer to current events, because that's how Plautus's plays were. Sometimes here the lines use phonetic spelling and nonstandard grammar; these features in the original Latin continue to plague editors and commentators. It has not been standard practice to translate so as to reproduce these aspects of Plautus, and the general approach taken in this book flies in the face of much current scholarly opinion. So why do it?

I was trained in a scholarly tradition that does not consider translation to be scholarship. But writing these translations taught me a lot. The plays are comedies, after all, and I figured that the first thing necessary to convey their meaning to students was for them to be funny—which meant coming up with humor that *is the equivalent now* of what the plays' humor was then. When you do that, you need to know a lot about the ancient context, and you need to think about what is funny *to us,* and which "us," and why. As the great papyrologist H. C. Youtie once remarked, "A translation is the most economical form of commentary" (thanks to Janet Martin); I hope classicists reading this book will take it seriously as a way of reading Plautus. Theater people already know that it don't mean a thing if it ain't got that swing.

All readers: I hope the translation is of use to you, but I strongly encourage you, at every point at which you would argue with my translation, or where it uses slang you wouldn't use, to work out your own version (the notes will give you a literal translation). Please go ahead and plug in what works for you, as in "Mad Libs." These plays were working scripts, not carved in stone.

With texts that were performed, their meaning must largely have been determined by how they worked *in performance.* To translate, you need to take the play off the page—to consider aspects like delivery, and action, and casting, and the space of the theater. You need to consider what would *play;* you need to see and hear it in your head, and laugh. Many studies of Plautus treat the text as a read text, as if the audience would have been composed of college professors (or the second-century B.C.E. equivalent) reading along with libretto in hand—or just reading, without any performance at all to distract them from the job of analysis.

For jokes, it is well established that the function of the form is precisely to discourage the recipient from analyzing the joke content (Richlin 1992a: 60–61, 73). I would postulate that the same must be true for comedy on a larger scale, and that any analysis we do must include an attempt to visualize what was a visual as well as a textual performance, to imagine it in a specific space at a specific historical moment (for expert advice on this, see Gamel 2002).

Or, rather, during a series of moments: plays shoot forward like cannonballs, while textual analysis moves back and forth over a text frozen in time. Though these plays may have been toured or revised, few spectators would have seen a given play more than once, much less read one, during Plautus's lifetime. So our analysis needs to be in terms of a single performance on a single day around 200 B.C.E., and in terms of an audience swept along through runs of gags, barred by laughter from giving any one line a lot of thought. Also, since this audience was composed of many different kinds of people, *the plays interpellate the audience segmentally and intermittently.* That is, different lines of the play address different audience members in their various social roles, thereby reinforcing those roles, and not all audience members are being addressed at any one time (see Althusser 1971 on interpellation). The one set of people who would have had the kind of intimate knowledge of the plays that we now associate with scholarship would have been the actors themselves.

There is a big problem with level in translations of Plautus. We don't know what to do with these plays. They're in Latin, they're classical, so that makes them highbrow; Shakespeare based plays on them, that adds another highbrow layer. We dress the players in togas (wrong, anyway, they wore Greek outfits, the *pallium*), keep the names as Plautus wrote them, and set them on the way to the forum. And, too often, we translate the Latin into a sort of scholarly humor, based closely on the original text. The translations in this volume take a shot at matching lowbrow with lowbrow and pop culture with pop culture.

Warning: these plays were not originally politically correct in the sense "not capable of offending an oppressed group." (They *were* politically correct in the sense "dumping on nations against whom Rome currently has troops deployed.") The plays include ethnic slurs—this is the point of translating these plays in particular, to trace the history of xenophobia. Translating the title of *Poenulus* as *Towelheads,* in particular, may seem problematic (for an explanation, see the introduction to the play). The amazing thing about *Poenulus* is that, though it was written very shortly after the peninsula of Italy had been steamrollered by Carthaginian troops, the main characters find out at the end of the play that they are all Carthaginians, and they are delighted. The attitude of these plays is not simple.

CONVENTIONS OF REFERENCE AND ABBREVIATIONS

Classicists refer to the plays of Plautus by their Latin title followed by the line numbers (i.e., they don't use conventions like "act 1, scene 2," though Plautus's plays were divided into acts and scenes in the Renaissance, and the Oxford text replicates these divisions; see Beare 1964: 196–218). Lines are numbered consecutively, starting from the first line of the play and going straight through to the end. The translations in this book are based on the Oxford Classical Text (OCT) edited by W. M. Lindsay and follow his line numbering; except as noted, the plays are translated word for word and line for line, so you can reliably compare a given line here with the Latin text. Sometimes Lindsay changed the order of the lines in the manuscripts; at those points, you will see out-of-sequence numbers here, too. In the few places where I have added words or phrases for clarity, I have enclosed them in curved brackets, {}.

When modern editors analyze ancient texts, they will sometimes print lines from extant manuscripts that they believe not to have been in the original but consider important enough still to be printed. These lines appear in square brackets, [], in scholarly editions like the Oxford Classical Texts, and such lines appear in this volume still in square brackets. Likewise, editors will sometimes insert words when they feel certain they were originally there, and such words appear between angle brackets, <>, in the OCT and here.

The Latin titles of the three plays in this volume are *Curculio* (this word literally means "Weevil," which luckily is still a funny word); *Persa* (this literally means "the man from Persia," a location that corresponds to modern Iran, hence *Iran Man*); and *Poenulus* (this literally means "The Little Punic Guy," but see the play's introduction). The plays are conventionally referred to by various abbreviations of their Latin titles, so that elsewhere you may, for example, see lines 1–10 of *Curculio* cited as *Curc.* 1–10 or *Cu.* 1–10.

The one standard reference work referred to throughout by its abbreviated title is the *Oxford Latin Dictionary,* abbreviated as *OLD.*

HOW THESE PLAYS GOT FROM PLAUTUS TO US

Plautus's plays were originally performed around the year 200 B.C.E., but they seem not to have been formally published or collected for about 150 years; scholars guess that actual scripts held by actors were collected for publication at that point, though others may have been in circulation previously. After that, these plays basically never quite went out of print—though until the fifteenth century, the only way they could be reproduced was by hand copying, which means that there was a great deal of room for errors to slip in (see MacCary and Willcock 1976: 233–35 for a quick description of the manuscript tradition). With the invention of the printing press, Plautus's popularity becomes evident; there are, for example, more than twenty-five editions dating from 1510 to 1605, printed all over Europe, in the Cambridge University Library. In 1594, Thomas Nashe gives one of the characters in his proto-novel *The Unfortunate Traveller* the chance to see famous men from antiquity, and his first request is for "pleasant *Plautus* [. . .] in what habit he went, and with what countenaunce he lookt when he ground corne in the mil" (cited by Riehle 1990: 1). Shakespeare would have been assigned the plays to read in Latin at the school he attended (Riehle 1990: 12, 279–83), and it is likely that he knew them well. The Elizabethans were big on performing both Roman plays and updated versions of them; schoolboys began performing Plautus's plays in Latin at Westminster School in 1560 (Zinn 1965).

Translating ancient texts was a highly charged political act in early modern England, part of a youth movement that aimed to shake up established ideas, and here Plautus played a small part; Edward Courtney, duke of Devonshire, translated *Amphitryo* in 1562/63 (Conley 1967 [1927]: 143). But until the twentieth century it would have been expected that a person interested in Plautus would know Latin and read, perform, or watch the plays in the original; the first translation of the collected plays into English does not appear until 1769–74—and, though charming, it's bowdlerized, despite the fact that it was organized by Bonnell Thornton, one of the great wits of eighteenth-century London (see Bertelsen 1986). In other words, Plautus himself was for the educated, while most people would have known Plautus, without realizing it, through plays in the vernacular that used Plautine elements.

The late nineteenth century saw the rise of affordable editions of Latin texts for use in teaching and for scholarly reference; these texts incorporate notes that show, in highly condensed form, what the text editor has learned about possible variants in the text from looking at manuscripts and the work of previous scholars. The Oxford Classical Text on which this translation is based is one such text, produced by W. M. Lindsay, a great scholar of early Latin, in the early twentieth century. Though such a text is recognized as standard, it is really an amalgamation of Lindsay's decisions at many points, and in this volume the introductions to *Iran Man* and *Towelheads* talk about their textual peculiarities.

Illustrations of the plays are rare, even in the sixteenth-century editions. Figures 1 and 2 show captioned illustrations from a 1511 edition printed in Venice from the collection of the Cambridge University Library (Sel.2.63). Figure 1 appears at the

Han/ no pœ.

Hanno pœnus loquitur punice:

FIGURE 1. Illustration at *Poenulus* act 5, scene 1, from a 1511 edition of Plautus's plays in the Cambridge University Library, Sel.2.63. By permission of the Syndics of Cambridge University Library.

head of act 5, scene 1, and carries the caption "Hanno Poenus loquitur Punice" ("Hanno the Punic speaks in Punic"); this caption appears at the head of the scene in many sixteenth-century editions. Though at this point in Venetian history we might have expected Hanno dressed as a Turk, he seems to be depicted as a Moor. This is clearer in the illustration from the head of act 5, scene 2, which shows Hanno with Milphio and Agorastocles (their order in the caption is reversed). The illustrations in this edition are, as it were, rubber stamps, repeated identically though not consistently from scene to scene (i.e., there were two stamps for "a young man"); Hanno is the only character to be shown consistently. The other Carthaginian characters are shown as Venetians; the characters disguised as Persian and Arabian in *Persa* are shown as Venetians; only Hanno is singled out. To these readers in the Renaissance, the color of his skin is as important as the language he speaks.

Dramatis Personae and Scene Headings

The lists of characters and roles at the beginning of each play do not come from the ancient manuscripts, but depend on the lists of characters and roles in the scene headings, which do (see Packman 1999; Lindsay 1904). However, the scene headings themselves were greatly battered over time, and have often had to be re-

FIGURE 2.   Illustration at *Poenulus* act 5, scene 2, from a 1511 edition of Plautus's plays in the Cambridge University Library, Sel.2.63. By permission of the Syndics of Cambridge University Library.

stored (i.e., guessed at). Names and roles are thus not only subject to editorial revision but have in some cases just been fashioned by editors. In most of the early printed texts I looked at, "Persa" is given as the name of the girl who is sold in *Iran Man* (today she's just "Virgo," and editors agree that the "Persa" is one of the male characters), the nanny in *Towelheads* is named "Giddeneme" (now she's "Giddenis"), and the pimp in *Iran Man* is called "Dorpalus" (now "Dordalus").

Stage Directions, Line Assignments, Sets

There are no stage directions printed in the Oxford text, and there probably never were any. The extant manuscripts do not assign lines to characters, either, but only mark where a new speaker begins, and sometimes even this is in question. Thus the line assignments in the OCT represent Lindsay's opinion, taking into account the opinions of centuries of scholars. The text itself provides a lot of explicit cues; working from this, like other translators, I have inserted stage directions, which here appear in italics. These should be taken as entirely hypothetical. Likewise with line assignments: in *Iran Man,* for example, I have incorporated quite a few changes to the OCT based on Erich Woytek's commentary.

The stage set for Plautus's plays is commonly the fronts of two or three buildings, with doors leading inward, while the stage L exit (on the spectators' right) represents "to town" and the stage R exit represents "to the harbor" (see Beare 1964: 255). For an experience-based hypothesis on the physical stage Plautus might have used, along with an account of a production, see Beacham 1991.

The doors are a major feature of every Plautine stage setting, and (as in all ancient drama) represent the barrier between inside and outside; they always make a loud creaking noise when opening, as cued by a thousand lines *(concrepuit foris,* "the door has creaked"). In Roman culture, this focus on doors matches a well-attested folk custom, *occentatio,* in which a person's enemies would stand in front of his house, exchange insults with him in front of the door, possibly write insults on it, and (I suppose in extreme cases) set fire to it (Lintott 1999: 6–10; Habinek 2005). The insults seem to have taken a specific, formalized pattern, like the Dozens in African-American culture, and Plautus's comedies include insult matches that follow this pattern; there is a good one in *Iran Man* between Toxilus (Bowman) and the pimp Dordalus (Dorkalot), and there are references to *occentatio* in both *Weevil* and *Iran Man.* (Indeed, there are insult matches in many of the twenty extant plays, and I think it is safe to assume that the audience would have looked forward to them, like the patter songs in the Savoy operas. They are fun to translate, but even better in Latin, for example *Towelheads* 1313: *manstruca, halagora, sampsa!*) All Roman comedy, as many have remarked, artificially yanks the inside action out into the street, turning the audience into rubberneckers. Readers should realize that this would not have been an unfamiliar position for a Roman audience to be in.

Prologues and Argumenta

The prologues that appear in some of the extant plays were, in their Roman form, something new: an effort to win over the audience (Beare 1964: 159–61). Some seem to have been added to the plays after Plautus, in revivals. No prologue is extant for *Weevil* or *Iran Man,* but the one for *Towelheads* is famous for its full depiction of the audience and stage crew, its double account of the play's content, its references to the play's sources, and its metatheatrical ending (see Slater 1992).

All three plays also have an *argumentum,* or synopsis of the play, something like the pitch that is now made for a screenplay: a short, punchy overview. The unusual thing about the Plautine ones is that, in some of them, the first letter of each line spells out the title of the play, reading down the lines—a sort of word game called an "acrostic." None of the *argumenta* were originally part of the plays; they were added by editors or owners of manuscripts, the acrostic ones probably in the fifth century C.E., when acrostics were popular (Lindsay 1904: 86–87). Though the *argumenta* were written as a feature of a read text, and not of a performance, especially in the case of *Iran Man* I think a production might want to perform the *argumentum,* perhaps using letters on placards to show the audience the point. The *argumenta* appear here on the title page of each play.

OTHER TRANSLATIONS

As noted above, translation of the collected plays of Plautus into English begins in the eighteenth century; Bonnell Thornton's five-volume set (1769–74) incorporates translations by various hands. In the nineteenth century, Bohn's Classical Library offered the collected plays translated by Henry Thomas Riley, which went through many printings (1881 [1852]); in the early twentieth, the Loeb Classical Library offered a five-volume set translated by Paul Nixon (1916–38; still in print). George Duckworth's *Complete Roman Drama* (1942) includes a translation of *Persa* by Charles T. Murphy, who titled the play *The Persian Girl,* though he noted that the Persa in the play is the man who sells the girl. The Slavitt/Bovie collection (still in print) brings us up to the late twentieth century (see Bovie 1995).

Collections matter because *Curculio, Persa,* and *Poenulus* have been infrequently translated and are relatively little known, compared with *Miles Gloriosus* (source of *A Funny Thing Happened on the Way to the Forum*) and *Menaechmi* (source of *The Comedy of Errors* and *The Boys from Syracuse,* among others). Among notable versions, *Poenulus* was produced in Latin in 1994 at Chapel Hill by John H. Starks Jr., who also provides a teacher's edition (1997, with condensed translation) and a video; both *Poenulus* and *Persa* are now being translated by James Tatum. In 1970, *Poenulus* was translated by Janet Burroway, who provides an extremely clever treatment that gives a much better sense of the wordplay in the original than I have been able to do; her goals are poetic, where mine have more to do with social history and performance. For details of C. W. Marshall's masked production of *Curculio,* see www.cnrs.ubc.ca/masc. On translations, see also the bibliography.

HISTORICAL BACKGROUND

Who Was Plautus?

You can look in any encyclopedia or handbook that covers Roman culture and find out that we don't actually know much about Plautus at all. His name is suspiciously meaningful—Titus Maccius Plautus. "Maccius," supposedly his family name, sounds like a fancy version of "Maccus," which was the name of one of the stock characters in the popular lowbrow ancient Italian drama form called Atellane farce, and "Plautus" supposedly meant "flat-footed" (Paulus ex Festo 275L; Beare 1964: 47) and was a term associated with the barefoot players in another popular lowbrow ancient Italian drama form, mime (nothing like Marcel Marceau, more like ensemble standup comedy). Or it might just mean "floppy." There is no contemporary information on him by other writers. We cannot even be 100 percent certain that he wrote under the name T. Maccius Plautus—the "Plautus" part is certain, the "T. Maccius" part is slightly iffy. Adrian Gratwick argues that even the "Titus" part was funny, in the same way that the name "Dick" is funny now (1973), and that in this period of Roman history a three-part name would have sounded hoity-toity. If this was his name, let us start right out by contemplating what it means to take a name that translates as "R. Harpoe Clownshoes III (just call me 'Dick')," or possibly "R. Harpoe Floppé (call me 'Dick')."

He is the earliest Roman writer for whom we have any complete works; there are twenty extant plays and a small part of a twenty-first. However, he probably wrote more plays than this (the first-century B.C.E. literary historian Varro picked these out of 130 circulating under Plautus's name [Gellius 3.3.3, 3.3.11, cf. Beare 1964: 45–46]); he is a sophisticated, complex writer of a form that already can parody its own clichés; and there were plenty of other playwrights around when he was writing—we just do not have their work. John Wright's book *Dancing in Chains* (1974) gives an excellent account of the fragments we do have, though (unfortunately for theater historians) he does not translate the Latin. The important ones are Caecilius Statius, a younger playwright whose work some major Roman critics preferred to Plautus's; Gnaeus Naevius; Livius Andronicus; and Quintus Ennius (all of these but Caecilius also wrote tragedies and nondramatic literature), and Wright convincingly shows that their comedy was a lot like Plautus's. Terence (Publius Terentius Afer), the other Roman comic playwright whose plays have survived, would make his brief appearance twenty years after Plautus's death; his comedy, as Wright and many others have felt and shown, is quite different from Plautus's (see Goldberg 1986).

We have very little to go on to date the plays or Plautus's life. *Didascaliae*—very brief headnotes on the circumstances of production—survive for two plays, *Pseudolus* and *Stichus*. Because they include the names of magistrates, we can date these plays to 191 B.C.E. and 200 B.C.E. respectively; however, even this minimal information is shaky (see Mattingly 1957). In addition, the prologue of one play, *Cistellaria,* contains two lines (201–2) cheering the Romans on to victory against the Carthaginians, which seems to date this play before the end of the Second Punic War in 201 B.C.E. And there may possibly be a reference in *Miles Gloriosus* (lines 211–12) to an incident involving the playwright Naevius that took place in

205 B.C.E. This is it—all other dating of Plautus's plays is conjectural. We have no idea how successful any of the plays were, except that the extant prologue of *Casina* suggests that it was revived, perhaps after Plautus's death. We do not in fact know when *Poenulus* was written relative to the Punic War. We know that Plautus came before Terence, because Terence in the prologue to his *Andria* lists Plautus, Naevius, and Ennius as his predecessors (see H. Parker 1996 for what we do not know about Terence).

The putative facts about Plautus come from four writers who lived long after him: Cicero (103 B.C.E.–43 B.C.E.); Pompeius Festus (late 100s C.E.), who made a condensed version of a dictionary written in the first century B.C.E. by Verrius Flaccus; Aulus Gellius (fl. 130s C.E.); and Jerome (fifth century C.E.). To put this in perspective, Cicero was as far distant in time from Plautus as we are from Gilbert and Sullivan; Jerome was a hundred years farther from Plautus than we are from Columbus. Cicero only says a few things about Plautus, but seems to have been relying on relatively fresh information. The rest are relying on literary historians whose work we know only through them. And even Festus is partly known to us only through an even later writer, Paulus Diaconus (late 700s C.E.), who made a condensed condensed version of Flaccus, known as "Paulus ex Festo."

Cicero says (*Brut.* 60) that Plautus died when Cato the Censor was censor, in what we call 184 B.C.E. If so, we might guess that the plays were mostly written between 210 and 184; Cicero says elsewhere (*Sen.* 50) that as an old man Plautus took pleasure in writing *Truculentus* and *Pseudolus,* but all this tells us is which plays Cicero liked (so, rightly, Beare 1964: 63), nor do we know *how* old. Let's be conservative and date the plays to a span of time from 224 B.C.E. to 184 B.C.E.

Paulus ex Festo (275L) and Jerome (s.a. 200 B.C.E.) say that Plautus came from Sarsina, in Umbria. What does that mean? If it is true, it is profoundly interesting. Sarsina is in the middle of nowhere: a small town in the Sapis River valley, tucked well back in the Apennines, a good twenty miles from the highway, the via Aemilia, down which lay the nearest large town, Ariminum, northward along the Adriatic (east) coast of Italy, in short about a million miles away from Rome. Umbria at the time of Plautus's birth was not exactly a Roman place; it was an ally of Rome—the mid-second-century B.C.E. historian Polybius says that "Umbrians and Sarsinates" (note the division) sent 20,000 men to help resist the Gauls in 225 B.C.E. (2.24), and that is about all he has to say about either Sarsina or Umbria. Indeed, according to the figures projected by the demographer P. A. Brunt (1971: 54), in 225 B.C.E., Umbria had the lowest population of free persons of all the regions of Italy, and the smallest territory; the number of free persons per square mile in Umbria is lower than that of any area except Etruria (then full of large grain-producing plantations), and the next regions higher are Apulia and Lucania (proverbially poor). People from Sarsina would not have had Roman citizenship in Plautus's time (see Salmon 1982: 96).

From a Roman perspective, the whole area was a backwater, barely mentioned by Roman historians of the period. It wasn't even Latin-speaking: Umbrian was a separate language, with its own alphabet. During Plautus's childhood, Umbrian would not yet have given way to Latin (Salmon 1982: 122–23). In short, Sarsina is exactly the sort of place that throughout the multiverse has always exported writers to big cities, each in turn slamming the door on the way out and trying out a stage name (Harpoe Clownshoes?). If [insert birth name here] was not from Sarsina, he should have been, or from someplace similar.

Jerome says that Plautus went to Rome, where he had *annonae difficultatem,* "trouble with the cost of living," and so hired himself out *(se locaverat)* to a miller to work in a *molae manuariae,* a "hand-operated mill." This story goes back to the first-century B.C.E. literary historian Varro, according to Gellius, who says (3.3.14)

> *Saturionem* et *Addictum* et tertiam quandam, cuius nunc mihi nomen non suppetit, in pistrino eum scripsisse Varro ait et plerique alii memoriae tradiderunt, cum pecunia omni, quam in operis artificum scaenicorum pepererat, in mercatibus perdita inops Romam redisset et ob quaerundum victum ad circumagendas molas, quae trusatiles appellantur, operam pistori locasset.

> Varro says, and many others have handed down the story, that he wrote *Fatso* and *Wage Slave* and a third play, the name of which now escapes me, in a mill. He had lost in trading ventures all the money that he had made in jobs related to the theater, and had returned to Rome, broke, and in order to make enough money to eat he had hired out his labor to a miller, for turning the mill (the kind they call a push-mill).

This story has him first come to Rome, [then] achieve some success in "jobs related to the theater" (this is a somewhat vague phrase and could mean acting or production as well as writing), [then] leave and lose it all in trade, and then return to Rome penniless to work in the mill.

What does that mean? Working in a mill was slave labor, and labor for slaves who were being punished, like a chain gang; some mills (where flour comes from) were powered by treadmills powered by human feet (for a harrowing description of what this did to the mill slaves, see Apuleius *Metamorphoses* 9.12; I can never look at the treadmills now pounded by well-heeled feet in gyms without thinking of it as a slave punishment). The extant plays of Plautus, which include neither

Fatso nor *Wage Slave,* are full of black-comedy allusions to the threat the mill posed for slaves. Whether this is what really happened to Plautus or only what later people liked to say about him, it implies that his social status was very low. In Roman law, *locatio*—working for pay—was much looked down upon, as if, like prostitutes, gladiators, and actors, you were selling your own body, as in self-imposed slavery; an *addictus* is a person who has been enslaved for debt or theft. Let us be conservative and say that this story at least does not conflict with the content of Plautus's extant plays—that the plays have a lot in them about trading ventures and losing all your money and slaves and mills. In Plautus's *Captivi (P.O.W.s)*, a freeborn person winds up working in the quarries, which were even worse than the mills.

Gellius says that Varro and his other, unnamed sources say that Plautus wrote three plays while actually working in the mill; Jerome says Plautus wrote and sold his plays in his spare time at the mill. Again, this is the kind of story people tell about writers now (think of Quentin Tarantino in the video store), but how normal was it for the period? Never mind the question of how you would write plays in your nonexistent spare time, by the light of an oil lamp—maybe in your head, this was an oral culture—is this story consistent with the time?

Very much so. A lot of people lost their homes and property in the late 200s and 190s B.C.E., though more from the aftereffects of war than from trade. And the writers of this period all reflect in their biographies the events of the time. (Note that all these "biographies" are known to us from much later sources and may be entirely fictitious. Or not.) Livius Andronicus was supposedly a Roman prisoner of war (i.e., he was enslaved—his name shows he was born Andronicus and freed by a man named Livius), from the Roman capture of Tarentum, in southern Italy. Naevius fought in the First Punic War, which ended in 241 B.C.E., and was said to have come from Campania, the area around what is now Naples; he is also said to have ended his life as a political exile. Ennius was a soldier who came to Rome with the Cato who later became censor; he is said to have come originally from Rudiae in southern Italy, which was a tiny town (Brunt 1971: 127 says it had about 500 male citizens in the second century C.E.), and to have said that he had three hearts because he spoke Greek, Oscan, and Latin (Gellius 17.17.1). Indeed, the story goes that Cato picked him up in Sardinia when on his way home from being stationed in Africa (Nepos *Cat.* 1; cf. Astin 1978); Cato had no military business in Sardinia that we know of, and it seems at least plausible that what made him add Ennius to his entourage was seeing him performing, not seeing him pitching a tent. Jerome says Caecilius Statius was an Insubrian Gaul, "some say from Milan" (a big Insubrian center in this period), and at first was Ennius's *contubernalis,* which could mean he served in the army with Ennius or that he was Ennius's roommate; Gellius (4.20.13) says he was a slave and that "Statius" is a slave name. If this is true, the name "Caecilius" would have come from his former master, and his birth name is unknown to us. Most of these are rags to rock star stories; all the writers come to Rome from elsewhere, most of them from the Greek- and Oscan-speaking south, Caecilius from the Celtic north.

Amongst the writers of the next generation, Accius is said by Suetonius to have been the son of freed slaves from Pisaurum in Umbria (land of Plautus). And Terence was supposedly born at Carthage around 185 B.C.E. and came to Rome as the slave of a man named Terentius Lucanus. His name, P. Terentius Afer, means "I was the slave of P. Terentius, who freed me," and "I come from Africa." It is unlikely that Latin was the first language of any of these writers, and, if these stories are at all true, all of them would have experienced hunger and war, several of them slavery and the loss of name and family. In this company it makes some sense to have lost your given name and write as Harpoe Clownshoes.

Plautus wrote his own material but, like his fellow writers, famously based his plays on comedies written in Greek and produced throughout the Greek-speaking Mediterranean in the late 300s and 200s B.C.E., known as New Comedy or *Nea.* In the nineteenth and early twentieth centuries, classical scholars did a great deal of work on Plautus, both to arrive at the best reconstruction of a text full of slang, rare or unique words, abbreviations, and jokes, and to try to decide what the relationship was between Plautus and his Greek originals. I personally find the scanty remains of these Greek originals so unfunny, and so different from Plautus, that I am happy to say that writers on Roman drama since the 1950s have been putting more emphasis on what is Roman about Plautus and on the (hypothetical) relation between what Plautus wrote and the (lost) very-low-culture genres of mime and Atellane farce. I think that Plautus and his lowlife companions on the Roman stage may have developed Roman comedy in the work farms and dives of war-torn Italy, the way James Brown came out of the county farm in the 1950s (Gourevitch 2002), and the way Public Enemy came out of the ghettos of the Reagan years. Maybe they used some pieces of plays they'd remembered or heard told, as in *Kiss of the Spider Woman,* but the music especially seems to have been all their own. Of the three plays presented here, only *Poenulus* has even the name of a Greek play given as source—*Karkhedonios* ("The Carthaginian")—and this is given in the prologue of the play itself, and may be a joke (see John Henderson 1999). No source at all is known for *Curculio* or *Persa,* and a great deal of both of them is so Roman that the idea of a "Greek original" becomes fairly meaningless.

It's true that this kind of comedy is known as *palliata*, "comedy wearing the *pallium*"(which was a sort of short cape worn by Greeks), and there are plenty of jokes in Plautus that show the actors were wearing the *pallium*. Another form of comedy developed later in the second century B.C.E. in which actors did wear the toga, and these plays were set in Italy, which the *palliata* were not. Actors in the *palliata* also wore *socci,* slippers or soft shoes, and this was one point of distinction between them and the barefoot actors in mime. But this clothing is worn self-consciously and often ironically, as will be seen in *Weevil* and *Iran Man.*

Background on Roman Culture

Other ways to read Plautus: it helps to understand the systems of Roman culture—slavery, marriage, sex/gender, law, war, performance, as well as politics. See "Suggestions for Further Reading" below. If you have only this book to go by, maybe the following will be enough:

- Roman slavery was a permeable institution in places. Urban household slaves were often freed, especially personal slaves who knew their masters; slaves who worked on the plantations that took over the Italian countryside in the second century B.C.E., or in the mines, mills, and shipping that fueled the Roman economy, had little hope of anything but an early death.

- Sources of fresh slaves included war (prisoners), sale (by impoverished parents), kidnapping (by pirates or other bad people). Because the whole Mediterranean was a war zone during this period, the number of slaves skyrocketed. Prisoners of war could be ransomed, but this was always dicey (see Leigh 2004: 57–97; Thalmann 1996).

- Once freed, Roman slaves owed specific kinds of allegiance to their former owners, and often continued to work for them and receive help from them. The ex-owner was now the *patronus* or *patrona,* the freed slave the *libertus* or *liberta* and a Roman citizen.

- Roman citizens could not legally be subjected to corporal punishment, whereas a whole array of punishments was meted out to slaves, of which crucifixion is only the best known today. An urban household slave could be punished by being transferred to the country or the mill. Freed slaves lived in a middle ground; their ex-owner retained some rights over their bodies.

- The Roman sex/gender system was different from current Western systems. It was normative for adult males to perceive both women and adolescent males as sex objects, though citizen boys were supposed to be off limits (see *Weevil* 33–38 for the classic statement of these norms). Girls could marry as young as age twelve, and would normally marry for the first time in their teens. Sex between women is little discussed in Roman texts. Adult males who wanted to be sexually penetrated by other men were the object of mockery and suffered civil disabilities. See Hallett 1997; Richlin 1992a, 1993, 1997a.

- All slaves were available for sex with citizens.

- Prostitutes could either be slaves, often owned by a pimp, or free, trained by a prostitute mother who brought them up to the trade. Prostitutes were *infames,* subject to civil disabilities; see Edwards 1997; McGinn 1998; McGinn 2004: 55–71. On the sale of children by their families, see *Iran Man* introduction.

- Slaves could not legally marry anyone; their unions were not recognized by law, and their children were the property of the master.

- Roman citizen women, though they married very young, did not lead sheltered lives, and (as well as participating in business, city life, and culture) they attended the theater; as did slaves (see Moore 1994; Goldberg 1998).

- The ideal adult male Roman citizen, for example, Cato, was involved in law, politics, and the army, which by the 180s B.C.E. had established Roman hegemony throughout much of the Mediterranean.

- The Roman army was organized by property classes; the rich were officers, the poorest were ineligible to serve. The army was filled by draft. After the Second Punic War, as Rome fought a series of preemptive wars in Greece and the Near East, the property qualifications for the infantry were lowered.

- The world of the ancient theater left quite a trail behind it: whole theaters, some still in use; souvenir figures; tickets (tokens); theater-inspired wall paintings; theater-fan graffiti still readable on the walls of Pompeii (for material remains, see Bieber 1961).

War, History, Geography

The period during which Plautus's plays were produced was crammed with major geopolitical events, with massive social changes within Italy, and with a huge boom in literary production. No one doubts that these phenomena were connected, but it is usually asserted that Plautus is not a topical playwright like Aristophanes (fifth century B.C.E., Athens), whose plays are full of jokes about persons then living. I wish to side with the small minority who have argued that Plautus was a topical writer (Gruen 1990; Harvey 1986; and see now especially Leigh 2004).

The map on page 18 shows all the places that feature in this volume; the shaded areas are places where Rome fought wars during this period. As Franco Moretti argues in *Atlas of the European Novel* (1998: 3), "geography is not an inert container, is not a box where cultural history 'happens,' but an active force, that pervades the literary field and shapes it in depth." Mapping the plays of Plautus shows us that they do not keep still; most of them involve travel, in war zones, between Here and There. And very often There is part of the Orient, a place of radical otherness. Edward Said, in *Orientalism,* begins by saying, "The Orient was almost a European invention, and had been since antiquity a place of romance, exotic beings, haunting memories and landscapes, remarkable experiences" (1979: 1). This is what defines Plautus's landscape, and forms the setting for playwrights, actors, and audience as well as characters and stories.

What people exactly were the Romans fighting? Plautus's adulthood runs at most from about 244 B.C.E. to about 184, and Rome was engaged with her neighbors on all fronts at this time. Most crucial were the wars with Carthage: the First Punic War, which started in 264, didn't end until 241, and the Second ran from 218 to 201. The twenty-year gap between them was occupied with, among other fights, a major invasion of Italy by Gauls from the north that got as far as Etruria. After this, Hannibal's invasion ravaged the peninsula and famously got up to the very gates of Rome.

Meanwhile, Rome was also involved in "pacifying" Italy itself. And the rest of the Mediterranean was a mess. During these years, Rome fought major wars and some good-sized interventions against or in Sicily, Sardinia, Histria, and Illyria (roughly what subsequently became Yugoslavia and Albania), Macedon, Rhodes, and other states in the Near East and Greece, including the Aetolian League. Leaders of these states—King Philip V of Macedon, King Attalus of Pergamum, the Seleucid kings of the former Persian empire including Antiochus the Great—show up in Plautus's plays embedded in catchphrases, as if everybody knows who they are. Greece was chaotic during this period, and the Romans were only part of the problem, amidst a welter of massacres, purges, forced exiles, and refugees. The scene was volatile; some areas, for example Caria and Lycia in what is now southern Turkey, were political footballs, much like the West Bank or Kashmir at present. Each war made new roles for people: soldier, veteran, prisoner of war, refugee, exile, slave, widow, orphan, prostitute.

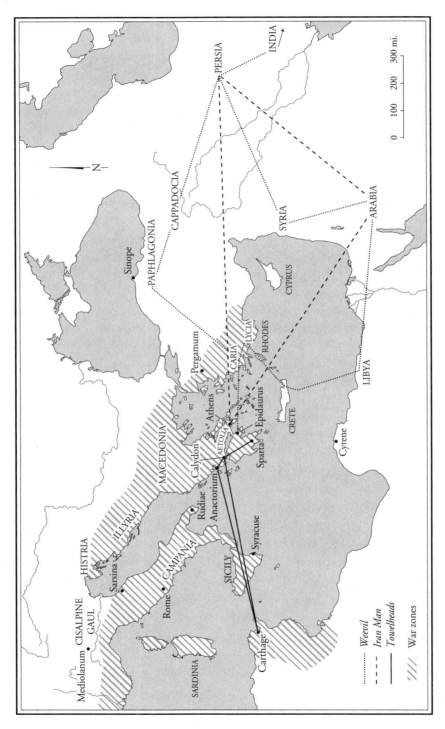

Travels in Plautus. Adapted from R. M. Errington, *The Dawn of Empire* (Ithaca, N.Y.: Cornell University Press, 1972).

Those who were enslaved did not always accept this as a permanent change in their lives. Military campaigns dumped batches of slaves all over the Italian countryside, and, though the new slaves came from different cultures, they still managed to band together and rebel (see Shaw 2001 for a collection of translated accounts). These stories are, for Roman narrators, stories of trouble for themselves. But even with this top-down view, we do get some idea of these slaves' agency and strategy.

Actors

Were the actors who performed Plautus's plays mostly slaves? We don't know for sure, but here at least there is some internal evidence from the plays. The only actor whose name is associated with Plautus is a male Roman citizen, T. Publilius Pellio, whose name appears in the *Stichus* didascalia, though the word "acted" there is a conjectural addition; Pellio is also mentioned in a joke in one of the plays *(Bacchides* 215) as having acted in *Epidicus.*

How about the rest of the cast? The prologues and epilogues of the plays, which have a liminal quality as if the actors were speaking as themselves, occasionally hint at the actors' status. The actors are a *grex,* a "herd" (*Asinaria* 2–3, *Casina* 22, *Pseudolus* 1334), with *domini* ("masters") and *conductores* ("bosses," i.e., men who hire people, *Asinaria* 2–3), and at the end of the *Cistellaria* the speaker(s) of the epilogue say that actors who did a bad job will be beaten, while those who did a good job will get a drink (785). At the end of the *Casina* prologue, the speaker implies that the actor who played Casina will have sex for money (84–86; cf. *Truculentus* 965–66). We do know of one participant in the plays who was definitely a slave: according to the didascalia, the music for *Stichus* was performed by Marcipor Oppii. This old-fashioned slave name means "Marcus's boy, [slave of] Oppius," that is, "slave of Marcus Oppius." Similarly, the didascaliae for all of Terence's plays list the same freed slave musician: Flaccus, freedman of Claudius. Again, by the first century B.C.E., we know that actors were *infames,* like prostitutes (Edwards 1997); indeed, "mime actress" is pretty much synonymous with "prostitute" in elite writers. Beare concludes that it is safe to assume that "the social status of the average actor in tragedy or comedy was probably not high" (1964: 167). This seems like a safe bet; put another way, there is nobody associated with the theater in the second century B.C.E. who is any kind of an aristocrat, except the sponsors.

Were all the roles played by male actors? We don't really know (Garton 1972; Rawson 1985), though this is normally assumed. There is plentiful evidence for male actors playing female roles in other types of drama in antiquity, but one Roman lowbrow form—mime—was co-ed. If male actors did play female roles in the *palliata,* were they thought of as effeminate? The *cinaedus* (originally a Greek word, *kinaidos*) is associated in Plautus with what the Victorian commentators called "lewd dancing"; by the 140s B.C.E., it is a rude word for an adult male who likes to be on the receiving end of anal sex (see Richlin 1992a: 93, 165; 1993). Could *cinaedi* have been playing the female roles, or some of them? Maybe parts like those of Tchotchka and Katya in *Towelheads* were played by *cinaedi,* who would then have been something like drag queens (see C. Williams 1999). The last act of *Iran Man* features a scene in which three male characters do a sort of mocking dance around the pimp, and one of the four is called a *cinaedus* (see notes at *Iran Man* 804).

Most of the roles in comedy are male. And it is easy to think of examples of modern comedy groups with few or no female players: the Pythons (but with Carol Cleveland), the Marx Brothers (but with Margaret Dumont), the Three Stooges, Firesign Theater. Arguably, comedy troupes just manifest the male-bonding aspect of comedy and humor (Richlin 1992a: 58–59, 74–75, 79), as seen in Harvard's Hasty Pudding Club, Princeton's Triangle Club, and the staff of humor magazines (notably the *National Lampoon* and *Mad*). *Saturday Night Live* is unusual in its gender balance.

Suppose all the roles in Plautus were played by male actors. Then *Towelheads* is not just a romantic comedy, it is a romantic comedy with a large drag-show element in it; *Weevil* likewise features both a romantic female lead played in drag and a drunken old bag played in drag. It is commonly argued that the concept of drag has no place in the ancient theater, in which men playing women was just a time-honored convention. Perhaps this was so at some time or place in the ancient Mediterranean, but Roman sources make it clear that the actor's transgressive skills were viewed as risqué (Richlin 1997b) and that men who dressed in women's clothing outside the theater were viewed as perverted; they formed a staple of Roman humor (Richlin 1993, 1995: 203–4; Corbeill 1996: 194–98). For the first-time theatergoers in the audience, this aspect of the comedies must have been hilarious (as in Robert Benchley's 1925 spoof of all-male college shows, "'The King of Razbo-Jazbo'"). And there are some jokes about the size of the "girls": see *Towelheads* 1167.

Or could there have been women onstage? Some historians of Greek drama have argued that the mute nude female characters in the plays of Aristophanes might have been played by actual naked women, rather than by male actors with comic female parts pasted onto them (Zweig 1992); compare the women on *Benny Hill* or *The Man Show.* And it does seem possible that some of the very small parts written for sexy women in Plautus's plays might have been done by female actors who were essentially showgirls (Georgia Moon in *Iran Man,* even Wanda in *Wee-*

vil). But *Iran Man,* anomalous in so many ways, includes two large and outspoken female parts—Brain Muffin and Cherry—and the social setting of this play seems so close to mime to me that I wonder whether the company might not have borrowed a couple of mime actresses for the occasion.

This is complicated by the question of whether the actors in Plautine comedy wore masks. We don't really know. All the textual evidence on masks long postdates Plautus, and there are no clear references to masks in the plays. The visual evidence (tchotchkes, mosaics, reliefs, wall paintings, even some actual masks) mostly does not come with labels explaining what it is showing, and the few examples that do are not showing Plautus in performance. This question is not resolvable on the basis of the current evidence, though historians of ancient drama lean toward "yes" (Beare 1964: 303–9), some with an enthusiasm based on stage experience (Marshall 2006; Wiles 1991).

In the normal Plautine play, then, the actors, probably all male, are, possibly, not native speakers of Latin, perhaps native speakers of a Celtic language, Umbrian, Oscan, or Greek, and performing on stage in Latin as people who act like native Romans but have Greek names and are usually supposed to be in "Greece." And some of them are playing women. In addition, some or most of them may well have been slaves, and they play both slaves and free people; within the play, as slaves, they joke about slave punishments. They act on a stage set in both a local and a geopolitical context.

Audience and Venue

So far I have been imagining a pretty trashy context for the production of Roman comedy: the actors, musicians, and playwrights are a bunch of rubes, runaways, army vets, ex-cons, ex-slaves, slaves, and lowlifes who may have done time together at the county farm and, when in Rome, may have met up at the local *popina* ("bar and grill"—a word of Umbrian origin; see McGinn 2004). What kind of audience could such a group possibly have pleased?

It is interesting to think about the subversive possibilities of slaves speaking to audiences that included both masters and slaves. Especially *Iran Man,* which takes place entirely in the absence of the master and utilizes his goods and authority to make things happen: how would that have played? To various audience members? And was the use of low-class language and jokes about slave torture entirely exploitative? The point is often made about Plautus that the uppity slaves in the plays are allowed such freedom due to the Saturnalian context of the religious festivals at which the plays were put on; this is freedom for only a day; why would the aediles pay for subversive plays? Usually, I agree with this; Roman satire and invective in general partake of the nature of rituals of reversal, which basically reinforce the status quo (Richlin 1992a: 75–76). But I do wonder about the multilevel Plautine audience and the ironically situated slave actors, and I want to side here with the very small minority who have seen these plays as in some way slave literature (Dunkin 1946; contra Anderson 1993, McCarthy 2000; Fitzgerald 2000: 10 allows briefly for an open-ended model). The plays are full of pointed comments, and the audience was full of people who had front-row seats on the process whereby citizens turned into prisoners of war turned into slaves. At the end of *Weevil,* Wanda protests to Weevil, "I was born a free woman," and he replies, "Yeah, like a lot of other people that are slaves now" (607). In *Iran Man,* a lot of Cherry's speeches in disguise can be taken as critiques of the enslavement of prisoners of war. And in *Towelheads,* Igor says (965–66), "Y'know it's a sin to let your fellow citizens / be slaves, right in your face, when they were free at home." Plautus, Terence, Caecilius: none of them is known to history by the name his parents gave him. How could they leave this subject alone?

Here I would like to reject two common models that are used for imagining Plautine theater.

(1) Highbrow, alien. Modern critics commonly use opera as an analogy for Plautine comedy. This is highly misleading. They draw this comparison because Plautus's comedy was musical, and because some other writers, going back to Horace, have dumped on this comedy as stupid and its audience as stupid, too. However, comparing Plautus to any kind of opera, for most readers today, means "Plautus is highbrow" (wrong) and "I wouldn't like it," because most people in the United States don't like opera (but Roman comedy seems to have been popular; I think that probably the writers who make this analogy like opera themselves). It would be reasonable to compare Roman comedy to opera in Italy in the nineteenth century, where it was popular across class lines.

This argument applies to another analogy writers sometimes draw, between Roman comedy and Kabuki theater. Again, what this conveys to most readers in the United States is "this drama is unintelligible," which is wrong. Writers make this argument to be honest about how different the conventions of the Plautine stage were from conventions now. But the best analogy for Plautine comedy is [something I find hilarious], because this comedy was performed for a wide audience, for whom it had to be intelligible.

(2) Rarely seen. Historians of Roman theater focus on how these plays came to be performed at major annual festivals instituted by the Roman government from the 240s through the 190s, so that eventually there were "seventeen days a year available for dramatic performance" (Wright 1974: 130; cf. Beare 1964: 162–63,

L. Taylor 1937). No, there were seventeen days a year for *state-sponsored* dramatic performance; we can only speculate about what went on for the rest of the year. It is true that at this point there were no permanent theaters outside of southern Italy; the whole stage had to be put up and taken down every time, and we do not even know whether plays had runs or not. There is a tiny shred of evidence for troupes going on tour, from around 150 B.C.E. (Lucilius 1034ff. Marx; Habinek 1998: 43). Occasionally during the next three hundred years a writer mentions performances way out in the country, with the audience sitting on the grass (Juvenal 3.172–79). Let's be conservative, and say that on the other 348 days each year the actors and writers had to be doing something. Maybe they gave lessons, maybe they took lessons, maybe they had day jobs, maybe they starved. But a lot of them must have been performing, and in non-state-sponsored venues. And this would have been the majority of their work; the seventeen days at festivals would have been, for them, the exception.

But we do need to think clearly about what went on during those seventeen days. First, what were these festivals? They are known as *ludi,* which is usually translated "games." Most of them were instituted by the Roman central government to keep up morale and foster social cohesion (Habinek 1998) at times of severe threat to Rome itself, especially the Second Punic War and the mess that followed as Italy tried to get back on its feet. Technically, they were religious festivals, including ceremonies that promised good things to the gods and dedicated the festivities to them. They were a central-government production—the job of hiring entertainers was delegated to the aediles, a set of junior magistrates—and if Rome had had a national anthem, the crowd would have been asked to stand and mumble along. During wartime—and Rome had armies in the field during the entire period from 224 B.C.E. to 184 B.C.E.—the stated goal of the festival would be to get [insert god's name here] to help Rome beat the tar out of [insert name of enemy here]. But the main feature of these *ludi* was indeed "games"—chariot races, gladiatorial combat, wild-beast hunts. We know from a much-discussed prologue of Terence that there were also other shows, like boxing matches and circus acts (see H. Parker 1996). As cultural events, these were the equivalent of stock-car racing and professional wrestling. This was the cultural context of Plautine comedy in its state-sponsored form.

And who would have been in attendance? Let's be safe and call it a mixed audience. We do not know where most of the performances took place, but Sander Goldberg (1998) has argued persuasively that in the time of Plautus performances would have been staged in front of the temple of the particular deity being honored, with people sitting squashed together on the temple steps. Each show would have accommodated about 1,600 people, and there might well have been multiple shows to accommodate a city with a population of about 200,000 and all the out-of-towners.

Who do we know were there? We can be sure of these at least: people who lived in Rome, first of all, as many as could cram in—the *Towelheads* prologue makes it clear that people of all ages, genders, and social classes were expected, including slaves (see Chalmers 1965). There would probably have been special seats for nobles and state officials—this was made law by 194 B.C.E. (Livy 34.44.4–5; cf. Goldberg 1998: 13–16, Moore 1994). Others who might have been there included refugees who had crowded into Rome from the countryside during and after the Carthaginian invasion in 213–12 (Habinek 1998: 40, 42); noble hostages taken by Roman armies from various states, and political exiles (the historian Polybius was one); immigrants; traders. And, depending on how easy it was to travel at a particular time, people presumably would have come from far and wide, like the crowd at Woodstock, or at the World Cup. This comes up casually in Plautus's plays, usually in the little histories of how somebody got raped or kidnapped: "It was the [whatever] festival, and people had come from all over, as people do. . . ." (Anybody here from Umbria today?)

It is important to remember this because of the argument commonly made about why Plautine comedy can't be subversive. Why would the aediles pay out good money for subversive entertainment? Well, why did Ed Sullivan host the Beatles and the Rolling Stones? Why did Nixon invite Elvis to the White House? What the aediles wanted was a happy crowd, including but certainly not limited to happy voters. Did the aediles limit what could be said? Probably (see the section on "Obscenity" below). Was there an element of selling out in doing comedy at the *ludi?* You bet *(ob quaerundum victum).* Does that mean Plautine comedy was squeaky clean, in any sense? No.

But the plays that we have do show signs of having been designed for the "national audience," as it were, that attended the *ludi.* Like radio, at the beginning of broadcast media in the United States, the plays had to be funny for farmers as well as New Yorkers as well as greenhorns, and Plautus's plays definitely include mixed levels of humor. We might assume that, if a *grex* really did go on tour to Umbria, the humor would have been less mixed and the whole effect would have been less elaborate, because we do know that the games cost the aediles a lot of money, that Terence was paid a record amount for one of his plays, and that the play's producer/director rented costumes and props through the aediles (there's a famous example of this in *Weevil* and another in *Iran Man*).

The large number of jokes that depend on technical terms from farming certainly suggests that people came in from the country to see the plays—or else that a lot of people had moved to Rome from the country. Generally, the country is a joke in Plautus, also the place a slave does not want to get sent to; Blini in *Towelheads* is funny partly because he is fresh up from the country and this is not really in keeping with getting disguised as an assassin fresh from the killing fields in the Balkans. Even he thinks it's funny. The prologue of *Mercator* includes a tour de force in which the young man recaps the speech his father made to him about "When I was a boy, how hard we worked down on the farm," including bona-fide-sounding farming proverbs. The boy and his dad are both *mercatores* now, though—traders who deal in import-export by ship—and this combination locates Plautus very securely in a landscape in which family farms were being overrun by agribusiness. Plautus has this in common with his contemporary, Cato the Censor, who in many ways seems to be Plautus's opposite (see Gowers 1993: 66–67; Habinek 1998: 42–43, 56; Leigh 2004: 98–157).

The plays themselves incorporate features that accommodate first-time theatergoers. In the prologues, and scattered here and there in the plays, we can recognize allusions to a few members of the stage crew; here, in the *Towelheads* prologue, we find the *praeco,* the announcer, who told everybody to sit down and keep quiet, as well as ushers who control the crowd. The actors' lines are full of cues and stage directions. And the combination of these lines with the prologues, which often tell the whole plot of the play—in the case of *Towelheads,* several times—reminds me of nothing so much as children's theater ("Uh-oh—here comes that bad man. I'll hide over here!"). This kind of cuing is also characteristic of effective rhetoric and preaching, and Plautine comedy cues even its own discourse: *animum advortite,* "pay attention," means "I'm going to tell you the story now"; *dicam,* "I'll tell you," means a lie is coming up; and lines like "enough foolishness" always signal the end of a run of gags and a return to dialogue. Opera companies that want to survive now use supertitles, because they can't depend on that sophisticated audience any more. The comedies are set up so that everybody can have a good time.

Let's run the tape back to another element of the audience: immigrants. Plautus inhabited a sort of ongoing world war, the streets always full of soldiers, many families short a son or two, refugees and exiles everywhere, a slave market swollen with the by-products of war, the whole Italian way of life teetering, along with the family farm. Rome, as readers of Terry Pratchett will recognize, was beginning to be Ankh-Morpork—the archetypal Big City—and this must have meant some fundamental changes in the city fabric (Pratchett 1990: 3–4): "No enemies had ever taken Ankh-Morpork. Well, *technically* they had, quite often; the city welcomed free-spending barbarian invaders, but somehow the puzzled raiders always found, after a few days, that they didn't own their own horses any more, and within a couple of months they were just another minority group with its own graffiti and food shops."

Terry Pratchett dubbed the part of his invented world that features deserts, turbans, and camels "Klatch," and Ankh-Morpork is full of Klatchian take-out joints, one of which plays a role in his novel *Jingo*, which is naturally about the war between Ankh-Morpork and Klatch. It is crucial to bear this Klatchian take-out side of things in mind when reading Plautus. It's not just that Plautus's audience included farm boys who had Seen Paree. That audience would have been peppered with the Pareesians themselves, present not only as prisoners of war turned slave (and invisible to us, even if we had their tombstones, under the glamorous new names bestowed upon them by the slave dealers), but as what the Romans called *peregrini*—noncitizens resident in Rome. Cubans in Miami. West Indians in London. Proprietors of Klatchian take-outs. What did they feel about the ethnic geography of comedy? Their children would have been at least bilingual, and doubtless spoke a fluent Latin full of urban slang. There was a whole court system just for legal issues arising with peregrines, dating, not surprisingly, from about this time period. So all the jokes where "this Klatchian goes into a bar, see," are being told in a context, familiar to us, of mixed ethnicity, stemming from a process of imperialism.

And even for the audience members who hadn't gone to war, a radical overhaul of the imagination must have been going on, as the Near East turned into Out There. Where anything could happen; where fabulous cities of gold lay waiting to be looted; inhabited by strange creatures, strange gods, exotic maidens, and gigantic mercenary soldiers, all with funny names. It's like the Pacific Rim as viewed by Ross Thomas's great con man Otherguy Overby: "'Well, when the war ended in Nam things went dead as a doornail out there,' he said, opening the refrigerator and taking out another beer. 'Out there' to Overby was the Far East—everywhere from Seoul to Sydney" (1978: 89; cf. 193, 255).

The Greeks had made the same sort of division between themselves and their near neighbors in Asia Minor and Egypt, but the Roman version feels different: *We* become so plain, so homespun, and *Out There* becomes so wondrous, so scary, so much fun. It was a formulation that lay for centuries waiting for Rudyard Kipling's wake-up kiss.

So for this audience, this huge, mixed audience that assembled on seventeen days a year, something was needed that would work for all of them, and why should it not have come up from below? Mass culture is not always hegemonic, and hegemonic culture is not always from below, for example ballroom dancing and the "palais de dance" culture in the 1930s–40s, where the lower classes dressed up. But sometimes hegemonic culture does come up from below. In the 1950s, suddenly blue jeans—workmen's clothing—became hegemonic; in the 1990s, white kids in the suburbs were flashing gang signs; maybe in the 180s, a lot of people liked to hear that slave style. But this genre is as ephemeral as "Be-Bop-a-Lula." Because by 50 B.C.E., it was all over, and Plautus was headed for the vocabulary museum, which is where most of his fragments come from: his language was a curiosity already by the time of Verrius Flaccus's dictionary.

Let's run the tape back again and think about the women in the audience. It is too rarely noted that these plays are highly sexist (see Rei 1998). In fact, I want to pay tribute here to John Wright, who in 1974 wrote: "Note how in both cases the girl's intransigence is met with a wheedling speech characterized by diminutives (a fact that might interest Simone de Beauvoir *et aliae*)" (1974: 174). OK, it's not radical feminism, but it's a start. Maybe the plays' sexism has always just seemed too obvious to mention; maybe we are used to it from TV and it seems normal. The range of female roles includes sexy prostitute, chaste prostitute, the occasional respectable girl (Cherry in *Persa*), shrewish wife, occasionally a clever wife *(Casina)*, old prostitute, female slave. "Take my wife" jokes are common (e.g., *Trinummus* 51–64, a whole sequence between two old men; *Cistellaria* 175, "and then she passed away—finally she was nice to her husband" [run laugh track]). After Elaine Fantham's thorough overview of women in New Comedy both Greek and Roman (1975), Zola Marie Packman (1993) is the only critic to have commented at length on the primary part played by rape in the marriage plots of Roman comedy (cf. on rape in Terence, James 1998; on Greek New Comedy, Henry 1985 and Lape 2004; on law, Scafuro 1997).

Rape makes no appearance in the three plays in this volume. But in all three plays, women are property, passed from hand to hand. Cherry in *Iran Man* is allowed by her father to be sold into slavery as part of an elaborate con game, just as he is literally lending her to Bowman in exchange for a meal, and, as she comments, will want to dispose of her to a husband some day; the selling of women into slavery as a by-product of war is central to the plot, and it comes up often in other plays. (What is somewhat unusual is that Cherry is also the sole voice of honor and reason in her play, though she could easily be played as whiny.) Georgia Moon in *Iran Man* starts out as a prostitute owned by a pimp, and at the end of the play evidently still has a master, although she is now supposedly free. Tchotchka and Katya in *Towelheads,* like Wanda in *Weevil* and numerous other girls in Plautus, have been kidnapped, taken far from home, and sold to a pimp. Wanda is already for sale, while Tchotchka and Katya are about to be turned out and, when first seen, are primping enthusiastically for the "slut market" at the local festival; when their father finally appears, they think he is a customer, and he lets them believe it (just at first; what a scream!).

Modern readers sometimes take Aristophanes' plays about women—*Lysistrata, Ekklesiazousai,* and *Thesmophoriazousai*—to be proto-feminist, and they can be played that way, as, for example, in Mary-Kay Gamel's production of *The Julie Thesmo Show* (see Gamel 2002). But it would be hard to play Plautus as feminist. Whereas the plight of (male) slaves fuels much of these plays' comedy, the plight of women as a class is less of an issue here. Old women are drunk, young women are desirable, wives in general are tyrannical bitches *(Menaechmi).* The one woman who really seems to run things, the prostitute Phronesium (Little Prudence) in *Truculentus,* is held up in the prologue as having "the morals common these days" (13)—greedy; and "that's how women are, / for they all do it, when they know they're loved" (16–17).

And how might women in the audience have received these plays? The plays define a set of roles and rules still too familiar in popular culture. The two central roles in Plautine comedy—the person in love and that person's tricky assistant—are never held by female characters. Women in the plays are always secondary, and two of the extant plays have no female characters at all *(Captivi* and *Trinummus).* And what if they were always, or usually, played by men dressed up amusingly as women? Oddly enough, considering that women played such a full part in Roman public life, we know of the names of very few female writers, none of them in the field of drama. So for Roman women this form of entertainment was male-designed, male-performed, and basically not theirs—addressed *to* them, sometimes played *at* them, often *about* them—but *not* them. Yet, as in the prologue of *Towelheads,* they are still presumed to be there for a good time. In other cultures that are this phallocentric, women often develop joking subcultures of their own; there are slight hints of this for Roman women (Richlin 1992b, 1992c), but basically this is something we just don't know.

And even talking about "Roman women" like this is wrong: the women were divided themselves, into slave, freed, and free; from Rome, from the country; speaking Latin or Greek or Oscan or Umbrian or a Celtic language or an African or Asian language; native or immigrant or exile or captive. And the slave/free divide was a big one; in some Roman religious rituals, free women acted out their superiority on the bodies of slave women (Richlin 1997a).

What we can safely assume is that some of the wellsprings of the comic plot in Plautine comedy—the exposure of infants due to illegitimacy or poverty; capture in war leading to enslavement and prostitution; rape at a festival, or, more likely, in war; the loss of children to war *(Captivi)* or kidnapping *(Towelheads, Weevil)*—would have been experienced by some of the women in that huge audience (see *Iran Man* introduction on the sale of children by their families). Very seldom do the plays show a mother's reaction to the loss or recovery of a child; *Epidicus* is a rare exception. It is a shock, toward the end of *Towelheads*, to hear Uncle Saddam give thanks (1253) "for what the good Lord is giving to me, to you, and to your mother"—this is the first we have heard of her. And in this same play, when the comic slave nanny Yasmin recognizes her own long-lost son among Saddam's slaves, this just enables a big laugh line calling her cries of greeting "womanish furniture" (1145). What would that mean to the women in the audience who had lost children? What would the hundreds of jokes about enslaved prostitutes mean to the female slaves in the audience? How about the plot line, in which the girl is miraculously found by her sorrowing parents?

And, if we can spare a short paragraph or so for the audience's sexuality: the plays are certainly not subversive sexually, except insofar as they credit slaves with feelings of romantic love (*Iran Man* is the big example, but there are others). Actually, the one unusual thing the plays do is give occasional voice to the *puer,* the boy sex slave who is a standard object of desire for adult males in Latin love poetry. In love poetry, the boys' attitude is sexy; here, Toyboy in *Iran Man* talks about the economy of sex from his own standpoint, saying to Einstein, "At least I don't do it for nothin, like you" (285). And the *puer* in *Pseudolus* complains about what it means to be a *puer* in the household of a pimp, saying he is too little (783) and fearing that tomorrow he'll have to drink "fuller's juice," that is, urine (782; fullers used urine to clean clothing). The plays make it clear that boys as well as girls were part of the flesh trade: Boris in *Towelheads,* and seemingly his adoptive father as well, had been kidnapped and sold. What would the jokes about the sex work of male slaves mean to the male slaves in the audience? As Sandra Joshel has so conclusively demonstrated, there is a big difference between what slaves thought about their own work and what elite writers said about it (Joshel 1992).

And what about *cinaedi?* The question of whether there was any sort of gay subculture in Rome is hotly debated (see Richlin 1993; C. Williams 1999), and, especially during this period, when the plays of Plautus and the fragments of other writers are the only contemporary evidence, it is impossible to speak with certainty. But the plays are certainly in keeping with the sexual norms of later periods. The main point of interest here, I think, must lie in the casting of men as women and the possibility that this might have read as drag and that *cinaedi* had an official role in the plays. Maybe there was a consciously cinaedic element in the audience as well, who might have especially liked this about the plays. But on this point there is no evidence at all, and as for lesbian identity and what any proto-lesbians might have found in the plays, who knows (on the Roman idea of lesbians, see Hallett 1997). *Cinaedus* is used as an insult in Plautus, as are imputations of cinaedic sexuality (e.g., *Pseudolus* 1180–81). Slaves insult fellow slaves with their sexual permeability (*Iran Man* 230, 284–86). The word *tribas,* later used by Roman writers to describe a butch lesbian, does not appear in Plautus, nor is there any clear mention of sex or love between women—though there may be some double entendres.

So, to sum up: even the audience at the *ludi* (or especially that audience) was not a unitary audience. Their needs would be variously met by Plautine comedy, and maybe some of them just liked gladiatorial combat better, anyway. Books about Plautus are full of arguments about what the plays meant to the "Roman audience," but while the audience at the *ludi* may have been physically in Rome at that moment, only some of it was "Roman." This is especially important in relation to the question of slaves, gender, ethnicity, and class in the plays. Do the plays reinforce the norms of the Roman class/gender system? Sure. Are they Rome-o-centric? Less clear. But the plays were acted by slaves (maybe) and non-Romans (maybe), and there were slaves and non-Romans in the audience, and these lines and plot lines would have played quite differently to slaves than to masters, to women than to men, to non-Romans of various kinds than to citizens. That is, the plays interpellate the audience segmentally.

Moreover, I cannot agree that these plays were made to order *by* the elite class *for* the elite class, or even that "socially dominant Romans" were an important target audience for them (contra McCarthy 2000). Not only were the writers not elite, most of the audience was not, either. Like television sponsors, the elite paid for the plays at the *ludi,* but they could not totally determine the plays' meaning. And comedy was bigger than the *ludi;* it had a whole other life, which shaped both plays and actors.

TRANSLATION ISSUES

Let's go back to the axiom that these plays should be funny in translation. The plays are certainly the equivalent of what is now dubbed "pop culture," like TV—a lot like sitcoms, which derive their dramatis personae and structure in direct lineage from Plautus. Or more like musical comedy, especially the kind with clever lyrics.

Like both these forms, Plautus's plays are, as often noted, formulaic, obsessively re-instantiating the Marriage Plot. It is therefore a mistake to translate these plays into scholarese, as sometimes happens. We cannot always reconstitute the sense of Plautine slang, but it is possible to get close to the tone. We have to remember, again, that the most popular forms of entertainment during this period were the equivalent of stock car racing, professional wrestling, and the films of the Farrelly brothers. Unfortunately in the early twenty-first century an ability to read Latin does not often go hand in hand with an appreciation of pro wrestling. During the past fifteen hundred years, the entirety of Roman culture has become the property of an intellectual elite. This poses a problem for reading Plautus accurately. Kathleen McCarthy, in a book published in the year 2000, refers to the players in *Persa* as "characters of the *demimonde*" (33). Such an archaizing, and arch, description fundamentally misleads non-Latin-readers about what Plautus is like.

Translate or Transpose?

In dealing with jokes, a translator has two choices: one, to put down what the original said as literally as possible; two, to put down an equivalent, to try to give the reader what will make sense in current context.

I found I could not translate at all without making up an ideal cast for the play—without hearing funny voices (see below on performance issues); then I could find words they would say. Plautus transposed his Greek originals into Roman contexts and Latin slang; I have opted to look for English equivalents that bring Plautus into focus as funny.

Example: Saturio, the parasite in *Persa,* compares himself to a Cynic philosopher (123–25), with his [globular or pear-shaped bottle or flask for holding oil], his [metal instrument for scraping off dead skin in the baths], his [concave vessel used for various purposes] or possibly [chamberpot], his [low-heeled shoes or slippers worn by Greeks and by comedians], his [mantle worn by Greeks and by comedians], and his [pouch]. The problem is (a) to achieve the same tone without a long explanation of what Cynics were like; (b) to deal with the fact that the Cynic's gear overlaps with the costume of the comic parasite. Solution here: Fat Jack in *Iran Man,* dressed in jeans and cowboy boots, talks about the "wise old cowboy" instead of the Cynic philosopher, and the list of gear becomes "just his canteen and his lariat, his tin pan, boots, and poncho, / and his leather pouch." The paradigm here is the narrator in the Coen brothers' movie *The Big Lebowski* (1998), but any solution would do that paired crusty wisdom with a costume overlap.

Comedy is by nature ephemeral in many of its aspects. Language is a big one. Plautus should sound funny, but what sounds funny changes subtly over time and per audience. These plays need to be updated often, and any translation used by a current production company will need to be thoroughly reworked so that it will sound funny on the day it is performed, in the place where it is performed. I did *Curculio* as vaudeville, *Persa* as a Kevin Smith project, and *Poenulus* as drawing-room comedy, but the options are infinite, and it is my hope that the translations I offer here will serve as a jumping-off point for a lot of improvisations.

Language (Latin/Greek)

As Thomas Habinek notes, Latin never fully dominated Italy (1998: 44; cf. Pulgram 1958). If Plautus really came from Umbria, he might well have learned Latin as a second language, and nobody can see the oddities and beauties of a language like a nonnative speaker. Indeed, even his name points to how outsider status can be marked by language (Paulus ex Festo 275L): "Those who have flat feet are called 'Ploti.' Whence also the poet Accius, because he was an Umbrian from Sarsina, from the flatness of his feet was first called 'Plotus,' and later was called 'Plautus.'" This is one of the sources that ties together Plautus's family name and cognomen, though confusedly—the text has Accius (a different poet), presumably an error for Maccius (we hope). What is interesting here is that the text seems to imply that being called "Plotus" is somehow connected with being from Sarsina. We do know that spelling (and presumably pronouncing) words with "o" instead of "au" was characteristic of common as opposed to upper-class Roman speech. So if—and it's a big if—we can believe any of this story, it would mean that Plautus's name not only had a funny meaning, it sounded either backwoodsy, or lower class, or both.

Could we expect a person from Umbria to come to Rome and make a hit putting on plays full of Umbrian slang? Maybe not; consider Danny Boyle's film *Trainspotting* (1995), which needed subtitles to make Scots slang intelligible to an English-speaking audience. But maybe so; maybe *popina* is not the only word that came into Plautus's Latin from the north. (It is possible that *leno,* "pimp," the word for Plautus's chief villain, is among these, along with *lena,* "she-pimp"; neither is originally a Latin word, nor are they Greek.) Habinek argues that the Roman elites, in their search for linguistic hegemony, could at least build on a state of basic mutual intelligibility; for the Hannibalic wars, Livy emphasizes the "incompatibility of Punic with the languages of Italy," but the Roman allies can talk to each other (1998: 41). And Livy did come from the north himself; but then he was teased about his accent.

What has always stood out in Plautus is the use of Greek words, some naturalized into Latin, some still in Greek letters. Embedded in a Latin play, these words are exotic, but exotic how? Again, here, there are multiple levels. The naturalized

Latin words could describe popular institutions (*balineum,* "public baths"); hybrid formations like *basilice* ("royally," but formed with a Greek noun and a Roman adverb ending) sound like slang—the effect is something like "kingissimo." Some words come out of the experience of war (*strategus,* "general"; *machaera,* "scimitar") or the luxury trade with the East (*murrinus,* "myrrh-scented"). Linguists have shown that Plautus's Greek, by and large, comes from lower-class trades and people (Habinek 1998: 43; Palmer 1954: 83; Shipp 1953; Wright 1974: 181).

Greek would have been the first language of many Roman slaves and prisoners of war, and when Bowman in *Iran Man* uses some Greek words in talking to his friend Einstein, this probably is not meant to sound like philosophy or tragedy. At *Iran Man* 29, he says, *basilice agito eleutheria,* "In a kingly manner (Greek/Latin) I am agitated (Latin) for the Festival of Freedom (Greek)." I turned this into "I'm royally loco, just like Cinco de Mayo." With *Persa* set in Los Angeles, now, Spanish is the right equivalent to Bowman's Greek; the play needs to be set in an urban, bilingual (or multilingual) setting.

Slang

Plautus's vocabulary may be low, but it is an extraordinarily rich one. Many of his words are used only once, not only by him, but in all of Latin. Some he clearly made up on the spot. But some things, like the oaths by Hercules and Castor and Pollux, or the repeatedly used adverbs *lepide, graphice, probe,* are clearly slang. And doing this translation made me think about how *located* slang is, both in English and in Plautus's plays. It is not just that the grandiose mercenary soldiers who clank through the plays talk like comic commandos (one of them even has a speech in which he says he's not going to talk that way, *Truculentus* 482–86). Certain kinds of slang and certain ways of talking belong to each of the various character types: pimps threaten, young men dither, and, as Gellius tells us (11.6.3), the oath *mecastor* was used by women in particular. There is no replication of accents or dialect (something Aristophanes does do), and the modes of speech are not as individuated as they are for characters in Dickens (Mr. Mantilini, Sam Weller). But the characters use language appropriate to their class and gender positions, and since a lot of them are slaves, pimps, and whores, no Gibbon periods here.

And no sort of language dates more rapidly than slang. This is one reason these plays need to be translated often; the Loeb translations are almost unreadable now, and they usually aren't funny, but Paul Nixon started writing them in 1916. At that point it probably made sense to translate the Greek into French, so that *Towelheads* 137 (*gerrae germanae, hai de kollurai lurai*), which I here translate "phony baloney, a lotta pastafazool," appears in the Loeb as "nothing but pure piffle, *rien que belles balivernes.*" To Nixon's audience, French was funny enough, I suppose; for an American audience today, I've used American immigrant slang.

At any rate, part of the raison d'être of slang seems to be to act as a generational marker. So Nancy Mitford (1975 [1931], ch. 9): "His correct and slightly pompous manner combined with the absence in his speech of such expressions as 'O.K. loo,' 'I *couldn't* be more amused,' 'We'll call it a day,' 'lousy,' 'It was a riot,' 'My sweetie-boo,' and 'What a poodle-pie' to indicate the barrier of half a generation . . . which more than any other often precludes understanding, if not friendship, between young and youngish people." Note that this novel was first published in 1931, and that most (not all!) of the expressions cited are now in the vocabulary museum along with Plautus. Indeed, this aspect of Plautus's writing surely played a part in sending him to the vocabulary museum, while Terence lived on as exemplar of the *purus sermo,* "pure speech." Plautus must have sounded very much of his time; let me postulate that to his huge mixed audience, he sounded desirably up-to-date and metropolitan, in short, hip.

Obscenity

Remarkably, Plautus was hip without using any of the common Latin primary ob-scenities, what in English we call "four-letter words." The lack of these words is so extremely marked in Plautus, compared with later writers of satire and invective, that it is hard not to wonder whether the aediles and the setting at the *ludi* had something to do with it ("We want clean family entertainment here"). Or, like Beare, you could attribute the cleaned-up language to self-policing, Plautus's "care never to risk a jest which might sully the honour of a free-born woman" (1964: 65). At least by the time of Cicero, who luckily wrote a long essay in a letter to a friend about what was and was not polite to say in Latin, there were rules about this, in-cluding respecting the presence of ladies (Richlin 1992a: 18–26). The satirist Lu-cilius, who wrote in the generation after Plautus, but who was not writing for per-formance to a wide public, felt free to use obscenities (Richlin 1992a: 164–74). In writing these translations, I was not able to approximate the class location of Plau-tus's Latin without using four-letter words sometimes. Though if I were writing them for TV, I would have to.

But this is not to say that Plautus's plays are clean. The insult matches noted above involve highly inventive obscenity, in which excrement plays a featured role—still without primary obscenities. Male characters commonly accuse each other of being on the receiving end of anal sex. And there are a lot of double en-tendres, some of which depend on stage business, like the candle scene at the open-ing of *Weevil.* Sometimes Plautus just relies on his own vigorous imagination, as in the phrase "fuller's juice" (see "Audience and Venue" section above, on sex slaves in the audience). I think what we see at work here is a skill that informs all of Latin literature, now commonly recognized in the literature produced under the repression of the Empire (Ahl 1984), but that, I would argue, was already hard at work in Plautus's plays: the ability to say something outrageous in the most innocent of words. We should probably assume that Plautus's audience picked up more than we will ever be able to.

Catchphrases and Parodies

If slang is ephemeral, consider the importance to comedy of the catchphrase, which always depends, at least originally, on the audience's familiarity with an intertext (see Farkas 2003, with John Ayto's prefatory comments, vii–ix). "Walk this way," which I use here at *Weevil* 87, can never be a simple invitation to anyone who's seen Mel Brooks's *Young Frankenstein* (1974). The triumphs of Monty Python have made it impossible for some people to hear the words "huge tracts of land," "shrubbery," or "pining for the fjords" without grinning. For them, "huge tracts of land" is always accompanied by a visualized hand motion that makes it have nothing to do with land. People who went to college when I did used to say, "He's no fun at all, he fell right over" or "hamburger all over the highway" and laugh, because of Firesign Theater. People who don't remember the original skits will still say "Vy a duck?" (Marx Bros., *Coconuts*) or "Who's on first?" (Abbott and Costello) or "Slowly he turned, step by step" (Lucille Ball, and evidently vaudeville before her). Inspired by *Saturday Night Live,* for several years those in the know hailed each other as (e.g.) "the Bobmeister!" Even non-Stoogologists know that "Mmm, wise guy, eh?" is a quotation. It's endless.

And Plautus is clearly full of this kind of thing, but we almost never have any idea of what it's about. The intertexts are long gone. But this is the kind of language the plays are written in, so a good translation will try to interlard itself with similar current catchphrases, as best it can. Some examples: When the pimp Dorkalot fails to express sufficient enthusiasm on first seeing the disguised Cherry, Bowman remarks, *ut contemptim carnufex,* which literally means "How contemptuously the executioner [is talking]!" (*Iran Man* 547). Phrases with this shape show up in *Asinaria* (*ut osculatur carnufex,* "how the executioner kisses," 892), *Bacchides* (*ut subblanditur carnufex,* "how the executioner wheedles," 876), and *Pseudolus* (*ut paratragoedat carnufex,* "how the executioner acts like a tragedian," 707), and, with a variation, in *Weevil* (*ut fastidit gloriosus,* "how the war hero turns his nose up," 633). The *carnufex* in Roman humor is a loathed figure (*carnufex* literally means "flesh-maker"), and all the activities in which he engages in these phrases are funny.

This looks like the kind of repeated catchphrase that Flip Wilson made famous in the 1970s with "The Devil made me do it."

A great line in *Iran Man* comes up when Bowman challenges Brain Muffin to get his instructions right and she replies (305), *magi' calleo quam aprugnum callum callet,* which literally means "I'm shrewder/tougher than a boar's hide is shrewd/tough." (It's here translated, "You know I'm hipper than hippo hide"; Mary-Kay Gamel suggests, though, that the reference is to the scars caused by flogging, and translates, "It's been beaten into me.") The jingle in the expression depends on the double meaning of *calleo,* "be tough"/"be shrewd." It comes up again, slightly altered, in *Towelheads,* spoken by the completely un-hip Blini (579): "Nope, hippo hide ain't gonna be hipper than me!"—again in response to a command. Are the lines playing off each other? Or off something else, familiar to the audience—or just to some segments of it? *Shrek 2* is full of intertextual references, some of which are only recognizable to residents of Los Angeles, others to fans of *Garfield* or *Mission Impossible,* many aided by recognition of the voice behind each character and other roles that actor has played. Here, in Plautus, we can only guess.

The melodramas and various previous dramatic forms Plautus often burlesques are also gone, but it is not so hard to see when he is doing this and to come up with a good equivalent. In the Savoy operas, Gilbert and Sullivan burlesque everything from sea chanteys to the mad scene in *Lucia di Lammermoor;* late-twentieth-century performance is full of burlesqued forms, both in music (Tom Lehrer, e.g., "Vatican Rag") and film (*The Rocky Horror Picture Show,* the Austin Powers films). When Plautus does a melodramatic flashback at the end of *Curculio,* it is easy to think of equivalent conventions with which to set this up on stage now, because the genres themselves have persisted. Mike Myers does the same thing in *Goldmember.*

Conversely, it is tempting to translate some Plautine jokes into current catchphrases. In act 4, scene 6 of *Iran Man,* there's a great bit where the pimp Dorkalot is paying out a large sum of money and announces that he's charging [a small sum of money] for a bag deposit. Bowman comments sarcastically (688), *sine, quaeso, quando lenost, nihil mirum facit* (literally, "Leave it, please. Since he's a pimp, he's doing nothing surprising," or, "He's a pimp. It's normal for him"). In the summer of 2002, I couldn't help translating this, "The guy's a pimp. It's Nature's way," having just seen Steve Irwin make this cheerful remark about numerous venomous reptiles and amphibians in *The Crocodile Hunter: Collision Course.* By the time you read it, this intertextual joke will doubtless be well on its way to unintelligibility. And the same must be true for dozens of slightly mystifying turns of phrase lurking in Plautus.

Topical Jokes

Occasionally Plautus's plays seem to refer to a specific current event, for example the reference in *Towelheads* to the city now at peace (524; see note ad loc.). And some of the plays include in their prologues a sort of political cheerleading in which the actors wish the audience members good luck with their war. The possible referents for such lines have been much discussed (see Gruen 1990, 1992; Harvey 1986), never conclusively, because the lines are always almost-but-not-quite specific.

Much more common than the tantalizing almost-specific references are lines that locate the plays in the current geopolitical landscape, often associating Out There with money and/or luxury and with war. One telling war itinerary comes from the slave Stasimus in *Trinummus*. If they lose their last field, he fears, he and his master will have to go to foreign parts (*peregre*, 596) and take up shield, helmet, and pack to go as *latrones* (brigands, thugs, mercenaries) "to Asia or Cilicia" (599). He repeats this fear at 718–26, adding that he will have to fasten heels to his *socci* (which are, again, the comedian's garb as well as the slave's) and become a *cacula*—a soldier's slave, like Harpax in *Pseudolus*—as they serve "some king" (722). What is fascinating about this is the hybridity of his imagined picture (see section below on "Locations"): they will lose the family farm and have to go into the army, only not the Roman army but "some king's" army, as *latrones*. But mercenary soldiers in Plautus have outlandish accoutrements; Stasimus dresses himself and his master as Roman soldiers. Again, to the audience at the *ludi* this picture would be only too familiar. In the Roman army, officers were rich men; the foot soldiers came from the common people.

Roman names in the plays are almost nonexistent, but the names of historical Greek persons in the plays also make a lightweight roster—fewer than a dozen; all are well known, but almost all were dead in Plautus's day. The names from Out There are much more interesting. They are all names of kings, many current, and again they are associated with power and money. King names show up in a joking catchphrase structure, the *mirum quin* construction; *mirum quin* basically means "It would be weird if. . . ." The miser husband in *Aulularia,* sniping at his wife, says (85–86): "It would be weird if Jupiter made me into / King Philip or Dareus *[sic]* on your account, triple witch." His point is that he has no money. Fat Jack in *Iran Man* says to his daughter, who has tearfully asked him if he is really going to sell her just to fill his own belly, "It would be weird if I sold you for King Philip or Attalus / rather than for me, since you *are* mine" (339–40). This is a "duh" joke, very snotty, and for it to work the audience has to be familiar with the people named: in *Iran Man* these kings are replaced by "Saddam or the Saudis." But note that "king" in Plautus often simply means "rich man."

The most common context for kings is in boasting, usually by a clever slave, usually making a favorable comparison between his own achievements and those of some Eastern monarch. The unnamed Slave of Lyconides in *Aulularia* says (701–4):

> I'm rich! Me! I'm richer than the dragons
> who hold the Gold Mountains! Hey, I'm not gonna even
> bring up those other kings—practically homeless guys:
> I am the actual King Philip!

He here identifies himself with the king whose name was identical with gold coins. This is topicality from the bottom up.

Once in a while we get a cue that a joke comes from current popular culture: at the end of *Iran Man,* Einstein and Bowman, taunting the pimp, threaten to strike dancing poses for him like ones evidently familiar to the audience (824–26):

> EINSTEIN: Pimp, I can't help but dance a little pose for you that Hegea
> once did. Really, see if you like it. BOWMAN: Me, too, I also want
> to give you my rendition of what Diodorus once did in Ionia.

These lines cause a big "?" to form over the head of the reader; I turned Hegea into John Travolta, Diodorus into Michael Jackson, and Ionia (known for effeminate dancing) into West Hollywood. But who knows.

Another common form of topicality in the plays is what I have called here "parabasis moments." In Aristophanic comedy, the parabasis is the part of the play where the chorus comes forward and gives a comic lecture on some current issue, full of the names of people and places. Plautus likes to do something similar without the chorus or the names: a character will suddenly start talking about some current issue. This happens several times in *Iran Man,* especially in Fat Jack's diatribe on bounty-hunting informers (62–74) and Cherry's on homeland security (550–60); in *Weevil,* the title character delivers a savage comparison of bankers to pimps (494–511). These sections are not that funny when translated, and in production they need to be transposed so as to deal with current events. In Tucson in 2004, for example, we rewrote to have Fat Jack discuss the ethics of turning in illegal aliens to the INS. This exercise made it clear that the "parabasis moments" must have been tied to breaking news: it's a choice between large dead spots in the plays or the shock of hearing Fat Jack or Cherry or Weevil sound off on a hot issue.

Locations

The plays' locations have to be translated into a current equivalent in order for them to mean anything at all; few Americans now know where Aetolia was, but it was a highly meaningful location in Plautus's day (see section on "War, History, Geography" above), as were Sparta and Carthage. Sicilians in the plays are evil (*Towelheads* 897, but also *Captivi* 888, *Rudens* 49–57) presumably because of feelings left over from the First and Second Punic Wars. Writing in 2000–2004, I used current and recent war zones as equivalents for the ones presented in these plays, and I have tried to make them reasonably parallel, in terms of geography and importance, to their original locations relative to Rome. So Carthage has become Iraq; Persia, Iran; Aetolia, the former Yugoslavia; Anactorium, Belgrade; Sparta, Kosovo; and Caria, Jerusalem. Arabia has stayed Arabia. Sicyon, a city involved in a siege during a complex peacekeeping mission, makes a brief appearance as Sarajevo in *Weevil;* Calydon becomes Sarajevo in *Towelheads.* Already, though, Iraq means something different than it did when I started, and Sarajevo looms less large.

Epidaurus, the site of *Weevil*, was harder; like Athens, it slips toward a sort of default mode in which the location is just a marker for hybridity. This poses enough problems, as, for example, Weevil comes running back into the streets of Rome/ Epidaurus saying that nobody can bar his way—"not a strategus or a tyrannus or an agoranomus / or a demarch or a comarch" (285–86). How to translate these words? Are they exotic in the Out There way, so that they should be translated as "not a paladin or a sultan or a caliph / or a vizier or a sheikh"? Are they only mildly foreign—say, British as opposed to American—so that they should be translated as "not a major-general or a monarch or a meat inspector [Henry Taylor trans., inspired] / or a Lord Mayor or a civil servant"? Because, in contrast to the Latin text in which it is embedded, the series is so strikingly Greek—it almost immediately precedes *isti Graeci palliati,* "those Greeks wearing the *pallium*" (288)—I decided they needed to be markedly foreign and wound up with "not a warlord nor an overlord . . . nor a border guard / nor a tribal chief nor a village chief."

Italian place-names are used extremely rarely in Plautus, but *Weevil* features the single biggest exception to this rule: the tour of the Forum that begins act 4. All the Italian place-names in Plautus appear in jokes, most of which depend on the spectators' local knowledge to be funny. The Forum tour is transposed here onto the map of New York City, but in performance would always work best with a city the audience knows well, since the places are repeatedly associated with bad behavior, which is not going to be funny in a list of places the audience has never heard of.

I made the Athens of *Iran Man* into Los Angeles, but it could be any big city—Athens is the default location of Plautus's plays. If you are using this book and thinking about production, please do choose a city well known to your audience.

Plautine comedy is also full of fantastic geographies, in which characters wander off the map (see map on page 18). In *Trinummus,* the Sycophanta says he has gone to Arabia (sort of) and then to the island of Rhadamanthes and up to the sky to visit Jupiter (928–47). In *Iran Man,* the action only gets as far as Arabia and the City of Gold (cf. the Gold Mountains in the section on "Topical Jokes" above); in *Towelheads,* the main characters bounce around a lot, but only in the Mediterranean. But the soldier in *Towelheads* has been to "Pentetronica," where he killed off the natives—a tribe of flying men (471–90). Soldiers get around. Thus when Weevil tells a tale of his supposed time with his soldier, he goes for quite a trip (442–46). In Latin, he visits the Persians, Paphlagonians, Sinopians, Arabs, Carians, Cretans, Syrians, Rhodes, Lycia, and the coast of Libya (real places), and Peredia (very hungry place), Perbibesia (very thirsty place), Centauromachia (place where the centaurs fought their [famous] battle), Classia Unomammia (Tribal One-tit-place), and Conterebromnia (place for screwing around with everything). As well as translating the joke names (see "Funny Names" below), the translation transposes the real places into comparable contemporary war zones and peoples: "the Iranians, / the Kurds, Tehranians, Arabs, Palestinians, Jordanians, Syrians / and Libya, Lebanon. . . ."

A certain ambivalence toward things Greek is suggested by the repeated use Plautus makes of the words *barbarus, barbaricus,* and *barbaria,* which he always uses to refer to Italy or to Italian writers, especially himself: as with his general take on geography, here he specifically plays with Italy as both here and there, the Greeks' despised Other, so called in fast and colloquial Latin. This running joke shows up in *Weevil* in Beauregard's serenade (150) and in *Towelheads* in a joke about stage money (598). As with the slave's vision of going to war in *Trinummus* (see section on "Topical Jokes" above), the plays manifest a hybrid identity.

Funny Names

Translations of Plautus almost without exception retain the original names, and this I feel to be a central mistake, because the names are meaningful and comic, and Plautus's audience would have recognized that. Even to a Latin-reading American audience today, the names are opaque, unfunny, just handles. At best, they sound like some names in Shakespeare. We are used to comic characters with comic names: Rocky and Bullwinkle, Olive Oyl, Mini-Me, Edina Monsoon, Sponge Bob Square Pants, Roseanne Rosannadanna, Dick Deadeye, Biggus

Dickus, Dixie Normous, Silent Bob. The Dude abides. . . . Most audiences watching Plautus in translation have to assume that what is funny about these names is that they are in Latin, which (a) is mostly not true and (b) would not have been what was originally funny about them. For students, all the names in a play often boil down to "Stringofsyllables."

Among the Greek features of Plautus's plays are the names of the locations (almost never in Italy) and the characters (many, though not all, are Greek). In Greece, these names wouldn't be comic unless the town name itself was funny (Schenectady, Cucamonga—now *Rancho* Cucamonga), and the names were funny (Jeeves, Pongo Twistleton, Charlotte Corday Rowbotham). It's hard to see from extant Greek comedies exactly how the names were funny, because most ancient Greek names seem somewhat funny to us (Aristophanes means "Best Looking," for example). But for a Latin-speaking audience, setting the plays in Greece and giving the characters Greek names is a big deal in itself.

For, although some of the actors, some of the people in the audience, and some of the playwrights were native speakers of Greek themselves, and might have been born with Greek names, in Roman ideology being Greek is heavily charged with meaning. As noted above, Rome was at war with various Greek-speaking countries throughout the third and second centuries B.C.E. But the Romans always admired Greek culture. And yet they consistently voiced contempt for Greeks, conceived of everything east of them as effeminate, weak, and corrupt, and found many things Greek laughable, if not disgusting. And among those things were Greek names, which were markedly different from Roman names.

A Roman male citizen's name has three parts: praenomen, nomen, and cognomen. Marcus Tullius Cicero. Gaius Julius Caesar. Titus Maccius Plautus. The first names are limited in number, only about ten of them; the second and third are family names, à la "John Quincy Adams." (Actually the third name often means something funny—Cicero means "Chickpea"—and if we translated these names they would sound even stranger to us than they already do. It's hard even to be sure that "Harpoe Clownshoes" would really have sounded funny to a Roman. But probably it did, even to somebody named Mark "Chickpea" Tully. And probably we should translate all the names, all the time, to get over our feeling that they sound like something that should be carved in marble.) Anyway.

A Roman woman's name is the feminine form of her family nomen: Tullia; Julia. And slaves likewise (hmm) just had a single name, which was often a Greek name, sometimes because the Romans took a lot of captives from places that spoke Greek, and sometimes because a slave trader or a new master would want to give a slave a Greek name because Greek slaves were classier than, say, Jewish slaves or German slaves. Greek citizen men, on the other hand, have one name: Socrates. Plato. Like women! And a lot like slaves! But these names aren't even family names. They're weird made-up names, like "Hippokrates" ("Horse-Strength") or "Agathon" ("Noble"). It's clear that they sounded funny to native speakers of Latin. Moreover, the Greek names in Plautus are not ordinary Greek names—most aren't found elsewhere. They're not just Greek names, they're funny Greek names: a double whammy.

And how do we translate that funniness? Funny like "Dances with Wolves"? Funny like "Franken*stien*"? Funny like "Yum-Yum"? In each of the three plays in this volume, I've taken a different approach.

The streetwise, lowlife world of *Iran Man* needs to be populated by people with lowlife names; I translated them as Bowman, Einstein, Fat Jack and his daughter Cherry, Toyboy, Georgia Moon, Brain Muffin, and the pimp Dorkalot. Each of these translations has a linguistic connection to the original Latin name (see the *Iran Man* introduction), and also tries to translate what is funny about the name. What I could not do was replicate the bilingual base of the humor—all these names except Fat Jack's and Cherry's were originally Greek; these plays might best be dealt with by a bilingual translator in a bilingual context like Los Angeles or Montreal.

Because I transposed *Towelheads* onto Sarajevo, I transposed the names as Slavic names: Boris, Igor, Tchotchka, Katya, General Popoff, Blini, Vodka. The Punic names in the play were transposed as (vaguely) Arabic. This double transposition gives something of the feel of a play that makes protagonists of two cultures that would have been recently at war with Rome. It also makes use of current comic ethnic stereotypes, pushing the question of how inherently ludicrous the names and settings would have been to their audience—or how offensive. The same goes for the comic Punic in *Towelheads,* which is made of a patchwork of Hebrew and Arabic words that have come into English, along with nonsense words (see *Towelheads* introduction).

In *Weevil,* I used light-romance English names for the normative characters and, as in *Iran Man,* tried to base the English name on the meaning of the original name (see *Weevil* introduction). All the names in *Weevil* are calculated to show class: Beauregard and Cornwallis have upper-class associations; Lt. Napoleon Plaza-Toro represents the military; Madame Lola, Mr. Wolf, Turk, Wanda, and Weevil have low-class associations. But even in *Iran Man* the names clearly show a white, academic standpoint, and could and should be rethought for your own context. Overall, I think translating the names will help an American audience get what is going on in the plays, though I know some readers like the original names; these appear in the cast lists at the head of each play.

An easier problem is posed by the name formations in the plays that are clearly jokes, like *Plautus Pultiphagonides* in *Poenulus* (line 54) or *Summanus* in *Curculio* (line 413) or the comic place-names in *Curculio* (see section on "Locations" above) or the string of names Einstein makes up for himself in *Iran Man* (lines 701–5). Example: *Virginesvendonides* (*Iran Man* 702), "Virgins-seller-[Greek patronymic ending]," the whole being a standard comic name formation with Eastern touches, turns into "Baima-i-Sistra," which plays on Eastern phonetics and name formations and on Western comic ethnic slurs and stereotypes.

Food

Food is often hard to translate, and in any case we do not know what many of the Plautine words for food referred to. In *Iran Man,* Bowman calls out the following instructions (87–88):

> Mix together the [wine mixed with honey]; get the [small variety of quince;
> sometimes used in double entendres for male genitalia] and the [pods of
> an unidentified tree] ready,
> so that it gets hot on the platters, and throw on the [sweet flags—a type of reed also
> used to make pens, musical instruments, and vine props].

(Definitions here come from the *OLD*.) You could, I suppose, speak this on stage so that it was funny, especially if you had an audience of undergraduate Classics majors accustomed to dictionary frustration and ready to laugh about it. But it wouldn't be the same kind of joke as in the original, though that joke is hard to get close to. Never mind that the text is corrupt and may be talking here not about food at all but about a sort of hot sangria (see notes ad loc.).

I translated the passage as follows: "Mix up the sangria, get out the nuts and the guacamole, / heat up the platters and throw on some fajitas." Why? *Mulsum* is sweetened wine; maybe the quinces are an hors d'oeuvre, anyway they're small and round, and we need a possible double entendre, hence "nuts"; the pods are clearly a lost cause, so (rejecting "edamame," which, though pods, would be hard to put over on stage) I made guacamole out of them; the platters (if they aren't pitchers) are okay as is; finally, stuck for something shaped like sugarcane that has to go on a heated platter, I opted for fajitas (flautas would be even closer to the Latin word, but not as recognizable). For, most important, all these words, except *mulsum,* are Greek; this is ethnic food, and, like other food lists in Plautus, has overtones of class. Think of translating [grain]: "popcorn" or "granola"? Or [cut of pork]: "hot dog" or "baked ham"? See *Weevil* 295 on "French-fried," *Towelheads* 54 on "corn-pone," and *Towelheads* 325–26 on "briquettes" or baked goods.

Animals

Plautus likes to use animal analogies, and sometimes these are hard to put directly into English. When Bowman tells his slave Toyboy to fly, on the run, Toyboy replies (*Iran Man* 199), "just like the ostrich does through the circus." This seems to refer to the presence of ostriches—N.B., an exotic creature, another by-product of conquest—in Roman public entertainment, where the usual point was to see them killed. As might very well be happening at the *ludi* at which this play might have been performed, hence a familiar sight to Plautus's audience. I first translated this line "like a pig through a slaughterhouse." But the proper analogy would probably be Demolition Derby, so I switched over to "like a Maserati at a Demolition Derby," going for foreign–fast–fragile–lower class, but losing the creature and the Orientalizing.

Money

Foreign coinage is hard to translate and, when specific names are used, gives a strong sense of location (pounds, pesos, yen . . .). The common denominations in Plautus are *Philippi aurei* ("gold Philips"), *minae* of silver, obols, and the generic *nummi,* here often translated "bucks" or "cash." Except for *nummi,* these are Greek forms of money and would have sounded either exotic or slangy or both to their audience. The one effort I made in this direction was to translate *Philippi* as "rubles" in *Towelheads,* but that misses the whole dimension of magic-wealthy-king (see section on "Topical Jokes" above); I tried "Krugerrands" first. The problem posed by translating money should at least lead to discussions of how money combines with nationality to produce meaning. And money is the Grail of all Plautus's plays.

But some things are just untranslatable, and if you transpose any of the plays into a modern setting, you get stuck at these points.

Slaves and Parasites

The most intractable one is slavery. These plays revolve around slavery; it is the central institution that governs what goes on. *Servus* and *ancilla* in Latin do not mean "servant" and "maidservant," they mean "male slave" and "female slave." *Erus* and *dominus* mean "master." In translating, I have often reduced these to "employee" and "boss," but all three plays hinge on buying a female slave out of her slavery. Luckily for us, there is no real modern equivalent; in this respect, the plays just cannot be translated out of their original cultural context.

Beyond this basic vocabulary, there is a whole range of roles and institutions that defy transposition. A freed slave, a *libertus* or *liberta,* would often go on working for his or her master, and would take the master's family name as his or her own. No English word conveys the social bond and status of the word *libertus*. Conversely, the former master or mistress is now the *patronus/a,* a person to whom the former slave owes loyalty as well as services. The chilling interlude at the end of *Iran Man* in which Bowman tells Georgia Moon that he expects her to do as he tells her and show proper gratitude provides a brief illustration of the hazards of such a relationship (and he is not even really her *patronus*). A person who was born free was an *ingenuus/a;* for the enslaved women of Plautus, facing prostitution, the proof of status as an *ingenua* was the magic news they awaited.

One of the most pervasive elements of the plays is the jokes revolving around the punishment and torture of slaves (see H. Parker 1989). This was evidently a surefire source of laughs, and there are a dozen insulting terms that not only cannot be directly translated into English but would not be funny if they were. Among these:

> *furcifer,* "fork-bearer": refers to a heavy wooden yoke used as a slave
> punishment (*Towelheads* 784)
> *mastigia,* "person suitable for flogging" (*Weevil* 567)
> *verbereum caput,* "head suitable for beating" (*Iran Man* 184)

These epithets are often located in a lowbrow context of insult matches; often they are used by one slave against another, so that the accusation of being a prime candidate for corporal punishment comes actually from one member of the oppressed group to another. *If* the plays are in any way an accurate rendition of the language of a subculture, we might compare the use of the term "nigger" within African-American culture, for example in the work of Richard Pryor. To see how far we are from really understanding these plays, imagine a translator setting *Persa* in the antebellum American South with an all-black or mostly black cast. Whereas Americans are used to laughing at the antics of poor folks and criminals, we have lost our taste for comedy based in slavery (but see McCarthy 2000 on comedy and the minstrel shows).

Another untranslatable role is that of the *parasitus*. Though the word is Greek, the position is basically that of the *cliens,* the freeborn person dependent on a more powerful or solvent free person, who would be his *patronus*. The *parasitus* in particular is dependent on his *patronus* for meals—the word in Greek literally means "next-to-the-food"—and in Plautus the *parasitus* is greedy, always hankering after food, which is used to motivate him (cf. Gowers 1993: 76–78; Tylawsky 2002). This

Rabelaisian element plays a large part in Aristophanic comedy (e.g., Dikaiopolis in *Acharnians*) and also in the Atellane farce, in which one of the four stock characters was Manducus, represented by a mask with huge, champing jaws. Food is one of the main topics of Plautine comedy, and the *parasitus* is a main source of food humor. There are two great examples in the plays in this volume—Fat Jack (Saturio) in *Iran Man* and Weevil (Curculio) himself—and it was very difficult to render the (derogatory) vox propria *parasitus* by which other characters often refer to them. In *Weevil*, I changed the translation depending on the speaker; Beauregard likes Weevil, so for him Weevil is his "associate"; to others he is his "sidekick," "that leech," "that bloodsucker," "that bum." Fat Jack is less problematically a bum. But his parasitic relationship to Bowman is all the more interesting in that Bowman is just a slave, and can only dispense food to Fat Jack insofar as he has control of his master's kitchen. Plautus's audience might have been more attuned than we are to the fact that the parasites are not just greedy, they are hungry. Some of them were familiar with hunger.

Pimps and Whores

Translatable, but odd to a modern audience, is the persistence of pimps and whores as main characters in these plays. The pimp is the archetypal bad guy of Plautus's plays, though actually a pimp appears in only five of the extant plays. But sixteen of the plays feature prostitutes or young women at risk of becoming prostitutes. Come to think of it, the fact that the young men at the center of these plays are so often in love with girls who are either prostitutes or on the verge of becoming prostitutes is not all that unfamiliar a plot element to current American audiences—see, for example, *Pretty Woman, Nightshift, Risky Business, Trading Places, The Girl Next Door,* and so on. And Plautus's prostitutes are often about as whorelike as Julia Roberts in *Pretty Woman*—that is, not very. They are usually potential wives. But the pimp has disappeared from modern romantic comedy and strikes a harsh note in these plays. Like slavery, he cannot be elided; the plots demand that the hero pay the pimp to get the girl.

Swearing

Another element is rarely fully translated in Plautus's plays: swearing. The slave insults discussed above, which must sorely vex any translator, have resulted in translations of Plautus littered with names nobody has been called in English for a long time: "you rascal!" "you scoundrel!" "you jackanapes!" A moment's reflection will assure us that, when Americans use bad language, we rely heavily on sex and excrement. This is rarely so in Plautus, although later Roman satire is full of sexual insults. But Plautus is full of other words that are evidently very rude. Translated literally, they fit comfortably with "scoundrel," "rascal," "jackanapes": "Go to a bad thing!" or "Go to the cross!" And Plautus is full to bursting with oaths, which are almost never really translated at all: *hercle*, "By Hercules!" and *edepol*, "By Pollux!" and *di deaeque te perdant*, "May the gods and goddesses ruin you!"

I have tried, in these translations, to use insults that are actually in common use in American English today and to translate oaths with oaths. This may be the most unsettling element in these translations; they often sound blasphemous. Oddly enough for plays produced at religious festivals, these plays often *are* blasphemous. My feeling is that to make these plays really understandable, the artificial gentility of "By Pollux, go to a bad place, you rascal!" needs to be replaced by what the Latin really meant, which is (roughly) "Jesus, get lost, asshole!" Since nobody has sworn by Pollux or Hercules for a long time, English translations need to pepper the plays with "God," "Christ," "goddamn," "bloody," "Jesus," and so on—as people actually do speak now, even godless humanists; once you substitute "Jesus" for every *hercle* on a page, suddenly it starts to sound like people talking. The long list of alternatives includes euphemistic substitutes like "golly," "gee," "jeeze," "egad," "By Jove," "By George," and so on, and I have used these as it seemed appropriate. For Catholic audiences, the polytheistic *di deaeque* might be translated "Jesus, Mary, and Joseph," but perhaps not elsewhere.

Similarly, jokes based on Roman religion need to be transposed into something recognizable to a modern audience. When Weevil describes how the soldier invited him to dinner, he says, *religio fuit, denegare nolui* (*Weevil* 350)—"It was [an impediment to action resulting from doubt, religious awe, conscience, etc.]—I didn't like to say no." I transposed this into "It was my Christian duty—I didn't like to say no," because this is a joke about the Weevil's cheerful greed, expressed here as hypocrisy, and that joke exists in English. I have translated almost all references to multiple gods and goddesses into references to the singular "God" or "Jesus"; like the use of Roman names and togas, the persistence of polytheism in these plays usually serves to distance them from current audiences. If you swear by one of that huge pantheon, to a modern audience it doesn't sound like swearing at all. But it was, and should be rendered as such. At one point (*Towelheads* 1220), I substituted Joseph and Mary for Jupiter and Juno, and the result sounds quite blasphemous, but so it was in the original. The one ancient deity who resisted translation here was Venus, and she stayed in; maybe she has never lost her following.

PERFORMANCE ISSUES

Students of theater will realize that this volume is the product of limited stage experience. For expert advice, see the website for MASC (Modern Actors Staging Classics) maintained by C. W. Marshall—www.cnrs.ubc.ca/masc—and Marshall's book on Plautine stagecraft (2006).

Imaginary Casts and the Comedy Troupe

As noted above, I not only transposed the plays to modern settings, I imagined an ideal cast for each, now included in each play's cast list. I found that I could not write speakable lines without hearing a particular comedian's voice in my head. Whether this will work for readers, I have no idea. If what I have done does not work for you, I still recommend that you try it for yourself; populate these plays with the people who make you laugh and see what happens.

However, this thought experiment has convinced me of two major points about Plautus's plays. (No, three; three major points. No . . . let me go out and come back in again.)

One: These plays were written for particular actors. If the *grex* referred to in various prologues really stuck together, the same actors would appear in play after play; the playwright would have known their range intimately, and the plays would reflect that. And I think the repetitiveness of the cast of characters has something to do with that (possible) fact of theatrical life.

Weevil has to be someone with a lot of manic energy: I imagined Michael Palin here, but it could be Roberto Benigni or Eddie Murphy or Jackie Chan—even Steve Irwin taking a break from hunting crocodiles. I have a hunch that Plautus played Weevil himself. Of the various soppy young men in love, Boris in *Towelheads,* with major episodes of inarticulate raving, cries out to be played by Hugh Grant, but Beauregard in *Weevil* is much more deadpan and has to carry off a ridiculous deadpan song: Owen Wilson. Bowman in *Iran Man,* though, is totally different: with his all-slave milieu and his nasty ways, he was made to be played by Jason Mewes. But maybe they were all played by the same actor originally.

Two: Each play has a feel to it, each different from the next. *Iran Man* has a Kevin Smith ambience, gritty and lowlife, but young and full of trashy force; also full of metatheatrics and self-reflexivity. *Towelheads* plays well as light romantic comedy in drag; *Weevil* is more like music hall or *Saturday Night Live,* more a series of bits than a play. What does this mean in terms of the first point and the idea of a troupe with a repertory of plays? Maybe it has to do with the fact that all comedy—and all drama—is a rehash of leftovers that have been lying around for-ever, and that the job of any troupe that wants to stay in business is to keep it fresh, to keep remixing that old hash (see Gowers 1993: 78–107, esp. 83, on Aeschylus's Homeric steaks. Even Homer didn't get to start from scratch.)

But thinking about Plautus's troupe made me think about how common a form that has been historically for comedy in the West. Not only do movie direc-tors do this now: Woody Allen, the Coen brothers, Christopher Guest, Kevin Smith. This tradition seems to move directly up from antiquity into the comme-dia dell'arte to Shakespeare, and on, visible in literature in *Nicholas Nickleby* (Vin-cent Crummles's melodrama troupe), and in J. B. Priestley's *The Good Companions* (pierrots), strongly in the D'Oyly Carte troupe, taking literary form in the novels of P. G. Wodehouse that paralleled his writing for musical comedy, and on into TV and situation comedy. The Savoy operas were so markedly written for partic-ular voices and talents that subsequent incarnations of the company have a prob-lem re-creating them across the board.

Writing funny lines is a lot easier if you can rely on a funny voice to put them over. Listen to Richard Suart sing "The Law Is the True Embodiment" in Gilbert and Sullivan's *Iolanthe,* and listen to him sing the lines "All very agreeable girls, and none / is over the age of twenty-one." Probably the word "twenty-one" has never before or since been pronounced with the degree of salivating lechery with which Suart infuses it. But Suart is the inheritor of a set of roles designed for George Grossmith, the original Savoy comic baritone, who started out as a sort of musical standup (or, rather, sitdown—like Victor Borge) comic. And Grossmith in turn was part of a company whose personnel in part determined the dramatis personae of many of the Savoy operas. There is always a brilliant young man (tenor), or two, and a comical older man (baritone), and a forbidding older man (bass), and a bril-liant young woman (soprano), with a couple of less talented soprano sidekicks, and a forbidding/comical, plump older woman (contralto).

The particular kinds of songs Gilbert and Sullivan wrote were likewise condi-tioned by the talents of their original troupe: the patter song, the soprano fire-works. (When Grossmith left, just before *The Gondoliers,* one result was that *Gon-doliers* is markedly short on funny songs.) This brings us to the issue of music.

Music

There is one huge problem of loss that has to be dealt with in translating these plays. They were originally musicals. This was one of Plautus's big innovations: he got rid of the Greek chorus, made the star actors into singers/dancers/actors, and wrote a lot of clearly very funny songs. All the tunes are gone.

As a child, I spent hours poring over a copy of *A Treasury of Gilbert and Sullivan,* edited by Deems Taylor. I couldn't read music, so I didn't know most of the tunes. I read the lyrics, though; anyone can see that they are funny. Nobody can turn a rhyme like W. S. Gilbert. But repeatedly listening to the operettas on CD made me think a lot about funny music, and what makes music funny. When Richard Dauntless in *Ruddigore* calls Rose Maybud a "right little, tight little, slight little, light little, trim little, prim little craft"—a list of diminutives that could come right out of Plautus—it's clearly a nice bit of rhyming and repetition, but it's the way the music exactly echoes what makes the words funny that makes this so brilliant: it's a right little, tight little jig, it sounds nautical, and it's also extremely catchy. The same goes for the gorgeous anthemlike tune Sullivan wrote for "When Britain Really Ruled the Waves" in *Iolanthe*—it would make a superb national anthem, except for the words ("The House of Peers throughout the war, did nothing in particular, and did it very well"). The wonderful tunes Sullivan wrote for the comic semi-heavy who pops up in every play, now memorably Richard Suart, often sound like funny dances: the Lord Chancellor in *Iolanthe* jigs irresistibly through "a pleasant occupation for, a rather susceptible Chancellor"; the Duke of Plaza-Toro in *Gondoliers* stomps like a flamenco dancer through "In Enterprise of Martial Kind" as "that unaffected, undetected, well-connected warrior, the Duke of Plaza-Toro." Similarly, Tom Lehrer's "Vatican Rag" is funny not only because of the words but because it's a rag, and the opening words are dance instructions ("First you get down on your knees . . .")—it's a takeoff on dance rags of the 1920s, and specifically on "Varsity Drag." And "Fugue for Tinhorns" is funny partly because it's a fugue—a classical form—sung by three gamblers, about horseracing.

If you think about what would be lost if *H.M.S. Pinafore* or *Guys and Dolls* were done without music, and without the songs even being read as metrical, you get a sense of how much is lost of Plautus. It's breathtaking, and disheartening.

However, it's also an overstatement. Sullivan is quoted as saying, "The first thing I have to decide upon is the rhythm, and I arrange the rhythm before I come to the question of melody" (D. Taylor 1941: 8). For a technical explanation of Plautine meter, see Beare 1964: 320–34, where he entertainingly illustrates many of Plautus's famously numerous meters from the lyrics to Gilbert and Sullivan songs. If you read the plays in Latin, you can, with training, read the original meters, and see what the patterns were. And it turns out that the number of real songs—production numbers—would have taken up a much smaller proportion of the show than the songs in a Savoy opera or a musical, never mind grand opera: only one long number in *Weevil* (it shows up in this translation as three songs linked by spoken lines); four numbers in *Iran Man;* and two in *Towelheads.* (N.B. of these seven songs, five involve female characters, and two that are sung by male characters are hymns: song type matched to voice type?) So the plays were more like comic revues with a few songs than like fullblown musicals. Moreover, Plautus had no chorus, and he didn't have much in the way of a pit orchestra, either; based on the scanty evidence, it seems likely that all he had was a woodwind player and maybe a couple of percussionists. So the loss is not so large in scope.

The meters are somewhat difficult to translate into English equivalents, though. And the plays were in meter almost throughout—though not rhymed; rhyme was not part of Roman poetry. We do not really have enough evidence to understand fully how these meters were used, but the evidence suggests that there were three modes of utterance in the plays: speech, recitative, and song (see Beare 1964: 219–32; Habinek 2005).

Long sections of the plays were spoken; these were set in iambic senarii, and the metrical effect of a single line of it is the same (with a lot of tinkering allowed) as a line and a half of "Stopping by Woods on a Snowy Evening":

Whose woods these are I think I know; his house is in

. . . or of a line of Shakespeare plus one iamb:

Whether 'tis nobler in the mind to suffer the slings

In translating the plays, I have generally adhered to this pattern where I found it (sometimes I used pentameter instead), though you could easily read the translations in this volume without realizing it. If you do read for meter, plenty of these translated lines won't look like smooth senarii, but that is emphatically true of the original, which was anything but metrically glassy. The original also clearly uses short words like "now" and "here" and "well" as grout to fill up the metrical line, and it is similarly fascinating to see how many ways you can translate a single line in order to take in both the sense and the meter.

The sense of loss is much greater for the songs and recitatives. The songs are marked as such by the complex metrical schemes they employ; with tunes, these would not have seemed like mathematical exercises, as they do now. I have turned the songs in *Weevil* and *Towelheads* into songs "to the tune of," and the songs in *Iran Man* into rhymed rap, and all I can say is that this kind of thing, though it seemed worth a try here, is funnier when you do not also have to translate Latin as closely as possible. A few short dialogues and transitions that were sung in the original I have translated as spoken.

Between songs and spoken lines were the recitatives—chanted lines—recognizable by their meters, most commonly the trochaic septenarius (trochaic tetrameter catalectic, seven trochees plus one syllable). Other recitative meters were the trochaic octonarius, iambic septenarius, and iambic octonarius (see Beare 1964: 221, 323, 328–29). These meters also appear in Roman folk forms like riddles and charms and the soldiers' nasty songs at triumphs. The trochaic octonarius amounts to a pair of lines from Longfellow's *Hiawatha:*

By the shores of Gitche Gumee / By the shining Big-Sea-Water

It also, interestingly, is basically the same meter used in hip-hop: just a coincidence? Listening to Public Enemy will give a fairly accurate idea of the beat and tone of *Iran Man.* So in *Iran Man* I reproduced these meters with some care, and they could be read or performed as unrhymed rap (see *Iran Man* introduction). In *Towelheads* and *Weevil,* here more genteel, I did them all, roughly, as trochaic octonarii, except for one run of iambic septenarii in *Weevil.* In English, the difference just boils down to starting on the downbeat or the upbeat. I have noted the meter of the original at change points and scene openings here; for exact lists, see Lindsay's OCT at the end of each volume.

The idea of a musical accompanied only by a woodwind player and a couple of percussionists often makes commentators on Roman comedy express doubt about its musicality. This has to be a mistake, abetted by the common translation of *tibia,* the word for the instrument used by the musicians of the *palliata,* as "flute." Based on visual evidence, and the fact that it could be heard above singing in an outdoor space, it must have been more like a clarinet or tenor saxophone. Plenty of vernacular music forms do not rely on big orchestration: rock, bluegrass, zydeco, polka, square dance, jazz, hip-hop. The cantina band in *Star Wars* is not a big band, but it really swings, and the main melody line is carried by something like a clarinet. We are hampered by having little idea of what ancient music sounded like, and by a suspicion that it may have sounded like Near Eastern music, which is hard to follow for most Western ears. Probably it did; who knows? But I feel certain that the songs in Plautus (a) had tunes, which (b) were funny, that is, parodying serious forms or echoing what was funny in the words, and (c) were marked by intricate, catchy rhythms. Both mime (Cicero *Cael.* 65) and, later, pantomimus, included a percussive accompaniment performed by a sort of tap dancer, the *scabillarius.*

For the songs in *Weevil,* I chose familiar tunes that tie in with the meaning and/or structure of the lyrics rather than with the original metrical scheme. In the two big songs in *Towelheads,* the tunes relate to the original rhythms: the bacchiacs of the girls' opening scene are interpreted via strip-tease beat, and the girls' final duet, which Plautus set in anapests, the "marching rhythm," appears here as a march (a little meter joke).

SUGGESTIONS FOR FURTHER READING

Of course, you do not have to limit yourself to Plautus to find out about Roman attitudes toward the cultures Rome was busily demolishing. But you do have to fast-forward. You can pick up an interesting angle from the histories of Polybius, a Greek exile living at Rome about a generation after Plautus. You can pick up a lot, with patience, from the speeches of Cicero, especially the Verrine orations (60s B.C.E.); or from Horace's *Satires* and *Epodes* (30s C.E.); or, with caution, from the histories of Diodorus Siculus (60s B.C.E.) and Livy (20s B.C.E.–10s C.E.). You can pick up a lot more from the (lesser-known) ethnographers: Caesar (40s B.C.E.), Strabo (10s B.C.E.), Mela (40s C.E.), the elder Pliny (70s C.E.), and especially the *Agricola* and *Germania* of Tacitus (98 C.E.). Most of all, you should look at three satirists of the empire: Petronius and his novel, the *Satyricon* (probably written around 60 C.E.); Martial and his epigrams (80s–90s C.E.); and Juvenal and his satires (110s C.E.; readers of this book should not miss Juvenal's fifteenth satire, on cannibalism in Egypt, along with his more famous third, on Greeks). All are available in translation, but it is well worth learning Latin to be able to read Petronius and Juvenal in the original. They are two of the greatest satirists who have ever written, and Juvenal is one of the greatest stylists; only Samuel Johnson ever really approximated Juvenal in translation. Satire was like the acme of standup comedy; if you are reading this book because of a general interest in comedy, do not miss Roman satire.

Meanwhile, for recommended translations and some starting points in secondary literature, see the last section of the bibliography at the end of this volume.

WEEVIL (CURCULIO)

Weevil, to help his boss Beauregard, goes to Jerusalem for cash.
Eventually he tricks Beau's rival, a soldier, out of his ring.
Eluding the soldier, he uses the ring to seal papers,
Virtuously tricking a pimp and a banker out of the girl.
In the end, the soldier returns, and sues for the girl—she's his
Long-lost sister, and he lets her marry Beauregard.*

INTRODUCTION

Of the three plays in this volume, *Weevil (Curculio)* has least to do with the Orient. True, the title character is in Caria during act 1, and returns in act 2 with a story of what happened to him there; later on, he makes up more elaborate stories to serve the needs of his plot. As in many other Plautus plays, Out There is the crucial source of money, food, and slaves—this shows up even in the name of the pimp, "the Cappadocian." What makes *Weevil* stand out amongst the plays is its juxtaposition of "here" and "there" and the way its location floats. Though it is set in Epidaurus, in Greece, at several key points it is explicitly in Rome, and has more explicit things to say about Rome than any of Plautus's other plays (see volume introduction under "Locations").

The first act is taken up by a night scene in which Beauregard, the stock young man, accompanied by his slave Cornwallis, achieves a visit with his sweetheart Wanda, with the help of the old woman Madame Lola. Beauregard and Cornwallis are both essentially straight men; I imagined them as Owen Wilson and Richard E. Grant, both understated comedians, notably funny even in deadpan (Wilson) or by means of facial expressions (Grant).

This opening act is a sendup of a stock scene in ancient love poetry, the *paraklausithyron* (literally "beside the closed door"). In drama, the earliest extant example is the scene at the end of Aristophanes' *Ekklesiazousai* (which also begins with a night scene); otherwise this kind of thing is more lyric than dramatic. In such scenes, the young man is imagined as outside the closed door of the house of his beloved. He has come there late, after a party, often wearing the lei left over from the party, sometimes drunk, and he wants to get inside. He calls on his girl to let him in, with protestations of love; he addresses the door directly, beseeching it not to be so cruel to him; he lies on the ground and waters the threshold with his tears. Here Beauregard talks to the door and sings a song to it, which is incredibly stupid in English and not much better in Latin. The scene would have to be done by someone with a talent for spoofing an amorous style of singing, like Bill Murray and his lounge singer act. One of the things that would make this scene funny for a Roman audience would be the way it gets the door into the act—the doors are

57

always a big feature of the action in Plautine comedy, and here the door is treated as if it were a character. This comic idea is picked up later in Latin literature by the love poets Catullus (poem 67) and Propertius (1.16).

The verb Beauregard uses for his serenade, *occento,* would call to mind for the audience the traditional Roman folk practice whereby a person's enemies gathered outside his house door to stage an insult match or make a demand (see volume introduction under "Stage Directions"). This practice is associated with chasing women several times in Plautus: once in *Iran Man,* when Bowman and Dorkalot envision how Dorkalot will be besieged by Cherry's wannabe lovers; and with details of street harassment in *Mercator* (405–11). Here Beauregard in effect draws the audience in with him to participate in his serenade.

The two female roles in this play are even more caricatures, and less important, than the female roles in *Towelheads,* where at least the female roles provide some great comic lines and a big musical number for a couple of drag queens. Madame Lola, the old woman who is guarding the door, is an example of a comic type common throughout antiquity and represented in art as well as in comic and erotic literature: the drunken old bag (there are three old bags in the *paraklausithyron* in *Ekklesiazousai*). Mme. Lola comes out, does her drunk scene with Beauregard and Cornwallis, brings Wanda out, and is not seen again in the play. She is more appropriately played by a man in drag (e.g., Terry Jones) than by an actress, even Lily Tomlin. Similarly, Wanda is pretty much a nonentity: in her first scene, she has little to do except get into a clinch with Beauregard and provoke Cornwallis; at the end of the play, she does have a flashback speech, but otherwise her lines are a foil for Beauregard's. Wanda is a good example of woman as commodity in Plautus; like Georgia Moon in *Iran Man,* she motivates the action without doing anything herself.

When Weevil appears in the middle of act 2, the play takes off. Weevil is what is called in Latin a *parasitus,* a Greek loanword that literally means "next-to-the-food" and in Plautus describes a professional sponger who gets meals by being funny (see volume introduction under "Slaves and Parasites"; Corbett 1986; Gowers 1993: 76–78). His entrance immediately plunges him into a couple of important comic monologues, the first of which is often cited by Roman historians as a picture of Roman street life in the mid-Republic. In opening with a monologue, Weevil follows a pattern established for the *parasitus* in other Plautine plays— Working Boy (Ergasilus) in *Captivi,* Little Dick (Peniculus) in *Menaechmi,* Fat Jack (Saturio) in *Towelheads,* Funny Boy (Gelasimus) in *Stichus*—and each of them is very funny, a star vehicle, and also presents a beef about some social issue. But this monologue not only sets up Weevil as the comic key to the play, it brings up what will be a recurring comic element in the play: the idea "foreigners are funny." However, though Weevil here gives a detailed picture of lower-class Greeks in the streets of Rome, he also tellingly identifies himself with them through costume.

The stipulation that all male characters wear loud sports jackets and ties derives from the Yale setting and is tied to a complicated joke made by Weevil in his opening speech. He complains that everywhere you go in what is evidently Rome, you run into *isti Graeci*, "those Greeks" (= "repulsive foreigners"), wearing the *pallium* (short cloak associated with Greeks, differentiated from the Roman citizen's toga). But the *pallium* was also the set costume for actors playing male characters in Plautine comedy, and this kind of comedy was called the *palliata*—that's how strong the association was. Moreover, as discussed in the volume introduction (see "Actors"), some of the actors themselves were probably native speakers of Greek and, if slaves, were not themselves entitled to wear the toga. In the translation in this volume, I have made Weevil complain about "those foreigners with the loud jackets" (288). The point is that the actors here are made to complain, self-reflexively, about themselves; Weevil should describe the foreigners as wearing whatever it is he wears himself. And in fact this self-reflexive joke will show up again in *Iran Man,* when Fat Jack describes the good *parasitus* as being like a Cynic philosopher (123–25)—again the accessories overlap with those of the comic actor and particularly the *parasitus* (cf. Gelasimus's auction in *Stichus;* volume introduction under "Translate or Transpose?"). Moreover, Weevil describes "those Greeks" as wearing the *pallium* "with their heads covered"—possibly referring to the way runaway slaves were depicted in mime—and soon thereafter calls them *drapetae* (290), the Greek word for "runaway slaves." Did runaway slaves hide behind theatrical masks? This speech, then, blends not only "here" and "there" but "them" and "us," actors and Others (on hybrid identity and ambivalence about Greece, see volume introduction under "Locations").

Weevil is defined in the play as someone who has been to the Near East and come back again, with tales to tell. Even the sort of boasting regularly associated with the mercenary soldiers in Plautus (compare the soldier's speeches in *Towelheads*) is here usurped by Weevil, who has all the best bits: he takes on the banker and the pimp, while Beauregard and Cornwallis sink into the background. For most of the rest of the play, everyone else is Weevil's straight man (as in his interchange with Mr. Wolf, 406–53, with Weevil's repeated *eloquar . . . dicam . . . dicam . . . dicam*—"I'll tell you"). If Plautus had the kind of theatrical company I envision (see volume introduction under "Performance Issues"), the man who played Weevil might have played all the other great *parasiti* too.

The play is ostensibly set in Epidaurus, a small city, southwest of Athens, of no major importance in the Greek wars of Plautus's time. It was famous for its theater and for its temple of Aesculapius, at which seekers after health would sleep overnight, in the belief that the dreams they had there would give them messages about their health (a process called "incubation"); naturally, a nice donation to the temple fund was acceptable. In *Weevil,* one house door belongs to the pimp who owns Wanda, the other to the temple of Aesculapius, and a third door would be Beauregard's front door. This is like having a pimp's front door abut the front of St. Patrick's Cathedral or the Mayo Clinic; it's a comic juxtaposition, though, surprisingly, not an unrealistic one (see McGinn 2004 on the lack of "moral zoning" in Roman cities). Moreover, the pimp initially comes out of the temple door rather than his own; he's a hypochondriac pimp, an unusual feature, and his concern for his health and for what the god can do for him is one of the only things that anchor the play in Epidaurus. Otherwise, it could be anywhere, and indeed it floats explicitly back to Rome for a piece of act 4 (see below). I set the play in New Haven as a city outside New York but near it, famous both for theater and for a major hospital or other temple to health. And that is basically the point of the setting of *Weevil:* it needs to be in a place that has a hospital that the audience knows well by name and reputation. I then wound up changing most of the references to Aesculapius to "the Big Doctor"; there is no real divine equivalent now to Aesculapius, and there really is no current equivalent to incubation. This constitutes a semi-untranslatable aspect of the play, but hypochondria remains easily recognizable.

The feel of the play is farcical: the bits are reminiscent of music hall, and the play is full of puns and elegant turns of phrase, ranging in tone from music hall to Oscar Wilde. Many of these are difficult to translate adequately (see notes below). This comic barrage perhaps sets the audience up for one of the key things in *Weevil,* the metatheatrical interlude that begins act 4, which I have set as a break featuring Alistair Cooke, as in *Masterpiece Theater.* The speaker treats the audience to a useful tour of the city of Rome, again contributing to the sense that Epidaurus is a notional setting at best. The tour focuses on the Forum Romanum, and there is a good possibility that the play itself might have been put on in the Forum, on a temporary stage, so that the Director could actually point to the spots he was naming (Beacham 1991: 63; Moore 1991: 358–60). Indeed, as Timothy Moore argues, the audience might have been sitting in bleachers actually located in some of the spots being pointed at, which would certainly have made the whole exercise even funnier.

The interlude would have been much more of a surprise in its Roman version than it is in translation, since as far as we know commercial breaks were not a conventional part of Roman theater; it might have reminded the audience of the choral interludes in Greek New Comedy, or even of the parabasis in Old Comedy, if there were any theater historians in the audience. In this translation, I have converted all the Roman landmarks to New York ones; any modern production should use a familiar nearby city, if possible the very place where the production is being staged. Again, here, the play highlights geography, "here" vs. "there"; at one point (400–403) this joke is projected onto the body of Mr. Wolf. Clearly, not only foreigners are funny. But which Romans are funny in the Forum scene? The rich, the pretentious, and those who break trust. And whores, who pervade every section of the Director's tour. Which is odd, because the protagonists of Plautus's plays are usually engaged in elaborate con games, usually in order to gain possession of female whores. Is this a form of social revenge? Is the play commenting on prostitution as Roman reality as well as theatrical fantasy? We know that actors later in the Republic suffered the same civil disabilities as whores (see volume introduction under "Background on Roman Culture"; "Actors").

Weevil's other big moment is the account he gives to Mr. Wolf of his supposed travels in the East with the soldier. As the map shows (see page 18), Weevil and the soldier have covered an improbable amount of territory, basically the whole Near East plus India, conquering everything, and with side trips into places like Tribal Onetittistan. For more on this sort of fantastic geography, see the volume introduction under "Locations"; you'll see something similar in *Iran Man* in the made-up letter from Bowman's boss about the sack of the City of Gold in Arabia, and in the amazing Persian name Einstein makes up for himself. The contrast between Out There and Right Here is nowhere more sharply or surrealistically drawn in Plautus than in *Weevil*.

PERFORMANCE

For an account of a masked staging of *Curculio,* with images, see C. W. Marshall's MASC website at www.cnrs.ubc.ca/masc/curculio.html.

MUSIC

The songs in *Weevil* are limited to a single long song sequence that constitutes act 1, scene 2. It begins with a solo by Mme. Lola, turns into a trio by Mme. Lola, Beauregard, and Cornwallis, and ends with Beauregard's serenade at the pimp's door. The translation suggests a music-hall feel for Mme. Lola's solo and a musical-comedy feel for the trio, associated with stage business and (probably) dancing; the serenade should sound sappy. Otherwise, *Weevil* does not exhibit much metrical variety. The translation treats the senarii as iambic but sometimes as pentameter; the long lines are mostly done as trochaic septenarii or octonarii, though there is a run of iambic septenarii at 487–532 (this is the meter of "Barbara Allen"—"In Scarlet Town where I was born there was a fair maid dwellin'").

THE NAMES AND THE CAST

CORNWALLIS

The name of Phaedromus's slave is a great joke and very difficult to translate. He is called "Palinurus," which was the name of the helmsman of Aeneas, who tumbled overboard just before landfall in Italy and was drowned: a sort of last bad travel day for the Trojans. A cape in southern Italy was named after him. But his name was also intrinsically funny; it can be read as meaning "Pee Again" (thus in Martial 3.78), which gives it the comic force of English names like Seaman or Hitchcock. Plautus doesn't go there, thus providing a neat index of the distance that separates even Plautus from Martial. (Well, except maybe at line 166; like many of Plautus's double entendres, this one could register or not with various audience members, but might be targeting native speakers of Greek.) A rendering of his name in American terms necessitates a not-that-major figure of a colonizing force who comes to a sad but somewhat ridiculous end and sounds historical and epic. Ponce de Leon would be pretty good, but a bit unwieldy. So, "Cornwallis," after the surrendering British general. Cornwallis's lines are here written for someone with an English accent who can sound snide; I was thinking of Richard E. Grant as in *Gosford Park.*

BEAUREGARD

The young man in love is named "Phaedromus," which means something like "Radiant Face." And he needs to be upper class. Hence "Beauregard," a Southern boy at Yale. Beauregard's lines are here written for someone with a slight, gentlemanly Southern accent, who can be funny while pretending to be serious; I was thinking of Owen Wilson as in *The Royal Tenenbaums.*

MME. LOLA

The old lady's name, "Leaena," is a stock prostitute's name in antiquity dating back to classical Greece; it means "Lioness." Hence "Madame" to indicate age and "Lola" as a stock showgirl's name. Mme. Lola's lines are here written for someone with a Cockney falsetto and visible beard stubble; I was thinking of Terry Jones (as also for Yasmin/Giddenis in *Towelheads*), because of his memorable old bags in various Python productions, for example as Mrs. Bloke in *Monty Python's The Meaning of Life*.

WANDA

"Planesium" means "Little Wandering One." This name is fancy, and not attested as a citizen woman's name, but it is not a common prostitute's name, either, though the *-ium* neuter diminutive ending is common for stage prostitutes. "Wanda" isn't so much a translation of "Planesium" as a bilingual pun. Mercedes? Mustang Sally? Runaround Sue? Feel free to send in suggestions c/o the publishers. I thought of Dana Carvey for this role; you would need a drag actor who could be demure.

TURK

The pimp's name in *Curculio* is "Cappadox," which means "person from Cappadocia." Cappadocia, in what is now east central Turkey and just west of what was even then Armenia, was a hinterland in the Near East, not prominent in the wars of the third and second centuries B.C.E. As a name for a pimp, "Turk" has more specific connotations than "Cappadox"—shades of the seraglio—and of course no Turks had yet arrived on the Mediterranean scene. But "Cappadox" is definitely an Orientalizing name (compare the Armenian at the end of Juvenal's second satire); John Wright suggests the name here derives from a connection between Cappadocia and the slave trade. I had Gene Wilder in mind, and Turk's lines are specifically written for Wilder's whining intonations and outraged innocence.

COOK

The Cook in *Curculio* is just named "Cocus"—Cook; he's a generic character. I was thinking of John Goodman.

WEEVIL

"Curculio" just means "Weevil." This was a funny word in Latin as well as in English: a little bug that eats up the food in your pantry. It's especially appropriate because Weevil is a *parasitus,* a guy who's always hungry and trying to scrounge a meal; see the volume introduction under "Slaves and Parasites" for the problems raised by this role. His lines here are written specifically for Michael Palin (formerly of Monty Python) speaking with a strong Cockney accent.

MR. WOLF

In *Curculio,* his name is "Lyco." Like the Wolf/Lycus in *Poenulus,* this is a name formed from the Greek word for "wolf," which is a stem found elsewhere amongst Roman sex workers; *lupa,* "she-wolf," shows up in later Latin as slang for a female prostitute. But here the wolf is scary as a banker, and is named with fond thoughts of Harvey Keitel as Mr. Wolf in *Pulp Fiction,* though this Mr. Wolf is not scarily efficient but pompous and conceited, like Dan Aykroyd in *Trading Places.* Mr. Wolf's ponderous, boring lines are written with Dan Aykroyd's delivery in mind. We might also think of Snidely Whiplash and the long tradition of melodramatic bankers he represents.

THE DIRECTOR

In *Curculio,* he is listed as "Choragus," which literally means "Chorus-leader," but was the technical term for the person responsible for organizing the nuts and bolts of the show. Both here and in *Iran Man* (159; also at *Trinummus* 858), the *choragus* is responsible for renting out the costumes, and the word is often translated "stage manager" or "props manager." The smarmy opening lines of his speech reminded me of Alistair Cooke. Martin Short as Jiminy Glick would also be good. Or Dan Aykroyd doing Alistair Cooke—roles in ancient theater were often doubled.

LT. NAPOLEON PLAZA-TORO

In the *Personae* of *Curculio,* he is listed as "Therapontigonus Miles." Like other Plautine soldiers, he has a ridiculously long name. But elsewhere in the play there is even more to his name: he is Therapontigonus Platagidorus. The parts of his name mean, roughly, "Squire-Antigonus Flat- [or Street-] [or Broad-] Mover-Gift." Hence "Lieutenant," for the "squire" part. Antigonus was the name of three awe-inspiring Macedonian kings/generals in the century before Plautus, hence "Napoleon." And "Platagidorus" is really just a nonsense name, a grand-sounding mush of Greek names (Plato? Agesilaus? Agis?); I have substituted here the title of the Duke in Gilbert and Sullivan's *Gondoliers,* in honor of that character's prowess in running away, and, well, because it sounds a little like "Platagidorus." Paul Nixon, in the Loeb *Plautus,* similarly gave up and used "Smackahead." As with the soldier in *Towelheads,* it was not possible to think of this role as belonging to anyone other than John Cleese. Well, maybe John Lithgow; but the lines are here written for someone sounding like a comic British army officer.

CAST OF CHARACTERS

Cornwallis, a slave   [Palinurus, a slave]

Beauregard, a young man   [Phaedromus, a young man]

Mme. Lola, an old woman   [Leaena, an old woman]

Wanda, a virgin   [Planesium, a virgin]

Turk, a pimp   [Cappadox, a pimp]

Cook, a cook   [Cook]

Weevil, a freeloader   [Curculio, a *parasitus*]

Mr. Wolf, a banker   [Lyco, a banker]

the Director   [Choragus]

Lt. Napoleon Plaza-Toro, a soldier   [Therapontigonus, a soldier]

Boy   [not listed]†

Scene

New Haven [Epidaurus].

Three house doors: R, Beauregard's house; center, pimp's house; L, Yale–New Haven Hospital and Health Spa (YNHHHS). An altar to Venus stands before the pimp's house. {Possible trim: flashing lights, neon, a wishing well, a prominent slot for donations, an ample tray for offerings. A comparable feature might stand before the YNHHHS. The flashing lights on the altar might well flash for each bad joke in the night scene that opens the play, of which there are quite a few.} Exit stage L goes to the forum, exit stage R goes to the harbor.

Costume Note

All male characters wear loud sports jackets and ties (except the soldier, who wears a military uniform including a trenchcoat). The goal is for the male characters' costumes to be on that unblushing borderline between preppie and garish, with a touch of Liberace. (By "sports jacket" is meant here not an item of outerwear bearing the logo of an athletic team but a jacket like the top half of a suit or a blazer.)

Songs

There is only one song sequence in *Weevil,* a long one in act 1 that incorporates dialogue: the songs appear in the body of the play set up as songs in English. A nonmetrical translation appears after the end of the play.

---

†See stage directions to act 1, scene 1 opening. This character was not listed in the manuscript scene headings and, though thought to be present by some modern commentators, does not seem to be entirely necessary.

ACT 1

SCENE 1: CORNWALLIS *and* BEAUREGARD *enter from Beauregard's house. Night.* BEAUREGARD *wears party garb along with his loud jacket, and holds a large, lit, cylindrical beeswax candle. He may be followed by a small boy carrying a large pile of party food (must include a rubber chicken or other item suitable for use in walloping and a huge punchbowl full of wine); the boy could pull, or be replaced by, a wagon. As soon as the play starts, the boy, if any, takes a break and goes to sleep until cued.*

CORNWALLIS: Where shall I say you are going at this time of night   iambic senarii
dressed up like that, and with all this fuss,* young Beauregard?
BEAUREGARD: Where Venus and Cupid command, and Love persuades me;
whether it's midnight or if it's barely nightfall,
even if I had a previous engagement—even a court date*—   5
still I must go where they bid me, even against my will.
CORNWALLIS: But really, really— BEAUREGARD: Really, you're starting to
             bother me.
CORNWALLIS: But *that*—indeed it's not only uncouth, it's unspeakable.*
(Leers.) You, holding your own candle—all dressed up and minding your own
             beeswax.*
BEAUREGARD: Am I not to take what's gathered by the little bees,*   10
welling from sweetness, to my sweet little honey?*
CORNWALLIS: So *where* shall I say you're going? BEAUREGARD: If you'd
             just *ask* me,
I'd tell you so you'd know. CORNWALLIS: If I kept asking, what would you say?
BEAUREGARD: This is the Yale Health Spa. CORNWALLIS: I've known that for
             over a year.
BEAUREGARD: And this next door is the door that I most madly adore.   15
(To the door.) Hello, hope I see you well? CORNWALLIS: O door most
             madly shut,
was your fever down yesterday? And the day before?
Did you eat a good dinner yesterday? BEAUREGARD: Are you laughing at me?
CORNWALLIS: Well, why are you asking a door if it feels well, you idiot?
BEAUREGARD: Because it looks so darned nice and so terribly shy—   20
it never makes a peep: when it's opened, it keeps its mouth shut;
when she sneaks out at night to me, it keeps its mouth shut.
CORNWALLIS: You're not doing anything that might disgrace your family
—or you—or thinking of doing the deed, young Beauregard?

You wouldn't be working your wiles on some innocent young girl 25
(or one that's supposed to be innocent)? BEAUREGARD: No, not one;
not even if the good Lord let me! CORNWALLIS: I certainly hope that's true.
You should always bestow your love *un*respectably if you're wise,
so that if people find out, they won't think ill of you.
You don't want to be cut out of your last will and testiclement. {By an angry
        father.}* 30
BEAUREGARD: What do you mean? CORNWALLIS: Just watch out where you're
        going, my boy, 32
and make sure you love what you love with intesticle fortitude.* 31
BEAUREGARD: No, it's all right . . . the pimp lives there. CORNWALLIS: No law
        against it.
No one says you can't buy what's for sale—if you've got the cash.
No one says you can't go down the public road— 35
as long as you aren't trespassing on posted land,
as long as you keep your hands off ladies, both married and un-,
off nice young men, and off boys, you can love whatever you like.*
BEAUREGARD: Well, this is Pimp Hall. CORNWALLIS: A plague on all his houses!
BEAUREGARD: What for? CORNWALLIS: Because they serve a nasty servitude. 40
BEAUREGARD: You keep interrupting me! CORNWALLIS: By all means.
        BEAUREGARD: Can you please be quiet?
CORNWALLIS: You *told* me to interrupt you. BEAUREGARD: But now please don't.
As I've been trying to tell you: she's his little slave girl.
CORNWALLIS: What, this pimp who lives here? BEAUREGARD: You've got it.*
        CORNWALLIS *(leers):* Good, then I
won't worry that it'll fall off.* BEAUREGARD: You're bothering me! 45
He wants to make her a whore, but she is dying for me;
yet I don't want to get her a loan {alone, get it?}.*
CORNWALLIS: Why not? BEAUREGARD: I want to make her mine! I'm a
        fair-trade lover.*
CORNWALLIS: A secret affair is a bad thing, ruin served straight up.
BEAUREGARD: Lord, you've got that right. CORNWALLIS *(leers):* And is she
        pulling your plow?* 50
BEAUREGARD: She's as safe from me as if she were my own sister;
unless she might be a little unsafe from kissing me.
CORNWALLIS: Just bear in mind that where there's smoke there's fire,
and you may not get burned from smoke, but you do from fire.
A chap who wants his peanuts* unshelled breaks the nutshell; 55

if he wants to go to bed, he breaks ground with smooches.*

BEAUREGARD: But she's a good girl, she doesn't go to bed with men.

CORNWALLIS: I'll believe that when I see a celibate pimp.

BEAUREGARD: How can you judge her? Every chance that comes to her
to sneak herself off to me—she smooches and runs.   60
And things are like this, because this pimp, who's taking the cure
in the Yale Health Spa, he's torturing me. CORNWALLIS: How so?

BEAUREGARD: Sometimes he asks me to pay him thirty thousand for her,
sometimes a hundred thousand;* you know, there's just no way
—I can't get a fair deal out of him. CORNWALLIS: It's you who's wrong—   65
you're trying to get a thing from him no pimp has.

BEAUREGARD: So now I've sent my associate* to Jerusalem*
in search of cash, a loan from an old frat brother* of mine.
And if he doesn't bring it, I don't know where I'll turn.

CORNWALLIS: If you want to say hi to heaven, you'd better turn right.*   70

BEAUREGARD: Yes! This shrine to Venus is here in front of their door;
I've vowed to give breakfast to Venus—myself.

CORNWALLIS: What? You're serving yourself to Venus for breakfast?

BEAUREGARD: Me, you, and all of these folks. *(Points at audience.)* CORNWALLIS:
        Ah, you want to make Venus de-breakfast.*

BEAUREGARD: Boy, give me that punchbowl. (BOY, *if this line is not addressed to*
        CORNWALLIS, *wakes up and holds up bowl for* BEAUREGARD *to take.*)
        CORNWALLIS: What are you doing? BEAUREGARD: You'll find
        out soon.   75
An old gal usually sleeps here as a door attendant—
name's Lola, she likes her drinks straight up and plenty of 'em.

CORNWALLIS: She is to drinking what the bottle is to Merlot-la.*

BEAUREGARD: Why mince words? She's the biggest drunk you ever saw;
and the minute I sprinkle this door here with this wine I've got,   80
she'll know I'm here from the smell, and she'll open it on the spot.

CORNWALLIS: And this punchbowl filled with wine is for her? BEAUREGARD:
        Unless you object.

CORNWALLIS: By Jove, I do, and I wish the chap who's got it was dashed.
I thought it was for *us.* BEAUREGARD: Could you be quiet for once?
Whatever's left over from her, that'll be enough for us.   85

CORNWALLIS: What river would that be that won't fit into the sea?

BEAUREGARD: Walk this way with me to the door, Cornwallis, be nice
        to me.

CORNWALLIS: All right, I will. BEAUREGARD: Come on, drink up, you
        party door;
have a drink, and may you be lucky and kind to me.
CORNWALLIS: Would you like some olives, some cocktail wieners,* some capers,
        perhaps?   90
BEAUREGARD: Awaken your guardian mistress and bring her here to me.
CORNWALLIS *(leers):* That wine is just *spurting* out; what's got you excited?
        BEAUREGARD: Lay off.
Do you see how the door is opening? She loves to party!
And the hinge doesn't make a peep? Sweet guy. CORNWALLIS: Why not give
        it a kiss?
BEAUREGARD: Be quiet. Let's hide our light and hush. CORNWALLIS:
        De-lighted.*   95
(Cue music.)

SCENE 2: MME. LOLA, BEAUREGARD, *and* CORNWALLIS
Enter MME. LOLA *from the pimp's house.*

LOLA *(to the tune of "The Man on the Flying Trapeze"):*
The smell of old wine on my nostrils is thrust,
enticing me here through the shadows with lust.
It's near me, hallelujah, and have it I must!
My darling, delight of the vine.

How aged ol' me lusts for aged you, too—
expensive perfume smells like puke* next to you.
To me you're Chanel No. 5 and Tabu—   100
wherever you're spilled, let me lie.

But this scent has enchanted my nose to the point   105
that my gullet's demanding a turn.
I'm not kidding: where is it? I just want a touch—
for your juices poured in me I burn!

I crave it in gulps—but now he's gone away;
{and I'm left alone, an old bag in a play.
If I don't have a drink soon, my guts will flambée—
I'm hot on the scent of old wine!}*   109a

BEAUREGARD *(spoken):* This old gal's thirsty! CORNWALLIS: How thirsty *is* she?

BEAUREGARD: Not a lot; holds about a keg.* 110

CORNWALLIS: Crikey, the way you tell it, one vintage isn't enough for this one old girl. 110a

She should have been a dog instead; she has a well-trained nose. LOLA: Thank you. 110b

(Cue music: trio, to the tune of "Fugue for Tinhorns.")

LOLA: I hear a voice, I think.

BEAUREGARD: I think she needs a drink,

but if she'd look this way she'd soon be in the pink.

CORNWALLIS: She's dry, she's dry, he says that the old bag's dry.

If he says the old bag's dry, she's dry, she's dry.

LOLA: Who is my valentine?

BEAUREGARD: The charming god of wine!

Don't hock another loogie, he will treat you fine. 115

CORNWALLIS: Why me? Why me? There's never a drink for me!

For me! For me! I just want a drink for me!

LOLA: I can't just see him quite . . .

BEAUREGARD: Now you can see the light!

LOLA: Just walk a bit more quickly, just to be polite.

BEAUREGARD: My dear, you're looking well! 120

LOLA: But I'm as dry as hell!

BEAUREGARD: Another step— LOLA: —or two—and I'll be feeling swell.

BEAUREGARD: Heads up! LOLA: Chin chin! CORNWALLIS: And now let the fun begin!

Begin, begin, oh when will the fun begin?

Pour it out, down the hatch, down the drain!

But not a drink—for—me!

LOLA *(spoken):* Venus, from the little I have I'll give you a tiny bit, (not very) gladly. *(Pours a few drops at altar.)*

Coz everybody who's in love, when they're drinking and craving your favor,

they give you wine; but me, I hardly ever get a legacy like that. *(Drinks.)* 125

(Cue music, reprise.)

CORNWALLIS: Now let me tell you what,

she's just a greedy slut,

look how she stands there gluggin' it down her gut!

BEAUREGARD: I think I might just die! 130

CORNWALLIS: You wanna tell me why?

BEAUREGARD: I have to make her bring me my sweetie-pie.

LOLA: Encore! CORNWALLIS: Want more? —She says that it tastes like more.

Just gimme a two-by-four, I'll give her more.

She's bending back, my friends,

just like the rainbow bends,

I bet we'll have some rain before the evening ends.

BEAUREGARD: I think I might just die!   135

I need my sweetie-pie!

If you could bring her out, I'd be a grateful guy.

LOLA: Oh, Beauregard, don't cry!

I'll get your sweetie-pie,

if you can just see to it I don't go dry.

(Exit MME. LOLA into the pimp's house.)

BEAUREGARD: If what you say is true,

I'll make a statue of you,

and plant a grapevine around it and paint it blue.   140

CORNWALLIS: I'd be blue too, if I were as broke as you!

BEAUREGARD: Just trust me, it will come through! CORNWALLIS: Sez

         you, sez you.

BEAUREGARD: Maybe I'll—sing a song*—to the door!   145

CORNWALLIS: And not a drink—for—me!

(Cue music.)

BEAUREGARD (to the tune of "Hey Jude"):

Hey, knob!* I say hello,

and I love you, and I implore you,

please be nice to me because I'm in love,

you're so far above,

and I adore you.

Hey, knob! Oh, just for me,

could you make like a native dancer?*   150

And spin round, and send my baby outside—

she's drunk my blood dry;

I need an answer.

Look—how—this—horrible knob—never wakes up—hey, knob!

Not—even—just to please me!—Won't even move—hey, knob!

I—see—you—don't even care—if I like you—hey, knob!   155

No—noise! Not—even a word! CORNWALLIS: Don't be absurd—you knob!

BEAUREGARD: And in the end, the knob I twist, is leading to the love I've
    missed . . .

SCENE 3: MME. LOLA, CORNWALLIS, WANDA, and BEAUREGARD
Enter MME. LOLA *and* WANDA *from the pimp's house.* WANDA *has on a lot of eye
makeup.*

LOLA: Quiet, go on, and don't let the door be noisy or the hinges
    be creaky,   trochaic septenarii
Sir shouldn't take any notice of what we're doing here, Wanda dear.
Hold on, I'll pour a bit of water on them. CORNWALLIS: Look at the shaky old
    bag! Playing doctor!   160
She's learned to drink liquor straight herself, but she's putting the door on a
    water diet.

WANDA: Where's the man who's set my bail with the bail bondsman of Venus?
I'm keepin' my court date with you and I want you to keep your court date
    with me.

BEAUREGARD: I'm present in court; and if I weren't, I'd be ready to take my
    punishment, honey.

WANDA: Baby, I reasonably doubt that a lover of mine should be far
    from me.   165

BEAUREGARD: Cornwallis, Cornwallis! CORNWALLIS: Talk to me, why
    Cornholler* like that?

BEAUREGARD: She's charming. CORNWALLIS: Too charming. BEAUREGARD: I'm a
    god. CORNWALLIS: No, still human, and fairly worthless.

BEAUREGARD: What did you ever see, what will you ever, more divinely
    comparatudinous?

CORNWALLIS: I see you're too healthy, it's making me sick. BEAUREGARD: I see
    you're not nice to me—pipe down.

CORNWALLIS: A chap tortures him*self* when he sees what he likes and doesn't
    grab it while he can.   170

BEAUREGARD: He's right to scold me. There's not a thing I've wanted more for a
    long time now.

WANDA: So hold me, put your arms around me. BEAUREGARD: Yes! This is my
    reason for living!

Since your master forbids you, I'll have you in secret. WANDA: Forbids me? He
    can't forbid me,

and he won't, unless death puts a restraining order on my soul. (BEAUREGARD
and WANDA *go into a heavy clinch.)*

CORNWALLIS: Indeed I can't hold back from bringing charges against
my boss;   175

it's a good thing to love a little, normally—*ab*normally can't be good,*

and this is truly, totally abnormal* love my boss is making here.

BEAUREGARD *(coming up for air):* Kings can keep their kingdoms, rich men can
keep their riches for themselves—

keep their honors, keep their virtues, keep their battles, keep their fights;

just let them keep their envious eyes off me, they can keep whatever
is theirs.   180

CORNWALLIS: Um, Beauregard? Have you taken a vow to hold an all-night vigil
for Venus?

Because, golly, it's going to start getting light here pretty soon. BEAUREGARD:
Pipe down.

CORNWALLIS: What, *I* should pipe down? Why don't *you* go to sleep?

BEAUREGARD: I *am* asleep, don't keep yelling at me.

CORNWALLIS: But you're awake. BEAUREGARD: But I'm asleep in my own way:
this is all my dream.

CORNWALLIS: Hey you, woman, it's boorish to hurt an innocent man who never
hurt you.   185

WANDA: You'd get mad if *he* pushed *you* away from your plate while you were
eating. CORNWALLIS: That's it!

I can see they both are dying of love, and they both are raving mad.

You see how grimly they're grinding away? They just can't squeeze enough.

Still saying goodbye? WANDA: No good thing ever lasts forever for anyone;

now to this pleasure this pain is joined. CORNWALLIS: What did you say, you
shameless creature?   190

You with your owl eyes, you have the nerve to say that I'm a pain?

You tipsy tart, you trashy makeup job.* BEAUREGARD: Are you vexing my Venus?

And should my own slave spew speeches? A slave I've offered up to be flogged?*

Talking back! By God, it's going to cost you a world of pain.

That's for your garbage mouth! *(Hits* CORNWALLIS *with the rubber chicken.)*
That'll help you keep a decent tongue.   195

CORNWALLIS: Help me, Venus of the Owl-Night Stand! BEAUREGARD: Are you
still at it, *(whack)* you deadbeat?*

WANDA: Please don't keep beating a dead horse;* I don't want you to hurt
your hand.

CORNWALLIS: Beauregard, you're making an eye-popping spectacle of yourself;
when someone helps you, you clobber him, but her you love—this
        90-proof trash.
Has it come to this, to behave yourself with such indecent behavior here?   200
BEAUREGARD: Show me a decent lover—he's worth his weight in gold; here, take
        my gold card.* (Flaps CORNWALLIS with rubber chicken.)
CORNWALLIS: Give me a sane master instead—I'm more the fool's-gold type.*
        (Creaky door sound from YNHHHS.)
WANDA: Farewell, my darling, for I hear the creaking sound of the locks on
        the door,
the temple keeper is opening the shrine. How long will we go on like this,
tell me, the two of us, always snatching at stolen love?   205
BEAUREGARD: No time—I sent my associate to Jerusalem three days ago
to get the money—he'll be here today. WANDA: Your planning phase is way
        too long.
BEAUREGARD: I swear by Venus, the goddess of love, I'll never let you stay in
        this house
another three days from now, before I set you free, you classy girl.*
WANDA: Make sure you don't forget. And now, before I leave, take one
        last kiss.   210
BEAUREGARD: Lord, if I were given a kingdom, I'd never go after it over this.
When will I see you again? WANDA: You better put your money where your
        mouth is.*
If you love me, buy me, and you won't have to ask—and make him an offer he
        can't refuse.
Take care of yourself. (Exit WANDA and MME. LOLA into the pimp's house.)
        BEAUREGARD: Am I left behind now? Cornwallis, I died happy.
CORNWALLIS: I, too, sir—from losing my skin as well as sleep. I'm beat.
        BEAUREGARD: Walk this way.   215
(Exeunt into Beauregard's house.)

ACT 2

SCENE 1: TURK and CORNWALLIS. Day has dawned.

TURK (entering from the YNHHHS): It's definitely time for me to move out
        of the spa,*   iambic senarii
since I'm pretty sure it's the Big Doctor's* diagnosis

that I don't count for much and he doesn't wish me well.
My health is dwindling, my pain's increasing;
'cause I'm walking around with my spleen binding me like a girdle,   220
and I feel like I'm carrying twin boys in my belly.
I'm not worried—except I might break in half. Oy veh!*
CORNWALLIS *(entering from Beauregard's house):* Beauregard, if you were thinking
        straight, you'd listen to me
and shake this sickness of yours right out of your head.
You're shook up 'cause that bloodsucker* isn't back from Jerusalem: 225
I believe he's bringing your money; because if he weren't,
he couldn't be held back by iron bars*
from taking himself back here to eat at his trough.
TURK: Who's this who's speaking? CORNWALLIS: What voice do I hear?
TURK: Isn't this Beauregard's man Cornwallis? CORNWALLIS: Who is
        this person   230
with the potluck* belly and the grassy eyes?
His shape looks familiar, but based on the color
I can't place him.—Wait—I see—it's Turk, the pimp.
I'll go up to him. TURK: You look well, Cornwallis. CORNWALLIS: And you,
you wicked man. How are you? TURK: Alive. CORNWALLIS: I'm sure it
        suits you.   235
What is your problem? TURK: My spleen's killing me, my kidneys hurt,
my lungs are in shreds, my liver is torturing me,
the roots of my heart are gone, and all my bowels hurt me.
CORNWALLIS: Ah, I see that liver makes you sick.*
TURK: It's easy to laugh at a poor sufferer. CORNWALLIS: Just you
        hang on   240
a few days more, until your guts get completely putrid,
while the pickling season's upon us; if you see to this,
you can sell your guts for more than you'd get for the whole package.
TURK: My spleen is crucified. CORNWALLIS: Keep walking, that's what's best for
        your spleen.
TURK: Enough with this, please, and just answer me what I'm asking you.   245
Could you give me an analysis* if I told you
what I dreamed last night as I was sleeping?
CORNWALLIS: Aha! You've come to the right man for analysis.*
Why, analysts come to me to ask advice,
and then they go back and diagnose what I told them.   250

SCENE 2: COOK, CORNWALLIS, TURK, *and* BEAUREGARD
Enter COOK *from Beauregard's house.*

COOK: Cornwallis, why are you standing there? Why ain't the stuff
        coming in   iambic senarii
I need, so that freeloader* can have dinner ready for him
when he gets here? CORNWALLIS: Hang on, while I interpret a dream for him.
COOK: Hey, when you have dreams yourself, you bring 'em to me.
CORNWALLIS: True. COOK: Go on, bring it in. CORNWALLIS *(to* TURK*):* Then go
        on, you tell your dream   255
to him, meanwhile; I refer you to one greater even than I.*
Everything I know, he taught me. TURK: As long as he's thorough. CORNWALLIS:
        He will be. *(Exit* CORNWALLIS *stage L; he comes in and out with many*
        huge bags of groceries.)
TURK: An unusual guy—look how he listens to his professor.
Fine, so give me the works. COOK: Even though I don't know you, I will.
TURK: Last night in my dreams I seemed to see   260
the Big Doctor sitting far away from me,
and he didn't come up to me and he didn't seem to care much for me.
COOK: Of course now all the others are gonna play god;*
naturally, they all hang together in harmony.
It's no wonder if you don't get better—   265
you should have taken your rest cure in the Head Doctor's place;*
he's been a big help to you in your court appearances.*
TURK: If every perjurer wanted to take the cure,
there wouldn't be room to breathe in the Mayo Clinic.*
COOK: Think about this: you'd better make peace with the Big Doctor,   270
so something really bad doesn't maybe happen to you,
like what was foretold to you in your sleep. TURK: You're good.
I'll go say my prayers. *(Exit* TURK *into* YNHHHS.*)* COOK: And I hope they all
        backfire on you! *(Exit* COOK *into Beauregard's house. Enter*
        CORNWALLIS, *with groceries, from stage L. Looks stage R.)*
CORNWALLIS: Good heavens, who is this I see? Who can that be?
Is that that leech* who was sent out to Jerusalem?   275
Hoy, Beauregard, out, out, out here, I say, quickly!
(Enter BEAUREGARD *from his house.)*
BEAUREGARD: Why are you making that racket? CORNWALLIS: I see your
        associate*

running—look, there he is—all the way up the final block.
Let's hear his story. BEAUREGARD: Absolutely, I agree.

SCENE 3: WEEVIL, BEAUREGARD, *and* CORNWALLIS
Enter WEEVIL *from stage R, staggering.*

WEEVIL: Make way, give over, friends and strangers, while I do my
        duty here;   trochaic septenarii   280
run away, all of you, go away and remove yourself from my path,
so I don't knock into you on my way with my head or elbow or chest or knee.
I've got such a sudden, urgent, and rapid piece of business thrust upon me,
there isn't anyone anywhere powerful enough to block my way,
no, not a warlord nor an overlord—none at all—nor a border guard*   285
nor a tribal chief nor a village chief nor anyone so high-powered*
that he wouldn't fall off the sidewalk, or stand on his head in the road
        {to avoid me}.
Then those foreigners with the loud jackets who walk around with their
        headrags on,*
who go around with their pockets stuffed with their books, and with their
        shopping carts,
and stand around, and gabble amongst themselves—mostly refugees*—   290
and stand in the way, and get in the way, and march around with their big ideas,
they're the ones you always see drinking in some smoky caff,*
when they've stolen something: with their noggins all muffled they drink it
        down hot,
and then they go on their way all gloomy and sloshed; if I bump into them,
I'll knock a French-fried fart* out of every one of 'em.   295
And then those slaves of smart-ass toffs,* who play with each other in the road,
I'll put the pitchers and the catchers* all under my boot, the lot of 'em.
So let 'em keep themselves at home, and they'll avoid a nasty accident.
BEAUREGARD *(to* CORNWALLIS*):* He's got it right, if he could carry through on it.
        For that's how it is,
that's how the servant classes* are: there's just no controlling them.   300
WEEVIL: Is there anybody here who could direct me to Beauregard, my
        guardian angel?*
My business is so pressing, I have urgent need to meet with that gentleman.
CORNWALLIS: He's looking for you. BEAUREGARD: Maybe we should go up to
        him. Hey there, Weevil, I'm looking for you.

WEEVIL: Who's calling me? Who's said my name? BEAUREGARD: Someone who
       wants to welcome you.
WEEVIL: You don't want it more than I want you. BEAUREGARD: Oh, my
       lucky break,   305
Weevil, I've pined away for you, welcome! WEEVIL: Well met. BEAUREGARD:
       Well, I'm really glad
you got here safely, let me shake your hand. Do you have what I hoped for?
Tell me, golly, I beg you. WEEVIL: Tell me, I beg you, do *you* have what *I*
       hoped for?
BEAUREGARD: What do you mean? WEEVIL: Darkness is falling, my knees are
       starting to buckle from hunger.
BEAUREGARD: Gee, I think he's tired. WEEVIL: Hold me up, hold me up, I
       beg you!   310
BEAUREGARD: You see how pale he is? Could you get him a chair so he can sit
       down? And quick!
And a basin of water! (CORNWALLIS *exits into Beauregard's house . . .*) Can't you
       go faster? *(. . . and returns with a bucket of water.)* WEEVIL: I don't
       feel at all well.
CORNWALLIS: Would you like some water? WEEVIL: If it's full of crumbs, give it,
       please, God, I'll suck it up.
CORNWALLIS: Bloody hell!* WEEVIL: Please, God, cut some cheese; make
       me happy.*
CORNWALLIS: Absolutely. *(Farts in his general direction.)* WEEVIL: What are you
       doing, eh? CORNWALLIS: Cutting the cheese. WEEVIL: No, I
       don't want   315
that kind of stupid cheese. BEAUREGARD: What *do* you want? WEEVIL: I want to
       eat, I want to *have* some *cheese.**
CORNWALLIS: May God have mercy on your soul.* WEEVIL: I'm done for, my
       eyes are growing dim,
my teeth are full of eye-boogers, my jaws are all gummy with hunger,*
I made it here with my food gauge on "empty" and my guts gave out.
BEAUREGARD: Soon you'll eat something. WEEVIL: God, I don't want
       "something": I want something a little more definite than
       "something."   320
CORNWALLIS: If you only knew what the leftovers were! WEEVIL: What I really
       want to know is
where they are, because my teeth have a really pressing engagement with them.

BEAUREGARD: We've got ham, bacon, pig's feet, pork chops* . . . WEEVIL: You
          really mean all that?
Maybe you mean they're in the freezer.* BEAUREGARD: No, they're out on
          platters,
we got them all ready for you, when we knew you were on your way.   325
WEEVIL: Don't fool with me. BEAUREGARD: I swear by my sweetie's love for me
          that I tell no lie.
But—why I sent you—I still know nothing. WEEVIL: And nothing's just what I
          brought you.
BEAUREGARD: You've ruined me. WEEVIL: I can *come up* with something, if you
          help me out.
After I set out, on your command, I duly arrived in Jerusalem,
and I see your old frat brother, and I ask him to stuff me with lots of cash.   330
You should know he wished you well, he didn't want you to be upset,
as is right for a chum to wish his chum, and to want to aid and abet;
he replied to me in a few short words, like a loyal chum—you bet,
that what's his is yours. A great lack of pots of cash.
BEAUREGARD: You're killing me with this news. WEEVIL: Nope, I'm saving you,
          and I want you saved.   335
After he thusly replied to me, I leave him, all sad-like, and go downtown,
thinking I'd come there in vain. And by chance I see a soldier.
I go up to the fellow, and salute him as I approach. "Cheerio," he says to me,
he shakes my hand, he takes me aside, he asks why I've come to Jerusalem;
I say I'm there on holiday.* So he starts to question me,   340
do I know Mr. Wolf, the banker, right here in New Haven.
I say I do. "And how about Turk the pimp?" says he, and I let on
as I've visited him. "But what do you want with him?" says I. "I bought a virgin
          from him,
for thirty thousand dollars,* clothing and jewelry extra; for them, it's another ten
          thousand."*
"Did you give him the money?" says I. "No," says he, "It's on deposit with
          the banker,   345
that Mr. Wolf I said, with instructions, that he should see to it, that the man
who brings him orders sealed with my ring, that man should pick up the woman
and take her away from the pimp together with her jewels and her
          clothing, too."
After he told me this story, I go to walk away. And he calls me right back,

and invites me to dinner. It was my Christian duty,* I didn't like to say no.   350
"Suppose we go off and grab a bite?" says he. Seems like a good plan to me;
"Time and tide wait for no man,"* says I. {"There's no time like the present!"}
"Everything's all ready," says he. "And here we are that it's ready for" (me).
So after we's et and had a few drinks, he calls for the dice to be brought to him,
and challenges me to a friendly game; so I go and bet my jacket,   355
and he antes up with his raincoat,* and calls on the name—Wanda.
BEAUREGARD: My beloved? WEEVIL: Wait for it. So he throws snake-eyes.*
I pick up the dice, and I call on my patron saint and nutritionist, Santa Claus,*
and I throw a seven;* and I call he has to chug; he drinks it up,
he puts his head down, he passes out. So I winkle the ring away from him,   360
and I sneaks my toes out from under the table, so the soldier doesn't hear me.
The slaves ask me where I might be going, and I say I'm going where you go
        when you're full.
And when I spied the front door, I got myself out of there on the spot
        and pronto.
BEAUREGARD: Good work. WEEVIL: Save it up for when I've got you what
        you want.
Let's go inside now and seal some papers. BEAUREGARD: Am I slowing
        you down?   365
WEEVIL: And let's snarf something down beforehand, some ham, some pig's feet,
        a few hot dogs.
These'll settle your stomach down, with some bread and a little rare roast beef,
and a nice pint, make that a pitcher, to help us get some good ideas.
You'll seal the documents up, *he*'ll be the waiter, and *I*'ll do the eating.
I'll tell you how you should word it. Just follow me inside. BEAUREGARD:
        Yes sir!   370
(Exeunt into Beauregard's house.)

ACT 3

SCENE 1: MR. WOLF, WEEVIL, *and* TURK
Enter MR. WOLF *from stage L. He has a hat in one hand and sunglasses in his pocket.*

MR. WOLF: I appear to be rich; I've cooked up a little calculation,   iambic senarii
re how much of my money is mine and how much is other people's.
I'm a wealthy man, if I don't pay those people back.
If I do pay them back what I owe them, more seems to be theirs.

But, by Jove, how nice it feels to bear in mind,   375
that if they start to press me, I can just go to court.
You'll find that plenty of money men have this custom—
they ask various people for money, but they never return it,
and they settle all questions with muscle, if someone complains too loudly.
Any man who sets out to get rich quick,   380
unless he gets stingy quick, goes hungry quick.
(Puts on hat and dark glasses.)
And now I'd like to purchase some kind of boy for myself,*
to rent out. Rental property is such a good investment.*
(Exit MR. WOLF *into the pimp's house.)*
WEEVIL *(enters from Beauregard's house, now dressed as a soldier, in a battered*
uniform, with a patch over one eye; speaks over his shoulder): You don't
have to tell me twice, now I'm full. I remember, I know.
I'll hand this to you nice and tidy. Keep yer knickers on.*   385
(To audience.) By George, I certainly filled up my insides proper,
and still I left in my tum a space for one small safe-room,
where I could store up the leftovers of the leftovers.
(Enter MR. WOLF *from the pimp's house; he goes towards the* YNHHHS, *looking*
for TURK.*)*
Who's this with his head covered up paying his respects
to the Yale Health Spa? Oho, the man I was looking for! Follow me.   390
I'll act as if I don't know him. Hey you! Can I have a word?
MR. WOLF: Good day to you, One-Eye. WEEVIL: Excuse me, are you
laughing at me?
MR. WOLF: I assume you must come from the stud line of the Cycalopses*—
they're all one-eyed. WEEVIL *(points to eyepatch):* I got this at Sarajevo.*
Knocked out of me by a grenade.* MR. WOLF: What do I care, anyway,   395
if it was gouged out with a broken bottle of dirt?*
WEEVIL *(to audience):* This chap's clairvoyant, he's got it exactly right;
coz grenades like that drop in on me all the time.
(To MR. WOLF.*)* Young man, in the name of our great nation, this thing
inside me
wot I cherish as a talisman, I beg you to spare me your filibuster.*   400
MR. WOLF: Then can I have sexual congress with you, if I can't filibuster?*
WEEVIL: You won't have sexual congress* with *me,* and I don't like
either your House or your Senator* very much.
But if you can direct me to the gent I'm seeking,

you will undergo my unyielding and king-size . . . gratitude.   405
I am looking for Mr. Wolf, the banker. MR. WOLF: Tell me,
what do you want him for? Where do you come from? WEEVIL: I'll tell you.
From Lt. Napoleon Plaza-Toro, the soldier.
MR. WOLF: By golly, I know that name; why, that name,
in my records, fills up four pages all by itself.*   410
But why do you want Mr. Wolf? WEEVIL: I have strict orders
to carry these documents to him. MR. WOLF: Who are you, anyway?
WEEVIL: I'm his former slave—everyone calls me Thunder God.*
MR. WOLF: Thunder God, how do. Why "Thunder God"? Do tell.
WEEVIL: Because when I go to bed drunk, when I wake up,   415
there's quite a me*th under* my clothes, so they all call me Thunder God.
MR. WOLF: I think you'd better look for another place to stay here;
I don't think I have room for the Thunder God.
But I happen to be the very man you're looking for. WEEVIL: No!
            You're him?
Mr. Wolf the banker? MR. WOLF: I am he. WEEVIL: Oh, Lt. Napoleon   420
told me to give you his very best regards,
and ordered me to give you these documents. MR. WOLF: Me? Really?
            WEEVIL: Yes!
Take them, and note the seal. Recognize it? MR. WOLF: And why shouldn't I?
It's got a man with a shield slicing an elephant in half* with his scimitar.*
WEEVIL: What's written here—he ordered me to request you   425
to kindly do it right off, if you wish to retain his custom.
MR. WOLF: Give it here, let me just look over the fine print. WEEVIL: By
            all means,
you're the boss (as long as I get what I've come for from you).
MR. WOLF: "From: Lt. Napoleon Plaza-Toro. To:
Mr. Wolf in New Haven. Dear Sir, sincerest greetings."   430
WEEVIL: He's mine now, he's swallowing the hook.
MR. WOLF: "I hereby request, with respect, that to the document bearer
shall be given the virgin I bought at your place of business,
a transaction I made in your presence and under your personal supervision;
also her jewelry and wardrobe. You already know our agreement;   435
you may give the cash to the pimp, and the virgin to this man."
But where's the man himself? Why isn't he here? WEEVIL: I'll tell you;
because three days ago we got to Jerusalem
from India; he's planning to donate a solid gold statue there now,

to be made of the Shah's melted-down gold bullion,* and it's to be   440
seven feet high—as a monument to his deeds.

MR. WOLF: And why put it there? WEEVIL: I'll tell you. Because he beat the
        Iranians,*
the Kurds, Tehranians, Arabs, Palestinians, Jordanians, Syrians,
and Libya, Lebanon, Hungristan, Thirststistan,
Klash-al-Titanz and Tribal Onetittistan,   445
the whole coast of Turkey, and Igonnascrewubad—
yea, even unto the half part of all nations*—
single-handed, in less than twenty days.

MR. WOLF: Whoa! WEEVIL: You sound surprised? MR. WOLF: Why, even if you
        put all those people
shut up in a coop, just like factory chickens,*   450
you couldn't get around 'em in a single year.
Lord, I believe you're from him, 'cause you babble the same bullshit.

WEEVIL: I could tell you more, if you like. MR. WOLF: I won't hold you up.
Follow me, and I'll complete the transaction that brought you here.
And look who's coming. (Enter TURK from YNHHHS.) Friend pimp, hope I see
        you well. TURK: God bless you.   455

MR. WOLF: What about that business I'm here about?* TURK: You could say what
        you want.

MR. WOLF: You'll have your money when you remit the virgin to him.

TURK: What about my guarantee? MR. WOLF: What difference does that make,
if you get your money? TURK: Look how he's full of advice—some favor.   459–60
Follow me, both of you. WEEVIL: And, pimp, don't make me late, please.
(Exeunt into the pimp's house.)

[Here a scene seems to be missing in which LT. NAPOLEON PLAZA-TORO arrives
        from the harbor and goes to the forum to look for MR. WOLF.]

ACT 4

SCENE 1: THE DIRECTOR, seated onstage in a large easy chair with books at his side.

DIRECTOR: By George, that Beauregard has jolly well found himself a jolly
        good liar.   trochaic septenarii
I don't know whether to call him a con artist or a cockroach.* {Aha ha ha.}
Why, I'm afraid I may not be able to get back the costumes I rented for him.
Though I don't have to deal with him personally; Beauregard, he's the one   465

I trusted; still I'd best keep an eye on things. But while he's offstage now
I'll explain to you where you can most easily find which kind of person,
so it won't be too hard for one to find whomever one might like to meet, {after
          the show,}
whether nasty or innocent, whether nice or not so nice.
(A map with a pointer, or a PowerPoint presentation, might work well here.)
To find someone to lie on oath, just go down to the county courthouse;*   470
Want a liar? Want someone glamorous?* Try Elaine's* (the restaurant);
rich husbands, deep in debt, you can look for down on Wall Street.*
You'll also find the overage toyboys* and the guys* who like to haggle;
contributors to charity banquets will be down at the Fulton Street Fish Market.*
On the Upper East Side* the true-blue Republicans* and the rich men are
          strolling;   475
in midtown, near the Lincoln Tunnel,* you'll find the purely ostentatious;
by the Reservoir* you'll find the big talkers, the loudmouths, the evil-minded,
those who are proud to make up libels against other people out of nothing,
along with those who have plenty that could be said about them themselves.
On the Lower East Side,* there are the loan sharks and their clientele.   480
Behind St. Patrick's* you'll bump into some people who you better not trust.
In Times Square,* there are the folks who keep peddling their own assets.*
In the Village* you can find a baker, a butcher, or an astrologer,
or the guys who turn their backs or the guys who give it to 'em when their backs
          are turned.*
[Rich husbands, deep in debt, you'll find at the house of {insert name of current
          scandalous call-girl entrepreneur here}.]*   485
(The door of the pimp's house creaks.)
But meanwhile the door is making that creaky door sound; must hold
          my tongue.
(Exit THE DIRECTOR *stage L.)*

SCENE 2: WEEVIL, TURK, MR. WOLF, *and* WANDA
Enter WEEVIL *from the pimp's house, leading* WANDA; TURK *and* MR. WOLF *follow.*

WEEVIL: Go on, then, virgin; I can't keep an eye on what's
          behind me.   iambic septenarii
(To TURK.*)* He said that all the jewelry and clothes that she might have
          is his now.
TURK: Who would deny it? WEEVIL: But, however, better safe than sorry.

MR. WOLF: Just bear in mind that you promised, if anybody should lay
claim to her   490
as a free woman, that all the money would then be returned to me,
thirty thousand dollars. TURK: I know, just leave it alone already.
(To WEEVIL.*)* And now the same to you. WEEVIL: I was just going to remind you
likewise.
TURK: I know, and I hereby give you title to her, guaranteed. WEEVIL: Will I take
any title guaranteed by a pimp? Pimps got one thing—one big tongue   495
for telling lies about matters of trust. You guarantee people that ain't yours,
you free slaves that ain't yours, and you order people around that ain't yours.
No one would guarantee your deals, nor you couldn't do it, neither.
In my opinion the race of pimps holds the same relation to humans
as flies, mosquitoes, bedbugs, lice, and fleas {—you're all bloodsuckers}.   500
You're good for nothing but meanness and malice, evil, and troublemaking,
and no honest citizen dares to deal with you in the market;
anyone who does, comes in for blame, abuse, and suspicion,
folks say he's lost both money *and* credit, even if he's done nothing.
MR. WOLF: By George, you've got those pimps down to a T, One-eye. Just
what *I* think.   505
WEEVIL: Christ, I lump you right in with them, you're just the same as
they are;*
at least they set up shop in shady places—you're right downtown here;
they mangle people by luring them into their lairs—you do it with interest.
The voters have passed plenty of propositions on account of you,
which you dodge as soon as they're passed; you always find some loophole;   510
if the law is boiling water, you just treat it like ice cubes.*
MR. WOLF: I should have kept my mouth shut. TURK: Not bad thinking for such
a trash-talker.
WEEVIL: If you talk trash to those who don't deserve it, that's what I call
trashy talk,
but if you dish it out to those who *do,* in my opinion it's well dished.
I won't hold you up, Mr. Title Guaranteed,* nor any other pimp.   515
Mr. Wolf, we through? MR. WOLF: Good day to you. WEEVIL: Goodbye. TURK:
Hey you! I'm talking to you.
WEEVIL: Speak up, what do you want? TURK: Please, if you just would take good
care of her.
I brought her up well in my home, like a lady.* WEEVIL: If you're feeling
sorry for her,

are you doing her any good? TURK: No, bad. WEEVIL: You need that for
    your*self* now.
TURK *(to* WANDA*):* Silly girl, why are you crying? Don't worry, I got a darn good
    price for you;   520
now save up your pennies like a good girl, and follow the nice man nicely.
MR. WOLF: Oh, Thunder God, d'you need me for anything now? WEEVIL:
    Goodbye, good luck now,
coz you've been very generous with your help and with your money.
MR. WOLF: Convey my very best wishes to your employer. WEEVIL: I'll give him
    your message.
(Exeunt WEEVIL *and* WANDA *stage R.)*
MR. WOLF: You want something, pimp? TURK: If you could just give me the ten
    thousand {for the clothes now},   525
so I can take care of myself, 'til I'm better. MR. WOLF: You'll have it; send round
    tomorrow.
(Exit MR. WOLF *stage L.)*
TURK: When I've done a deal, I like to offer a prayer up in the chapel.
I paid for her a long time ago as a little girl—ten thousand,*
but after that I never saw the guy who sold her to me again;
I think he's passed on. And what's it to me? I got the cash in hand now.   530
When God feels kindly towards a man, he throws him a profit, no question.
And now I'll attend to my spiritual side. It's sure to do my health good. *(Exit
    into* YNHHHS.*)*
*(*WEEVIL *and* WANDA *sneak back into Beauregard's house from stage R.)*

SCENE 3: LT. NAPOLEON PLAZA-TORO *and* MR. WOLF
Enter LT. NAPOLEON PLAZA-TORO *from stage L. With him is* MR. WOLF; *they are in
mid-argument.*

LT. NAPOLEON: I don't stand before you now, enraged with any
            common rage;   trochaic septenarii
but with that very rage with which I've learned to plunge cities into ruin.
If you don't give me back my thirty thousand, chop chop, on the double,   535
that I left with you, prepare to give up living, on the double.
MR. WOLF: I don't afflict you now, by George, with any commonplace affliction,
but with that same affliction I like to inflict on a man I don't owe a thing to.
LT. NAPOLEON: Don't you act all fierce with me, and don't think you can beg
            for mercy.

MR. WOLF: You'll never force *me* to return a deposit to you that's already been
      returned,   540

and I'm not about to. LT. NAPOLEON: That's just what I gave you credit for
      when I gave you my credit,

that you'd never give it back. MR. WOLF: Then why are you trying to get it from
      me now?

LT. NAPOLEON: I want to know who you gave it to. MR. WOLF: Why, to your ex-
      slave, the one-eyed fellow,

he said he was called Thunder God—he's the one I gave it to.

He brought me those sealed documents, after all—the ones you sent me—   545

LT. NAPOLEON *(interrupting)*: What are these one-eyed wonders you're raving
      about? *Thunder Gods?*

I don't have any ex-slave at all. MR. WOLF: Well, you're playing it smarter

than some of these pimps, who *do* have them and then leave them in the lurch.*

LT. NAPOLEON: Well, what now? MR. WOLF: I followed your orders, as per your
      excellent credit rating*—

I wasn't going to turn my nose up at a messenger who came bearing your seal. 550

LT. NAPOLEON: You were thicker than a brick* to put your trust in a piece
      of paper!

MR. WOLF: I shouldn't trust the cornerstone of all business, public and private?

I'll take my leave; your deal is done up proper. Warrior, be well.

LT. NAPOLEON: What's this "be well"? MR. WOLF: Go ahead and be sick, if you
      want, all your life, for all I care.

(Exit MR. WOLF *stage L.)*

LT. NAPOLEON: Now what do I do? What use is it to me to have forced it
      on kings   555

to follow my orders, if this shady character can laugh at me?

SCENE 4: TURK *and* LT. NAPOLEON PLAZA-TORO

Enter TURK *from* YNHHHS.

TURK: When God feels kindly towards a man, I think God isn't
      mad at him.   trochaic septenarii

After I did my spiritual duty, it occurred to me,

before the banker takes a powder, I should get that money from him,

better I should eat it up than him. LT. NAPOLEON: I *said*, I hope that
      you are *well*.   560

TURK: Lt. Napoleon Plaza-Toro, I hope *you*'re well; and since you are here

today in New Haven, healthy and happy, please have a bite* at my
     house—never.
LT. NAPOLEON: Thank you for your kind invitation, but it's all arranged—that
     you should get stuffed.*
But how's my package doing with you, eh? TURK: You got nothing with me,
don't you go calling witnesses,* I don't owe you a darn thing. LT. NAPOLEON:
     What's this?   565
TURK: What I was pledged to do, I did. LT. NAPOLEON: Will you or won't you
     hand over the virgin,
before I subject you to my scimitar, you person suitable for flogging?*
TURK: Go ahead and beat yourself up, by all means; don't try and scare me.
She was picked up, and I'll have you removed yourself, if you go on
insulting me, of all things. I don't owe you a thing except a hard time.   570
LT. NAPOLEON: *You're* threatening *me* with a hard time? TURK: By George, I'm
     not just threatening, I'll do it,
if you keep on making a nuisance. LT. NAPOLEON: A *pimp* threaten *me!*
And my magnificent military might just *lies* here, a mockery?
But I swear by my scimitar and shield, <my mighty boots, my trenchcoat>*—
long may they guard me in the line of battle: unless the virgin's
     delivered to me,   575
I'll fix you so the ants will be carrying you away from here in the form of
     crumbs.
TURK: But *I* swear by my tweezers, my comb, my mirror, and by my curling
     iron,
my scissors, and the towel I use to wipe them on—long may they love me—
that I don't count those fancy-shmancy words of yours or those big threats
as meaning any more to me than the girl* who cleans my toilet.   580
I handed her over to the fellow who brought the money from you.
          LT. NAPOLEON: Who *is* this person?
TURK: He said that he was your ex-slave—name of Thunder God.
          LT. NAPOLEON: Mine?
Aha! The Weevil has played a trick on me, egad—now I understand.
He stole my jewel from me. TURK: Oh, really? You lost your jewels?*
Soldier, it's a lucky thing you're enlisted in the Butthole Brigade.*   585
LT. NAPOLEON: Where would I find the Weevil now? TURK: Probably
     in the flour;*
I can fix it so you get five hundred weevils and not just one.

Well, I'm leaving now, goodbye and good luck. *(Exit* TURK *stage L.)*

      LT. NAPOLEON: Bad bye and bad luck to you!

What am I going to do? Should I go or should I stay? With egg on my face?*

I'm willing to offer a big reward to whoever will show me where he is.*   590

*(*LT. NAPOLEON *canvasses audience.)*

ACT 5

SCENE 1: WEEVIL

Enter WEEVIL *from Beauregard's house.*

WEEVIL: I've heard a poet in ancient times once wrote in a

      tragedy   *trochaic septenarii*

that two women are worse than one. Well, that's the way it is.

But a worse woman than this girlfriend is of Beauregard's

I've never seen or heard of, and, Christ, you couldn't find words to describe or

      make up

a worse one. When she got a look and spied that I had on this ring,   595

she asks where I got it. "Why d'you want to know?" says I. "Because I need to,"

      says she.

So I say I'm not telling. And to rip it off me, she rips into my hand with

      her teeth.

I could hardly rip myself away and get out the door. Get rid of the bitch!

SCENE 2: WANDA, BEAUREGARD, WEEVIL, *and* LT. NAPOLEON PLAZA-TORO

Enter WANDA *and* BEAUREGARD *from Beauregard's house.*

WANDA: Beauregard, hurry. BEAUREGARD: What should I hurry for? WANDA: So

      you don't lose your sidekick.*   *trochaic septenarii*

It's a big thing. WEEVIL: Well, *I* don't have it—whatever I had I ate it

      up quick.   600

BEAUREGARD: I've got him. What's the deal? WANDA: Ask him where he got

      that ring.

My daddy used to wear it. WEEVIL: Oh yeah? Well, so did my auntie.

WANDA: My Ma gave it to him to wear. WEEVIL: And I bet your father gave it

      back to *you.*

WANDA: You're talkin' trash. WEEVIL: As usual: trash is how I make my living.

WANDA: Well? I'm beggin' you, please don't keep my parents from me. 605

WEEVIL: What, me? You think I've got your mum and dad hidden under
this ring?

WANDA: I was born a free woman. WEEVIL: Yeah, like a lot of other people that
are slaves now.*

BEAUREGARD: I'm definitely getting angry. WEEVIL: I *told* you how this thing
got to me.

How many times do I have to say it? I tricked the soldier playing dice, I tell you.

LT. NAPOLEON *(takes notice and stops canvassing audience):* I'm saved, here's the
chap I was looking for. What's the deal, my good man? WEEVIL:
I hear you. 610

If you want, for three rolls of the dice—how about for your trenchcoat?*

LT. NAPOLEON: Will you go to hell?

Rolls, shmolls!* Give it back—either my money or the virgin.

WEEVIL: What money, what mishmosh *are* you talking about? What virgin do
you want back

from me? LT. NAPOLEON: The one you took from the pimp today, you rotten
excuse for a man.

WEEVIL: I never. LT. NAPOLEON: I certainly seem to see her right here.

BEAUREGARD: This is a *free* virgin. 615

LT. NAPOLEON: How can my slave girl be free, when I never set her free?

BEAUREGARD: Who gave you the right to own her? Or where did you buy her?
Do let me know.

LT. NAPOLEON: I paid for her myself, out of money on deposit with
my banker;

and I'll have that money back in quadruplicate from you and that pimp.

BEAUREGARD: Oh, since you're the expert here at dealing in stolen and freeborn
virgins,* 620

let's take a walk downtown. LT. NAPOLEON: I'm not going. BEAUREGARD: Can
you call on outside testimony?* LT. NAPOLEON: No.

BEAUREGARD: Then, God damn you, you can live without testiclemony;*

but I *can* call, and I call *you.* *(To* WEEVIL.*)* Come here. LT. NAPOLEON: A slave
bear witness?* WEEVIL: Look.

Watch and you'll see how free I am. Let's walk downtown. LT. NAPOLEON: I'll
show you! *(Grabs* WEEVIL.*)* 624–25

WEEVIL: Help! Help!* LT. NAPOLEON: What's with the shouting? BEAUREGARD:
And you? What's with the grabbing?

LT. NAPOLEON: I felt like it. BEAUREGARD *(to* WEEVIL*):* Come over here, you,
and *I'll* give him to you. Be quiet.

WANDA: Beauregard, I'm beggin' you, keep me safe. BEAUREGARD: As myself and
        my guardian angel.*

Soldier, I would like you to tell me where it is you got that ring,

the one my associate tricked you out of. WANDA: I'm beggin' you on my knees*
        (Falls to her knees and grabs Lt. Napoleon Plaza-Toro's knees.)   630

to tell us the truth. LT. NAPOLEON: What does this ring have to do with
        you all?

You might as well ask where I got this trenchcoat and this scimitar.

WEEVIL: Ooh, the war hero's* getting fussy!* LT. NAPOLEON: Get rid of him, I'll
        tell you everything.

WEEVIL: What he says is worthless. WANDA: Tell me the truth, please, I'm
        beggin' you.

LT. NAPOLEON: I'll tell you, just stand up. Pay attention now
        and focus.   iambic scenarii   635

My father, Gottawanda, had this ring. WANDA: Gottawanda!*

LT. NAPOLEON: Before he died, he gave the ring to me,

as was proper to do with his own son. WANDA: Dear God!

LT. NAPOLEON: And he made me his heir. WANDA: O my family values,*

save me, since I have kept you safe so carefully.   640

My brother—hello. LT. NAPOLEON: Can I believe my ears? Go on,

if you're telling the truth, what was your mother's name?

WANDA: Fiona.* LT. NAPOLEON: And what was your nanny's name? WANDA:
        Gwendolyn.*

(Lights fall, spotlight on WANDA *for flashback.)*

She had taken me to see the Shakespeare festival.*   644–45

We get there, and suddenly, when she has me settled,

there's a tornado!! The bleachers are collapsing,

and I'm very frightened; then someone—I don't know who—grabs me,

frightened and shaking, more dead than alive.

And I can't tell you how he stole me away.   650

LT. NAPOLEON: I remember that brou-ha-ha. But you tell me,

where is the man who stole you away? WANDA: I don't know.

But I always saved this ring along with myself;

with it I was lost long ago. LT. NAPOLEON: Let's have a look. WEEVIL:
        Are you mad,

to hand it over to him? WANDA: Let him look. LT. NAPOLEON: By God!   655

It's the very one I sent you on your birthday.

I know it like my own face. Hello, my sister.

WANDA: My brother, hello. BEAUREGARD: I hope God will make all this

turn out fine for you. WEEVIL: Me too, for all of us:
you've just showed up—so give a Sister Supper, 660
tomorrow he'll give the Bridal Banquet. We'll be there.
BEAUREGARD: Quiet, you. WEEVIL: I won't—everything's turning out perfect.
Bestow her hand on him, soldier. I'll be giving the dowry.
LT. NAPOLEON: What dowry? WEEVIL: Me? That she should feed me as long as
         she lives.
Christ, I'm telling the truth. LT. NAPOLEON: It's all right with me. 665
And I think this pimp owes us thirty thousand dollars.
BEAUREGARD: How so? LT. NAPOLEON: Because he made a deal with me:
if anyone should lay claim to her as a free woman,
he'd return my money in full, no questions asked.
Now let's go see the pimp. WEEVIL: Hear, hear. BEAUREGARD: But
         first I want 670
to take care of my business. LT. NAPOLEON: What's that? BEAUREGARD: That
         you should give me her hand.
WEEVIL: What are you waiting for, soldier? Why not give him his bride?
LT. NAPOLEON: If she's willing. WANDA: Oh, brother, I'm willing.
         LT. NAPOLEON: Make it so. WEEVIL: Well done!
BEAUREGARD: Soldier, do you promise me this woman in marriage?
         LT. NAPOLEON: I do.
WEEVIL: And I do, too. I promise. LT. NAPOLEON: Very good of you. 675
But here's the pimp waltzing along—my jackpot. 676–78

SCENE 3: TURK, LT. NAPOLEON PLAZA-TORO, BEAUREGARD, *and* WANDA
Enter TURK *from stage L.*

TURK: People who tell you you can't trust the bankers—they're just talking
         through their hat;   trochaic septenarii
I say it's both good and bad to trust 'em—that's how it went today, anyway. 680
When they never pay you—credit isn't the problem. It's a total lack of money.*
For instance, this guy, to pay off the ten thousand, he went to every
         bank in town.
So then when nothing's doing, and I'm starting to yell, he says "So sue me";
I was positive he'd never pay me off today in front of the judge.
But my colleagues made him do it; he's paying back the money from his
         personal account. 685
And now I'm headed for home myself. LT. NAPOLEON: Hey you, pimp,
         I want you!

BEAUREGARD: And *I* want you. TURK: But I don't want either of you.

LT. NAPOLEON: Stay right where you are.

BEAUREGARD: And cough up that money, chop chop, on the double. TURK:
What do you want me for?

Or you? LT. NAPOLEON: Because today I'm going to make a grenade*
out of you,

and I'm going to ratchet you back by your pin, just like a grenade
launcher does.*   690

BEAUREGARD: And I'll turn you into a girly man,* so you can eat dinner with
your poodle*—

I mean the iron poodle.* TURK: But I'll see you both in a high-security prison,*

so you can die there. BEAUREGARD: String him up, take this guy away to
be hanged.*

LT. NAPOLEON: Whichever it is, he's going to beg for death. TURK: For the love
of God and humanity!

Am I to be taken away like this, unconvicted and without testi(cle)mony?*   695

Help me, Wanda, and you, Beauregard, you gotta help me here!

WANDA: Brother, I'm beggin' you, don't destroy him, even if you get a
conviction.

He kept me well in his home, like a lady.* LT. NAPOLEON: Not because he
wanted to;

you can thank the Big Doctor that you kept your virginity.

If he'd been a well man, he would have sold you wherever he could by now.   700

BEAUREGARD: Now, consider this; maybe I can settle this amongst you.

Let him go.—Come over here, pimp. I'll give you my legal opinion,

if you're willing to abide by my decision. LT. NAPOLEON: You have our
permission.

TURK: As long as you judge, God willing, that no one should take money away
from me.

LT. NAPOLEON: What about what you promised? TURK: How so? BEAUREGARD:
With your tongue. TURK: And with this tongue I now deny it.   705

This tongue was given to me so I could talk, not so I could throw money away.

BEAUREGARD: He's no good—string the guy up. TURK: I should have done it
myself a long time ago.

LT. NAPOLEON: Since you're such a gentleman,* answer my question. TURK: Ask
whatever you like.

LT. NAPOLEON: Didn't you promise, if anybody should lay claim to her as a
free woman,

that you would pay back all my money? TURK: I don't recall saying that.   710

LT. NAPOLEON: What? You deny it? TURK: Of course I do. Who else was there?
Where was this?

WEEVIL:* I was there myself, and Mr. Wolf the banker. TURK: Can't you
be quiet?

WEEVIL: No, I can't. I don't care tuppence* for you; so don't you try to
scare me.

It was done in my presence, and Mr. Wolf, too. BEAUREGARD: I think you're
creditable.

So now, pimp, that you may know the judgment I have settled on: 715
this is a free woman, this is her brother, and that makes her this man's sister,
and she's going to marry me: so you give him his money back. That's my
decision.

LT. NAPOLEON: And you'll be all tied up in jail,* if the money isn't
returned to me.

TURK: Golly, you judged this case of yours very sneakily, Beauregard.
It'll be on your head, and you, soldier—may God punish you.   720
OK, you can follow me. LT. NAPOLEON: Where should I follow you? TURK: To
my banker—

I mean to court.* Because that's where I pay everyone I owe money to.

LT. NAPOLEON: I'll put you in jail, not in court, unless you pay me my
money back.

TURK: I very much wish you were dead, just in case you don't know.

LT. NAPOLEON: Is that so? TURK: Of course it is. LT. NAPOLEON: I know these
fists of mine.   725

TURK: So what? LT. NAPOLEON: "So what," you ask? With these fists I, if you
annoy me,

will make you stress-free today. TURK: All right, take your money.

LT. NAPOLEON: And pronto. TURK: Fine.

BEAUREGARD: And you, soldier, will dine with me. Today will be my
wedding day;

and I hope it turns out great for me and you all! Cue the audience: applause!

NONMETRICAL TRANSLATIONS OF SONGS

Mme. Lola's Song

LOLA: The flower of old wine has been thrust upon my nose,
the love of it lures me here, full of desire, through the shadows.   96a–97
Wherever it is, it's near me. Yippee, I have it!   97a

Hello, my darling, charm of the wine god.

How old me desires old you! 98a

For the smell of all perfumes is bilgewater next to yours,

you're my myrrh, my cinnamon, my rose, 100

you're saffron and [aromatic tree bark], you're [ointment made with
        fenugreek]; 101–2

where you're poured out, there I'd wish to be buried. 103–4

But since your smell has chased my nose this far, 105

do my gullet a favor and give it a turn.

I'm not kidding: where is the thing itself? I want

to touch it, let me pour your juices into me,

swigwise. But it's gone away, this way, so I'll follow it this way.

The Wine-Jar Trio

LOLA: Whose voice do I hear far off?

BEAUREGARD: I think the old lady needs a call.

I'll get her.—Come back and look this way, Mme. Lola.

LOLA: Who's giving the orders here? 113a

BEAUREGARD: The dear Lord of wine—what a charmer.

Here you are, dry and half-asleep and hocking loogies,* 115

and he's bringing you a drink and coming to quench your thirst.

LOLA: How far away from me is he? BEAUREGARD: You can see the light.

LOLA: So take bigger steps toward me, I'm begging you.

BEAUREGARD: You look well, Lola. LOLA: How could I be *well,* when
        I'm so dry?*

BEAUREGARD: But soon you'll be drinking. LOLA: It's taking long enough. 119a

BEAUREGARD: Hey, you charming old lady. 120

LOLA: You look well, you adorable man. 120a

CORNWALLIS: Go on, pour it all out quick! Into the abyss! Pronto, right down
        the drain!

BEAUREGARD: Be quiet. I don't want her talked to that way. CORNWALLIS: All
        right, I'll *do* her that way.

Wine-Jar Trio, Reprise

CORNWALLIS: God, look at her, the greedy slut, look how she's glugging it down
        straight! Full to the gaping maw! 126–27

BEAUREGARD: God, I'm dying! I don't know what to say to her first.

        CORNWALLIS: What you said to me. 128–29

BEAUREGARD: What's that? CORNWALLIS: Just say that you're dying.

BEAUREGARD: Damn you! CORNWALLIS: Say it to *her.*   130

LOLA: Ah! CORNWALLIS: What is it? You like that? LOLA: I like it! CORNWALLIS:
    And I'd like to drive a spike into you.

BEAUREGARD: Be quiet. *(Grabs rubber chicken off party tray and threatens*
    CORNWALLIS *with it.)* CORNWALLIS: Don't, I'll be quiet. *(*MME. LOLA
    arches back to finish off the bowl.) —But look, dammit, she's over the
    rainbow . . . I think we're in for a shower.*   131a

BEAUREGARD: Now should I talk to her? CORNWALLIS: What'll you say?

BEAUREGARD: That I'm dying.

CORNWALLIS: Go on, say it. BEAUREGARD: Old lady, listen to me.

I want you to know this: poor me, I'm lost.

LOLA: But, Lordy, I'm totally found.

But what is it? Why do you want to say   135

you're lost? BEAUREGARD: Because I don't have what I love.

LOLA: Beauregard, sweetie, don't cry, please.

You just see to it that I don't go thirsty, I'll bring you out what you love right
    now. *(Exit* MME. LOLA *into the pimp's house.)*

BEAUREGARD: If you are true to me, I'm going to dedicate a vineyard to you,
    instead of a golden statue,*

as a monument to your gullet.   140

Who on earth will be as lucky as me, if she comes sashayin'* out to me,

Cornwallis? CORNWALLIS: Christ, a chap who's in love, without money, has a
    terrible problem.

BEAUREGARD: No, it's not like that, because I'm sure my associate will be
    here today,

with the cash for me. CORNWALLIS: You're taking on a lot, if you're going to wait
    for what doesn't exist.

BEAUREGARD: Suppose I go up to the door and serenade it? CORNWALLIS: If you
    like, I won't say yes or no,   145

since I see you're sadly changed, sir—body and soul.*

Beauregard's Serenade

BEAUREGARD: Bolts, hey bolts, I greet you gladly,

I love you, I want you, I seek you and beg you.

Be nice to me, a lover, you very charming guys; ·

for my sake, turn into native dancers.   · 150

Leap up, I beg you, and send her outdoors—

the girl who's drinking the blood from poor me, her lover.

Look at this, how these very bad bolts sleep on,

and they don't get a move on for me!

I see how you don't even care what I think of you.   155

But quiet, quiet! CORNWALLIS: Christ, I'm quiet already. BEAUREGARD: I
       hear a sound.

Golly, this knob is finally being nice to me.*

NOTES

Weevil . . . Beauregard: This section translates the acrostic *argumentum,* or brief precis,
affixed to the beginning of the play; the original one is longer, since the acrostic
is CURCULIO rather than WEEVIL. But the sense is roughly the same.

2   With all this fuss: Literally, "with this parade"; a *pompa* was a public ceremonial
parade, and hence came to mean "ostentation," though maybe later than Plautus. This word is the grounds on which scholars have posited the existence of
slave(s) with party apparatus accompanying Beauregard.

5   Court date: Latin *condictus . . . dies;* see Lodge 1962 [1924] s.v. *condico.*

8–11   Romans usually used oil lamps for light and candles only for processions and
Saturnalia gifts. Beauregard seems literally to be holding a wax candle *(cereus,* 9),
per his jokes about beeswax in 10–11; Cornwallis's "that" (8) points at something,
and later in the scene there are lines about seeing or hiding a light. In line 9,
Cornwallis literally says, "You're the boy for yourself, you're dressed up and making your own candle shine" *(tute tibi puer es, lautus luces cereum).* The last three
words sound like a proverb or a tag line, and may also be a phallic joke; imagine
a *big* candle.

30–38   It was a stock joke in Roman humor that free men who had illicit sex risked a
range of punishments at the hands of their sex partner's outraged male kin, including castration (cf. *Towelheads* 862–63). At line 30, Cornwallis tells Beauregard to watch out that he doesn't become *intestabilis,* literally "unable to make a
will" but (punningly) "testicle-less." At 31, he tells Beauregard to love "with wit-
nesses/testicles present"; cf. *Towelheads* 447 on the double meaning of *testis.*
Lines 35–38 give an often quoted list of illicit sex partners; the "public road" then
= slaves and prostitutes.

44–45   You've . . . off: Probably a phallic joke; cf. *Towelheads* 116–17, 565–66.

47–48   A pun on *mutuum,* "loan" (cf. 68); jokes about love as property are common in
Plautus.

50   Is she pulling your plow: Literally, "does she bear the yoke"—crude.

55–56 Peanuts . . . smooches: These two lines seem to continue the agricultural/sexual double entendre with plays on *nuce/nuculeum/nucem* (phallic?) and *pandit saltum,* "opens up the pasture" (ref. female genitals?).

63–64 The price: Literally, "thirty *minae*" (= a half talent) or "an Attic talent"—large sums.

67 Associate: Literally, *parasitus* (see introduction). Jerusalem: Literally, *Caria* (now southern Turkey)—a continuous war zone in the Near East during this period.

68 Frat brother: Literally, *sodali*—"friend," with overtones of fellow membership in a secret society that held parties together.

70 Cornwallis here refers to the onstage altar.

74 Literally, "you want to make Venus vomit."

77–78 Lola . . . Merlot-la: Also a really bad pun in Latin: the old woman's name is Leaena, and Cornwallis says, "I thought you said *lagoena* [wine bottle], the kind Chian wine comes in."

90 Cocktail wieners: Latin *pulpamenta,* bits of meat used to start a meal; the word occurs in an obscene insult at Terence *Eunuchus* 426, supposedly quoted from the early Roman playwright Livius Andronicus: "You're a bunny yourself and you're hunting for meat?" (= "You're a male sex-object and you're acting like a he-man?"). The line appears in the late ancient life of Carinus (*Historia Augusta, Carinus* 13) in a complicated context: the writer says Diocletian used to boast of having killed Aper (whose name means "Boar") by quoting a line of Vergil, and that this is the kind of thing military men do—witness the soldiers in comedy, e.g., the *Eunuchus* insult, spoken by the soldier in that play and quoting Livius Andronicus. The word is, oddly, used again soon afterwards in a joke attributed to Diocletian ("I always kill the boars, but the other man enjoys the *pulpamentum,*" *Carinus* 15).

95 De-lighted: Latin *licet,* "that's fine"; possibly a pun on *lucet,* "that's clear / it's light out."

99 Puke: Literally, "bilgewater." See nonmetrical translations of songs after end of play.

109a Scent of old wine: These last three lines are just here to fill out the verse.

110 Keg: Latin *quadrantal,* "a unit of liquid measure having the volume of a cubic Roman foot" *(OLD),* equal to an amphora.

145 Sing a song: Latin *occentem;* see introduction to *Weevil* on the folk practice of chanting before the house door. Cf. notes on *Iran Man* 406–26, 569.

147   Knob: Literally, "bolts"; see nonmetrical translations of songs after end of play.

150   Native dancer: Beauregard asks the bolts to become *ludii barbari*, "barbarian stage performers" or "dancers." He gives them the command *sussilite*, "jump up"—appropriate for bolts, and presumably for barbarian dancers. For *barbari* as "native," see volume introduction (under "Locations") on the ambiguous use Plautus makes of *barbarus* to mean "Italian."

166   Cornholler: Literally, "Why are you calling 'Palinurus' like that?" This line has the format of a joke; it's possible that this is a bilingual pun on Cornwallis's last name (see section on names in *Weevil* introduction). As a pun (if it is one), this would not be intelligible to the whole audience, much like the substitute given here.

176–77 Normally, *ab*normally . . . abnormal: Latin *sane, insane . . . insanum. Sane* basically means "healthily," but came to be used most commonly to = "sure(ly), certainly, really," and so here that double sense is being played off against "insanely"; see also 187, all possibly echoing the health theme embodied in the Temple of Aesculapius and recurring in vocabulary throughout the play.

192   You . . . job: Lindsay prints *ebriola persolla, nugae* (literally "tipsy little mask/person [female], nonsense," i.e., "You tipsy tart, fiddlesticks"); others read *ebriola, persollae nugae,* translated here. Beare takes *persollae* as a diminutive of *persona,* "theatrical mask," = "ugly face." This might be taken with the two "owl" jokes at 191 and 196, which seem to point to an effect in Wanda's mask or makeup. On Roman attitudes towards makeup, see Richlin 1995.

193   Offered up to be flogged: Literally, "given as an offering to the rods." For slaves being beaten with rods, cf. notes at *Iran Man* 28, 279; *Towelheads* 18.

196   Deadbeat: Latin *verbero,* literally "person who deserves flogging"—a common slave insult in Plautus. On the punishment of slaves as a source of humor in the comedies, see H. Parker 1989.

197   A dead horse: Literally, "a stone."

201   Take my gold card: Literally, "take gold from me."

202   I'm more . . . type: These two lines play on *auro contra* (201), "as good as gold," and *contra aurichalco* (202), "as good as fool's gold."

209   Classy girl: Literally, "you who are like a free person." Cf. *Iran Man* 130 for *liberalis* as a compliment.

212   Better . . . is: Literally, "Look, by that word prepare the claim of my freedom."

216, 217 Spa, Big Doctor: Literally, "shrine," "Aesculapius" (god of medicine).

222   Oy veh: Literally, "wretched (me)."

225   Bloodsucker: Latin *parasitus.* To Beauregard, he is an "associate"; to Cornwallis, a leech.

227   Bars: Latin *tormento,* probably here = "shackles"; the Latin plays on *ferre* "bring" / *ferat* "bring" / *ferreo* "iron."

231   Potluck: Latin *conlativo.* Paulus ex Festo explains a *conlativum sacrificium* as one that is supplied by multiple contributions (33L).

239   Liver makes you sick: Cornwallis says Turk is suffering from *morbus hepatiarius,* "liver disease," and Turk says this is a joke, so it must be on the double sense of *hepatia(rius)* as both organ and food.

246, 248 Analysis: Literally, "interpretation of a dream" or "prophecy through dream analysis"; this was considered a science in antiquity, as seen in the *Oneirocritica* of Artemidorus.

252   That freeloader: Again, the *parasitus.*

256   One greater . . . I: This cook, though he has only a small part, manages to double as a dream interpreter. On the major part played by cooks in Plautus generally and their function as doubles for the poet, see Gowers 1993: 78–107, esp. 82 on the cook in *Weevil.*

263   All . . . god: Literally, "Now the other gods will do the same thing."

266   You . . . place: Literally, "It would have been better for you to do your incubation in the temple of Jupiter."

267   In . . . appearances: Literally, "in taking your oath"; implies the pimp has sworn by Jupiter many times in court, probably falsely.

269   In the Mayo Clinic: Latin *in Capitolio.* The Capitoline Hill in Rome was the location of the temple of Jupiter.

275   Leech: The *parasitus.*

277   Associate: The *parasitus.*

285–86 A list of titles of Greek authority figures: *strategus* (general), *tyrannus* (dictator), *agoranomus* (market inspector), *demarchus* (chief official of an Attic tribe), *comarchus* (chief official of a village). In the following lines, Weevil will separate himself from Greeks as invasive foreigners, so this list of titles should sound foreign and contemptuous.

288   Foreigners, loud jackets, headrags: Literally, "Greeks wearing the *pallium,* with their heads covered." The irony of this line is important, since Weevil is himself wearing the *pallium,* which was the conventional dress of comedy as well as of

Greeks. See volume introduction under "Translate or Transpose?" and *Weevil* introduction. This scene plays on Roman fear of the eastern cultures that were simultaneously providing the vehicle for the expression of that fear. The comedian is then a liminal figure here; is he co-opted into the mainstream culture or mocking it? On the connection between the covered head and runaway slaves, see note on *Towelheads* 743–44; cf. below, lines 293, 389.

290   Refugees: Latin *drapetae,* literally "runaway slaves" (but this is the Greek word for them).

292   Smoky caff: Latin *thermopolio,* literally "low-class place where hot drinks are sold" (again, this is a Latinized Greek word); hence "caff," the low-class Anglicized form of "café."

295   French-fried fart: Latin *crepitum . . . polentarium,* literally "polenta crack." *Crepitus* is the word for the sound made by the onstage door opening, by fingers snapping, and by farts; polenta (crushed grain) was similar to *puls,* the common food of poor Italians, though Pliny tells us it was Greek rather than Roman. So, here, "French-fried" as a reference both to fast food and to the ironic combination of xenophobia and cultural appropriation in this passage. What could be more American than French fries? On polenta and the association between foreignness and food here, see Gowers 1993: 63–64.

296   Smart-ass toffs: Latin *scurrae*—young men in the city who spent their time partying and saying clever things; see Corbett 1986.

297   Play . . . pitchers and catchers: This cryptic vignette seems to refer to a street game and also to convey a sexual insult.

300   Servant classes: Literally, "slaves." This line has the potential to address not only slaveowners in the audience but slaves, especially through Cornwallis's reaction. See line 607 below.

301   Guardian angel: Latin *genium,* "guardian spirit of the family"; the Romans believed each man had one, derived from his paternal line (a problem for slaves, who had no legal parents). *Parasiti* paid their way not only in jokes but in flattery. See 628 below.

314   Bloody hell: Literally, "Woe upon your head."

314–16   Please . . . *cheese:* A long play on Weevil's setup line (314), *facite ventum ut gaudeam,* which can mean either "make me glad I came" or "fan me to make me happy" or "make wind to make me happy." Other translators take the joke to be not that Cornwallis farts but that Cornwallis fans Weevil with his jacket. Either is of course possible.

317   May . . . soul: Literally, "May Jupiter and the gods ruin you."

318 Eye-boogers . . . hunger: Plautus has many jokes about an illness that made the eyes gooey (cf. *Iran Man* 11); here they are transferred to other parts of the body. Maybe better to translate with current comic afflictions: "I'm so hungry I've got athlete's foot in my teeth and heartburn in my jaws." On parasites' "drooling speeches," see Gowers 1993: 62.

323 Ham . . . pork chops: Literally, "ham, pork belly, sow's udder, sweetbreads"—favorite Roman parts of the pig. On the special significance of pork in Roman comedy, see Gowers 1993: 69–73; G. Williams 1968: 286–87.

324 In the freezer: Literally, "on the meat-rack."

340 On holiday: Literally, "for my own gratification," "because I feel like it."

344 Money amounts: Literally, "thirty *minae*," "ten *minae*."

350 It was my Christian duty: Literally, "It was a religious obligation."

352 "Time . . . man": Literally, "It's not right [for me] to delay a day, nor hinder the night." This sounds like a proverb, or a quotation, maybe from a tragedy.

356 Raincoat: The manuscripts read *anulum,* "ring"; but at 611 Weevil teases the soldier by challenging him to throw dice for his *chlamys,* "military cloak" (here translated "trenchcoat"), so Leo conjectured *amiculum* here (= "cloak"), which might also fit better with Weevil betting his *pallium* (355).

357 Snake-eyes: Latin *volturios,* "the vultures." Cards did not exist in antiquity, but dice games were very popular, and the various throws had names, as they do now.

358 My patron saint . . . Santa Claus: Latin *almam meam nutricem Herculem.* Weevil calls on Hercules as his patron god—a joke because Hercules was proverbially a glutton. *Almam* and *nutricem* mean both "guardian," "taking care of" and "feeding," "nursing" (as in nursing a baby).

359 Seven: Literally, "the king's [throw]"; on kings, luck, money, and poor men's dreams, see volume introduction under "Topical Jokes."

382–83 And now . . . investment: Mr. Wolf here seems to be going in for the not uncommon Roman investment of buying a prostitute (here an adolescent male) and making money by a little pimping on the side. This is not a respectable thing to do; Weevil notes Mr. Wolf's efforts at disguise (389). See McGinn 2004.

385 Keep . . . on: Literally, "Be quiet."

393 Stud line, Cycalopses: Latin *prosapia,* "family line" (rel. *Priapus*); *Coculitum.* This word seems to be a Latin vernacular version of Greek *Kuklops* (Cyclops), but it seems possible that a further joke underlies this; Roman jokes sometimes describe the penis as "one-eyed," and a string of sexual double entendres follows.

394   At Sarajevo: Latin *apud Sicyonem* (395 in the OCT). Sicyon was a Greek city be-sieged several times in the third century B.C.E., though probably some time pre-vious to the date of this play; substitute the name of any city besieged in the not too recent past. Or Leningrad.

395   Grenade: Latin *catapulta* (394 in the OCT). Cf. lines 689–90; *Towelheads* 201–2.

396   Broken . . . dirt: Literally, "with a broken jug with ashes (in it)." Hitting some-one over the head with an *aula* full of ashes is also suggested in *Amphitryo* (frg. IV [III]—after 1034); maybe it was the equivalent of a rotten tomato or a cream pie.

400–403   Filibuster . . . congress . . . House . . . Senator: The Latin is a series of puns set off by *incomities* (400) "abuse," which sets up *inforare* "perforate," "bore into"— playing on *forum* and *comitium* (part of the forum where the people assembled for legislation and speeches). In 403, *forum* and *comitium* are probably anatom-ical jokes, perhaps based on the association of the roots of these words here with, respectively, perforation and coming together.

410   A joke on the length of the soldier's name.

413   Thunder God: Latin *Summanus,* Jupiter's title as god of high places and light-ning. This name appears just to trigger the pun on *vestimenta . . . summano,* "I drip onto my clothes" (= "I wet myself"), 415–16. In Marshall's production, he was "Wet Blanket."

424   Slicing in half: Lindsay prints *diligit,* usually "adores," possibly here "cuts up"; the codices have *dessicit* (= *dissicit* = *disicit*), a more usual expression. Scimitar: Latin *machaera,* a Greek loanword.

440   The Shah's . . . bullion: Weevil says the statue is going to be made out of Philip's gold (compare Lola's statue at 139). In the plural, this refers to gold coins minted by Alexander the Great's father, Philip II of Macedon (died 336 B.C.E.); these coins will show up in *Towelheads* translated as "rubles." This gold should be translated as gold belonging to (or possibly minted by) a fabulously wealthy and powerful man in recent history.

442–47   Iranians . . . nations: In Latin, this list of peoples and places is made up of (a) real ones—all war zones or scarily exotic, and (b) comic names; see volume in-troduction under "Locations." It's a long trip (see map on p. 18), and includes Arabia and Persia. The last comic place name, *Conterebromnia,* tells what's up; cf. *Iran Man* 702–5, and Kalman and Meyerowitz 2001.

450   Factory chickens: Latin *pulli gallinacei,* "baby chicks," or possibly the sacred chickens used by the Romans to provide omens. *Cavea* ("coop") was also a word for the theater building, including the spectators' seats.

456–57   Some editors think this scene has been condensed and that these lines substitute for something longer and less flat. The play also seems to need a scene after line 461 in which the soldier arrives, so that we can see him with the banker at 533.

463   A con artist or a cockroach: Latin *halophantam an sycophantam,* two Greek loanwords that literally mean "harvest informer" and "fig informer." *Sycophanta,* which originally meant "a person who informs on people who dodge the Athenian fig-growing rules," hence "slanderer," had come to mean "sponger"/"flatterer," and is the non-name given to a character in *Trinummus.* The word *halophanta* seems to be made up, but perhaps plays on Weevil's name from the Greek words *halos* "harvest" and *phagein* "eat."

470–85   All the place-names in this list are in or near the Roman Forum; see *Weevil* introduction.

470   The county courthouse: Literally, the *comitium* (see note on lines 400–403).

471   Glamorous: Latin *gloriosus,* an adjective often applied to the boasting soldiers; could = "war hero" here, see 633 below. Elaine's: Literally, "the shrine of Cloacina," the sewer goddess.

472   Wall Street: Literally, "by the basilica."

473   Overage toyboys: Latin *scorta exoleta,* literally "grown-up whores." *Exoletus* is used commonly of male sex objects, usually prostitutes and/or slaves, who are past the most desirable age, i.e., over eighteen or so. Cf. *Towelheads* 17. Guys: Or "ones"—could include women (not likely, though).

474   Fulton . . . Market: Literally, "the fish market."

475   Upper East Side: Literally, "at the bottom end of the Forum." True-blue Republicans: Latin *boni homines,* "good men"—what conservative upper-class Romans called themselves.

476   Midtown . . . Tunnel: Literally, "in the middle near the gutter," probably meaning the Cloaca Maxima, the main sewer.

477   Reservoir: This *(lacus)* is usually taken to refer to an unidentified cistern; why not to the *lacus Iuturnae,* a spring at the end of the Forum near the temple of Vesta?

480   Lower East Side: Literally, "by the Old Shops."

481   St. Patrick's: Literally, "the Temple of Castor."

482   Times Square: Literally, "Etruscan Street." Peddling . . . assets: Literally, "who themselves keep selling themselves" (this may refer to prostitutes both male and female).

483   The Village: Literally, "the Velabrum" (a neighborhood).

484   Guys . . . turned: This line probably refers to men having sex with men. Cf. *Towelheads* 612.

485   {Insert . . . here}: Literally, "at the house of Leucadia Oppia." This is one of a tiny number of names in Plautus that seem to belong to real people—a marked contrast to Aristophanes. The name would be that of a freed female slave who had belonged to a man named Oppius and whose slave name had been Leucadia, probably meaning she had been an entertainer, since Leucas was a place associated with Apollo; compare the famous Volumnia Cytheris who became Antony's mistress (she belonged to a Volumnius, and "Cytheris" is an epithet of Aphrodite). This line is a doublet of line 472 and is bracketed in the OCT (on bracketing, see the volume introduction under "Conventions of Reference"). It seems possible that topical allusions like this were pasted into the text on an ad hoc basis, and that this is a trace of that practice.

506–11   This unexpected tirade from Weevil constitutes another "parabasis moment," in which a character comments on Roman social institutions—here banking, also unpopular elsewhere in Plautus (cf. *Iran Man* 432ff.). See volume introduction under "Topical Jokes."

511   Ice cubes: Literally, "cold water."

515   Mr. Title Guaranteed: Latin *mancupem,* a legal technical term.

518   Like a lady: Literally, "well and chastely."

528   Ten thousand: Literally, "ten *minae.*"

548   Mr. Wolf's point seems to be that the soldier is repudiating someone he says he never had in the first place—the pimps are "worse" because they acknowledge their obligation, i.e., pimps are better than the soldier. Ex-masters were supposed to take care of their ex-slaves.

549   Credit rating: Latin *honoris,* "respectability," "high position in the world," "good credit."

551   Thicker than a brick: Literally, "dumber than dumb."

562   Have a bite: Literally, "lick salt."

563   That . . . stuffed: Literally, "that it go badly for you."

565   Witnesses: Latin *testis* (the source of jokes at lines 30–38, 622, 695). The pimp is litigious, and here refers to the self-help process used in Roman courts, whereby a plaintiff in a lawsuit rounded up his own witnesses and the defendant—as we see later in the play, and at length in *Towelheads.*

567   Person . . . flogging: Latin *mastigia,* a Greek loanword, from *mastix* "whip"; part of the standard Plautine vocabulary of abuse for slaves. Cf. above, line 196; *Towelheads* 382, 390.

574 Half of this line is missing in the manuscripts; this sense is a guess by editors.

580 Girl: Latin *ancillam*, "female slave," as "girl" so often in English.

584–85 Lost your jewels . . . Brigade: There's certainly a joke here, and it must be playing on the sense of *perdidistin anulum* (584), "you lost your ring." Cf. the joke about King Antiochus's eyes at *Towelheads* 694. The punchline (585) says literally, "Soldier, you are well/beautifully [arranged into centuries] in the [unit of infantry consisting of two centuries] that has been [pricked thoroughly / marked off on a list]." The *OLD* notes one obscene use of *expungo* (= "bugger" at *Iran Man* 848), but takes it here to mean "unpaid." A pun on *anus* "ring"/"anus" seems possible, esp. since *perdo* can mean both "lose" and "ruin/destroy/hurt." This joke would have had to be put over with physical business. "Butthole Brigade" is much coarser than what Plautus says here, and indeed he avoids direct obscenities; "Ma-reamed Corps" would be closer to what he says, but hard to put over onstage.

586 Flour: Literally, "wheat."

589 With egg on my face: Literally, "with my face smeared up like this." Cf. *Towelheads* 1195.

590 This line is perhaps directed to the audience.

599 Sidekick: Latin *parasitum*.

607 This is one of a set of lines scattered throughout Plautus's plays that seem to address a slave audience and appeal to its life experience. Cf. also line 300 above; *Towelheads* 965–66.

611 Trenchcoat: Latin *chlamydem;* see note on line 356 above.

612 Rolls, shmolls: Latin *cum bolis, cum bullis* (literally "with throws, with amulets"). Weevil has used the Greek word *bolis* (611) for "rolls"; this irritates the soldier into childish wordplay.

620 Freeborn persons could not legally be bought or sold, though of course they were sold all the time as prisoners of war, or, like Wanda, after being kidnapped. Beauregard here plans to start the legal process whereby such a person was claimed back out of slavery. Buyers were supposed to do a title check, sellers to provide one. On the return of P.O.W.s, see Leigh 2004: 57–97.

621 The line assignments in this scene are unclear; Beauregard's question here may be addressed to Weevil, in which case it means "Can you testify against him?" and the soldier says, "No, he can't."

622 Without testiclemony: Latin *intestatus*, literally "without the power to make a will," punningly "without testicles." See notes on 30–38, 565 above; 695 below.

623	Is Weevil a slave? Parasites by definition aren't. Is the soldier confused? Slaves' testimony was accepted in ancient courtrooms only under torture.
626	Help! Help!: Weevil is performing a traditional Roman act when threatened by force—calling on his fellow citizens (*o cives, cives!* he cries). See Lintott 1999: 11–16 on *quiritatio.*
628	Guardian angel: Latin *genium* (see note on 301 above).
630	On my knees: Literally, "by your knees." Wanda here performs a formal ritual/religious act: *supplicatio,* in which the one begging grabs the knees (and sometimes also the beard) of the beggee.
633	War hero: Weevil calls the soldier *gloriosus*—the stock adjective for the stock soldier in comedy—cf. Plautus's play titled *Miles Gloriosus,* usually translated "The Swaggering Soldier," and 471 above. Ooh . . . fussy: This line follows a pattern repeated elsewhere in Plautus (e.g., *Iran Man* 547) and seems to be some kind of catchphrase or pattern. See volume introduction under "Catchphrases."
636	This line is corrupt in the manuscripts; the sense seems clear. The name of Planesium's father is Periplanes, "Wanders-around."
639	Family values: Latin *o Pietas mea.*
643	Fiona, Gwendolyn: Wanda has given both her mother and her nanny very hoity-toity Greek names, Cleobula and Archestrata.
644	Shakespeare festival: Literally, the Dionysia, the festival of Dionysus—i.e., a theater festival.
681	The sense of this line is unclear; this is a guess.
689–90	The soldier threatens to make Turk into a catapult bolt and twist him back by his string (*nervo,* 690); *nervus* can also mean "chain" or "penis." So this threat works on three levels: the image itself, the association between *nervus* and prison, and stage business. Cf. line 395; *Towelheads* 201–2.
691–92	Girly man: Latin *delicatum.* Turk has already given some indications of effeminacy with his list of accessories at 577–78. Cf. the General insulting Saddam and Boris at *Towelheads* 1303–18. Poodle: Latin *catello,* "puppy." This is the only example I know of that associates puppies with effeminate men, but that must be the joke; "poodle" here then = "foo-foo dog." The iron poodle: Beauregard qualifies *catello* (691) with *ferreo* ("the iron one") in 692; this is a play on *catellus* "puppy" and *catella* "lightweight chain."
692	High-security prison: Latin *in robusto carcere.* The *carcer* was the only official prison in Rome, a small building in the forum, next to the senate house; cf. *Towelheads,* note on 690–92. It figures in Latin literature as an awe-inspiring and

fearful place, for people went there mainly to be executed (by strangling). It was for citizens only.

693   String . . . hanged: Literally, "put a rope around his neck, take him away to the bad cross." Citizens executed in the *carcer* are often described as being dragged by a noose afterwards; crucifixion, a recent import from Carthage, was a punishment for slaves and noncitizens. The Romans generally did not use hanging as a means of execution.

695   Testi(cle)mony: A joke by now familiar; see above at 30–38, 565, 622.

698   Like a lady: Echoes what Turk says himself at 518.

708   Gentleman: Latin *vir bonus,* "good man"; see note on line 475.

712–14   Lindsay gives Weevil's line here to the soldier, and Weevil's line in 713 to the soldier and Turk, and Weevil's line in 714 to the soldier.

713   Tuppence: Literally, *flocci,* "a hair"—a common expression.

718   Be all tied up in jail: Literally, "you'll be lying in chains"; same in 723.

722   To court: Literally, "to the praetor"; same in 723.

NOTES ON NONMETRICAL TRANSLATIONS OF SONGS

115   Hocking loogies: Latin *screanti,* "clearing the throat of phlegm," a mimetic word; related forms appear only in comedy.

119   Well . . . dry: Replacing Plautus's string of S's with a bad pun.

131a   She's . . . shower: Literally, "the rainbow is drinking, I think it's going to rain today, by God."

139   A vineyard . . . statue: Or possibly "a grape statue instead of a golden one."

141   Sashayin': Latin *bitet,* a verb that may derive from Umbrian, the language of Plautus's supposed hometown (see volume introduction under "Who Was Plautus?").

146   Body and soul: Literally, "in customs and spirit."

157   Being nice to me: Latin *mihi morigeri.* The adjective *morigerus* means "obliging," sometimes with sexual overtones. Cf. 149, *gerite mihi morem;* below, 169; *Iran Man* 605.

IRAN MAN (PERSA)

Rap, but with touches of "Iron Man," by Black Sabbath:

I am Iran Man—I'll tell you my story if I can.
Rockin you today—is my friend named Bowman and his boss is away.
A ho named Georgia Moon is his girlfriend—he's gonna buy her freedom in the end.
Not enuf to set her free—he got to fool her pimp with some help from me.
Me, I'm his buddy, but I fake like I am—a bad foreign dude and I come from Iran.
And I sell the pimp a stolen virgin—but really she's the daughter of a citizen.
N we get the cash and the girl is cool—and we get high and treat the pimp like a fool.*

INTRODUCTION

Iran Man (in Latin, *Persa*) is noted as the only extant play by Plautus in which the central character is a slave and accomplishes on his own behalf what the "clever slave" usually accomplishes on behalf of his young master. The characters in this play are all either slaves (Bowman, Einstein, Georgia Moon, Toyboy, Brain Muffin) or lowlifes (Dorkalot the pimp; Fat Jack the freeloader and his hapless daughter Cherry—a rare case of a *parasitus* with family).

Western literature is full of parallels for this kind of setting; stories about poor people evidently have wide appeal, and comic stories about poor people are very common. Literary elites love to glamorize the lower classes, and to make fun of them, which is in a way the same thing, since poverty is not actually, in itself, fun (though it may develop the sense of humor). As I've argued in the volume introduction, Plautine comedy doesn't really give a top-down view, and especially this amongst Plautus's plays seems pitched *to* a lower-class audience *from* a lower-class standpoint; here I differ vigorously from the reading of *Iran Man* in McCarthy 2000, which takes this play as an elite-oriented pep talk on good citizenship and brotherly affection. Amongst all possible parallels, it seems to me that the films and comic books of Kevin Smith provide a really excellent current parallel for the kind of humor in *Iran Man.*

It should be noted that not every character in Plautus speaks the same way. Slaves use all kinds of slang that more genteel characters avoid, and use Greek words much more than any other sort of character. *Iran Man* is full of this kind of language, and I think it would have come across in the 190s–180s B.C.E. much as the obscenity-riddled slacker vernacular of Kevin Smith's cast of characters does today.

Smith's films even include an oddly Plautine staging: a favorite place of his is a convenience store in Leonardo, New Jersey, called the Quick Stop, which forms part of a two-store mini-mall; its neighbor is the RST video store. Two of Smith's central characters, the dope dealers Jay and Silent Bob, regularly hang out in front of the two stores, which present a classic *scaenae frons* (Roman stage set): two doors side by side, with exits to either side—there's even a mysterious third door in the middle, as also in the *scaenae frons*. Smith's first feature film, *Clerks*, was set entirely in and around the Quick Stop; the owner of the store never materializes as we follow a day in the life of the harassed Dante, the clerk who has to keep the store open on his day off, not much helped by his friend Randal, who is supposed to be taking care of the video store.

Smith followed *Clerks* with three films involving the same characters and others: *Mallrats, Chasing Amy,* and *Dogma.* Recurring in these films are Jay and Silent Bob, Silent Bob being played by Smith himself. As, indeed, Bob almost never speaks in these films, he has no equivalent in Plautus other than the silent but absent Plautus himself, though then again Plautus might have acted in the plays. But Jay, played by Smith's real-life high school buddy Jason Mewes, makes up for Bob's silence with a constant stream of manic, self-aggrandizing, self-deluded, obscenity-riddled raving. In Smith's 2001 film, *Jay and Silent Bob Strike Back,* these two characters moved to center stage, making Jay the Aristophanic entrepreneur of their metatheatrical endeavor: to travel to Hollywood to stop the production of a film based on their alter-ego identities as comic-book heroes. Bowman in *Iran Man* is not at all self-deluded—he is the manipulator of all the other characters—but his attitude, his drive to party, would be perfectly played by Jason Mewes.

Bowman's friend Einstein, loyal but slightly whiny, if tough, would be well played by another Smith actor, Jason Lee, who has played not only the cartoonist Banky Edwards, loyal sidekick of Ben Affleck as Holden McNeil, but the demon Azrael in *Dogma.* The running joke in Smith's films and comic books about the homosocial/homoerotic bond between both Edwards and McNeil and Jay and Silent Bob also parallels the sort of male friendship seen in *Iran Man* between Bowman and Einstein, and so typical of Roman culture, as well as of untold thousands of comic odd couples in the history of Western comedy.

Cherry, the virgin daughter of Fat Jack, needs to be cast as blue-collar but noble. I imagined Marilyn Ghigliotti here as Cherry; in *Clerks,* she plays Dante's good girlfriend, who tries to talk him into going back to school (as opposed to the sluttish Caitlin). This goody-goody role usually belongs, in New Comedy, to the hero's love object; interestingly, in *Iran Man,* Cherry is not the beloved—this role belongs to Georgia Moon, who is given little to say for herself. Cherry's speeches provide some of the numerous "parabasis moments" in this play—moments when a character editorializes, as in the parabasis in the plays of Aristophanes (see volume introduction under "Topical Jokes"). The audience may be moved to feel sorry for her, but neither she nor her father gets to participate in the final party scene.

Like *Iran Man,* Smith's films push the issue of audience. At one level, they seem to be directed at fifteen-year-old boys. But the films are also highly literate, sophisticated in their use of intertextuality and metatheater, and at times deeply concerned with questioning the Catholic Church (most notably in *Dogma;* compare Smith's writing for hero comics, esp. DareDevil). In that regard they are more Aristophanic than Plautine—Plautus does not overtly take on anything as serious as established religion, reserving his direct attacks for people everybody hates, like bankers, informers, and foreigners. Still, both *Iran Man* and *Jay and Silent Bob Strike Back* are capable of being enjoyed both as mass culture and by a literary elite. Perfect for the *ludi,* the Roman festivals for which these plays were commissioned.

In the play, two of the most entertaining characters are Brain Muffin and Toyboy, who engage in a memorable confrontation/seduction. Each is a *vicarius*—a slave's slave; Toyboy belongs to Bowman (247), Brain Muffin belongs to Georgia Moon (181). Having imagined the rest of the cast played by actors with a record of playing white lower-class characters, I imagined actors of color playing Brain Muffin and Toyboy; in *Iran Man,* there are layers of slavery, somewhat as, for a current audience, class is complicated by race. In the play, Brain Muffin and Toyboy are pretty clearly marked as even further removed from freedom than the rest. Each is also an adept at the snappy comeback; each has a smart mouth; Toyboy is the only character to tell Bowman off, and Brain Muffin's opening tirade is made to a nonspeaking Georgia Moon. As Kevin Smith's characters have a lower-class white parasitic cultural relationship to African-American culture (*Jay and Silent Bob Strike Back* ends with them being invited on stage by Morris Day and the Time), and constantly show their admiration by imitation, so the two slaves' slaves in this play are the coolest characters. But in fact the language they use is not, in Latin, marked by increased use of Greek words or other unusual slang—that is, it is not really differentiated from the speech of the other characters; they're just fast.

The Orientalism of this play appears in the title, in the fictive location of Bowman's absent master, and in the scam worked against the pimp by Bowman, Einstein, and Fat Jack. As in *Towelheads,* where the advent of the Carthaginian is emphasized in the prologue, it seems that the idea has been present in Bowman's mind from the start (136), and the audience gets some clues to the exotic element in it at 155–58. The plan entails stereotyped costuming (463–64), though initially Bowman seems pretty vague about this (155–58), and the disguises are set up to be laughably flimsy. The plan also entails imaginary geography (the City of Gold, 506) and a bravura list of imaginary Persian names (702–5). The faraway places of *Iran Man* are outside the sphere of Roman influence: Persia the seat of the Seleucid empire, Arabia a fabulous land from which spices come. As in *Weevil,* the Orient here serves as the deus ex machina, the place that enables the crew to pull off their scam. And they don't even have to go there; just a few costumes—which they get, metatheatrically, from the director—will do the trick. The Orient, like theater itself, becomes a way out, an escape. Bowman also locates his master there for the purposes of the scam; of course, the absence of the master is also a necessity here, and it becomes identified with the Orient.

The plan also involves selling a citizen girl onstage, as she voices her feelings in a long sequence of speeches with double meaning. This play is one of the most fascinating potential sites of veiled resistance in Latin literature, in which (slave?) actors spoke lines that talked about what it feels like to be sold. Throughout the play, slaves ventriloquize and mock their absent masters and the obsequious voice slaves use to masters (Brain Muffin and Toyboy at 240–42; Einstein at 260, 262, 310–11, cf. 7–9). Maybe this tallies with Bowman's brutality to Georgia Moon after he has bought her out of slavery. Or maybe not. This play could be read in many ways—like a lot of Latin literature, shaped by a culture in which free speech was both highly valued and dangerous. *Satura tota nostra est,* as Quintilian said—satire is all ours.

It should be noted that parents in Plautus's world really did sell their children into slavery and prostitution—as they still do today, if perhaps not in the United States. Such sales were a topic of jokes from Aristophanes in the fifth century B.C.E. at least to Lucian in the second century C.E., in the work known somewhat misleadingly today as *Dialogues of the Courtesans.* Aristophanes' *Acharnians* features a long scene (729–835) in which a Megarian man, impelled by starvation during the Peloponnesian War, comes to the market opened by the main character, bringing with him his two little girls to sell. He has the brilliant idea of disguising the girls as "piggies," a conceit that plays (throughout) on the crudest Greek slang term for the female genitalia; see D. Parker 1969: 61–73 and J. Henderson 2003: 61–67 for translations. The *Acharnians* scene has many points in common with the selling of Cherry by Fat Jack and may well be a direct ancestor; a major difference is that Cherry gets to describe her feelings, while the little girls' lines consist of "Sell us! Sell us!" and "Oink oink." This joke is still functional, as in the comic name "Baima-i-Sistra" at *Iran Man* 702; in English, it is still a joke to associate this practice with the Third World. For modern writing by sex workers, see, for example, Delacoste and Alexander 1987.

THE SETTING

The play is set in Athens, which is the central location of Plautine comedy (twelve of the twenty extant plays are set there) and roughly means "the big city." There is no real sense of setting in the play, except that the Near East is elsewhere in regards to it, and Einstein's master sends him to Eretria, which is near Athens. I would take this to be a sort of default mode, and though I set *Iran Man* in Los Angeles and substituted Spanish for Greek, the play would work well in any gritty setting definable as "here."

PLOT POINTS

Many readers have noticed that Bowman actually gets the money he needs to buy Georgia Moon twice; the money he gets from Einstein shouldn't really be necessary, since he knows early on that he's going to get the money from the pimp. But his problem is that the pimp won't sell him Georgia Moon on credit; by paying for her with Einstein's cattle money, he sets the pimp up for the con he proceeds to run on him. The idea then is that the money from the con will replace the cattle money and Einstein will not be in trouble. However, Bowman gives several signs (681–82, 767a–768) that he does not intend to pay his friend back right away. And yet he knows that Einstein is fresh from a year of punishment in the mill (21–22). The last act makes it clear that Bowman is not a nice guy.

The play also never explains why Bowman chooses to pay Dorkalot the money to free Georgia Moon, rather than buying her himself and setting her free himself, which would make Bowman rather than Dorkalot her *patronus*—a sore point at the end of the play. Bowman already owns at least one other slave (Toyboy), so why not another? The answer is that, though a Roman slave could own another slave, he couldn't free a slave—only a citizen could make a citizen. Everything Bowman "owns" is really part of his *peculium* (see notes on lines 192, 201 below): the real owner in law would be Bowman's owner, who also has the right to have sex with any of his slaves. Buying Georgia Moon wouldn't enable Bowman to set her free, and act 5 makes it clear how important this is to him. And yet act 5 makes it clear that she isn't exactly free.

As in other plays of Plautus, the last act is set at a party. The character most interested in eating, Fat Jack, is conspicuous by his absence from the table, along with Cherry, who has explicitly suggested (675) that some reward or acknowledgment for all she has done is in order. The problem here may have been heightened for the audience by Fat Jack's speech (99–100) aligning Bowman with Jupiter and himself with one of those celebrating the feast of Jupiter Epulo (see note ad loc.). There is a chance that the play may have been performed at the Plebeian Games, of which the feast for Jupiter formed a part.

MUSIC

This play has a lot more music in it than *Weevil* does, is full of rhythm, and ends with a scene that clearly involved dancing. If the play's musical passages could be set in a reasonable facsimile of hip-hop, it might come fairly close to the feel of what Plautus actually did. Listening to Public Enemy sets the reader up well for the play. (For a comparison of rap with Aristophanic comedy, see Rosen and Marks 1999.) Basically, all the passages that were spoken in the original (the senarii) are translated line-for-line into iambic senarii, or sometimes iambic pentameter. Most of the passages that were in recitative meters in the original—iambic septenarii and octonarii, trochaic septenarii and octonarii—are done here line-for-line into the same meters in English, without rhyme. In English, the trochaic meters are used in Longfellow's *Hiawatha;* the iambic meters are like the meter of "Stopping by Woods on a Snowy Evening" or Shakespeare's plays, but with longer lines. In a scene toward the beginning of *Jay and Silent Bob Strike Back,* Jay has a run-in with some youthful clients and starts to talk to them in a sort of chanted rap; this is trochaic septenarii (could it really be a direct descendant?). There are long stretches of it in *Iran Man;* it could probably be performed either as prose or as chanted rap, and can certainly be read without really noticing the meter. An interesting thing about this meter is that it can be felt either as seven and a half trochees or as four groups of cretics—long-short-long. This is useful not only because it matches the way we might feel this line (listen to Jay in *Jay and Silent Bob Strike Back*), but because the Romans themselves had a favorite beat called the tripudium, the "triple stomp," and may well have felt trochaic septenarii this way, too.

Finally, I have turned most of the lyric passages, which were sung in the original, into rhymed rap; like the songs in *Weevil* and *Towelheads,* this is not line-for-line, and a closer translation is provided after the end of the play. Please note (I'm not just making this up) that Plautine meter is notoriously rough, with syllables pushed around shamelessly to make the line work; the same is true here. Occasionally, I have italicized a stressed word to help the reader figure this out, if desired. The final act of the play, like some others in Plautus (*Stichus* is the most obvious example), is something of a grand musical finale, with dancing; like the last act of *Stichus,* it represents a slave drinking party.

LANGUAGE

The level of diction used in *Persa* corresponds with a level of diction in English that uses "primary obscenities" (= four-letter words), which Plautus does not, and a lot of excretory language that does not exist in Latin in the same way. In addition, the characters' constant use of oaths like *edepol* and *hercle* corresponds with the common use of Christian god-names. *Iran Man,* then, is not written in polite language; readers may of course tone it down as suits them. Startling as the slang may be, the translation is close to word-for-word.

Similarly, nonstandard English spelling and grammar in this translation reflect similarly nonstandard Latin spelling and grammar in Plautus. Readers of Plautus in the original have to get used to this and are usually taught to think of the Latin in terms of the classical and proper equivalents, but proper English does not really convey the tone of the original.

Throughout the play, "Iran" is pronounced as in "I ran down the street." This (a) fits with the play's general level of diction, (b) points to the connection the play makes between the Orient and slave fantasies of escape.

THE TEXT

I have followed the Latin of the Oxford Classical Text, originally produced by W. M. Lindsay, a great scholar of early Latin, in 1905, with some updates since. But I have also made use of Erich Woytek's 1982 commentary. This commentary is in German, is difficult to obtain, and in any case does not address the usual concerns of teachers and students, dealing in large part with the relation between this text and its putative Greek original, with meter, and with early Latin vocabulary and syntax. But Woytek is a radical critic in that he does not take the text for granted, questioning both the words and the line assignments. The ancient manuscripts do not tell us who spoke which line, but just put a mark to indicate speaker changes, and the line assignments in modern editions are the result of centuries of discussion and the volume editor's opinion. Moreover, both speaker changes and the words of the play have taken a beating during two thousand years of transmission, via hand copying until relatively recently. It's good to be reminded of this, and to know that readers should feel free to experiment: the "real" original text is not available to us, and many scholars think the original text was based on actors' working copies that were full of variations. The translation given here, then, sometimes follows Woytek's ideas, as indicated in the notes.

THE TITLE

The title of the play in Latin is *Persa,* which looks like a feminine noun and has caused a lot of confusion (see Faller 2001: 178–79 for a summary going back to the nineteenth century; the identification of Fat Jack's daughter as the Persa is standard in the pre-1600 editions I surveyed). On first glance, it means "The Persian Girl."

But Bowman addresses Einstein as "Persa" (line 676), and allusions to the "Persa" later in the play can easily be read as referring to Einstein. And Cherry is supposed to be from Arabia, not Persia. It is still interesting to think about the form of this proper noun: masculine nouns ending in -*a* are rare in Latin, this one belongs to a set of nouns that transmute the ending from Greek, and Romans strongly associated the Orient, and sometimes Greece, with effeminacy. *Iran Man* may sound much more macho than the original title did to its audience. We might compare the critique of the term "Chinaman" within ethnic studies, and the factors that led Maxine Hong Kingston to title her second novel *China Men*.

THE NAMES AND THE CAST

BOWMAN

The main character in the Latin original of *Iran Man* is named "Toxilus," which sounds as if it means "Bowman" in Greek. (Or "Bow-like Person"—I suppose he could be called "Bowie.") See Woytek 1982: 131 for reasons why this is probably a false etymology; I still think it would have been so understood by its audience. See above for reasons why I thought of Jason Mewes in this role. Bowman's lines here are written for Mewes's Jersey-inflected rant.

EINSTEIN

In the Latin, this character is called "Sagaristio," which seems to be an Asiatic ethnic name (Woytek 1982: 131–32). The "*Sag*" element in it means "wise" in Latin. But Sagaristio is no mental giant, and plays second fiddle to Bowman, as the play's ending makes clear (no girl for him, maybe no money either). Hence the name "Einstein" in its current common sense of "not too smart." See above for reasons why I imagined Jason Lee in this role. The lines are written for Lee's slightly whiny, smart-ass voice.

FAT JACK

In Latin, this character is called "Saturio," not only a Greek name but also a very Latin name based on the word that gave its name to the genre of satire. The word *satur* meant "full" or "stuffed," and filling up on food is Saturio's main goal in life. "Fat Jack" just seemed to suit him—and also enabled me to match a pun at 103. Fat Jack is a *parasitus,* like Weevil in *Weevil:* a person who scrounges meals in return for flattery and jokes (much like a comedian, which is the source of many jokes in Plautus). Saturio, who has a daughter old enough to sell to a pimp, could well be older than the other characters; I thought James Garner would make a perfect Saturio, and Fat Jack's lines here are written for his oily, sanctimonious, yet lovable voice.

BRAIN MUFFIN

This character's Latin name is "Sophoclidisca," which probably means "Little Female Sophocles" (see Woytek 1982: 132). The first part of the name, "*Soph-*," means "wise" in Greek; the *-id-isca* ending on a woman's name is a double diminutive (cf. Blini/Collybiscus in *Towelheads;* Igor as *Milphidisce* at *Towelheads* 421), and can appear in the names of whores (cf. Lycisca in Juvenal's sixth satire). Hence the peculiar equivalent "Brain Muffin." I originally saw her as a smart-mouthed Chicana, like Rosie Perez in *White Men Can't Jump.* But she could also be like Marisa Tomei in *My Cousin Vinnie,* or like Ariyan Johnson in *Just Another Girl on the IRT.* In theory, this role should be played by a male actor in drag (John Leguizamo *doing* Rosie Perez, as in *To Wong Foo, Thanks for Everything! Julie Newmar*); but Brain Muffin's femininity is not a joke here. Contrast the whores in *Towelheads,* or Madame Lola in *Weevil;* I like to think of her being played by a *mima* (mime actress), though there is no historical basis for such a guess and most theater historians would reject this idea.

GEORGIA MOON

This character's Latin name is "Lemniselenis," which roughly seems to mean "Moon Goddess of the Island of Lemnos"; Lemnos was a Greek island famous in myth for the slaughter of a lot of husbands by their wives. I thought this idea would come across better in "Georgia Moon" than in "Lemniselenis." This is a small role, sexy and fluffy but with a few important moments; I imagined Tara Reid in the part, as in her performance in *The Big Lebowski.* Again, this role was probably originally played by a male actor in drag.

TOYBOY

This character's Latin name is "Paegnium," which is a Latin spelling of a Greek word, *paignion,* that exactly means "toyboy" (more generally "plaything," "darling"; but it has the specialized sense elsewhere as well—see Woytek 1982: 133). The name suggests that this character is an adolescent boy of the sort that commonly appears in Latin literature as a sex slave, whose job within a household would often be that of "cupbearer" (i.e., doing what Ganymede did for Zeus)—Toyboy appears in this role at the end of the play. He seems to have no sexual relationship with

Bowman, but there is a hint that he has been making some money on the side by sex work at 284–85. Stereotypically, he would have long curling hair, look somewhat girlish, and appear Greek or Near Eastern. However, Toyboy in *Iran Man* is tough and smart-mouthed, not swishy; I thought of Chris Rock, as in his role in *Jay and Silent Bob Strike Back,* and wrote lines for his voice, but ideally Toyboy would be markedly younger than the other characters and look androgynous. On Roman sex slaves, see Richlin 1993; C. Williams 1999.

CHERRY

This character has no name in the Latin original, and is simply listed in the *Personae* as "Virgo," "a virgin." I tried out "Angela" and "Virginia" before settling on "Cherry," a joke not really present in Plautus, who makes her generic. But he also makes her important, and I thought she needed a name. No one ever uses it, which probably underscores the pathos of her situation. Her father and others address her as *virgo,* but this is not a name. See above for the reasons why I thought of Marilyn Ghigliotti in this role; it could also be done by someone like Reese Witherspoon or Scarlett Johansson. Again, this role was probably originally played by a male actor in drag. Lines here are written for a female actor with a strong New Jersey accent who sounds self-righteous.

DORKALOT

The pimp's Latin name was "Dordalus." This is a somewhat mysterious name form, and may be meant to recall the name "Daedalus"; the first element, *dor-,* could mean "gift" or "spear," among other things. I made "Dorkalot" on the analogy of "Lancelot" as a version of "Dordalus" on the analogy of "Daedalus," to fit the play's level of diction (also thinking of "Dork Knight," Jay to Silent Bob, in Kevin Smith's graphic novel *Chasing Dogma*). I imagined Tim Allen as the pimp because Dorkalot is smarter than pimps usually are in Plautus, but that's not saying much—a level Tim Allen plays very well. Dorkalot's lines are written here for a neutral voice like Allen's but could easily be taken in other directions.

CAST OF CHARACTERS

Bowman, a young guy (and slave)   [Toxilus, a slave]

Einstein, a young guy (and slave)   [Sagaristio, a slave]

Fat Jack, a bum (not a slave)   [Saturio, a *parasitus*]

Brain Muffin, the maid (a slave)   [Sophoclidisca, a female slave]

Georgia Moon, a hooker (and slave)   [Lemniselenis, a prostitute]

Toyboy, a teenaged guy (and slave)   [Paegnium, a boy]

Cherry, a virgin (not a slave)   [Virgo]

Dorkalot, a pimp (not a slave)   [Dordalus, a pimp]

The text possibly, but never explicitly, indicates the presence of a couple of nonspeaking house slaves.

Scene

Los Angeles [Athens].

There are two house fronts side by side: one house belongs to Bowman's master (who's away), the other to Dorkalot the pimp; Georgia Moon and Brain Muffin also live there. Onstage there needs to be a feature behind which first Einstein and Cherry and then Fat Jack can hide in act 4—a dumpster would be appropriate; it needs to be stage R. Exit stage R = to the Harbor Freeway, exit stage L = to Downtown.

Costume Note

Several of the male characters—Bowman, Einstein, Fat Jack, Toyboy, and/or Dorkalot—should wear cowboy boots and ponchos or jeans jackets, to tie in with lines 123–25 here. Or, however the lines are translated, there should be a visual correspondence between costume and these lines. Toyboy should have long hair, at least down to his shoulders. The pimp Dorkalot carries a swagger stick, which can also be used as a weapon.

ACT 1

SCENE 1: BOWMAN *and* EINSTEIN
BOWMAN *enters from his house;* EINSTEIN *enters from stage L.*

BOWMAN *(to himself):* The dude who first set out to go on the road of Love
        without no dough,   iambic octonarii and septenarii
this guy had to go through way more shit than all them Labors of Hercules.*
Man, I'd rather duke it out with the lion, the snake, the deer, that
        A-rab mummy,*
the birds in that swamp in ancient Greece, or even with the Incredible Hulk,*
than with Love; that's why I'm goin nuts and tryin to borrow some dough,   5
but folks I ask don't know how to say nothin to me but "ain't no way."
EINSTEIN *(to himself):* A slave who wants to slave for his boss like a good slave
        just slaving away
damn well better take good care to save up a lot inside his head—
stuff he thinks will please his boss whether he's there to see it or not.
But I don't slave just for fun, and my boss doesn't think much of me,   10
just like I'm a case of pinkeye, he can't keep his hand off me,*
he's just got to tell me off, just got to stick me with his bizness.
BOWMAN: Who's this I see in front of me? EINSTEIN: Who's this who be in
        front of me?   trochaic octonarii
BOWMAN: Looks like Einstein. EINSTEIN: Yes indeed, it's the Bowman, it's
        my homes.
BOWMAN: Yup, it's him. EINSTEIN: I believe it's him. BOWMAN: I'll check him
        out. EINSTEIN: I be checkin him out.   15
BOWMAN: Yo, Einstein, you're lookin good.* EINSTEIN: Bowman, good to see
        you, dude.
How's it hangin?* BOWMAN: Best I can. EINSTEIN: Whussup? BOWMAN: I'm just
        gettin by.   17–17b
EINSTEIN: Good enough for you? BOWMAN: If things turn out how I
        want, not bad.
{But, Jesus, I can't win for losin—my friends won't loan me a fuckin dime.}*   18a
EINSTEIN: You're treatin your friends real stupid, dude. BOWMAN: Why's that?
        EINSTEIN: You gotta be the boss.   iambic septenarii
BOWMAN: Hey, I thought that *you* was dead, cuz I didn't see you around.   20
EINSTEIN: Jeeze, it was bizness— BOWMAN: Juvie bizness?* EINSTEIN: Yeah, a
        little more than a year

I was the Beat Officer in charge of handcuffs down at County.*

BOWMAN: That's an old tour of duty for you. EINSTEIN: Ever make out?

       BOWMAN: No, not rightly.

EINSTEIN: That's why you're so damn pale.* BOWMAN: No, I'm wounded in the
      war of love:

Cupid pierced my heart with his dart. EINSTEIN: What, so now slaves fall in
      love here?*   25

BOWMAN: What could I do? Can I take on the superheroes?* Can I
      make war   trochaics

on beings that I can't match up to? What is this, *Clash of the Titans?**

EINSTEIN: Just watch out that your *butt* don't get pierced by bolts from the
      boys in blue.*

BOWMAN: Right now I'm royally loco, just like Cinco de Mayo, dude.*

EINSTEIN: What's up? BOWMAN: Cuz my boss is out of town.

          EINSTEIN: No shit,   29a

(Rap.) the boss is away? BOWMAN: And we can play!

If you got the time I'm gonna treat you fine,   30

we'll live la vida loca like a pair of jokers.*   30a

EINSTEIN: Whoa! It makes my shoulder blades burn just to hear you
      talk like that.

BOWMAN: But there's just one thing that burns my ass.* EINSTEIN: Oh, yeah?
      What might that one thing be?

BOWMAN: Cuz today is the final day of decision, whether my girl goes free

or slaves away forever and ever. EINSTEIN: So—what do you want?

BOWMAN: You got the power to buy yourself a pal forever and ever.

          EINSTEIN: How might that be?   35

BOWMAN: Just give me the six hundred bucks so I can pay for her freedom now,

and I promise I'll pay you back right away, or could be in three–four days.

Go on, be a sport, help me.

EINSTEIN: Where do *you* get the nerve to ask for so much money from me,

bitch?* Shit, if I sold myself including my clothes,* I couldn't get   40

what you're askin me for; you're tryin to get blood out of a stone

that's pretty anemic itself.* BOWMAN: That's it? EINSTEIN: What do you want
      from me? BOWMAN: Wanna know?

Get a loan from somewhere. EINSTEIN: Why don't *you*
      get one, then?   iambic septenarii

BOWMAN: I tried, I couldn't get one nowhere. EINSTEIN: I'd try too, like I could
      get credit.

BOWMAN: For sure, it's out there.* EINSTEIN: If I had any at home, I'd
        promise it to you;   45
the only thing I got is get busy. BOWMAN: Whatever you get, get
        back to me.
Just get going, I'll get busy, too. EINSTEIN: Whatever I get—you'll be the first to
        know.
BOWMAN: I'm tellin the whole truth— EINSTEIN: And nothin but the truth!*
        BOWMAN: Just help me out, homes. EINSTEIN: Hey, you're killin me
        with boredom.
BOWMAN: It's all for love, not my fault you hear me talkin loco* to you.
EINSTEIN: Shit, man, I gotta leave you now. BOWMAN: So soon? OK, well—have
        a nice walk.   50
But get back here as soon as you can, and don't make me come lookin for you.
I'm stayin home to cook up* somethin evil for that pimp. Oh yeah.
(Exeunt, EINSTEIN *stage L,* BOWMAN *into his house.)*

SCENE 2: FAT JACK
Enter FAT JACK *from stage L.*

FAT JACK: The ancient and honorable profession of my ancestors   iambic senarii
I keep, maintain, and cultivate with extreme care.
For there never was a single one of my ancestors   55
that didn't feed his belly by sponging off folks:
my pappy, my grandpappy, my great-grandpappy, *his* pappy, *his* pappy, and *his,*
they always ate other people's food—like mice.
And there wasn't anybody could beat them in eating ability—
that's how they got their name—the famous Suckerfish.*   60
That's where I get this profession and the place of my ancestors.
I wouldn't be a snitch* {to feed my gut},
it's rude to grab other folks' goodies, no risk to me;
and I don't like folks who do that. May I speak frankly?
*(In legal singsong.)**
For whosoever shall do this for the sake of the public good   65
rather than for his own benefit, the conclusion can be reached
that he be a citizen both faithful and good.
{But I want this penalty established legally from now on:}*   67a
If anyone shalt fail to convict the lawbreaker, let him pay

a fine of half to the public exchequer; and also in that law be it written:
when a snitch shalt point the finger at a certain party, 70
just so much the party of the second part shalt lay hand on the party of the first
                part in return,
so that they shalt proceed in equal part to see the judge.
Should this be law, they'd make 'emselves scarce, I guarantee it
—those guys who set a paper trap* for other folks' goodies.
(Returns to his normal mode.)
But aren't I dumb to trouble my head about my civic duty 75
when there are politicians who *have* to think about it?
Now I'll mosey in here, I'll pay my respects to yesterday's leftovers,*
did they sleep well or not, or did they run a fever,
or have they been covered or not, so nobody tries to steal 'em.
—But the door's opening, I better go into slow-mo. *(Freezes.)* 80

SCENE 3: BOWMAN *and* FAT JACK
Enter BOWMAN *from his house.*

BOWMAN: I got it all set up, so today that pimp   iambic senarii
should make my girlfriend a free woman with his own money.
But, whoa, here comes that bum—I need his help—
I'll act like I don't see him; that's how I'll rope the dude in.
(Yells into house.) Hey, you, watch out and snap it up in there, 85
I don't want to have to wait around when I'm ready to go in.
Mix up the sangria, get out the nuts and the guacamole,*
heat up the platters and throw on some fajitas.*
Jeeze, he'll be here any minute, I believe—my homeboy.
FAT JACK: Oh boy, he means me! BOWMAN: I think he's on his way here 90
fresh from the gym. FAT JACK: Look how he's got it all organized!
BOWMAN *(yelling into house):* Make sure the spaghetti ain't too al dente!
                And the steaks,*
don't give 'em to me raw. FAT JACK: He really knows his stuff.
Raw food is no good, unless you gulp it down with a nice marinade;*
when your spaghetti sauce isn't thicker than oatmeal* 95
it's no-good and puny, like eating see-through chiffon.*
Spaghetti sauce ought to have cojones.*
I want what'll go to my belly, not my bladder.

BOWMAN: Hey, somebody's speaking near me. FAT JACK: Oh, my God!
Your earthly dining companion doth address you.*   100
BOWMAN: Oh, Fat Jack, you got here just in time.
FAT JACK: I'm afraid you're telling a lie, and it doesn't become you:
for I'm here not as Fat Jack but as Hungry Jack.
BOWMAN: So you'll eat! I got somethin on the grill just for your gut.*
I've had 'em heat up the leftovers. FAT JACK: Mmm, I think with ham   105
the rule is to serve it *cold* the following day.
BOWMAN: That's what I had 'em do. FAT JACK: Hot salsa?* BOWMAN: You
                need to ask?
FAT JACK: You're a genius in the kitchen. BOWMAN: But did you think about
that piece of bizness I mentioned to you yesterday?
FAT JACK: I remember: that you shouldn't heat up the crab legs*   110
cuz it's much easier to comb through 'em* cold. *(Primps hair.)*
But why are we holding back from diving in?*
A good breakfast is the start of a healthy day.*
BOWMAN: Mmm, it's a bit too early for me. FAT JACK: Whatever you get
an early start on goes well for you all day long.   115
BOWMAN: I want you to listen to this. Yesterday I told you all about it
and I explained it to you—how you should give me six hundred bucks
just to use as a loan. FAT JACK: Oh, I remember and I know
that you explained it to me and that I don't have a thing to give you.
Do I look like the Guggenheim Foundation? I'm a bum!*   120
What bums like to do is have dinner right now,
and scarf down anything they happen to have at home.
A good bum ought to be poor, like the wise old cowboy*—
just his canteen and his lariat, his tin pan, boots, and poncho,
and his leather pouch, with a little assistance inside   125
—just enough to keep his home life happy.
BOWMAN: OK, I don't want money now: just give me your daughter
to borrow for a while. FAT JACK: Dang, I never loaned her to anyone before.
BOWMAN: It's not for what you're thinkin. FAT JACK: So what for? BOWMAN:
                I'll tell you.
Cuz her bod's bodacious but classy.* FAT JACK: I can't deny it.   130
BOWMAN: This pimp don't know you or your daughter either.
FAT JACK: Does anybody know me who's not giving out free meals?
BOWMAN: No shit. And this is how you can get me some money.
FAT JACK: Goddamn, I'd like to. BOWMAN: So let me sell her to the pimp.

FAT JACK: You're going to sell her? BOWMAN: Actually I'm gonna get
                another guy   135
to sell her—he's gonna say he's some foreign guy.
{It's really my buddy Einstein—he's been in jail for a year,}*   136a
and, like, this pimp, it's not six months since he moved here
from Orange County.* FAT JACK: The leftovers are getting cold.
Can we talk about this later? BOWMAN: You know what we can do later?
You ain't puttin a damn thing in your mouth, {fat boy}, don't think it,   140
before you promise me you're gonna do what I'm askin you;
and unless you bring your daughter here with you on the double,
by God I'll kick you out of this Breakfast Club.*
Capisce?* What is it?* Why don't you tell me what you're gonna do?
FAT JACK: Jesus, go ahead, you can sell me, too, while you're at it,   145
if you sell me on a full stomach. BOWMAN: Gonna do it? Get to it!
FAT JACK: I'll do whatever you want. BOWMAN: All right! Go on, get home;
clue her in scientific, teach your little girl how to be sharp,
and explain the story she's gonna have to tell—
where she was born, who her parents were, where she was snatched from.   150
But she better say she was born someplace far away from L.A.;
and she should cry when she talks about it. FAT JACK: Will you shut
                up already?
She's three times as wicked as you want her to be.
BOWMAN: God, now you're talkin. But y'know what to do? Just get
a bathrobe and belt, a trenchcoat, and throw in a floppy hat*   155
for the guy to wear who's gonna sell her to the pimp. FAT JACK: Good thinkin!
BOWMAN:—like he's some foreign guy. FAT JACK: I like it! BOWMAN: And your
                daughter—
get her here decked out nice in one of those foreign costumes.*
FAT JACK: *De donde** costumes? BOWMAN: Gotta get 'em from the director,*
that's his job: the producers* hired him to hand 'em out.   160
FAT JACK: OK, I'll get 'em here right away. And I don't know a thing about it.
BOWMAN: Not a damn thing. Cuz the minute I get the bucks for her,
that's when you claim her from the pimp as a U.S. citizen.*
FAT JACK: He can have her if I don't grab her from him then and there.
BOWMAN: OK, get goin, get it done. Meanwhile I want to send my boy   165
to my girlfriend, to tell her to think cheerful thoughts,
I'm gonna do it today. Man, I'm talkin too much.
(*Exeunt,* FAT JACK *stage L,* BOWMAN *into his house.*)

ACT 2

SCENE 1: BRAIN MUFFIN *and* GEORGIA MOON
Enter BRAIN MUFFIN *from the pimp's house. She holds an envelope.*

BRAIN MUFFIN *(yells back into the pimp's house):** It's bad enough to explain it to a
        brainless, witless *puta* so many times—   anapests
but I think you even take me for a hick from the sticks on top of it.
OK, I drink a little wine, but I don't drink away what you tell me with it.   170
I thought me and my character was tried and true enough for you.
In fact I'm workin for you five years now, and that's enough time, I think,
you could send a sheep to school and it'd be able to read and write.
But in all this time you still couldn't figure me out, you baa-baa Barbie™ doll.*
(Rap.) Can you shut up? Can you quit your naggin?   175
I'm with it! I'm cool! So stop your raggin.
Poor you, you're in love: it's boilin your brain.
I'll fix it so it don't make you act insane.
Poor him, he's in love.—Sure, a guy's a disgrace
if he ain't in love: his whole life is a waste.   180
(To herself.) I ought to go, like a model employee, and so I can help her get
        free sooner.
I'll go see this Bowman guy: I'm gonna stick her orders in *his* ears. *(Freezes.)*

SCENE 2: BOWMAN, TOYBOY, *and* BRAIN MUFFIN
Enter BOWMAN *and* TOYBOY *from Bowman's house.* BOWMAN *holds an envelope.*

BOWMAN: Is this all plain and clear to you? Are you gonna
        remember it all?   trochaic septenarii
TOYBOY: Better than you, and you said it, dude. BOWMAN: Oh really,
        shit-for-brains?*
TOYBOY: For sure, dude. BOWMAN: What'd I say then? TOYBOY: I'll tell her
        right away.   185
BOWMAN: Damn, you forgot, didn't you? TOYBOY: Jesus, wanna bet I don't got
        the whole thing down cold?
Yeah, wanna bet you know how many fingers you got on your hand today?*
        (Gives BOWMAN *the finger.)*
BOWMAN: You want me to bet you? TOYBOY: If you got the nerve and want to
        lose your money.

BOWMAN: I'll just let you live.* TOYBOY: Then lemme go. BOWMAN: I'm tellin
  you, not lettin you;
but here's what I want: run so that you get home when I think you
  should be *there*.   190
TOYBOY: I'll do it. BOWMAN: So where are you goin? TOYBOY: Home, so I'll be
  home when you think I'm *there*.
BOWMAN: You're a rotten kid, and that's why I'm gonna give you a little advance
  on your allowance.*
TOYBOY: I know you can trust what your damn boss promises you
  like a queer*—
what am I gonna do, get you down and sue you? Then who's gonna be
  the judge?*
BOWMAN: Just get outta here. TOYBOY: Gonna make you proud of me.
        BOWMAN: But this envelope, Toyboy?   195
Make sure you give it to Georgia Moon herself and tell her what I want done.
        (Gives envelope to Toyboy.)
BRAIN MUFFIN: I think I'll slow down on my errand.
TOYBOY: I'm going. BOWMAN: So go! I'm going home. Make sure you do a
  good job, OK?
Fly, man, full speed. TOYBOY: Just like a Maserati at a Demolition Derby.*
(Exit BOWMAN *into his house.)*
—OK, he's finally gone in. But who would this girl be who's walkin
  toward me?   200
BRAIN MUFFIN: Hey, it's Toyboy. TOYBOY: Oh, it's Brain Muffin, she the
  personal slave* of the girl
I'm bein sent to. BRAIN MUFFIN: They say there's nobody badder than this
  boy today.
TOYBOY: I'll stop her. BRAIN MUFFIN: I better catch him. *(She stands directly in
  front of him.)* TOYBOY: I better stop at this roadblock.
BRAIN MUFFIN: Toyboy, sweetie boy, hello there. How ya doin? Feelin healthy?
TOYBOY: Brain Muffin! God bless—me.* BRAIN MUFFIN: What about me?
        TOYBOY: God could go either way;   205
but if he treated you like you deserve, he'd diss you and do you down.
BRAIN MUFFIN: Stop talkin trash. TOYBOY: If I talk like you deserve, I'm tellin
  truth, not trash.
BRAIN MUFFIN: Whatchu doin? TOYBOY: I'm standin on top of you checkin you
  out, you bad, bad girl.
BRAIN MUFFIN: For sure I never knew no badder little dude than you, no way.

TOYBOY: What am I doin that's bad? Who'm I dissin? BRAIN MUFFIN: Any damn
   body, whenever you get the chance.   210
TOYBOY: There were no witnesses. BRAIN MUFFIN: Damn, but lots of people
   know that's the way it is.
TOYBOY: Good golly! BRAIN MUFFIN: Miss Molly!* TOYBOY: You're judgin other
   people by your own behavior.
BRAIN MUFFIN: I'm just exactly the way I should be, seein as how I work in a
   whorehouse.
TOYBOY: You don't have to paint me a picture. BRAIN MUFFIN: I know I am, but
   what are you?*
TOYBOY: I'd admit it, if I were. BRAIN MUFFIN: Get away, you win. TOYBOY: *You*
   get away, *now.* BRAIN MUFFIN: Tell me one thing,   215
where ya goin? TOYBOY: Where're *you?* BRAIN MUFFIN: Tell me! TOYBOY: Tell
   me! BRAIN MUFFIN: I asked first. TOYBOY: You'll be the last to know.
BRAIN MUFFIN: I'm not goin far from here. TOYBOY: Me neither, not far. BRAIN
   MUFFIN: So where you goin, bad boy?
TOYBOY: Unless you tell me first, you'll never find out what you want to know.
BRAIN MUFFIN: Shit,* you're never gonna find out today before *I* hear it
   from *you.*
TOYBOY: Is that so? BRAIN MUFFIN: That's so. TOYBOY: You're bad. BRAIN
   MUFFIN: You're wicked. TOYBOY: I take it as a compliment. BRAIN
   MUFFIN: Me too—more so!*   220
TOYBOY: What chu mean? Are you really gonna hide where you're wending
   your way, you extremely bad girl?
BRAIN MUFFIN: Are you seriously gonna keep it secret where you're takin
   yourself, you extremely bad boy?
TOYBOY: Do I hear an echo around here?* BRAIN MUFFIN: So go, since that's
   how it's gonna be.
TOYBOY: Don't care if I know. Bye-bye. BRAIN MUFFIN: Wait. TOYBOY: Sorry,
   I'm in a hurry. BRAIN MUFFIN: God, me too.
TOYBOY: Got anything? BRAIN MUFFIN: You? TOYBOY: Not a thing. BRAIN
   MUFFIN: So gimme your hand. *(She feels in his pockets.)* TOYBOY: Is
   that a hand?*   225
BRAIN MUFFIN: Where's that left hand—that five-finger discount?* TOYBOY: I
   left it home. I got no hand there.
BRAIN MUFFIN: You do have somethin. TOYBOY: Don't feel me up, you massage
   parlor queen.* BRAIN MUFFIN: But if I love you?

TOYBOY: You're wastin your time. BRAIN MUFFIN: Why? TOYBOY: You love
      nothin when you love a guy who don't appreciate it.
BRAIN MUFFIN: Y'know, it's time you woke up this little body of yours, this little
      teen bod,*
so when it's time to grow up and turn butch,* you ain't still slavin the
      nasty way. 230
I bet you don't weigh eighty pounds drippin wet. TOYBOY: But, baby,
it ain't the meat, it's the emotion that does the job in this man's army.*
But I'm wastin my time with this. BRAIN MUFFIN: What now? TOYBOY: I'm
      lecturin to an expert.
But I'm stoppin now. BRAIN MUFFIN: Stay. TOYBOY: You're a pain. BRAIN
      MUFFIN: I definitely *will* be, unless I know
where you're goin. TOYBOY: To you guys' house. BRAIN MUFFIN: Me, too—to
      you guys'. TOYBOY: Why? BRAIN MUFFIN: What's it to you? 235
TOYBOY: Cuz you're not goin anywhere, unless I know too. BRAIN MUFFIN: I
      hate you. TOYBOY: Good. (BRAIN MUFFIN *physical business.*)
Jesus, you'll never *screw* it out of me! Like you're badder than I am.
BRAIN MUFFIN: It's a business to compete with you in badness.* TOYBOY: You're
      a piece of work.
What are you afraid of? BRAIN MUFFIN: Same as you.* TOYBOY: So tell me.
      BRAIN MUFFIN: But I was forbidden
to tell a single soul; the mute should speak, every one, before I tell.* 240
TOYBOY: Yeah, I was strictly forbidden too, to trust a single soul with this—
the mute should speak, every one, before I should tell. BRAIN MUFFIN: But—
      just do it.
Let's pretend we trust each other. TOYBOY: I knew it: you can't trust a ho,*
the eensy-beensy spider* weighs more than a ho's promise does.
BRAIN MUFFIN: *Please* tell me. TOYBOY: *Please* tell me. BRAIN MUFFIN: Don't
      you "please" *me.** TOYBOY: No problemo. 245
BRAIN MUFFIN: Keep it to yourself. TOYBOY: And you keep your mouth shut.
      BRAIN MUFFIN: I can keep a secret. TOYBOY: It'll be kept.
BRAIN MUFFIN: I'm bringin this note to your boss Bowman. TOYBOY: Make like
      a tree and leave! He's home.
But I'm bringin these sealed-up parchment leaves* to your boss, Georgia Moon.
      (*They trade envelopes and examine them.*)
BRAIN MUFFIN: What's in there? TOYBOY: Between you and me, if you don't
      know, I don't know;

unless maybe some sweet talk. BRAIN MUFFIN: I'm leavin. TOYBOY: I'm leavin
     too. BRAIN MUFFIN: So long, {Toyboy}. *(They trade*
     envelopes back.) 250
(Exeunt, TOYBOY *into the pimp's house,* BRAIN MUFFIN *into Bowman's house.)*

SCENE 3: EINSTEIN
Enter EINSTEIN *from stage L. He holds a bulging wallet or fanny pack, which at some
point he sticks in his pocket or straps across his hips.*

EINSTEIN *(rap):* I wanna say a prayer to the Lord* and I'm gonna,
you rich and you famous and Plenty is yo Mama.
Almighty, strong, and all-powerful,
you give us bucks, hope, and a belly full.
I celebrate you gladly, and that's no lie,
cuz you help out my homeboy* in the nick of time. 255
I got the cash to lend him that he needs,
a thing I never hoped for in my wildest dreams:
that chance would come my way—like now it fell out of the sky,
{and now I'm gonna tell you the reason why}.
Cuz my boss sent me to Bakersfield* to buy some prize cattle* at the
        market, see,   trochaic octonarii
and he gave me some money, and he's like, the market's a week from
        now there; 260
the fool, to give me this money, when he *knows* what I'm like.
Cuz I've got other uses for this money: "There just weren't any cattle worth
        buying."
Now I'm gonna do my homeboy a favor and do my karma* a lot of good;
for a while, it's all good, one day I'll pay the price; wham! bam!* on my back, but
        I don't care.
Now I'm gonna bankroll my homes out of my own pocket,* using these guys as
        the prize.* 265
Cuz that's what's really cool, to get these super-stingy, little old, greedy,
        dried up guys,
and bite 'em good—the kind of guys who lock up the food along with
        the silver.*
(Rap.) It's a good deed, when opportunity knocks.
Think it over. What choice has he got?
He'll have me flogged, he'll have me put in leg irons; yeah, *he's* beat,

if he thinks I'm gonna beg for mercy: fuck him!* Nothin new he

      can do to me   270

that I'm not already an expert in.—But, whoa, here's Bowman's boy, Toyboy.

SCENE 4: TOYBOY *and* EINSTEIN
Enter TOYBOY *from the pimp's house.*

TOYBOY *(rap):* I've done my little job that was given to me—

now I'm hurryin home. EINSTEIN: Wait, don't hurry.

Toyboy, listen. TOYBOY: You want a slave, you gotta pay the price. EINSTEIN:

      Stand still.   *trochaic septenarii*

TOYBOY: You'd be a real pain, know what I mean, if I owed you a

      damn thing,

since you're already such a pain anyway. EINSTEIN: Hey, bad boy, you

      lookin at me?   275

TOYBOY: I know how old I am, that's why you can get away with that trash.

(Rap.) EINSTEIN: Where's your boss Bowman? Better tell me true.

TOYBOY: Wherever he wants—he didn't ask you.   277a–b

EINSTEIN: Little man, little witch,* better tell me, yo.   278

TOYBOY: I'm tellin you, jailmeat,* that I don't know.

EINSTEIN: You're insultin your elders. TOYBOY: You started it, you earned

      it, you gotta suffer.   *iambic septenarii*   280

My boss told me to do a slave's work but keep a free tongue in my head.   280a

EINSTEIN: Will you tell me where Bowman is? TOYBOY: I'll tell you how you're

      gonna die forever.

EINSTEIN: You're gonna get the strap today.* TOYBOY: And all for you,

      cuckoohead!

Dang,* if I popped you right in the mouth,* I wouldn't be scared of you,

      roadkill.*

EINSTEIN: Now I see you, you fresh-laid egg.* TOYBOY: So I am, and

      what's it to you?

At least I don't do it for nothin, like you. EINSTEIN: You're so sure. TOYBOY:

      Damn, I am.   285

Cuz I'm sure I'll be free, which you have no hope you'll ever be.

EINSTEIN: Could you possibly not be annoying. TOYBOY: You're talkin about

      what *you* can't do.

EINSTEIN: You go to hell.* TOYBOY: No, you go home—hell's already there and

      waitin for you.

EINSTEIN: This'll* bail me out. TOYBOY: I wish there was no bail, and you was in jail. *(Lines interspersed with physical/phallic threats.)*
EINSTEIN: What's this? TOYBOY: Yeah, what? EINSTEIN: Still dissin me, bad boy?
     TOYBOY: As long as it's still legal   290
while you're a slave, for a slave to diss you. EINSTEIN: Oh yeah? Just look
what I've got for you. TOYBOY: Nothin, cuz you got nothin. EINSTEIN:
     Goddamn me if I don't—*
TOYBOY: I'm your man, I want all your prayers to come true. EINSTEIN: Good,
     so be it,
if I don't catch you today and hammer you into the ground like a nail.*
TOYBOY: You nail me? No, I think they'll be nailin *you*—with a lethal injection,*
     real soon.   295
EINSTEIN: You! Goddamn! . . . — you know what I was gonna say back
if I couldn't watch my mouth. Can't you just leave? TOYBOY: You can easily
     make me.
Cuz my evil twin* is gettin beat up in there already. *(Exit* TOYBOY *into Bowman's house.)* EINSTEIN: Damn him to hell!
He's like the beast that crawls on the ground with forkèd tongue: very bad.
Jesus, I'm glad he went away.—The door is opening, whoa, and look,   300
the guy I wanted most to see is comin out here from inside.

SCENE 5: BOWMAN, BRAIN MUFFIN, *and* EINSTEIN
Enter BOWMAN *and* BRAIN MUFFIN *from Bowman's house.*

BOWMAN: Tell her that it's all set now where the bucks are gonna
     come from,   iambic septenarii
tell her she better keep her mind right, say that I love her a lot;
when she's OK, then I'm OK.—OK, you got that? Gonna tell her
everythin I'm tellin you? BRAIN MUFFIN: You know I'm hipper than
     hippo hide.*   305
BOWMAN: OK, get goin, go home. *(Exit* BRAIN MUFFIN *into the pimp's house.)*
     EINSTEIN: And now I'm gonna look mucho cool* for him.
I'm just gonna flap my wings and put me on my Superman suit.* *(*EINSTEIN
     struts with hands on hips.)
BOWMAN: Hey, who's the little teapot swishin down the street?* EINSTEIN:
     Gonna hock a royal loogie.*
BOWMAN: Hey, it's Einstein, yes indeed. Whussup, Einstein? How ya doin?

Remember what I asked you to get me? Got a little hope for me? EINSTEIN:
        Come over here.* 310

Let's see. I want this taken care of. Step this way. State your business.*

BOWMAN: What's that bulge growin out of your pocket?* EINSTEIN: It's a zit and
        don't you squeeze it;

cuz when you touch it with your dirty hands, it just makes it start to hurt.

BOWMAN: When'd you start gettin that? EINSTEIN: Today. BOWMAN: You ought
        to get it cut off you.

EINSTEIN: I'm afraid if I cut it off before it's ripe, it'll just make more
        trouble for me. 315

BOWMAN: I wanna take a look at your disease. EINSTEIN: Ah ah! Get off, better
        watch out

for the horns. BOWMAN: Excuse me? EINSTEIN: Cuz I got a couple of bulls* here
        in this wallet.

BOWMAN: Better let 'em out, you don't wanna starve 'em; better let 'em out on
        the range.

EINSTEIN: I'm afraid I might not be able to get 'em back in the barn—they
        might wander off.

BOWMAN: I'll get 'em back, don't worry, be happy. EINSTEIN: Somehow I believe
        you—I'm gonna help you out. 320

Get this, if you please. That cash you asked me for before? I got it right here.

BOWMAN: What do you mean? EINSTEIN: My boss sent me to Bakersfield to buy
        some cattle.

But now somehow your house is lookin like Bakersfield. *(Hands wallet to*
        BOWMAN.) BOWMAN: Now you're talkin. Too cool!

And I'm gonna finance all this dough safe back to you right away;

cuz now I got all my scams ready for battle and good to go, 325

how I'm gonna get this dough from the pimp. EINSTEIN: Even better.

BOWMAN: He's not just gonna set my woman free, he's gonna pay for it himself.

But stick with me—I need your help for this scam too. EINSTEIN: I'm yours.

(Exeunt into Bowman's house.)

ACT 3

SCENE 1: FAT JACK *and* CHERRY

Enter FAT JACK *and* CHERRY *from stage L.* CHERRY *is dressed up like a stage Arab woman.*

FAT JACK: May this happy occasion turn out fine* for me (and you) and my
      tummy, too,   *iambic senarii*
and for the foreseeable future, so long as we both *(shakes stomach)*
      shall have . . .   330
food to spare, food in abundance, food-o-rama:
just follow my lead, daughter dear, in God's holy name.
You know the deal, you got it, you understand it;
I communicated the whole plan carefully to you.
That's why I got you all dolled up* in this getup;   335
you're gonna be sold today, young lady.* CHERRY: Please, Dad.
I know you're always tryin to scam a meal off somebody,
but would you really sell your own daughter on account of your gut?
FAT JACK: Well, it'd be weird if I sold you on account of Saddam or the Saudis,*
and not on account of me—you are *mine,* after all.   340
CHERRY: Do you think I'm your daughter or your slave girl?
FAT JACK: Jesus, whichever looks like it'll do my belly most good.
I believe *I'm your* commanding officer and not vice versa.
CHERRY: You've got every right to do it, Dad. Really.* But still,
even though the way things are for us, Dad, we're pretty broke,   345
it's better for us to live a plain and simple life.
Cuz if a bad reputation moves in with you when you're broke,
being broke gets heavier, and your good name gets lighter.
FAT JACK: You're really obnoxious. CHERRY: No, I'm not, and I don't think I am,
when I'm tryin to teach my dad right, and I'm just a kid.   350
Cuz your enemies say stuff about you that's not true.
FAT JACK: Let 'em say it, and let 'em all go straight to hell;*
cuz I don't count all my enemies as a bigger problem
than if I had to sit down to an empty table now.
CHERRY: Dad, a bad reputation never dies away;   355
it stays alive even when you'd think that it was dead.
FAT JACK: What? Are you scared I'll actually sell you? CHERRY: I'm not
      scared, Dad.
But, really—don't let them *say* it happened. FAT JACK: Too bad for you;
I'm the one who's calling the shots around here, not you.
CHERRY: OK. *(Sobs.)* FAT JACK: Now what's all this? CHERRY: Think it
      over, Dad: 360
if a boss threatens to do something bad to his slave,
even if it's not gonna happen, when they pick up the whip,

when they strip off his shirt, the poor guy—how he suffers!
So now—something that's not gonna happen—I'm still scared of.
FAT JACK: No young lady will ever be born who isn't bad— 365
as long as she thinks she knows better than her parents.
CHERRY: No young lady will ever be born who isn't bad,
who keeps her mouth shut when she sees something wrong going on.
FAT JACK: You better watch out for something bad. *(Physical threat.)* CHERRY:
      And what if I can't
watch out, then what do I do? Cuz I want to watch out for *you*. 370
FAT JACK: Are you saying *I'm* bad? CHERRY: You're not, and I'd be
      wrong to say so,
but, really, I'm trying to fix it so folks who *can* say it, *don't*.
FAT JACK: People can say what they want. I'm not gonna change
my decision. CHERRY: But if you were just OK with *my* way,
you could play it smart instead of stupid. FAT JACK: Fine. 375
CHERRY: I know it's fine with you for it to be OK with me,
but if it was fine with me, really, it wouldn't be OK for it to be fine with you.
FAT JACK: Are you about to obey your Daddy's word or not?
CHERRY: I will. FAT JACK: And do you understand what I told you to do?
      CHERRY: Everything.
FAT JACK: How you were kidnapped at gunpoint?* CHERRY: I
      studied. I'm hip.* 380
FAT JACK: And who your parents were? CHERRY: I got it memorized.
You're just forcing me to turn into a bad girl.
Just make sure, really, when you want to marry me off,
this bad reputation doesn't leave me divorced at the altar.
FAT JACK: Shut up, dummy. Don't you see how people are today, 385
how girls with a bad reputation get married every day here?
As long as a girl's got money, even a rap sheet won't start the tongues flappin.*
CHERRY: Then maybe you'd like to think this one over, pal—
I don't *have* any money. FAT JACK: Don't say that out loud.
Jeeze, thanks, may I say, to the good Lord and my ancestors, 390
you should not say you have no money when your dowry's at home:
looky here, I've got a trunk just full of jokebooks.*
If you take good care of this bizness we got in hand,
you'll have from me for your dowry six hundred surefire gags*—
all Hollywood; you won't find a bush league* one in the bunch. 395
With a dowry like this you could even marry—a squeegee man.*

CHERRY: Why don't you just take me, if you're taking me somewhere, Dad?
You can either sell me or you can do—what's "fine with you."
FAT JACK: Can't say fairer than that. Step this way. CHERRY: I hear what
      you're saying.
(Exeunt into Bowman's house.)

SCENE 2: DORKALOT
Enter DORKALOT *from his house. He carries a stick—part accessory, part weapon.* *

DORKALOT: What should I tell you this neighbor of mine is
      going to do,   iambic senarii   400
the guy who swore to me he'd give me the cash today?
But if he hasn't paid up by the end of the day today,
I'll be out the dough, and he'll be out of a credit rating.*
But, hey, the hinges are creaking. *(Door sound.)* Who's that coming out?

SCENE 3: BOWMAN *and* DORKALOT
Enter BOWMAN *from his house, carrying the wallet.*

BOWMAN: You guys inside look sharp, cuz I'll be back soon.   iambic senarii   405
DORKALOT: Whoa, Bowman, whussup? BOWMAN: Whoa, you pimping dirtbag,*
you public shithouse, with extra dung on top,
you cocksucking, lowdown, sleazy, skeezy,* national grease stain,
you greedy, beady-eyed, evil-eyed money vulture,*
you mouthy, grabby, pushy*—nobody could   410
run through your scum-sucking shit* in three hundred lines—
you want your dough? You gonna take your dough, bitch?*
You wanna have your dough? You still want your dough?
Can I possibly convince you to take your dough, dirtbag?
You didn't think I could get my hands on the dough,   415
so you wouldn't risk giving me credit unless I swore to it?
DORKALOT: Hey, let me breathe, so I can get on with *my* lines here.*
The national bigshot!* You slave-girls' motel,
you savior of sluts, you're makin the whips sweat,*
you're wearin out all the shackles, you chain gang green card,*   420
you permanent slave! You Slurpee! You fat-ass, jacking slacker*—
bring me my dough! Gimme my dough, bitch!
Can I squeeze the dough out of you? Bring me my dough, I tell you,

ain't you gonna gimme up my dough? Have you no shame?
Hey, the pimp is askin you for dough, Mr. Solid Slavery,   425
to set your girlfriend free—everybody listen up!
BOWMAN: Jesus, shut up, please. You got a set of lungs on you.
DORKALOT: I got a tongue that's born for returning favors.
I gotta pay the same for food* as you do.
Unless this tongue defends me, it's not gonna get a lick.   430
BOWMAN: OK, stop bein mad. I was just pissed at you
cuz you said you wouldn't trust me for the money.*
DORKALOT: It'd be weird if I trusted you, for you to pull
the same stuff with me that the bankers mostly do:
when you trust 'em with money, they're out of town as fast   435
as a rabbit out of the starting gates at the dog track.*
BOWMAN: Take this, OK? DORKALOT: Well, gimme! *(Takes wallet from
        BOWMAN.)* BOWMAN: That'll be six hundred clams,
all bona fide, cash on the barrel. Now set my woman free,
and bring her here right away. DORKALOT: OK, I'll get her here.
Jesus, I don't know who I should get to check this out.* *(He holds up the money to
        see if it's real.)*   440
BOWMAN: Maybe you're scared to hand her over to me on trust?
It's weird how the bankers are closing up shop downtown already,
quicker than a tire goes spinning round on a racetrack.*
Go on, take the back alleyways* and get downtown;
and while yer at it, send that woman over to me   445
through the garden. DORKALOT: OK, I'll get her here. BOWMAN: But
        not openly.*
DORKALOT: Sure, that's smart. BOWMAN: Let her go to church and thank
        God *tomorrow.*
DORKALOT: Jesus, good idea. BOWMAN: You coulda been there and back already.
(Exit DORKALOT *into his house.)*

ACT 4

SCENE 1: BOWMAN

BOWMAN: If you take care of bizness honest and serious*   iambic senarii
your bizness comes out perfect every time.   450
And, Jesus, the way any guy carries out his bizness,

that's the way it goes for him, from start to finish.
If he's bad or no good, his bizness turns out bad,
but if he's honest, things always turn out honest.
I set this bizness up all cool and hip,*   455
that's why I know it's gonna come out just fine.
N now I'm gonna mess up this pimp today
so bad, he ain't gonna know which way is up.
(Calls into his house.) Einstein, hey, come out and bring the girl
and also those papers I signed and sealed for you, *(winks)*   460
the ones you brought me from my boss all the way from Iran.

SCENE 2: EINSTEIN, BOWMAN, *and* CHERRY
Enter EINSTEIN, *dressed up à la Arab, leading* CHERRY, *ditto, from Bowman's house.*
EINSTEIN *has a knapsack or bag full of paperwork.*

EINSTEIN: Am I too slow? *(Hands* BOWMAN *some papers.)* BOWMAN: Wow! Royal
        disguise there, hombre!*   iambic senarii
Sweet turban! Really gives that Hollywood touch.*
And nice shoes* on this fair stranger, too—she looks mucho* good!
So, got it all rehearsed? EINSTEIN: Hey, professional actors*   465
never rehearsed it so good. BOWMAN: You're a damn fine assistant.
OK, get out of sight and keep your mouth shut, dude.
When you see me talkin with the pimp over there,
that's when you make your move. *(To both.)* OK, get yer ass in gear!
*(*EINSTEIN *and* CHERRY *hide behind the dumpster, stage R.)*

SCENE 3: DORKALOT *and* BOWMAN
Enter DORKALOT *from his house, without the wallet.*

DORKALOT: A guy the gods are gonna be good to, they're gonna throw him a
        little cash;   trochaic tetrameter   470
today I figure I saved myself—let's see—a good two McBurgers* a day.
Cuz that slave girl—mine this morning, now her own woman—in
        cash we trust—
from now on she's gonna be eatin on *his* credit card, not chewin up mine.*
Ain't I a fine upstanding American citizen, ain't I a righteous guy,
makin our great nation greater by plus one lady citizen?*   475
What a nice guy I was today! I trusted everybody!*

Didn't take no security deposits—that's how I trusted all of 'em;
I don't worry a single one is gonna welsh on what they owe me.
I wanna be a good guy from now on—like I might do that. Not!
BOWMAN: Gonna lead this guy right into my trap today, with serious
        sneakiness, 480
and everything's set up nice and tight. I'm gonna go right up to him.
Whussup? DORKALOT: I got trust! BOWMAN: Whussup with this shit now,
        Dorkalot? DORKALOT: Got trust in you!
May all your dreams come true. BOWMAN: Yo, dude, did you set my woman
        free already?
DORKALOT: I trust, yes, Jesus, I mean I trust in you. BOWMAN: She free?
        DORKALOT: You're killin me.
I'm sayin I trust in you. BOWMAN: True/false: she's free? DORKALOT: Jesus, I'm
        tellin you. 485–86
Go downtown, and ask the judge if you don't want to trust in me.
I say she's free: what, are you deaf? BOWMAN: Whoa, God bless you, and
        all the saints!*
I'll never wish evil on you and all your kinfolk ever after this.
DORKALOT: Go on, don't swear,* I trust you already. 490
BOWMAN: So where's your former girl slave? DORKALOT: You got her. BOWMAN:
        I got her? DORKALOT: You got her, I'm tellin you.
BOWMAN: God love me if there ain't a lot of good things comin at you from me
        on account of this.
Cuz there's somethin I've been keepin secret from you: and now I'm gonna
        tell it to you,
how you can make some serious bucks;* you'll never forget me as long
        as you live.
DORKALOT: My ears are beggin to hear you're puttin your money where your big
        mouth is. 495
BOWMAN: And you so richly deserve for me to do so. And so you can
        be real sure,
just take these papers here and look 'em over. DORKALOT: What's it to me?
        BOWMAN: It's *so* to you,
cuz they was just brought here to me from my boss—he's in Iran. DORKALOT:
        When? BOWMAN: Just now.
DORKALOT: What do they say? BOWMAN: Ask them: they'll tell you.
DORKALOT: Gimme that. BOWMAN: But read it out loud. DORKALOT: Shut up,
        lemme read this. BOWMAN: I won't say a word. 500

DORKALOT: "Mr. James Van Pelt the Third. {July 12.}*

       Dear Bowman,   iambic senarii

and all the servants: Hope you're all in the best of health.

Having a great time, getting a lot done, making a lot of money,

and I can't get back to town for another eight months or so,

and here's the special business that's detaining me.   505

The Iranian army has seized the City of Gold

in Arabia, an ancient citadel, full of luxury goods:

the loot is being convoyed here for an auction,

a public one, and that's what's keeping me away.

I want you to offer help and hospitality   510

to the guy who brings these papers. Do whatever he wants,

because he's treated me as an honored guest."

What's it to me or my bizness what the hell the Iranians do?   trochaic septenarii

Or your boss, either? BOWMAN: Shut up, dumbass;* you don't know what's in

        store for you

or what a lucrative Bic it is that Lady Luck wants to flick for you.*   515

DORKALOT: What lucrative Lady Luck is this? BOWMAN: I think you better ask

        someone who knows. *(Points to papers.)*

I only know as much as you, except I read it earlier.

But go on, figure it out from the papers. DORKALOT: You're giving me

        good advice.

Keep quiet. BOWMAN: Now you're just gettin to the part that has to do with you.

DORKALOT: "The guy who brings this letter has brought

        with him   iambic senarii   520

a very nice girl*—a virgin—with a very choice body—

stolen—she was carried off from deepest Arabia.

I want you to see to it that she gets sold here.*

But the guy who buys her does so at his own risk:

she can't be formally purchased and no one can guarantee title.   525

See that the guy gets righteous cash on the barrel.

Take care of all this, and see that my host is well hosted. Yours truly."

BOWMAN: So? Now that you've read out loud the contents of this private

        communiqué,   trochaic septenarii

now d'you trust me? DORKALOT: Where's this "guest" at now—the guy who

        brought you this?

BOWMAN: I trust he'll be here: he was bringin her from the ship. DORKALOT: I

        really got no need   530

for legal messes. And why should I shell out cash extracurricular?*

If I can't have formal title, what do I need with goods like this?

BOWMAN: Will you shut up or not? I'd never a believed you was such a
           toilet bowl.*

What? Are you scared? DORKALOT: God, really scared. I been around this
           block before.*

Me get stuck in shit* like this when I'm no dummy? It ain't gonna happen.   535

BOWMAN: *I* don't see nothin to worry about. DORKALOT: I know, it's *me* I'm
           worried about.

BOWMAN: I'm not doin this for me, I'm doin this on your account,

so I could give you the very first chance to make out like a bandit* on this.

DORKALOT: Thanks a lot. But it's sweeter to see you learn from others than see
           others learn from you.   539–40

BOWMAN: Like anyone's gonna follow her here all the way from deepest Arabia.

Why doncha snap her up right now? DORKALOT: Well, lemme just check out
           the goods.

BOWMAN: Now you're talkin. But luckily, whoa, looky here, the guy is
           comin now—

that guy who brought the letter. DORKALOT: That's him? Really? BOWMAN: Yup,
           the man himself.

DORKALOT: And that's the stolen virgin? Really? BOWMAN: I know just as
           much as you,   545

except that, Jesus Christ, she's quite the lady,* whoever she is.

DORKALOT: By God, she's fairly easy on the eye, I guess. BOWMAN: Ooh, the
           Devil's gettin fussy!*

Let's shut up and check her out, OK? DORKALOT: I like your plan, my man.

SCENE 4: EINSTEIN, CHERRY, BOWMAN, *and* DORKALOT

Enter EINSTEIN *and* CHERRY, *as if from stage R, but actually from behind the
dumpster.*

EINSTEIN: So, does L.A. look lucky to you? A fertile source
           of revenue?   *trochaic septenarii*

CHERRY: I saw the appearance of the city, but it's still a city of
           appearances to me.*   550

BOWMAN: Hey, did she talk smart right from the get-go or what?

DORKALOT: I couldn't see how smart she is just from the first thing that she says.

EINSTEIN: What *did* you see? Does the city seem well set up, security-wise?*

CHERRY: If the folks who live here are good people, that's enough
          security for me.
If they've deported the top ten offenders: cheating and graft and greediness;   555
fourth would be envy; five, crooked elections; six would have to be backbiting;
number seven, perjury— BOWMAN: OK! CHERRY: Number eight, laziness;
nine, injustice; and then there's ten (the hardest to deal with of all)—
          that's crime;
once they're out of town, a city's secure enough with a single wall;
when they're *in* town, a hundred walls would be too little to save the day.   560
BOWMAN: What do you say? DORKALOT: What should I? BOWMAN: You're one
          of the ten frat brothers*—
you better get out of town. DORKALOT: Why's that? BOWMAN: Cuz you're a
          p . . . erjurer.
DORKALOT: I gotta admit she makes a lot of sense. BOWMAN: Your bonus!
          Buy her now.
DORKALOT: Jesus, the more I look at her, the more I like her. BOWMAN: If
          you buy her,
God almighty! No other pimp will be rollin in cash like you.   565
You'll peel guys away from their homes and families by snappin your fingers,
you'll be dealin with the biggest guys, they're gonna be suckin up to you,*
they'll come to you to get down. DORKALOT: And then I'll tell 'em they
          can't come in.
BOWMAN: But then they'll yell outside your house at night, they'll burn your
          front door down;*
and then you should order your house to be shut in with iron security doors,   570
you'll have your house rebuilt in iron, you'll put in iron burglar bars,*
and iron bars on the door, and an iron knob; don't flinch, don't spare the iron—
and while you're at it you should get some fat iron shackles put on yourself.*
DORKALOT: Go burn in hell.* BOWMAN: The same to you—or go buy her. You
          listen to me.
DORKALOT: I wish I knew how much he's asking. BOWMAN: Want me to call
          him? DORKALOT: I'll go over.   575
BOWMAN: Whussup, Mr. Guest? EINSTEIN: I'm here, I got her here for you, the
          way I said.
The ship got into port last night. I want to get her sold today,
if possible; and if it's not, I wanna get out of here soon as possible.
DORKALOT: Lookin good, young man. EINSTEIN: If I can sell this one at a
          decent price.

BOWMAN: You know you're gonna make a nice sale to this guy or to nobody. 580

EINSTEIN: Are you a friend of his? BOWMAN: As much as God and all the saints
        in heaven.*

DORKALOT: Then you're definitely my enemy. Cuz the noble tribe of pimps
never had God on their side at all, or not enuf to do any good.

EINSTEIN: Go on, then. Do you need to buy her or not? DORKALOT: If you
        really need to sell her,

then I need to buy her; if you're in no rush, well, then it's all the same to me. 585

EINSTEIN: Go on, name your price. DORKALOT: She *is your* merchandise, *you*
        name your price.

BOWMAN: He's only sayin what's fair. EINSTEIN: You wanna good buy?
        DORKALOT: You wanna make a nice sale?

BOWMAN: Jesus, I know you both wanna do it. *(To* DORKALOT.*)* Go on, name
        yer price—you're the expert here.*

EINSTEIN: Gotta warn you: nobody will give you title to her. Capisce?
        DORKALOT: I understand.

Tell me the least you'll give her away for, just to get her off your hands. 590

BOWMAN: Shut up, shut up.—Jesus, you are so dumb, just like a little kid.

DORKALOT: Now what? BOWMAN: Becuz I want that you should ask the girl
        some questions first,

for background info. DORKALOT: Yeah, Jesus, lucky thing you reminded me.

Check it out, me, a pimp of the world, I almost fell right into a trap,

if you wasn't here. So key to bring a friend along when you do bizness! 595

BOWMAN: I want you to ask her what's her family or what's her hometown,
        who's her folks;

I don't want you sayin you bought her on impulse or that I pushed you into it,

or set you up. DORKALOT: I gotta tell you, guy, that's really a good idea.

BOWMAN *(to* EINSTEIN*):* If it ain't too much trouble, he'd like to ask her a coupla
        questions. EINSTEIN: By all means,

he can take his time. BOWMAN *(to* DORKALOT*):* Why're you standin there? Go
        on, go up to him 600

and ask him yourself if it's OK to ask her your questions. He did tell *me*

he'd give permission to talk to her: but I'd rather see you do it yourself,

so he won't go disrespectin you. DORKALOT: I gotta admit, you have a point.

(To EINSTEIN.*)* Mr. Guest, I'd like to question her. EINSTEIN: Go round the
        world,* whatever you like.

DORKALOT: Just order her to come over here by me. EINSTEIN *(to* CHERRY*):* Go
        on, be nice to him.* 605

(To DORKALOT.*)* Ask her whatever you want, work her over. BOWMAN *(to*
    CHERRY*):** Go on, to battle, {Princess Leia,}*

just check the Force is with you now. CHERRY: Shut up, the Force is
    crystal clear.

I'll see that you get back to base well loaded down with enemy loot.

BOWMAN: Go over there, I'll bring her to you. DORKALOT: OK, if you think
    that's best.

BOWMAN: Ahem, now, young lady. Watch what you're doin. CHERRY: Shut up,
    I'll take care like you want.   610

BOWMAN: Follow me. *(To* DORKALOT.*)* I got her, if you want to ask her a few
    questions now.

DORKALOT: But I want you to stay right here. BOWMAN: How could I not attend
    to my guest,

when my boss told me to? What if *he* don't want me to stay here? EINSTEIN: Go
    on, it's OK.

BOWMAN: I'm at your service. DORKALOT: And also your own, when you
    help a friend.

EINSTEIN: Go on, ask her. BOWMAN: Hey you, wake up. CHERRY: Nuff said:
    though I'm a slave,   615

I know my duty, and what I'm asked, I should state the truth, as best I know.

BOWMAN: Young lady, this is a righteous man. CHERRY: I believe it. BOWMAN:
    And you won't be his slave for long.*

CHERRY: Lordy, I hope not, if my parents do their duty the way they should.

DORKALOT: I don't want you to be surprised, if we should ask you pressingly

to name your hometown, or your parents. CHERRY: Why should this surprise
    me, mister?   620

Becoming a slave has seen to it that I'm not surprised by anything bad.

Boo-hoo. DORKALOT: Don't cry. BOWMAN *(to himself):* Whoa, damn the bitch!*
    Who knew she was so sly and hip?*

What a smart brain* she has! She says just like she should! DORKALOT: What is
    your name?

BOWMAN *(to himself):* Now I'm afraid that she'll screw up. CHERRY: Back home
    they used to call me Casha.*

BOWMAN: The name and the game* worth any price. Go on, why don't you
    buy her now?   625

(To himself.) I was too scared she'd screw up. She nailed it. DORKALOT: And if I
    should buy you now,

I'm sure you'll also be Casha for me. BOWMAN: In fact, if you do buy her,

I bet she won't still be your slave before the next month comes around.

DORKALOT: By God, I hope you're right. BOWMAN: And God helps those who
   help themselves.

(She hasn't made a boo-boo yet.)* DORKALOT: Where were you born? CHERRY:
   As my mama told me,   630

in the kitchen, right in the corner as you come in on the left-hand side.*

BOWMAN: She's gonna be a good-luck ho for you: she was born in a
   real hot place,

where there's always plenty of good stuff comin at you all the time.

(Tag, you're it, pimp! Like he's askin her to tell him where she was born,*

she goofed him up real cool.) DORKALOT: But I'm asking you what country
   you're from.   635

CHERRY: What should it be, if not the one where I am now? DORKALOT: But
   what *was* it?

CHERRY: To me everything that used to be is nothing now—it's in the past—

just like when somebody gives up the ghost, why would you ask him
   who he was?*

BOWMAN *(to himself)*: Jesus love me, she is smart! And look, he's feelin
   sorry for her.

DORKALOT: But, young lady, right now, come on, tell me what country you
   come from.   640

Why don't you say something? CHERRY: OK, I say that when I'm a slave here,
   this is my country.

BOWMAN: You better stop askin her about this (don't you see she don't
   want to tell?)—

you don't wanna give her post-traumatic stress syndrome.* DORKALOT: What
   is it, then?

Was your dad also captured? CHERRY: No, he wasn't, but he certainly lost
   everything.

BOWMAN: Must come from some high-class family: she don't speak nothin
   but the truth.   645

DORKALOT: Who was he? Tell me his name. CHERRY: Why should I recall who
   he was, poor man?

The right name for the two of us now would be Mr. and Ms. . . . erable.*

DORKALOT: And what kind of lifestyle did he maintain? CHERRY: Nobody was a
   more frequent guest;

he was loved by slave and free alike.* BOWMAN: You make this poor man
   sound so great

(considering how he screwed himself and screwed the folks who were
　　good to him).　　　　　　　　　　　　　　　　　　　　　　650

DORKALOT: I'll buy her, I think. BOWMAN: Oh, still "I think"? In my opinion
　　she's a real class act;*

you're gonna make a fortune on her. DORKALOT: God willing! BOWMAN: Just
　　buy her now.

CHERRY: I'm telling you now: as God is my witness,* the minute my dad finds
　　out I'm sold,

he'll be here and rescue me from you. BOWMAN: What now? DORKALOT: What
　　is it now?

BOWMAN: You hear what she says? CHERRY: Cuz even if we're totally broke, we
　　still have friends.　　　　　　　　　　　　　　　　　655

DORKALOT: Don't cry, Miss, please; you'll soon be free (if you spend enough
　　time on your back, that is).

Wanna be mine? CHERRY: As long as I don't belong to you for too long a time.

BOWMAN: Is that a free spirit or what? She's gonna bring you in quite a haul,*
　　my friend.

Do it if you're gonna. I'll see this guy. (To CHERRY.) Follow me. (To EINSTEIN.)
　　I'm handin her back to you.

DORKALOT: Young man, wanna sell this girl? EINSTEIN: Better that than waste
　　her, don't you think?　　　　　　　　　　　　　660

DORKALOT: Then just tell me in so many words: what's the price you're
　　setting on her?

EINSTEIN: I'm gonna make you a very affordable price. You can have her for a
　　thousand bucks.*

DORKALOT: Too much. EINSTEIN: Eight hundred. DORKALOT: Too much.

　　EINSTEIN: I can't take a penny away from *this* price, then,

that I'm gonna say now. DORKALOT: What is it, then? Spit it out and set
　　your price.

EINSTEIN: At your own risk I can let her go to you for six hundred pesos, cash
　　on the barrel.*　　　　　　　　　　　　　　　665

DORKALOT: Bowman, what do I do? BOWMAN: God does hate you—She's*
　　drivin you nuts, you jerk,

if you're not snappin that up right now. DORKALOT: <You got it.>* BOWMAN:
　　Go bring the cash here now.

Jeeze, she'd be cheap at *three* thousand.* I'd say you made some cash-a today.*

DORKALOT: {I gotta admit you're right.}* EINSTEIN: She's yours, dude!

　　BOWMAN: Yeah! You made a righteous score.　　　　　668a

EINSTEIN: Ahem, but then to cover her outfit I gotta add on a hundred bucks.*

DORKALOT: That's gonna be taken off, not added. *(Leers.)* BOWMAN: Shut up,
don't you see what he's doin? 670

He's lookin for a handle to undo the deal. Are you gonna go and get the cash?

(DORKALOT *starts to leave.*)

{And that's the ball game, folks. Done deal,} and down he goes, like
he deserves.* 671a

DORKALOT *(turning back):* Just keep an eye on him. BOWMAN: Will you get
goin? DORKALOT: I'm goin, I'll bring the cash.

(Exit DORKALOT into his house.)

SCENE 5: BOWMAN, CHERRY, *and* EINSTEIN

BOWMAN: Damn, young lady, you just did a most outstanding job: iambic senarii
neat, discreet, good enough to eat.* CHERRY: When good things happen
to *good* people, one good turn normally rates another. 675

BOWMAN *(to EINSTEIN):* You hear me, Iran Man? When you get the cash
from him,

make believe you're goin straight to the ship. EINSTEIN: Don't lecture me.

BOWMAN: Then get yourself back here to me through the alleyway,

through the garden there. EINSTEIN: You're just announcing* what's
gonna happen.

BOWMAN: I mean you better not take off straight back home with the cash,* 680

I'm warnin you. EINSTEIN: Think the shit you pull is stuff I'd do?*

BOWMAN: Hey, shut up, keep your voice down: the loot's walkin out the door.

SCENE 6: DORKALOT, EINSTEIN, BOWMAN, *and* CHERRY

*Enter DORKALOT from his house, carrying the wallet. Einstein's hands are now full of
papers from his knapsack.*

DORKALOT: Voy-la, you see six hundred bona fide bucks in cash,   iambic senarii

—less two bucks. EINSTEIN: And what could two bucks have in mind?

DORKALOT: That's to pay for the bag,* or to see that it finds its way home.   685

EINSTEIN: What, God forbid you wasn't enough of a pimp already,

you sorry, suckass thief*—you was worried you'd lose your baggy?

BOWMAN: Leave it, please. The guy's a pimp, it's Nature's way.*

DORKALOT: My horoscope* said today was a day I'd make a profit:

there's no amount so small I wouldn't mind losing it. 690

Go on, take this. EINSTEIN: Just put it in my pocket,* then,
if you don't mind. DORKALOT: OK. EINSTEIN: And now, is there anything else
you need me for? BOWMAN: What's the rush? EINSTEIN: I got a lot to do:
I want to deliver these letters that people sent with me;
and then I heard my own twin brother's* a slave here now,   695
I want to track him down, I want to buy him out.
BOWMAN: And, Jesus God, lucky thing you reminded me.
I think I seen a guy here who looks a lot like you,
same height as you. EINSTEIN: Of course! The guy must be my brother!
DORKALOT: Hey, what's your name? BOWMAN: Hey, what's it to ya,
       {buddy boy}?*   700
DORKALOT: Hey, what's it to ya that I don't know? EINSTEIN: So listen,
       you'll know:
My name is Osama bin Blabbin,* son of Baima-i-Sistra,*
son of Ali Blabba,* son of Sheikh Daoun,*
son of Yomammed,* son of Khayyam Allah Khan,*
son of Whataisteali,* son of Younevergetbacki.* There you go!   705
DORKALOT: God almighty! Your name is written a lot of ways.
EINSTEIN: Well, that's our quaint Iranian custom—long names,
very combobulous, that's what we have. Anything else
you want? DORKALOT: Take care. EINSTEIN: Same to you; and now, my mind's
       on my ship.
BOWMAN: Aw, leave tomorrow, you should eat here today. EINSTEIN:
       Nope. Bye.   710
(Exit EINSTEIN *stage R.)*

SCENE 7: BOWMAN, DORKALOT, CHERRY, FAT JACK, *and* EINSTEIN

BOWMAN: Well, now he's gone, and we can say whatever we want.   iambic senarii
I'll say this day dawned on you as truly cashworthy,
cuz you didn't *buy* Cash-a, no, you *made* cash-a.*
DORKALOT: He definitely knows his bizness, now, I have to say,
he sold me stolen goods, and at my own risk, too,   715
he took the dough, he's gone. And how do I know now
if somebody's going to claim her? How can I track him down?
To Iran? Shit! BOWMAN: And here I thought you was gonna be
grateful for all my kindness. DORKALOT: No, I really am grateful
to you, Bowman, I am; I know that you tried real hard   720

to do me a favor. BOWMAN: I did? For you? Oh, yeah, real hard.
DORKALOT: Sheesh!* *(Headslap.)* I forgot to explain to my people just now
what I wanted done at home. Watch her. BOWMAN: She's safe with me.
(Exit DORKALOT *into his house.)*
CHERRY: My dad is late. BOWMAN: Should I give him his cue? CHERRY: It's
       time you did.
BOWMAN: Hey, Fat Jack, come out of there. Now's the moment, dude,   725
to strike the enemy. *(Enter* FAT JACK *from Bowman's house, probably showing signs*
      of food.) FAT JACK: Here I am. What, am I late?
BOWMAN: Go on, go over there, get out of sight, keep yer mouth shut;
and when you see me talkin with the pimp over here,
then throw yer shitfit. FAT JACK: A word to the wise is always enough.
BOWMAN: I mean, after I go away— FAT JACK: Will you shut up? I know what
      you want.   730
*(*FAT JACK *hides behind dumpster stage R.)*

SCENE 8: DORKALOT, BOWMAN, *and* CHERRY
Enter DORKALOT *from his house.*

DORKALOT: When I got home I gave 'em all a taste of my belt,   iambic senarii
the way the upholstery's filthy, and the whole house, too.
BOWMAN: You're finally back? DORKALOT: I'm back. BOWMAN: Damn if I
      didn't do you
a lot of good today. DORKALOT: I'm tellin ya, man, I'm grateful.
BOWMAN: Want anything else from me? DORKALOT: Just have yourself
      a nice day.   735
BOWMAN: Jeeze, you said it, and I'm gonna take that thought right
      back home,
cuz now I'm gonna do the horizontal boogie* with your old slave girl.*
(Exit BOWMAN *into his house.)*

SCENE 9: FAT JACK, CHERRY, *and* DORKALOT

FAT JACK *(jumps out of hiding):* If I don't waste that guy, I'm hosed. And,
      whaddaya know,   iambic senarii
here he is in front of the house. CHERRY: Great to see you, Dad.
FAT JACK: And you, my child. DORKALOT: Whoa! Iran Man just
      ran me over!*   740

CHERRY: This is my dad. DORKALOT: Um, what? Your dad? I'm totally hosed!
Time to start in on singin the out-of-luck lament
for my six hundred bucks. FAT JACK: Jesus, I'll fix you, you scum,*
so you sing the lament for yourself to boot. DORKALOT: I'm totally dead!
FAT JACK: Let's mosey over to the courthouse, pimp. DORKALOT: What do you
          mean, court?   745
FAT JACK: I'm savin it for the judge. But I'm takin you to court.
DORKALOT: Got witnesses? FAT JACK: For your sake, you dirty devil,*
do I need to slap a subpoena on any decent man?*
You, carrying on your trade in freeborn citizens!
DORKALOT: Lemme explain. FAT JACK: No way. DORKALOT: But listen! FAT
          JACK: I'm deaf. Now march!   750
Walk this way, you rotten virgin-stealing polecat.
Walk this way, my child, let's go to the judge. CHERRY: I'm coming.
(Exeunt DORKALOT, FAT JACK, *and* CHERRY *stage L.)*

ACT 5

SCENE 1: BOWMAN, GEORGIA MOON, EINSTEIN, *and* TOYBOY
Center stage: a beer keg, two plastic lounge chairs at right angles, and between them a low table set for dinner with flowers, food, and lots of things that can be used to beat on the pimp—rubber chickens, loaves of French bread, rubber salamis . . .
Enter BOWMAN *from his house.*

BOWMAN *(sounding like a walkie-talkie):** Roger, the hostiles are down, civilians
          secure, we're at green alert, the ceasefire is operative;
enemy fire's eighty-sixed, mission accomplished, troops and garrisons accounted
          for. {Let us pray.}
Almighty Father and all the saints in heaven,* thanks for seeing us through,   755
I want to thank you all, and express my gratitude, because I took righteous
          vengeance on my enemy.
And now in recognition I will divide the loot among those who have shared
          my struggle, and will take my share. *(Ends military cadence;*
          breaks into rap.)
Get out here! In front of my door,
I'm gonna set up my flag of war.*   758a
Set up the beach chairs, get out the customary,
I want my fellow soldiers to make merry.   759a

(Enter GEORGIA MOON, EINSTEIN, *and* TOYBOY *from Bowman's house; they carry various party trappings including plastic cups and a pitcher.* TOYBOY *carries a keg tapper. They may be accompanied by a couple of nonspeaking house slaves.)*

And I'm gonna get everybody here to get happy get down get high*— 760
you guys who got it going for me to get good what I wanted to get good.
A guy's no good if he only knows how to take and not give back.

GEORGIA MOON: My Bowman, why aren't I with you, and why aren't
     you with *me?*

BOWMAN: Come on then, honey, come here and gimme a squeeze. GEORGIA
     MOON: I'm sure! BOWMAN: Ooh, there's nothin sweeter than this.

But please, darlin, why don't we just recommend ourselves to this beach chair*
     right now? 765

(They sink down on one of the lounge chairs.)

(Rap.) GEORGIA MOON: Whatever you want is OK with me.

BOWMAN: N I gotta say that goes double for me. 766a

Come on, yo, Einstein, set yourself at the head.* *(Points to the lounge chair
     at his left.)*

EINSTEIN: Don't let me slow you down. Pay me back like I said.* 767a

BOWMAN: You'll get it back eventually.

EINSTEIN: Yeah, well, eventually's too late for me.

BOWMAN: Get your butt over here while you are able.

Let's pretend it's my birthday.* You*—set this table! 769–69a

Here's some flowers for my flower. *(To* GEORGIA MOON.*)* Girl,
     you're on top.* 770

GEORGIA MOON: Come on, boy, pour the drinks, and don't you stop.

From the top*—a pitcher each*—let the games begin. 771a

*(*TOYBOY *serves* EINSTEIN, *who chugs his pitcher.)*

BOWMAN: Hey, Toyboy, move yer ass, just bring it on in.

*(*TOYBOY *takes pitcher from* EINSTEIN, *refills it, and starts pouring cups
     for* BOWMAN.*)*

You guys, lissen up, I'm gonna make a toast:
to me, to you guys, and to my girl—she's the most.
God let me see the day I put my arms around
a free woman. Yeah! GEORGIA MOON: You the man. BOWMAN: Drink it down! 775
I pass my cup to you, baby, cuz I'm yer man.

GEORGIA MOON: Gimme. BOWMAN: Take it. GEORGIA MOON: An I want you all
     to understand—

I'm drinkin right now to the folks that begrudge me
right along with you—my homeys, who love me!*   776a

SCENE 2: DORKALOT, BOWMAN, EINSTEIN, TOYBOY, *and* GEORGIA MOON
Enter DORKALOT *from stage L.*

DORKALOT: Of all the men who are, who will be, who have been, and who'll
        come after that,
I easily outdo them all as the miserablest living human being.
I'm hosed! I'm wasted! This scamming day that dawned for me today
        was the worst,   779–80
the way that Bowman faked me out and ripped off most of my bank account.
I threw away a truckload* of cash, I lost it, and I got nothin to show.
Goddamn the man from Iran and all Iranians and—I ran lines with them!*
That's the way Bowman messed this up but good for me! Poor me!
Just cuz I wouldn't trust him for the cash, he worked this scam on me;   785
so help me if I don't have him shackled and tortured—if God gives me the
        strength!
And if his boss ever comes back here, and I hope he does—but what do I see?
Look! What's this, a comedy?* God, they're drinking. I'll go up to them.
        Excuse me, sir,
good evening, and you, gentle lady (ex-slave).* BOWMAN: It's Dorkalot!
        EINSTEIN:* Why not have him join us?   789–90
BOWMAN: Join us, if you want. EINSTEIN:* Let's give him a hand! BOWMAN:
        Hello, Dorkalot, what a suavé gent.
Here's a place for you, have a seat. Wash his feet!* Boy, let's have some service!
DORKALOT *(to* TOYBOY*)*: Don't you lay one finger on me, or I'll throw you down,
        you evil boy.
TOYBOY: Then I'll just mash out your eye with this kegtapper*—right
        now, scumbag.*
DORKALOT *(to* BOWMAN*)*: What do you say, you lethal injection,* you cattle-
        prod meat?* How you screwed* me today?   795
How you got me into this mess? How you hoodwinked* me about Iran Man?
GEORGIA MOON:* You'd quit yer bitchin, if you was smart.
DORKALOT: Gentle lady (ex-slave), did you know about this? Did you hide it
        from me? GEORGIA MOON: It's foolishness,
when a man could be fine, to get all wrapped up in legal stuff. It's
        better for you*   799–800

by far, to deal with this stuff later.

(Rap.) DORKALOT: My heart's on fire.

BOWMAN: Give him a cup, put out that match;

if his heart's on fire, his head is gonna catch.

DORKALOT: I know you're just treatin me like a fool.

BOWMAN: Hey, Toyboy, here's yer bitch;* all nice and new!

Fool with him, do yer thing, this is the land of the free.   805

*(*TOYBOY *performs crude physical insults.)*

Hoo, baby!* Way to shake it! Royally cool with me.*

TOYBOY: It's my job to be cool and I love to be drummin

on this pimp, what a fool, cuz he's got it comin.

BOWMAN: Keep it up, doin fine. TOYBOY: Pimp, this Bud's for you!

(Further crude physical insults.)

DORKALOT: I'm dead! He's whupped my ass!* *(Insults continue.)* TOYBOY: One

       more time, comin through!   810

DORKALOT: Fool with me all you want, while your boss is out of town.

TOYBOY: I'll do just like you say, {wanna see how?}

But why don't *you* be *my* slave when *I* say,

and do like I tell you? DORKALOT: You want *me* to obey?

TOYBOY: Grab this rope, hang yo ass,* it's nice and thick. *(Obscene gestures.)*   815

DORKALOT: Don't you try and touch me or you'll feel my stick!*

       (Obscene gestures.)

TOYBOY: Go on, use it yourself, you got my permission.

BOWMAN: OK, Toyboy, now it's time for intermission!

DORKALOT: God, I'm gonna root you out. TOYBOY: But that guy upstairs gonna

       root *you* out,   trochaic septenarii

cuz he hates you and he's gonna mess you up. And this comes from me

       personally, not these guys.   820

BOWMAN: C'mon, pass the beer,* and come fill up these pitchers again so

       we can drink.

Seems like a long time since the last round; we're too dry here for way

       too long.

DORKALOT: May God make you all suck down something that'll never pass

       through you.*

EINSTEIN: Pimp, I can't help but dance a little pose for you like Travolta*

       used to do.

Take a look, and see if you like it. BOWMAN: Yeah, and I wanna do it, too,   825

I wanna show you what Michael Jackson used to do in West Hollywood.*

DORKALOT (mumbling): Gonna show *you* something, if you don't beat it.
           EINSTEIN: You still bitchin, smartass?
If you make me mad, I'm gonna bring back Iran Man again.
DORKALOT: Jesus, I'm not talkin. And *you're* the Iranian guy—you pruned me
           down to the skin.*
BOWMAN: Shut up, stupid: this is that guy's twin brother. DORKALOT: He is?
           Really? BOWMAN: Twinissimo.   830
DORKALOT: Goddamn you and your twin brother to burn in hell! EINSTEIN: *He*
           wasted you;
I don't deserve nothin. DORKALOT: Yeah, well, whatever he deserved, I want
           should happen to *you.*
BOWMAN: Come on, you guys, let's goof him up!* GEORGIA MOON: If he don't
           deserve it, there's no need.
Not fair for *me.** BOWMAN: I trust this ain't cuz he snaked you when
           I'm buyin you.*
GEORGIA MOON: But—no—I mean—but— BOWMAN: Better watch out, and
           stick with me.   835
Girl, you better be listenin to *me* when I'm talkina you, cuz, Jesus, without me
and my timely assistance, he'd have you on the street in no time flat.
But that's how these freed slaves are: unless they're raggin on their benefactor,*
they don't think they're free enuf, or solid enuf, or respectable enuf,
if they ain't done it up, if they ain't dissed him, if thank-you ain't turned
           into no thanks.   840
GEORGIA MOON: Gee, the way you took care of me gives me every reason to take
           orders from you.
BOWMAN: I'm your real benefactor, obviously, cuz I paid this guy the
           cash for you.*
I wanna goof him up righteously.* GEORGIA MOON: I'll mind my manners, I
           know my place.
DORKALOT (to audience): I'm sure these guys are planning to do something bad
           to me. EINSTEIN:* Hey you guys!
BOWMAN: Whussup? EINSTEIN:* Is this the pimp Dorkalot who deals in
           American* virgins here?   845
Is this the guy who was once so tough? DORKALOT: What's this? Hey! He's beatin
           me up! (Brawl.)
I'll screw you all. BOWMAN: But we screwed you, and we'll do it again.
           DORKALOT: Ow! He's pullin out my butt hair!*

TOYBOY: Sure: cuz your butt got well reamed out a long time ago. DORKALOT:
      You still talkin, crumb boy?

(Rap.) GEORGIA MOON *(to* DORKALOT*):* My benefactor, go and eat your
      dinner, please.

DORKALOT: My Wimp Goddess,* now you're mockin me?   850

GEORGIA MOON: Because I'm callin you to have a good time? DORKALOT: I
      don't want a good time. GEORGIA MOON:
      OK, fine.   trochaic octonarii/septenarii

BOWMAN: How about it? What are those six hundred bucks doin now, they
      gettin you all shook up?

DORKALOT: I'm so dead! They righteously know how to pay back
      their enemy.

(Rap.) EINSTEIN:* We've slaked our thirst for vengeance—I think
      we're through.

DORKALOT: I give up—I surrender to you.   855

BOWMAN:* N later you'll surrender to a rubber hose.*   855a

EINSTEIN: We wanna welcome you—come on in to Death Row!*

DORKALOT: They're workin me out {like some ancient Roman}!

BOWMAN: {Next time think twice before}* you mess with the Bowman!   857

Hey, fans, bye for now. This pimp is wasted. ALL: You can applaud now!

NONMETRICAL TRANSLATIONS OF RAP SECTIONS

Bowman Meets Einstein

EINSTEIN: You mean it?

He's out of town? BOWMAN: If you can stand

to get down, come on; you'll live with me,   30a

you'll be treated to stuff to eat *como el rey.*

Brain Muffin's Solo

BRAIN MUFFIN: Could you shut up? Could you not nag me?   175

I remember and I know and I'm hip and I'll bear it in mind.

Jeeze, poor you, you're in love: your brain is boilin with it.

I'll fix it so things calm down for you.

He's a poor guy, who's in love. Well, a guy's nothin

who loves nothin; a guy like that might as well not be alive.   180

Einstein's Prayer

EINSTEIN: Oh God, thou art rich and famous, son of Wealth,
almighty, strong, all-powerful,
thou who providest us with wealth, hope, and lots of stuff,
I celebrate you gladly, as you deserve,
because they bestow upon my buddy, as buddies do, this copious amount of
      good times,   255
that I might bring him the boon of a loan in his hour of need;
a thing I never dreamed of nor hoped for nor expected,
that this chance would come my way, this chance that now has fallen as if
      from heaven.

Einstein Meets Toyboy

EINSTEIN: Where's your boss Bowman?
TOYBOY: Wherever he wants to be—   277a
he didn't ask you. EINSTEIN: Will you   277b
tell me where he is, witch?
TOYBOY: I'm tellin you I don't know, jailmeat.

Bowman Rallies His Troops

Get outside! Right out here in front of the doorway
I want to treat my associates well.   758a
Set up the couches here, get out the customary.
I wanna set up my eagle standard here.   759a

The Party Starts

GEORGIA MOON: Whatever you want, I want.   766
BOWMAN: That's mutual with me. C'mon c'mon c'mon then,   766a
you, Einstein, take the head of the bed.
EINSTEIN: Don't let me hold you up. Gimme the payback I bargained for.   767a
BOWMAN: All in good time, my man. EINSTEIN: Yeah, well in good time's
      too late for me. BOWMAN: Just get over here and lie down. This
      sweet day   768
let's celebrate my excellent birthday.   769
You!—come wash our hands and set the table.*   769a
(To GEORGIA MOON.) Here's some flowers for my flower. You be our
      lady dictator.   770
GEORGIA MOON: C'mon, boy,   771

from the top—a pitcher apiece—let the games begin. 771a

Shake a leg,* get goin. 772

BOWMAN: Toyboy, you're gettin slow with the pitchers; 772a

keep 'em comin. Here's to me, to you guys, and to my girlfriend here; 773

this day was a long time comin 773a

but God let me live to see the day when I could put my arms around you as a

free woman. 774

GEORGIA MOON: All your doin. BOWMAN: Here's to all of us. 775

My hand puts this cup in yours, like lover to lover. 775a

GEORGIA MOON: Gimme. BOWMAN: Take it. 776

GEORGIA MOON: Here's to the one who begrudges it to me, right along with the

one who's glad for me. 776a

The Taunting of Dorkalot

DORKALOT: My heart's on fire. 801a

BOWMAN: Give him a cup, put out the fire; 801b

if his heart is burning, we don't want his head to catch. 802

DORKALOT: You're makin a fool of me, I know it.

BOWMAN: Hey, Toyboy, you want a new bitch just for you?

Go ahead, fool with him, the way you do, it's a free country. (TOYBOY *performs*

crude physical insults.) 805

Hoo, baby! You shook it up royally cool.

TOYBOY: It's my job to be cool and I love to goof on

this pimp, because he deserves it.

BOWMAN: Keep goin, you're doin fine. TOYBOY: This to you, pimp. *(Further*

crude physical insults.)

DORKALOT: I'm dead! He almost whupped my ass. TOYBOY: Hey,

think fast. 810

DORKALOT: Goof on me all you want, while your boss is out of town.

TOYBOY: Your slightest wish is my command!

But why don't *you* be *my* slave when *I* say,

and do what I tell you to? DORKALOT: What's that?

TOYBOY: Take yourself this nice thick rope and hang yourself.

(Obscene gestures.) 815

DORKALOT: Don't you dare touch me, or I'm gonna give you a big hit

with my stick here. *(Obscene gestures.)* TOYBOY: Go on, use it, you got my

permission.

BOWMAN: Now, now, Toyboy, take a break.

Farewell Song

EINSTEIN: We've slaked our thirst for vengeance now.

DORKALOT: I give up, I surrender to you.   855

BOWMAN: And later you'll surrender to a rubber hose.   855a

EINSTEIN: Welcome—to Death Row. DORKALOT: They think I didn't get
        enough of a workout yet?

BOWMAN: {Next time think twice before} you mess with the Bowman.

NOTES

1 . . . fool: This section translates the acrostic *argumentum,* or brief precis, affixed to the beginning of the play; the original one is shorter, since the acrostic is PERSA rather than IRAN MAN. But the sense is roughly the same.

2   Labors of Hercules: Hercules was a popular Roman god; among the most common oaths in Plautus are *hercle* and *mehercule,* and Hercules had an altar in the cattle market in Rome that dated well back into the Republic. He is Weevil's patron deity in *Weevil* (see note there at 358) and also seems an appropriate role model for Bowman in light of the B movie series about Hercules.

3   That A-rab mummy: In the original, "the Aetolian boar." Toxilus (Bowman) lists Hercules' labors and gives the appropriate adjective to the birds (Stymphalian). But he calls the boar "Aetolian," which is a mythology mixup and a joke. Hercules' boar was the Erymanthian boar; a different boar, traditionally known as the Calydonian boar, was hunted by the hero Meleager. Calydon is in Aetolia, a part of Greece that was a war zone in this period (see notes on *Towelheads,* which is set there). Hence here "A-rab" as a parallel jarring geographical reference, and "mummy" as a sidestep into the wrong myth.

4   The Incredible Hulk: The Latin refers to Hercules' giant opponent by his name, Antaeus.

11   Pinkeye . . . me: This is another eye-disease joke (see note on *Weevil* 318), and also probably a slave-beating joke. For the punishment of slaves as a source of humor in Roman comedy, see H. Parker 1989.

16   Lookin good: Literally, "may the gods love you," to which Einstein replies in kind; a conventional greeting.

17   How's it hangin: Literally, "How's your health?" or "How do you do?"

18a   A transition in thought seems to be missing between lines 18 and 19; this is my guess at the approximate content of the line.

21 Juvie bizness: Initiates a series of plays on words involving the punishment of slaves. Literally, Einstein says, "By Pollux, business—" and Bowman replies, "Iron [business], perhaps?"—a reference to shackles.

22 Beat . . . County: Literally, "I was the ironclad Tribunus Vapularis (= Beating Tribune, a play on Tribunus Militaris) in the mill." The mill was where slaves were sent as a severe punishment, to work the treadmill that turned the mill-stones; Plautus is said to have worked in one when he fell on hard times. See volume introduction under "Who Was Plautus?"

24 Pale: Probably a joke on "not rightly" (23), which also can mean "improperly." In later Latin jokes, playing the passive part in male-male sex is said to cause paleness (Richlin 1992a: 189, 250n26; 1993: 549–50). Or else just a bad-health joke triggered by 23 *satin tu usque valuisti,* literally "Have you been healthy all this time?" = colloquial "Have you been doing well?"

25 What . . . here: Marks the unusualness of having a slave be the lovelorn hero of a comedy, and the license afforded by the location ("Athens" / the stage).

26 Superheroes: Literally, "the gods."

27 *Clash of the Titans:* Bowman says he cannot make war on the gods as the Titans did.

28 Just . . . blue: Literally, "Just see to it that catapult bolts made of elmwood don't pierce your side." Einstein turns Bowman's war-in-heaven images back to the subject of slave punishment: elmwood was evidently used for the sticks used to beat slaves, as there are repeated jokes about it in Plautus; see note on 279 below.

29 Royally . . . dude: Latin *basilice agito eleutheria,* literally "I'm running around / celebrating royally in freedom." The vocabulary here is a Latin/Greek hybrid ("Gratin"?); cf. blends of English like Spanglish or Yinglish. *Basilice* is a hybrid of Greek *basilikos* and a Latin adverb ending; Greek *eleutheria,* "freedom," was also the name of various festivals around the Greek-speaking Mediterranean. *Basilice* shows up four more times in Plautus—twice in *Iran Man* (462, 806), once in a slave speech in *Epidicus* (56), and once in *Towelheads,* in a speech by the young gentleman (577). These words almost certainly mark nonelite speech, with familiar/foreign overtones, hence *eleutheria* is translated here as Cinco de Mayo, Mexican Independence Day, also celebrated in Southern California.

30a We'll . . . jokers: Literally, "You'll be getting the royal treatment"—Latin *basilico* (see note on 29).

32 Burns my ass: Literally, "tortures me," "puts me on the cross."

40 Bitch: Literally, "shameless one." Including . . . clothes: Literally, "entire."

41–42   Tryin . . . itself: Literally, "asking for water from pumice, which is dry with thirst itself."

45   For . . . there: The text is corrupt at this point; the OCT prints *nempe habeo in mundo*, "For sure, I have it to hand." Woytek suggests the association of *mundus* with the horizon as surveyed by the augurs (Roman priests who based prophecies on the flight of birds). Others correct the Latin to *habes*, "You have it to hand," which makes sense with Einstein's response.

48   I'm . . . truth: Here Bowman and Einstein swap oaths; this translation accepts Woytek's suggestion that they come from the context of official hearings.

49   Talkin loco: Latin *morologus fio*, "I'm turning into a crazy talker." More hybrid Greek/Latin (see line 29).

52   Cook up: On the use of culinary vocabulary for the Plautine plot, and on the way this word seems to summon up Fat Jack, see Gowers 1993: 90, 93.

60   That's . . . Suckerfish: A corrupt and puzzling line. The OCT starts the line with *neque*, which would make this mean (literally) "nor did they have the nickname . . . "—which doesn't make sense. Leo's simple correction to *atque*, "and," would be helpful, and the error would be easily explained by the *neque* directly above it. The words here translated "famous Suckerfish" are corrupt; the OCT prints *duris Capitonibus*, literally "hard Bigheads." *Capito* is a Roman cognomen, and there may well have been contemporary politicians by that name; *capito* was also the name for a fish, a type of mullet or suckerfish (cf. Huey "Kingfish" Long). The translation here is based on reading *claris*, "famous," for *duris*. See Woytek 1982: 97, 173, for other ideas.

62   Be a snitch: Latin *quadruplari*, "act as the bringer of a criminal accusation that paid a fourfold penalty" (the accuser would get a cut of the penalty). Fat Jack claims that he has *some* scruples, and that there are some things lower than being a *parasitus*. In the following lines (through 74) he speaks at length against informers—a "parabasis moment" like that in the speeches of other *parasiti*. Cf. Weevil's opening speech, against foreigners in Rome; volume introduction under "Topical Jokes."

64   Singsong: Lines 64–74 are full of legal wording.

67a   As after line 18, a line seems to have fallen out here, making a transition from line 67 to line 68, with roughly the sense given here. See Woytek ad loc.

74   Paper trap: Literally, "a white net"; the "white" is perhaps a reference to the white tablets on which laws were posted, but cf. Woytek 1982: 162–63.

77   Pay . . . leftovers: For the personification of food in Plautus, see Gowers 1993: 77–78. Fat Jack is performing the action of a respectful *cliens*, whose job it was to pay a morning call on his *patronus*.

87–111 These lines are full of words for various Roman dishes; see volume introduction on translating food, and Gowers 1993: 62 on the Plautine menu. The food names are mostly Greek—i.e., ethnic food—and have to be funny, or the scene would be boring.

87 Sangria: Latin *mulsum,* wine with honey in it. Nuts: Latin *struthea,* a small variety of quince, sometimes used in a double entendre for male genitalia. Guacamole: Latin *colutea,* pods of an unidentified tree—the original reference may have been to the hot water to be mixed with the wine. This line is corrupt; Woytek argues that lines 87–88 describe the process of making hot spiced wine.

88 Fajitas: Latin *calamum,* sweet flags, a type of reed also used to make pens. This line may be referring to heating pitchers and putting in spices.

92 Spaghetti . . . dente: Literally, "Make sure the *collyrae* and meat are well soaked / cooked through"; *collyrae* was bread soaked in soup, or possibly a kind of pasta. Cf. note on *Towelheads* 137.

94 With . . . marinade: Literally, "soaked / cooked through."

95 When . . . oatmeal: Literally, "when the *collyrae* broth isn't like thick oatmeal."

96 It's . . . chiffon: Literally, "that thin, see-through saffron robe is no good."

97 Cojones: What the sauce should be is hidden under a corruption in the text. The sense has to contrast with the thin and effeminate image of line 96; maybe a word for some manly garment was there ("ought to be like a lumberjacket").

99–100 Woytek's punctuation; Fat Jack addresses Bowman as his Jupiter and calls himself Bowman's earthly *coepulonus,* "fellow diner." This probably refers to a Roman festival for Jupiter Epulo, instituted in 196 B.C.E., in which Jupiter was given a public feast that took place during the Plebeian Games (November 4–17; they also featured dramatic productions). The feast was run by three public priests called Epulones; these would be male politicians, for whom it was an honorary position like being grand marshal of a parade. So Fat Jack's speech has overtones of self-aggrandizement as well as flattery. Note that Fat Jack is not among the guests at the feast in act 5.

104 I got . . . gut: Literally, "the grills are smoking for bellies inside (the house)."

107 Hot salsa: Latin *hallex,* "fish sauce," a popular condiment.

110 Shouldn't . . . crab legs: Literally, "the *murena* and *conger* shouldn't get hot"; these were types of eel, a favorite delicacy in antiquity.

111 To comb through 'em: The metaphor treats either the eels or their bones as hair.

112 Diving in: Literally, "engaging in battle."

113 A good . . . day: Literally, "While it's morning, every human being ought to eat."

120   Do I . . . bum: Literally, "There's no bum whose name is [or "who has a"] Mon-eygiverson." The text here is corrupt; the OCT prints *Argentumdonidest,* which is a grandiose comic name formation like those in lines 702–5 below. But the original might just have said *argentum domi est,* "[who has] money at home."

123–25   Wise old cowboy: Literally, "like the Cynic philosopher." See volume introduction under "Translate or Transpose?" for his actual list of accessories and the reasons for converting him to a cowboy. Whatever he is, he is dressed a lot like a comic actor—Fat Jack should be wearing gear similar to what he describes, and so should the other male actors. The same joke plays a key part in *Weevil;* see notes there at 288. On the Cynics, see Branham and Goulet-Cazé 1996; on the Cynic/*parasitus* tie, see Corbett 1986.

130   Classy: Literally, "like a free person"; the same expression is used at *Weevil* 209.

136a   As after lines 18 and 67, a transitional line seems to have fallen out here; the words given here are an approximation of the sense.

138   From Orange County: Literally, "from Megara"—a city near Athens.

143   Breakfast Club: Literally, "from this club," "from this [organization of ten people]" (Latin *decuria*). "Breakfast Club" is chosen here as (a) close in meaning, (b) appropriate in context, and (c) a reference to Kevin Smith's interest in the films of John Hughes.

144   Capisce: Latin *quid nunc,* "What now?" or "Well?"

        What is it: Woytek suggests these words are Fat Jack's.

155   A bathrobe . . . hat: Latin *tunica, zona, chlamys, causea.* The point of these items of clothing must be to make Einstein look like a traveling foreigner (explicitly so at 157). A *tunica* was just a standard unisex undergarment—like a long T-shirt—and a *zona* was normally a sash worn by unmarried girls; these items do show up on male travelers elsewhere in Plautus (e.g., on Uncle Saddam in *Towelheads,* but then he is said to look exotic). The *chlamys* was a cloak worn by soldiers and riders (in *Weevil,* it's also translated "trenchcoat"); a *causea* was a broadbrimmed hat, like a sombrero. In Plautus's *Trinummus* (851), when the old man sees the con man disguised as a traveler, he says he looks like a mushroom; cf. *Tri.* 766–67, 857–59, lines that echo *Iran Man* 157, 159–60. Bowman here requests no specifically exotic clothing, though at 463 Einstein shows up wearing a turban *(tiara).*

158   Those . . . costumes: Bowman tells Fat Jack to bring Cherry "*ornatam* like a foreigner." *Orno* means both "adorn" and "costume"—it's a theatrical technical term, going with the metatheatrical joke in 159–60. See also *Towelheads* 123.

159   *De donde:* In text, *Pothen* (Greek), which means "From where?"

159–60   Director, producers: The choragus (cf. *Weevil*, act 4, scene 1) and the aediles (Roman officials who bankrolled the theatrical shows).

163   Claim . . . citizen: Literally, "by hand lay claim to her from the pimp (as a free person)." As with many Roman legal transactions, a symbolic physical act was central here.

168   *(Yells . . . house):* Georgia Moon is supposedly in this scene, according to the list of actors in the scene heading, but she has no lines; it's possible that she stands on stage, mute, while Brain Muffin berates her, then goes back inside without saying anything.

174   But . . . doll: Literally, "when meanwhile you haven't yet even gotten to know my brainpower, *fans infans*." Woytek 1982: 222–23 argues that *fans infans,* literally "speaking" and "unspeaking/babyish," is a translation of a similarly jingly expression in the Greek of the original play, comparing Georgia Moon's brains unfavorably with those of a sheep.

184   Shit-for-brains: Latin *verbereum caput,* literally "head/person suitable for flogging."

186–87   Toyboy's jeer here may be based on a Roman betting game something like "Rock, Scissors, Paper" or "Once, Twice, Three, Shoot" (cf. Cicero *De Officiis* 3.77; Petronius *Satyricon* 44.7). It would make more sense if the Latin in 187 said *habeam,* "I got," rather than *habeas,* "you got" (the adjective "your" is supplied from the verb, so it would then change to "my"). The text, as always, indicates no stage directions, but the gesture of "giving the finger" was a Roman one and would fit here (see Richlin 1992a: 90). Throughout this and the next scene, many speeches seem to be metaphors for physical threats.

189   I'll . . . live: Literally, "let there be good peace instead"; "Truce!"

192   I'm . . . allowance: Latin *alioqui peculiabo,* "I'll peculiate you a bit." The *peculium* was the allowance given to slaves and adult sons still under their father's legal power; though they could not legally own anything, they could do business up to a point. This would be a chief source of a slave's savings toward buying his freedom. Note that Toyboy's usual line of work is sexual. Cf. Plautus *Pseudolus* 1188, where a similar joke is made; there a soldier's slave is accused of having been his sex slave, and the *peculium* is "what [his] thighs hold up"—i.e., his rear end. *Pedico* is the verb used in classical Latin as the four-letter word for "penetrate the anus"; it does not appear in Plautus, but *peculiabo* may suggest *pedicabo* here.

193–94   These two lines are difficult, but the meaning seems clear. Literally, "I know that *inpudicitia* is always brought up against a master's credibility *(fide . . . erili)* as a reproach, / nor can they ever be forced to have a judge for that *fides*." I.e., Bowman says he'll give Toyboy money, Toyboy thinks his promise is worthless (a repeated theme as the play goes on). *Fide* is dative here, as at *Amph.* 391. *Inpudicitia*, "unchastity," is a common euphemism in Latin for the willingness to play the passive part in sexual intercourse between males, and though the noun is used only rarely elsewhere in Plautus and then = "unchastity," the adjective *impudicus* is used in the common sense at *Mi.* 282 (slave conversation); *Ru.* 115 (slave insults young man, also in comparison with *peculiosum*); and *As.* 475 (same context). It is also one of the insults flung at the pimp in *Pseudolus* (360). So this metaphor compares the master's credibility with a penetrated male or male whore; Toyboy turns the tables on Bowman's implied threat in 192. The sexual permeability of slaves is a theme in this and the next scene.

199 Like . . . Derby: Literally, "like an ocean sparrow at the Circus"; "ocean sparrow" is said by Paulus ex Festo (248L) to be vulgar slang for "ostrich." Ostriches, a North African import, would have been a fairly recent arrival on the Roman cultural scene after the defeat of Carthage. This joke attests that the Roman public already had a nickname for ostriches and was already seeing them serving as targets in *venationes* (wild beast hunts), which were entertainments going on at the same time as Plautus's plays; see line 436 below. The first *venatio* on record, however, took place in 186 B.C.E., and *venationes* in this early period are not otherwise attested in the Circus Maximus, which was designed for chariot races. The image is of something fast and exotic that is publicly destroyed for entertainment and the survival of which depends on its speed.

201 Personal slave: Latin *peculiarest*. Slaves indeed could own slaves—another use for the *peculium*.

205 God bless—me: Same joke at *Towelheads* 859.

212 Good . . . Molly: More elaborate than the Latin, which is just *Heia!* and *Beia!* These could just as well be rendered "Nyah nyah" and "La di dah," or "Suck me!" and "Fuck me!": reflexive rhyming taunts.

214 I know . . . are you: Literally, "But what about you? Do you confess [that you are] as I judge you?"

219 Shit: Literally, "by Castor."

220 Me . . . so: Accepting the conjecture *addecet* for OCT *hau decet* (see Woytek ad loc.).

223 Do . . . here: Latin *par pari respondes dicto*, "Equal to equal statement you reply"; the point is the echo effect in the first two words. Line assignments in 223–24 accept Woytek's suggested changes.

225–27   These lines are usually interpreted as Brain Muffin trying to see and grab what Toyboy has in his hand (i.e., the envelope). Ostensibly, this is what she is doing, but line 227 makes it clear that she is feeling inside Toyboy's clothing.

225   Is . . . hand?: Most editors take Toyboy's line here to mean "Oh, you mean *this* hand?" [holds up right hand].

226   Left hand . . . discount: Latin *furtifica laeva,* "theft-committing left hand"; the left hand was conventionally associated with stealing.

227   Massage . . . queen: Latin *subigitatrix,* a word (as far as we know) made up by Plautus for this scene and meaning "female sex worker specializing in sexual fondling."

229   This . . . bod: Latin *formulam,* "little form/body"; *aetatulam,* "little teenage-hood." *Aetatula* is often used to refer to male adolescence in a sexual context, and especially in invective referring to the time when a boy is sexually vulnerable, perceived as feminine.

230   When . . . butch: "When you become *vorsicapillus.*" This Latin word is an emendation to the manuscript; it would be a play on *versipellis,* "werewolf" (literally, "skin-changer"). At the end of adolescence and sex-object-hood, the long hair of young male sex slaves was cut short and they turned into adult males, who might expect no longer to be used as passive sex partners by their owners (but see Richlin 1992a: 289; Richlin 1993: 534–35, 547–48).

232   Ain't . . . army: Literally, "But self-confidence does more service in that kind of military duty than weight." Pace McCarthy 2000, Toyboy is not here claiming that his good character will win his freedom.

238   Business . . . badness: Latin *miseria, malitia.*

239   Same as you: The OCT includes Lindsay's insertion, *mora* ("delay," "lateness").

240   Before I tell: Here and at 242 Brain Muffin and Toyboy mimic themselves acting loyal to their owners.

243   A ho: Latin *lena.* This word is usually translated "madam" or "bawd," and some have deduced from this that Brain Muffin is an old woman. But the complete lack of old woman jokes in this passage rules out the possibility; contrast the opening scene in *Weevil* (yes, Brain Muffin confesses to drinking at 170, but she is not in a class with Mme. Lola).

244   The . . . spider: Latin *tippula,* defined in the *OLD* as "an aquatic insect." The form is diminutive.

245   Don't . . . me: This is exactly the same joke in Latin as in English, for once. It depends on the colloquial use of *amabo,* literally "I will love you," to mean "please."

248 Sealed-up parchment leaves: Latin *opsignatam abietem,* a sudden switch into the language of epic poetry. *Abies* means "fir tree," hence anything made of wood, hence as here "writing tablets" (cf. *tabellas,* 195). Romans wrote notes on thin sheets of wood painted black and coated with wax, using a stylus; two of these would be put face to face and then sealed. The word *abies* is used only here in Plautus; Quintilian (8.6.20) says it can't be used in this sense in prose. The use of the word seems to be motivated by a play on sound in 247–50: *abi eccillum* (247), *abietem* (248), *abeo . . . abiero . . . ambula* (250), moving from "leave" to "fir tree" to "leave." Hence the English joke in 247 here.

251 Lord: Jupiter, here identified as son of the goddess Ops (Plenty). A line or so may have fallen out of this song—lines 255–56 have a plural verb in the original, so more gods may have been addressed. See nonmetrical translation after end of play.

255 Homeboy: Literally, "friend"; also at 263, 265.

259 Bakersfield: Literally, "Eretria"; this was a town not that far from Athens, probably here connoting "cowtown," since Eretria was in Euboea, a part of Greece famous for its cattle. Prize cattle: Literally, "oxen trained to the plow." This wording recurs in the joke at 265; see below.

263 Karma: Latin *genio meo,* "my guardian spirit"; see note at *Weevil* 301, and note Einstein's claim to a family line, which slaves did not have. Cf. note on line 769 below, on birthdays.

264 Wham! bam!: Latin *tuxtax.*

265 Pocket: Latin *crumina.* This *crumina* seems to have been a purse worn around the neck, as a fanny pack is worn around the hips; in this scene it's a wallet or fanny pack, and a prop, and Einstein needs to gesture with it. See the joke at 312–19, and later in the play. The double entendres produced by translating *crumina* "pocket" or "wallet," as seems unavoidable, are not present in the Latin.

Using . . . prize: Latin *hominibus domitis,* lit. "trained/subjugated men" (cf. 259); the text is corrupt. The translation relies on the double meaning of "guys" in English (people/items); this isn't present in *hominibus,* but the line works like a riddle, and Einstein must be pointing to the *crumina.* The joke (if the text is right) must make a transition between the *domitos boves* in 259 and the *homines* Einstein wants to punish in 266, who stand for slave owners in general.

267 Who . . . silver: Literally, "who seal off from a slave the saltcellar with the salt." *Salina,* "saltcellars," were a standard item of family silver; *sal,* "salt," is often used in Plautus to mean "food" (see note on *Weevil* 562; below, line 429). Note use of *opsignant,* "seal off," here; cf. 248, where Bowman's letter is *opsignatam,* off limits to his slave.

270   Fuck him: Latin *vae illi,* "woe to him!"

278   Little witch: Latin *venefice,* "(male) poisoner," "male witch"; this term of abuse is mostly reserved for women.

279   Jailmeat: Latin *ulmitriba,* "one who wears out the elm"; see note on line 28.

282   Gonna . . . today: Literally, "you'll be flogged today with ropes."

283   Dang: Literally, "by Hercules."

     If . . . mouth: Latin *si os perciderim tibi;* elsewhere in Latin invective, this expression = "if I fucked you in the mouth," a meaning that may be present here, though it would be unexpected from the (younger, smaller, sex toy) Toyboy to Einstein.

     Roadkill: Latin *morticine,* "animal that has died a natural death."

284   You fresh-laid egg: Latin *incubitatus es,* "you have been sat on [the way a hen sits on an egg]." In 284–88, Einstein and Toyboy taunt each other with their sexual vulnerability as slaves. Toyboy is a sex toy, but Einstein, like any slave, is also vulnerable (flashback to line 11). In 285, Toyboy implies that he (Toyboy) makes money on the side by prostituting himself; Einstein has just seen him come out of the pimp's house.

288   Go to hell: "Go away to a bad thing."

289   This: The word *hic* in this line must mark a gesture or use of a prop; that Einstein has pointed to his crotch is suggested by 290.

292   God . . . don't: "May all the gods and goddesses ruin me." Here Toyboy interrupts Einstein in the middle of this oath, which he picks up in 294; at 296, Einstein starts to make it again, only with "you"—"Oh, if the gods and goddesses . . . you . . ."—he interrupts himself before the verb gets there.

294   Hammer . . . nail: The Latin specifies that Einstein will do this *colapheis,* "with punches" (slang)—"by sluggin you."

295   With a lethal injection: Literally, "to a cross."

298   Evil twin: Latin *umbra mea,* "my shadow." A mysterious line. There are other shadow jokes in Plautus, all on the dumb side. In any case, this has to be Toyboy's parting shot at Einstein.

305   Hipper . . . hide: Latin *magi' calleo quam aprugnum callum callet,* "I am [tough/in the know] more than a boar hide is." A great line in Latin and clearly a catchphrase; it's repeated in similar form at *Towelheads* 579, and cf. 380, 455 below. See volume introduction under "Catchphrases." The verb *calleo* literally means to be tough or calloused, and Mary-Kay Gamel suggests that this expression refers to the scars formed by flogging, as in "It's been beaten into me."

306   Mucho cool: Latin *graphice facetus.* The adverb *graphice* (another Greek/Latin hybrid, see line 29) appears only in speeches by slaves. It = "as though worthy to be painted," "exquisitely," like "Beauty!" (Canadian), and functions like "way." Sp. *de pelicula,* "like in the movies" = "fabulous," would be a closer translation, but hasn't made it as far into the U.S. vernacular as "mucho." *Facetus* = "clever/witty."

307   Flap my wings: Stance possibly derived from cockfighting; cf. the two Logics in Aristophanes' *Clouds.*

       Put . . . suit: Literally, "I'll be robed [gloriously/like a war hero]," "I'll wear my hero suit." For *gloriosus* used of soldiers, cf. *Weevil* 633. Einstein, about to throw money around, is acting like a tycoon.

308   The little teapot . . . street: Bowman asks, "Who is walking here with handles?" Einstein must be walking with his hands on his hips, a gesture associated with effeminacy in Latin invective (Richlin 1992a: 258n3; Richlin 1993: 542).

       Hock a royal loogie: Latin *magnifice conscreabor,* an oxymoron. For this evidently gross verb, see *Weevil* 115. Einstein seems to be planning to clear his throat to get attention ("ahem!"), and to do so like a prince.

310–11   With this string of commands, Einstein may be trying to sound like a master.

312   Pocket: See note on 265. Bowman asks what the bulge is on Einstein's neck; he must be trying to reach inside the purse. The joke purse/zit in English acquires a third layer, "bulge in the pants," but this is not in the Latin, though the specification "a couple of [bulls]" might just conceivably suggest male genitalia.

317   Bulls: Riddle format; Einstein makes the money an equivalent for the oxen he was supposed to buy. Bowman jumps over the riddle to get at the money, and in 318–20 Bowman and Einstein both speak on a double level.

329   May . . . fine: This expression in Latin is a formula for good wishes, especially for an engagement; see Woytek ad loc. The parody of ritual language continues through line 332.

335   I've . . . dolled up: Latin *exornavi;* includes the sense "I've costumed you." See note on line 158.

336   Young lady: Latin *virgo,* "virgin"; this is how Cherry is addressed not only by her father but by others later in the play, and it is each time translated "young lady."

339   On account . . . Saudis: Literally, "on account of King Philip or Attalus." There were several ancient kings by these names, and we cannot be sure which are meant here; any of them would signify the East, power, and wealth, and need to be represented by modern equivalents. Likely candidates are Philip II of Macedon, father of Alexander the Great (382–36 B.C.E.); his descendant and Plautus's contemporary, King Philip V of Macedon (238–179), Rome's enemy; Attalus I of

Pergamum (269–197), friendly to Rome, involved with the fighting in Greece in Plautus's time, and renowned for wealth. Philip II, whose conquests included major gold mines, actually had a type of coinage named after himself, and his name is thus synonymous with "money"; see *Weevil* 440, *Towelheads* introduction under "Settings." For this form of king joke in Plautus, see volume introduction under "Topical Jokes."

344   Really: Cherry loves the adverb *verum,* which pops up in most of her speeches in this section.

352   Let 'em . . . hell: Literally, "let 'em go to the biggest bad cross."

380   Kidnapped at gunpoint: Literally, "how you were stolen away by force."

      I studied. I'm hip: Latin *docte calleo*—see note on line 305.

387   As long . . . flappin: Literally, "as long as there's a dowry, no vice is counted as a vice." The "money" in the next few lines is Cherry's dowry; it was a matter of family pride to provide one.

392–96   Here Fat Jack says he will dower Cherry out of his stock in trade as a *parasitus.*

392   Trunk . . . jokebooks: Woytek gives references for the "trunk" as a theatrical accessory. For jokebooks, see Hansen 1998: 272–82.

394   Gags: Latin *logei,* a Latinized version of Greek *logoi,* "sayings."

395   Hollywood . . . bush league: Literally, "Athenian" / "Sicilian." This probably derives from the origin of Plautus's plays in Greek New Comedy, for which Athens was the big time and Sicily the provinces. But see Woytek on Athenian and Sicilian humor.

396   A squeegee man: Literally, "a beggar." Like line 394, this line is set up as a *para prosdokian* (ends in an unexpected way).

Scene 2   He . . . weapon: See Woytek on 816, where Dorkalot threatens Toyboy with the stick; Woytek cites the ancient theater historian Pollux, who says that stage pimps carried a stick as a standard prop.

403   He'll be out of a credit rating: Literally, "he'll have lost his sworn oath."

406–26   This is one of the major insult matches in Plautus and, like others, has a pimp as its object. The structure of the insults is traditional and probably recalls the folk practice of *occentatio* (see *Weevil* introduction and note on *Weevil* 145; line 569 below). On this passage see Opelt 1965: 91.

406   Pimping dirtbag: Literally, "pimpish dirt."

408   Cocksucking . . . skeezy: Latin *impure, inhoneste, iniure, inlex,* "sexually perverted [implied: performing fellatio], dishonorable, illegal, illicit."

409	Beady-eyed, evil-eyed: Latin *invide* (on the unlucky figure of the envious man in Roman culture, see Barton 1993). Vulture: literally "hawk."
410	Mouthy . . . pushy: Latin *procax, rapax, trahax,* literally "rude, rapacious, robbery-prone."
411	Scum-sucking shit: Latin *tuas impuritias* (see note on 408).
412	Bitch: Latin *impudens* (also at 422). Like *impure,* this word suggests sexual passivity in a male.
417	This line, like 411, steps outside of the theatrical fiction.
418	National bigshot: Literally, "highest man of the public."
419	You're . . . sweat: Latin *suduculum flagri.* The meaning of *suduculum* is not clear, but the phrase conveys the idea of heat and sweat in connection with flogging.
420	Chain gang green card: Latin *pistrinorum civitas,* "citizenship of the flour-mills." See note to line 22 for the mills as the locus of slave punishment.
421	Fat-ass . . . slacker: Latin *edax, furax, fugax,* "greedy, thieving, runaway," echoing 410; pathetically, slaves were faulted for tending to run away. Cf. *Towelheads* 147, 427.
429	Food: Literally, "salt"; see note to *Weevil* line 562; above, line 267.
432	Trust . . . money: The issue of credit, both monetary and verbal, pervades the rest of the play, and forms of the verb *credo,* "believe/trust/credit," are everywhere. For banking and credit as social issues, see note on *Weevil* 506–11.
436	At the dog track: Literally, "at the games"; the rabbit presumably is a way to start the action at a *venatio.* See note to line 199 above.
440	Check this out: Compare the aside to the audience about stage money in *Towelheads* (lines 595–98); this is a similar joke.
442–43	Woytek assigns these lines to Bowman; the OCT assigns them to Dorkalot.
444	Back alleyways: Refers to part of the setup of the Roman *scaenae frons*—a corridor/alleyway ran behind the housefronts.
446	Not openly: This otherwise superfluous plan is driven by a problem in staging: Dorkalot needs to return the *crumina* containing the money to his house so that he can exit to get it out of the house at line 671. This business with Georgia Moon gives him a reason to go home the back way. It also conveys Georgia Moon to Bowman's house so she can exit from there in act 5.
449	Honest and serious: Latin *sobrie aut frugaliter,* "seriously" and "honestly," "doing the right thing." The basic Roman virtue of being *frugi* recurs in this passage at 454.

455 Cool and hip: Latin *facete . . . callide;* see notes on lines 306 and 305.

462 Royal . . . hombre: Latin *exornatu's basilice.* For *orno* as a theatrical term (= "cos-tume"), see note on line 158. For *basilice,* see note on line 29. Part of the joke seems to be that Einstein's getup is obviously a disguise.

463 Really . . . touch: Literally, "dresses up your disguise/costume with a clever dec-orating scheme." Note that Einstein now wears, not the floppy hat of line 155, but a turban.

464 Nice shoes: Latin *crepidula,* "little sandals," a normal Greek item of clothing—there must be something special on Cherry's feet, but it's hard to say what.

Looks mucho good: Latin *graphice decet* (see note on line 306).

465 Professional actors: Latin *tragici et comici.* Same joke at *Towelheads* 581.

471 Two McBurgers: Literally, "two loaves of bread"; Dorkalot here identifies him-self as miserly, both as master and ex-master.

473 Eatin . . . mine: Literally, "she will dine on another's (property), she won't taste a bite of mine."

474–75 Literally, "Am I not upright, am I a charming citizen, who made the greatest Athenian state today / greater, and augmented it by a female citizen?" A mix of Greek setting and Roman customs: freed slaves became citizens under Roman law, but not under Athenian law.

476 I trusted everybody: See note on 432; Dorkalot plays with *credo* "I believe" and "I give (monetary) credit."

488 God . . . saints: Literally, "All the gods do well to you!"

490 Don't swear: Both Dorkalot and Bowman play with the idea of swearing an oath, which Dorkalot had evidently made Bowman do (see line 416). One problem here is that slaves' oaths were held to be no good, as in the custom of the *iusiu-randum liberti,* the freedman's oath of loyalty to the master that had to be taken twice—once before and once after a manumission.

494 Bucks: Latin *lucrum,* "money," "profit," "cash." This word is repeatedly used in this and subsequent scenes, which helps set up for Cherry's joke when she says her name is "Lucris" (line 624).

501 "Mr. . . . {July 12}": The letter follows Roman salutation rules and identifies the sender as "Timarchides," an aristocratic name. There's no date, but we would put one in a formal letter, so there's one here to convey what the Roman format does: "this is a letter." In performance, any recent date would do.

514 Dumbass: Latin *stultiloque,* "stupid-talker."

515   What . . . you: Literally, "what a profit-bearing torchette the goddess Fortune wants to light for you."

521   Very nice girl: Latin *liberali,* literally "appearing like a free person." See notes on *Weevil* 209; above, line 130; below, line 546.

523   Here: That is, at home, in Athens.

531   Extracurricular: Latin *foras,* "out of doors."

533   Toilet bowl: Latin *matula;* could be translated "noisy pisspot."

534   Been around this block before: Literally, "I've experienced (this) now many times."

535   Shit: Latin *luto,* literally "dirt" (see note on line 406).

538   Make out . . . bandit: Literally, "of doing well for yourself."

546   Quite the lady: Latin *specie . . . liberalist;* cf. note on 521. Note that looking free(born)—which the fictive captive claims to be and Cherry really is—is a selling point in a slave, and is expected to draw customers; cf. 130, 521.

547   Ooh . . . fussy: Literally, "how contemptuously the executioner." *Carnufex,* literally "meat-maker," is a highly derogatory term. For the format, see *Weevil* line 633; volume introduction under "Catchphrases."

550   But . . . me: Literally, "but I have inspected the mores of the people too little." Cherry's comments in 550–60 constitute another parabasis moment (see volume introduction under "Topical Jokes"); she is the Voice of Wisdom here, as in the scene that follows. The tone is lofty, and there is a faint echo of the opening lines of the *Odyssey.*

553   Security-wise: This section is expressed in Latin in terms of city walls.

561   Frat brothers: See note on *Weevil* 68.

567   They're . . . you: Literally, "they will crave your favor."

569   Yell . . . down: See note on lines 406–26, and cf. note on *Towelheads* 539. This line clearly refers to the practice of *flagitatio* and *occentatio,* which could climax with the burning down of the front door; see Lintott 1999: 6–10. The excluded lovers also resemble the young man in a *paraklausithyron* (see *Weevil* introduction), but this is an analogy.

571   Burglar bars: Literally, "thresholds."

573   While . . . yourself: Only slaves wore shackles.

574   Go burn in hell: Literally, "Please go to the bad torture."

581   As . . . heaven: Literally, "As much as all the gods who live in heaven."

588	Woytek assigns this whole line to Bowman; the OCT assigns the second part to Dorkalot, addressing Einstein.

588   Woytek assigns this whole line to Bowman; the OCT assigns the second part to Dorkalot, addressing Einstein.

604   Go round the world: Literally, "from the earth to the sky."

605   Be nice: Latin *morem . . . gere,* a phrase with slight sexual overtones.

606   BOWMAN *(to* CHERRY*):* Woytek assigns this speech to Einstein, based on problems in blocking the scene, but Einstein is not usually the one giving instructions.

{Princess Leia}: Lines 606–8 use the language of battles and epic poetry; the *Star Wars* movies provide a current analogy (here "the Force" substitutes for the Roman practice of taking the auspices before a battle). See *Iran Man* introduction; the Kevin Smith films all include *Star Wars* references.

617   You . . . long: Bowman means Dorkalot to understand that a rich buyer will immediately take Cherry off his hands; Bowman obviously means this in a double sense, to which Cherry replies in the first of a long string of double entendres. In keeping with line 616, she does not actually tell a lie. Woytek gives Bowman's lines in 617 to Dorkalot, speaking of himself.

622   Damn the bitch: Literally, "may the gods ruin her."

So sly and hip: Latin *catast et callida;* see note on 305.

623   Brain: Literally, *cor,* "heart."

624   Casha: Cherry says her name is "Lucris," a woman's name formed from Latin *lucrum,* "profit" or "cash." Note that this name is Greek in form, and does not sound "Arabian" at all (see Faller 2001: 194–95); contrast the name Einstein makes up for himself at 702–5.

625   The name and the game: Latin *nomen et omen,* "the name and the omen."

630   She . . . yet: Is this a reaction to something Cherry has just said? Woytek suggests assigning Dorkalot's line in 629 to Cherry.

631   In . . . side: A similar joke also appears in the *Aesop Romance,* a second-century C.E. comic biography of a legendary slave; it's not impossible that both derive from oral tradition (Hansen 1998: 121). The left side was considered lucky. For comedy "dragging the tone of the drama down to the level of the kitchen," see Gowers 1993: 79.

634   Tag . . . born: This line is corrupt, but the sense seems clear.

638   Just . . . was: An interesting analogy; the sociologist Orlando Patterson writes of slavery as "social death" (1982).

643   You . . . syndrome: Literally, "Don't lead her into the memory of her miseries."

647 Mr. and Ms. . . . erable: That is, "Mister and Miserable." Cherry says their names should be *Miserum* and *Miseram*, "Poor Man" and "Poor Girl."

649 By slave and free alike: The Latin says he was loved by slaves and *liberi*, which can mean either "free people" or "[his] children"—another double meaning in Cherry's speech.

651 Real . . . act: Literally, "born from the highest family/class."

653 As . . . witness: Literally, "by Castor."

658 Quite a haul: Latin *grandis bolos; bolos* < Greek "throw," as in casting a fishnet.

662 A thousand bucks: A hundred *minae*.

665 Six . . . barrel: Literally, sixty *minae* in cash.

666 God . . . She's: In the Latin, "the gods and goddesses"—a possible reference to the Furies, whose job it was to make people crazy after they committed murder.

667 Dorkalot's speech in this line is a blank in the manuscripts; the translation here is of a guess at its content. Woytek assigns the next speech to Einstein.

668 Three thousand: Three hundred *minae*.

Made . . . today: Latin *fecisti lucri*, "you made a profit." Throughout these scenes, Bowman and Dorkalot use variants on this expression; while they don't use the exact name Cherry made up for herself, they probably are playing with it.

668a <I . . . right>: Another hole in the text; Woytek suggests a question here, Dorkalot needing reassurance: "So I got her for six hundred bucks?" Woytek assigns the response (*habeto*, "She's yours!") to Einstein; the OCT leaves it with Dorkalot ("You got it!").

669 A hundred bucks: Ten *minae*.

671a {And. . . .} . . . deserves: This is another fragmentary line; from the few words left, it seems to be an aside on the downfall of the pimp. The translation here is a guess at the sense of the missing words. The idea that the pimp deserves the scam recurs throughout the play.

674 Neat . . . eat: Latin *probam et sapientem et sobriam*, "righteous and wise and serious."

679 Announcing: From Latin *praedico, -are*.

680 I mean . . . cash: Why does Bowman make this request? The money is more Einstein's than his. But this positions Einstein for act 5. Cf. at 446.

681 Think . . . do: Literally, "What's fit for you, you want to be fit for me?"

685   Bag: Latin *crumina*—a wallet like Einstein's (see note on line 265); indeed, probably the very wallet Einstein gave to Bowman and Bowman gave to Dorkalot.

687   Sorry . . . thief: Latin *miser, impure, avare:* "wretched, sexually perverted, greedy person."

688   The . . . way: Literally, "Since he's a pimp, he's not doing anything amazing."

689   Horoscope: Literally, "auspices."

691   In my pocket: Literally, "on my neck"—Einstein's *crumina* again. Einstein has his hands full; it seems key to make Dorkalot put the money directly into Einstein's possession. Cf. Slater 1985: 49–50, who suggests that this action completes the narrative arc that begins when Einstein arrives with the cattle money in his *crumina*.

695   Twin brother: A further ruse to disguise Einstein from Dorkalot, who will see him in the last act without his Iran Man costume.

700   {Buddy boy}: This translation represents a guess that the hole in the text of this line originally held a term addressing Dorkalot.

702–5   Einstein's name: Einstein fires off a string of comic names; these are not Persian names, though in Greek literature there are stereotypes of Persian names as being long and ending in "s" (see Faller 2001: 189–93). The names here mostly have Greek patronymic endings and are Latin/Greek hybrid formations, geared to seem funny to a bilingual Greek/Roman audience in Rome; they also tell Dorkalot exactly what is going on, except that he doesn't get it. See note on *Towelheads* 54.

702   Osama bin Blabbin: *Vaniloquidorus,* "Empty-speaker-[Greek name ending]."

        Baima-i-Sistra: *Virginesvendonides,* "Virgins-seller-son."

703   Ali Blabba: *Nugiepiloquides,* "Trash-upon[Greek]-speak-son."

        Sheikh Daoun: accepting Woytek's suggestion *Argentumexterebronides,* "I-screw-cash-out-of-[you]-son." Cf. *Weevil* 446.

704   Yomammed: *Tedigniloquides,* "[I]-speak-what-you-deserve-son."

        Khayyam Allah Khan: ("Hi, I'm all a con"), accepting Woytek's *Nuncaespalponides,* "Now-I-squeeze-money-out-son."

705   Whataisteali: *Quodsemelarripides,* "What-once-steal-son." Younevergetbacki: *Numquameripides,* "Never-get-back-son."

713   You . . . cash-a: Literally, "You didn't buy this girl, you really made a profit."

722   Sheesh: Latin *attat.*

737	Do the horizontal boogie: Latin *inclinabo me,* "I'm gonna bend myself over."

Your old slave girl: Latin *liberta tua,* "your freedwoman." Georgia Moon is now Dorkalot's freed slave and stands in the special relationship to him (her *patronus*) this entailed: she still owes him both obedience and service. This will be a problem, since Bowman sees himself as her *patronus.*

740	Iran . . . over: The Latin puns on *Persa / pessum dedit,* "gave me the treatment."

743	Scum: Latin *scelus,* "crime."

747	Dirty devil: Latin *carnufex,* "executioner"; see note on line 547.

748	Any decent man: Latin *mortali libero,* "a free human being," echoed by the next line. Fat Jack's point is that he hardly needs witnesses for Dorkalot's heinous crimes.

753	*(Sounding like a walkie-talkie):* The song in lines 753–57 is dense with military language. Almost the whole of act 5 is sung, except for 819–42, 851–53, which are in the chanted meter that takes up much of the earlier acts.

755	Almighty . . . heaven: Literally, "Jupiter and all the other gods who rule the sky."

758a	Flag of war: The text (at 759a in the original) has *aquilam,* "eagle," which most editors reject. Surely this is just the end of the military metaphor; the eagles were the Roman military standards. Woytek here adduces Roman descriptions of triumphs, in which soldiers are said to have enjoyed public banquets.

760	Get . . . high: Latin *hilaros ludentis laetificantis,* "cheerful, partying, happy-making."

765	Beach chair: The *lecti* at Roman dinners were like poolside lounge chairs; Roman men ate dinner lying on their sides, propping themselves up on their elbows. Wives supposedly sat next to them in chairs. The prostitutes who worked at drinking parties, though, might share a *lectus* with a man.

767	Head: I.e., the head of the *lectus,* a place of honor.

767a	Pay . . . said: Here it becomes evident that Bowman plans to keep the pimp's money rather than pay back his friend.

769	Birthday: Freeborn persons celebrated their birthdays, but it seems doubtful that slaves did so in any officially recognized way; see Joshel 1992: 64–65, with note on Martial 10.27 and 11.12. Slaves legally lacked parents, and their births would have been recorded only in their capacity as property, and then only if they were born in captivity. Cf. Einstein's casual allusion (263) to his *genius,* the natal spirit derived from the patriline. Under the empire, an ex-slave could get his *natales* (birthright/birthday) restored by the emperor (*Digest* 40.11), but no such action

was available in the Republic. This looks like an act of wishful thinking—or a recognition of what slaves did amongst themselves.

You: Bowman here addresses helpers in the plural—possibly nonspeaking actors playing house slaves.

770   On top: Literally, "You will be our lady dictator." At ancient drinking parties, one guest would often be given the job of dictating the rules for drinking.

771a   From the top: I.e., starting from Einstein.

A pitcher each: Literally, "seven *cyathi* apiece." Toyboy is the cupbearer; his job is to keep the glasses filled at the instructions of the partygoer appointed by the others to rule the drinking. A *cyathus* was a metal wine ladle with a long handle; this is actually what Toyboy is holding, and will soon use as a weapon.

776–76a   Folks . . . me: In the Latin, Georgia Moon drinks to singular representatives of each class; or she may literally mean Einstein (grudging) as opposed to Bowman.

782   Truckload of cash: Latin *vehiclum argenti.*

783   Man . . . them: Latin *Persam . . . Persas . . . personas,* "man from Iran . . . Iranians . . . theatrical masks." Woytek argues that Plautus does this just for the jingle and the group of three; cf. Slater 1985: 51–52 for interpretation. The translation here assumes a metatheatrical point to the pun.

788   A comedy: Latin *fabula,* "play."

789–90   Gentle . . . ex-slave: Latin *bona liberta,* something of an oxymoron, picking up on *bone vir,* "gentleman," addressed to Bowman at the end of 788. Woytek assigns the third speech in this line to Georgia Moon, and all of line 791 to Bowman.

792   Wash . . . feet: Again, this command is addressed to slaves in the plural.

794   Kegtapper: Actually, the *cyathus.*

Scumbag: Woytek suggests that the last word in this line (*tuom,* "your") was originally some insult directed at Dorkalot.

795   Lethal injection: Latin *crux,* "cross."

Cattle-prod meat: Latin *stimulorum tritor,* literally "wearer-out of prods."

Screwed: Latin *vorsavisti;* Woytek says this metaphor derives from turning meat on a spit.

796   Hoodwinked: Literally, "your hand was put upon me," a Plautine idiom = "cheat, swindle," possibly from a game; or it may have been a metaphor from wrestling—cf. note on *Towelheads* 457.

797   Woytek assigns this line to Georgia Moon; the OCT gives it to Bowman.

799–800 Woytek treats this metrically as a single long line.

804 Here's yer bitch: Literally, "Do you want a new *cinaedus* to be given to you?" Woytek takes this to be a sarcastically polite question addressed to Dorkalot; Bowman will give him Toyboy as his *cinaedus* (sexy dancer, in Plautus; in later literature and perhaps here as well, an effeminate adult male who enjoys sexual penetration by other men—see volume introduction under "Background on Roman Culture" and "Audience and Venue"). In the following lines, then, Toyboy's actions are both a dance and a mockery. But other editors take this line to be addressed to Toyboy, and Bowman to be dropping the pretence of entertaining Dorkalot at this point. Dorkalot is then Toyboy's *cinaedus,* a particularly demeaning insult since it makes Dorkalot the sex toy of a sex toy. Since Toyboy et al. in the rest of the scene go on to act out the anal rape of Dorkalot, this seems like the logical reading here. The original manuscript had no punctuation; either meaning is obtainable here depending on how you punctuate.

806 Hoo, baby: Latin *hui, babae!*

Royally cool with me: Latin *basilice . . . et facete;* see notes on lines 29 and 306.

810 Whupped my ass: Latin *perculit me prope,* "he's nearly knocked me down." But *perculit* plays with Latin *per culum,* "through the ass."

815 Hang yo ass: Latin *suspende te,* "hang yourself." But what Toyboy offers Dorkalot is clearly not a rope but a phallic object (or he points to his own crotch)—this is a rape threat.

816 Stick: A reciprocal rape threat. See above on Dorkalot's stick (after line 396).

821 Beer: Latin *mulsum,* wine sweetened with honey; see note at line 87.

823 May . . . you: Dorkalot's wish takes the form of a riddle; Woytek cites editors who think the answer is "poison," or a weapon. But surely this is another oral rape threat.

824–26 Travolta, Michael Jackson, West Hollywood: Einstein says he wants to dance like Hegea; Bowman, like Diodorus in Ionia. These are two of a very short list of evidently real people mentioned in Plautus's plays, though they are not otherwise known. Ionia was the coast of Asia Minor, notorious as a hotbed of effete luxury and the source of exotic dancing. Male dancers generally were considered effeminate by Romans. Translators should insert the name of any well-known male dancers (especially ones known for striking poses), plus the name of any place with a similar current reputation. See volume introduction under "Topical Jokes."

829 You . . . skin: Latin *me usque admutilasti ad cutem.* This is usually taken to be the equivalent of the English "you fleeced me good" (see *OLD* s.v. *admutilo* and *cutis*

for parallels). But I wonder whether the reference might not also be to the making of eunuchs, a practice associated by the Romans with Asia Minor and one that was common among slave traders. The verb *mutilo* is closer in meaning to "castrate" than it is to "shear."

833   Goof him up: Latin *ludificemus.* Forms of *ludus* recur in this passage, recalling the setting of the plays at the *ludi* and the overall ludic quality of the plays.

834   Not fair for me: Here Georgia Moon seems not to want to torment the pimp herself, perhaps out of a sense of duty as his *liberta.*

      I . . . you: The sense here is not certain: Bowman either says this (meaning Dorkalot tricked Georgia Moon into having sex with him before Bowman came up with the money) or says sarcastically that Georgia Moon doesn't want to hurt the pimp now because he "did not annoy you" during the sale (Woytek).

838   Benefactor: Latin *patronus*—ex-master of ex-slave; see note on line 737. "Benefactor" translates *patronus* throughout this scene. See introduction to *Iran Man* for discussion of why Bowman does not buy Georgia Moon and free her himself.

842   I'm . . . you: Wishful thinking; see *Iran Man* introduction.

843   Righteously: Latin *graphice.* See note at 306.

844   Woytek gives Einstein's line here to Dorkalot.

845   American: Literally, "free." Woytek gives Einstein's speech here to Dorkalot.

847   Pullin out . . . hair: Literally, "he's plucking my butt."

850   Wimp Goddess: Latin *mea Ignavia,* addressing Georgia Moon as a personification of the quality of laziness, cowardice, and/or weakness. Cf. note on *Towelheads* line 846, with further examples of this kind of joke.

854   Woytek thinks this line should belong either to Bowman or (better) to Georgia Moon, to go with earlier remarks of hers which he reads as placatory. He then gives line 855a to Toyboy, because he takes it to be obscene and feels Toyboy should get the obscene lines. Directors should realize that these lines are up for grabs.

855a Rubber hose: Latin *sub furcis,* "under the forks"; this image combines (a) the use of the yoke as a slave punishment; (b) the symbolic action in which the soldiers of a defeated army were marched under the yokes (subjugated).

856   To Death Row: "To the cross."

857   {Next . . . before}: The words here represent a guess at the content of the words missing from this line.

NOTES ON NONMETRICAL TRANSLATIONS OF
RAP SECTIONS

769a   You . . . table: This command is actually addressed to [slaves] in the plural.

772   Shake a leg: Literally, "move your hands."

TOWELHEADS (POENULUS)

This seven-year-old boy gets kidnapped from Baghdad—
Once he's in Sarajevo, a rich old guy who hates women,
Wanting an heir, buys him . . . and adopts him—
Eventually makes him his heir. Then this kid's two girl cousins,
Loitering in the Casbah one day, with their nanny,
Help! get snatched themselves. The Wolf, a pimp,
Educates them and turns them out for hire,
And teases the kid (who now loves one of the girls).
Deceiving him, the kid gets the girl. Meanwhile Uncle Saddam
Searching, finds him (his nephew), and his own lost girls.*

INTRODUCTION

Poenulus poses important problems for making Plautus funny in English, problems that have a lot to teach about what this play originally meant and can still mean.

The problems start with the title; *Poenulus* means "The Little Punic Guy." Based on an unscientific survey I took while working on this project, nobody now finds this title funny, and most people had no idea what "Punic" meant. But originally it was a funny title—funny in the way *Towelheads* is funny (or not). When the play was produced, the Romans were in the midst of the Punic Wars, a series of devastating wars against the Carthaginians, who were their biggest rivals and enemies in the Mediterranean. The Romans hated the Carthaginians and had special stereotypes for them (see Franko 1994; Leigh 2004). In particular, they thought they were untrustworthy, sneaky, slimy; and trustworthiness was a particularly Roman virtue, one of the foundation stones of being a good Roman man (the acme of Romanness). The *vox propria* for "Carthaginian" in Latin is *Carthaginiensis*. But another word for "a Carthaginian person" in Latin is *Poenus* (the adjective *Punicus*, as in "Punic Wars," comes from the earlier form *Poenicus*). This word literally means "Phoenician"; the Carthaginians were so called because they were originally from Phoenicia in the eastern Mediterranean, and the Romans knew this, in a mythic kind of way. (The Carthaginians were a Semitic people; their language is a Semitic language, close to Hebrew, while Latin is an Indo-European language. This means the vocabularies of the two peoples would share no words except loanwords, and there are very few Punic loanwords in Latin.) When the Romans talked about Carthaginian untrustworthiness, they used the term *Punica fides,* "Phoenician trustworthiness," which is untrustworthiness.

Moreover, the diminutive ending *-ulus* was affixed in Latin to ethnic adjectives to produce an ethnic slur; the classic example is the *Graeculus* in Juvenal's third satire, which literally means "little Greek." But that sounds more affectionate than what the Latin means. Interestingly, the Carthaginian in the play is never called "Poenulus" or referred to as "Poenulus," though on his first entrance he is the butt of a long series of jokes on his appearance and language; the word appears only as the title. And in the prologue to the play, the title of the play is stated to be *The Uncle*. (In the translation, I have added two lines after line 54 in order to take in the current translated title along with the Greek and Latin titles.) Anyway, the play must have acquired its nasty title sometime before it was canonized in the first century B.C.E., maybe as a result of escalating anti-Punic feeling.

The bottom line is that "The Little Punic Guy" is not much of a translation of *Poenulus*. A good translation would be an ethnic slur, applicable to a recently defeated and commonly insulted enemy of the mainstream culture. It should be dismissive (that's one force of the diminutive ending). And, if possible, it should be Orientalizing, as in the process described by Edward Said in *Orientalism* whereby the West defines an "East" by means of fantasies (see volume introduction under "War, History, Geography"). It should be pandering to a mainstream audience that's known to speak of this recently defeated enemy using ethnic slurs. A close linguistic equivalent in English would be "Jap" as used in the United States during and after World War II: a deformalized form of an ethnic name, used to express contempt. Hence, today, *Towelheads*. Well, really it should be *The Towelhead*, singular; I made it plural to refer to the play's discovery of *multiple* Carthaginians. But there is no way to translate this title accurately and have it not be an ethnic slur.

Indeed, *Poenulus* is a crucial text for the question of ideas of race in antiquity. In a lot of Plautus's plays, the plot revolves around a secret of birth (cf. *H.M.S. Pinafore; The Importance of Being Earnest; Goldmember*)—often with echoes of epic, as in *Star Wars*. The old nurse holds the key (cf. *Pinafore; The Pirates of Penzance; The Gondoliers*). Somebody, often a young woman, is now a slave (often a prostitute), sexually available and about to be sold to someone she doesn't like. Surprise! By the end of the play, the secret is revealed, and it turns out that the young woman is freeborn (*My Fair Lady*: " . . . of royal blood. She is . . . a princess!": Eliza Doolittle, Cinderella). And she can marry the boy next door, who has long loved her but couldn't afford to buy her.

In *Poenulus,* though, there's a twist. In the normal Plautine play, as noted in the volume introduction, the actors, probably all male, are, many of them, native speakers of Greek, born in the south of Italy, and performing on stage in Latin as people who act like native Romans but have Greek names and are supposed to be in "Greece." And some of them are playing women. When they're in a Greek city, it's usually Athens. This time, the main actors play people who act like native Romans but have Greek names and live in a Greek city and then, by the end of the play, discover or disclose that they're not Greeks at all, they're Carthaginians! And they're delighted about it! (Again as in *My Fair Lady*: "Not only Hungarian, but of royal blood. She is . . . a princess!") Funny, they didn't *look* Punic . . .

Most amazingly, the central character in the play, the title character, the Poenulus, is not only a Carthaginian, his name is Hanno. Hanno is a historical name; it's attached to a Greek wonder-geography that (purportedly) predates Plautus, and, even more pertinently here, it was the name of a Carthaginian general in the First Punic War, as well as of numerous Carthaginian officers and statesmen in the Second. Here he's the friendly uncle who saves the day; the prologue of the play tells us that the play's title is *Karkhedonios* (the Greek equivalent of *Carthaginiensis*), or "in Latin, *The Uncle*" (54). But his name, Hanno, translates as a generic enemy name like "Fritz" or "Adolf" in World War II; or it may be more specific, like "Saddam" (America, 2005). Kindly Uncle Saddam.

This is where the race part comes in. Hanno and Carthage actually figure only in the prologue and act 5. The rest of the play is just your standard Plautine let's-trick-the-pimp plot, interesting in itself (here the sexy ingenue and her sexy sister are explicitly whores in training), but without much racial anything. But when Hanno appears, he's dressed up like a stage Carthaginian; his whole getup and appearance are clearly hilarious. He looks Punic. The leading man and the two leading girls are going to turn out to be Punic, but did they look Punic all along? Could you tell before the discovery scene? And what about the nanny, who (unlike the girls and the boy) has kept her Punic name, Giddenis? And what about the incidental Ethiopian jokes in this act, where did they come from? What about the scattered blackface jokes, two of which seem to apply to the girls? And what about the fact that some readers have seen Hanno as the most serious character in the play—pious, dedicated, just?

Of course, they were probably all wearing masks. But what did the masks look like? Did they change in act 5?

Let's rewind to the setting of the play. The city in "Greece" inhabited by these Roman/Greek/Punic actors isn't Athens or Epidaurus, it's Calydon, off the beaten track, in the country, like a fairy tale. But the fairy tale was over. Five places that figure in this play—Calydon, Aetolia, Anactorium, Histria, and Sparta—would have been constantly in the news during the time at which *Poenulus* would have been written, probably between the end of the Second Punic War in 204 B.C.E. and the death of Plautus, supposedly in 184 B.C.E. Yes, one major association an ancient audience would have had with Calydon would have been a mythical one: it was the site of the hunt for the Calydonian boar, in which Meleager sealed his doom (see joke at *Iran Man* line 3). The whole region in which Calydon is located—Aetolia, in the west central part of Greece north of the Peloponnesus—was wild and rugged, a remote, backwoods area until past the classical period of Greek history. However, by the time this play was written, important things had changed. Calydon became a fortified city during this period. Aetolia zoomed from "backwoods mythical place" to "world power," and was first Rome's ally against King Philip of Macedon and then changed sides, also taking up with the Seleucid King Antiochus III. The Aetolians are a laughingstock in later histories of the period by Polybius and Livy—troublemaking, complaining, self-important—and their folly cost them a Roman invasion. At one point in *Poenulus* (lines 524–25), one of the characters says that the play is set during a time of peace, which might just possibly point to a date of 189 B.C.E., when the Romans conquered the Aetolians and put an end to their sovereignty (see Errington 1972: 171–86; for conjectures on the date of the play, see Maurach 1988: 32–33). As for Anactorium, it was a port city in a region of western Greece called Acarnania—Aetolia's next-door neighbor and, naturally, enemy.

How about Histria? The complicated pun on *histricus* "theatrical/Histrian" (*Poenulus* lines 4, 44) points to the year *before* the Second Punic War began, when Rome was involved in the Second Illyrian War, partly over Histria and its dreaded pirates (for a stereotype of them as such, see Livy 10.2.4). Like the Aetolians, the Illyrians took a beating. Sparta, meanwhile, throughout this period was a seething mass of revolution and counterrevolution, and one of its major issues was the predicament of political exiles, some of whom were in Rome.

So the play's air of light comedy in a pleasant country town takes on some jarring notes. As seen in *Weevil* and *Iran Man,* the setting of Plautus's plays often appears to be notional; often, clearly, the play is in Rome all along, or in a sort of hybrid location. But in *Towelheads,* there are recurring references to Calydon and Aetolia that make it hard to forget where it is set. The play is set on the Aphrodisia, the local Festival of Aphrodite, and references to the festival at the temple and the sacrifices offered there recur throughout the play. What is peculiar about this is that Calydon was famous for a temple to a particularly bloodthirsty manifestation of the goddess Artemis—not Aphrodite—at which there was a famous sacrifice that involved burning birds and animals alive (noted in the second century C.E. by Pausanias, *Description of Greece,* 7.18.8–13; it was still going on, though it had moved). Meanwhile, the *vilicus* Collybiscus pretends to be a mercenary who has been fighting in Sparta, in the pay of King Attalus of Pergamum (see note on line 664)—and Pergamum did send relief troops to Sparta when Sparta was threatened (by Rome!) in 195 B.C.E. But the combination of this Balkan-equivalent setting with the arrival of the Iraqi-equivalent Carthaginian in act 5 is really pretty thought-provoking.

One of the most important things in this play is the long speech that opens act 5, which seems to be in a sort of Punic. Was it really in Punic? Or in a sort of Punic melange? Or was it a comic Punic? How much Punic would Plautus's audience, fresh from Hannibal's invasion, have recognized? Or found amusing? Some scholars have hypothesized that an audience in Rome at this time would have known quite a lot of Punic; others have pointed to the language barrier that existed between the invading Carthaginians and all their Italic-speaking opponents. Semiticists and classicists since the sixteenth century have argued that the speech is in real Punic (which they reconstruct in different ways) and that the lines in Latin that immediately follow it provide a translation. In the OCT, the first line of this speech—*Ythalonimualonuthsicorathisymacomsyth*—is followed by nineteen more lines of alphabet soup that look something like a transliterated Semitic language. The next scene contains more blobs of alphabet soup in exchanges between the Punic-speaking Hanno and the slave who's pretending to understand him. Real Punic had its own alphabet, like Hebrew, so at best this scene started out with something phonetic and not Phoenician. It does seem clear that the lines printed as 930–39 in the OCT are a doublet of lines 940–49, and Lindsay chose to bracket the first version.

For further insight into this vexed question, a good place to start is still Sznycer 1967. His approach is lucid and relatively cautious, and he repeatedly stresses the obscurity of the text and the often contradictory results obtained by various scholars. Though tempted, like many, into detailed speculation about a putative Greek original of which no trace exists, he provides good cultural background on Hellenistic Greek interest in things Carthaginian, and sensibly argues that the doublet speeches are just another example of *Poenulus* as a patchwork of various revisions of the play, as seen in the double ending. Yet he less sensibly says (in French), "It is normal that after the end of the Second Punic War . . . the Romans would have taken a passionate interest in the Carthaginian world" (1967: 37). How many comedies about Germany were there in France in 1950?

Adrian Gratwick, a leading expert on *Poenulus,* in his essay on the Punic speech (1971) thinks, more than others have, about how it could be staged. He argues compellingly that an incomprehensible speech could work onstage as the actor made its meaning clear through gesture and emotion; after all, the audience is told what to expect in the prologue. And he lists plays, from antiquity through the Renaissance to the modern, that have used the same trick (1971: 34); to this list should certainly be added Larry Shue's *The Foreigner.*

Unfortunately, there is not enough room in any one person's head for all of Roman comedy plus all of Semitic linguistics. The authoritative current statement on the speech in Charles Krahmalkov's *Phoenician-Punic Grammar* takes many speculative ideas about the play's putative Greek original as certain, and on the basis of lines 1023 and 1017 deduces that Plautus was relying on a translation of the original Greek play into Punic (2001: 3–5). How this play would have gone over in Carthage is hard to imagine, though not impossible, I guess; readers just need to realize that Krahmalkov is pushing the evidence, as also in his 1988 essay.

At any rate, one party of scholars believes that the lines are in real Punic and constitute a prayer, so I've translated the first five lines into two common Hebrew prayers, presuming that at least some members of the audience will recognize them and say "Amen" at the appropriate moments. But on the basis of my first axiom for these translations, which is that they should be funny, I've put the rest of Hanno's speech into comic Punic, and have continued this in the comic mistranslation scene that follows. This whole sequence is set up to be funny, so I don't want to translate it into an exercise in historical linguistics. Productions of the play that want to take Hanno's speech as entirely in real Punic should substitute ten lines of Arabic. Would that get a laugh? Maybe not from everybody. If we think about the problems that might be raised by inserting an Arabic prayer into this text now, that might give us an index to the problems that might have been raised by inserting a prayer in Punic then.

The point here is that we don't know what kinds of prayers the Carthaginians made, never mind what jokes they made about the Romans, because all their literary texts are gone. In 146 B.C.E., the Romans wiped out Carthage, texts and all—the historian Polybius was present; ancient sources refer to (lost) Punic libraries and a range of (lost) Punic literary genres. Today this not exactly respectful passage in Plautus constitutes one of the major pieces of evidence Semiticists have to work with—otherwise, it's mostly inscriptions. Yes, the destruction of Carthage still lay in the future in the time of Plautus. However, after the Second Punic War, it's hard to believe that any Punic merchants formerly living in Italian cities were carrying on as before. Yes, there were Punic speakers in the vicinity; they formed the main body of the first slave uprisings of the 190s (Shaw 2001: 69–71). If they were somehow in Plautus's audience, it's hard to imagine them in a sunny mood, and indeed the shows at Setia provided them with an opportunity to strike. Acilius Glabrio, who brutally put down another rebellion near Rome in 196, had previously served as peregrine praetor (judge for noncitizens) and later was the general in the war against the Aetolians. Punic in a play at this time has to be an under-language and an out-language.

Not surprisingly, the Carthaginians themselves don't have an angelic reputation. To the victors belong the archives. Most notoriously, they are said to have sacrificed their own children: a stark contrast with Hanno. No Roman source contemporary with Plautus tells this story, and it appears first after him, interestingly, in the work of Diodorus Siculus in the 60s B.C.E. (20.6–7); as this writer's name indicates, he was a Greek speaker from the island of Sicily. Sicily was the Belgium of the First and Second Punic Wars, and, just as Sicilians are bad guys in Plautus (see volume introduction under "Topical Jokes"), so Sicilians themselves manifest a certain ambivalence about both Rome and Carthage. For an archaeological view of the child-sacrifice question, see Brown 1991.

Perhaps less controversially, the Carthaginians are associated with extreme forms of torture and execution and are thought to have introduced Romans to the practice of crucifixion, which certainly caught on (there are already a lot of crucifixion jokes in Plautus). In the First Punic War, the Carthaginians crucified their own generals if they failed; Hanno was one of them (241 B.C.E., Dio Cassius 12, = Zonaras 8.17). Another, Hasdrubal, was impaled after a defeat in Sicily in 251 B.C.E. (Dio 11, = Zonaras 8.14). This custom, like crucifixion, is also associated with the Persians (e.g., at Herodotus 1.128). Truth? Orientalism?

In particular, the Carthaginians are said to have tortured to death a famous Roman hero of the First Punic War, Marcus Atilius Regulus. All schoolchildren who took Latin used to be familiar with the uplifting story told by Horace in his fifth Roman Ode: how Regulus, held as a P.O.W. with his men, was sent back with a delegation from Carthage to seek terms from the Senate, offering the Roman prisoners in exchange for concessions. Regulus, so the story goes, told the Senate not to do it and was too honorable to break his parole, though his family clung to him; he returned to Carthage, "knowing full well what the barbarian torturer had in store for him." The details show up in Dio: the Carthaginians cut off his eyelids and made him stand in the sun in a barrel full of spikes, until he died; in revenge, the Romans gave his sons Carthaginian captives to torture (book 11, = Zonaras 8.15). But Dio wrote in the late 100s C.E.; Diodorus Siculus tells the story quite differently, though his description of Regulus's death, if any, is lost. He picks up with Regulus's wife (24.12). "Taking the end of her husband hard, and believing he had departed this life on account of neglect," she took two Carthaginian prisoners of war and had her sons torture them. They were kept in a space so small they could barely both fit into it; when one died, the other was left there with his corpse. The household slaves told the authorities and there was a public scandal.

This story, so resonant in the year of Abu Ghraib, is further complicated by the long afterlife of the Regulus tale. It shows up again in Kipling, in one of the lesser-known chapters of *Stalky & Co.* King, the Latin teacher, figures prominently in these boarding-school stories, and it is a basic part of the context that the boys are being trained in preparation for entrance into the army. The whole point of the story "Regulus" (Kipling 1929) is that learning Latin endows the boys with a fundamental code of ethics that they will need in fighting for the British Empire. This being so, then, we should note that King, in explaining Regulus's state of mind as he left the Senate house, says Regulus knew Carthage "was a sort of God-forsaken nigger Manchester." In reading Latin texts, then, we must cope not only with what they meant in their own time, but how they have been recycled through two thousand years of wars and empires.

So this is the magic erasable race joke of Plautus's *Poenulus,* and it forces the reader and/or director to think a lot not only about Roman history but about current events—at any time. This play could be produced in the aftermath of any major military engagement, with the names and nationalities adjusted. What would it mean? W. V. Harris, writing in the *Cambridge Ancient History* on the extreme hostility to Carthage in the years leading up to the Third (and Last) Punic War, remarks: "The Carthaginians were cruel and above all untrustworthy, according to the clichés which go back at least to Ennius and probably much further. But in the years 201–150 the Roman attitude toward the Carthaginians was not simply one of blind detestation, as Plautus's *Poenulus,* probably produced in the 190s, demonstrates" (154; see full reference in Bibliography sub fin.). Saddam Hussein in *South Park* is not a positive character, the jokes about him are not friendly; are the Punic jokes in *Poenulus* friendly jokes? Is there such a thing?

In *Poenulus,* race/ethnicity is a costume that can be put on and taken off; the girl puts on Punicity and leaves behind poverty, prostitution, and low class, and with her similarly metamorphosed Prince Charming will learn the attributes of an imaginary upper class. Where would Plautus and his troupe of (possibly) slave actors stand in relation to the fantasy they were enacting? How about their audience, which would have included slaves, citizen men and women, and (maybe) proprietors of Carthaginian, Aetolian, Acarnanian, Illyrian, and Spartan takeout restaurants? How were audience and actors related to the uprisings of slaves and Carthaginian prisoners of war in the 190s? When Igor/Milphio says (lines 965–66), "Y'know it's a sin to let your fellow citizens / be slaves, right in your face, when they were free at home," is this a manifesto? Does this play connect with Cherry's big scene in *Iran Man?* With Wanda's comments on freedom in *Weevil?*

POINTS OF INTEREST IN THE PLAY

Uncle Hanno among the Whores

An odd but marked detail in the prologue is the description of the good uncle hitting every port city in the Mediterranean, going straight to the first brothel, and renting girls by the night so that he can cross-question them (lines 106–10). This same plot element is a main feature of two very popular late-ancient stories: the novel *Apollonius, King of Tyre,* and the *Life* of St. Mary the Harlot, which was also made into a play at least once—in the tenth century C.E., by the German nun Hrotsvitha. As in *Towelheads,* these stories dwell on the logical outcome, a sort of striptease in which the uncle finds out the truth in the nick of time (in *Towelheads,* it's only the girls who, at least at first, believe that Saddam/Hanno is a customer; and he colludes in letting them believe it). This story must have been a basic type in ancient Mediterranean popular culture; there is a Jewish version featuring Rabbi Meir and the sister of his famous wife, Beruria, who was captured by the Romans and put in a brothel in Rome (Boyarin 1993: 190). Here the story definitely works to subvert the ostensible piety of Hanno, and emphasizes the whorishness of the two girls. The girls, as well as Hanno, have been read by some as virtuous, particularly Tchotchka/Adelphasium, because of her speeches in act 1; this translation takes these speeches to be comic.

The Wild Boar Chase

Plautus loves to work on multiple levels; a lot of his jokes are too complicated to translate fully. The myth of Meleager and the hunt for the Calydonian boar seems to circulate around in this play in all sorts of ways: why? Just an extra for the myth lovers in the audience? When Boris is recognized at the end of the play by means of the scar of a monkey bite, this is a mock-epic version of the recognition of Odysseus in the *Odyssey* by means of the scar made during his rite-de-passage *boar* hunt. There are frequent mentions of the setting of the play on an Aphrodisia, which would have been pronounced "Aprodisia"—*aper* is the word for "wild boar." Meleager's basic problem, in the myth, is with his uncles. And so on (see John Henderson 1999).

The Location of the Play's Performance

As seen in *Weevil,* the plays may have been performed in the Forum Romanum, on the occasion of major religious festivals which were supposed to benefit the state in wartime; the whole idea of having a drama festival at Rome was tied in with this religious function. In *Weevil,* a Forum setting would obviously have given special point to the Director's travelogue. John Henderson (1999) suggests that for *Poenulus* the presence nearby of the first Temple of Venus Erycina, dedicated in 215 B.C.E. during a low point in the Second Punic War, would have given point to the bits about the Aphrodisia. The idea is that the temple, up on the Capitol, would have been visible to the spectators. Thinking about it as a war monument and reminder of yet another theater of war (this Venus was lifted from Eryx in Sicily as a deliberate cultural appropriation, a favorite Roman technique) adds yet another current-events dimension to this play.

The "William Tell *Overture" Effect*

Commentators, most pertinently John Henderson (1999) and James Tatum, remark on the lengthiness of the play, as occasioned by the endless scenes of greeting and goodbye—it takes everyone forever to get off the stage—and by redundancies large and small, especially in the final recognition scene. It's not as if this joke is unique to *Towelheads*—compare the clinch in act 1 of *Weevil*—but *Towelheads* is in fact almost twice as long as *Weevil,* and these repetitions are part of the reason why. Henderson and Tatum both argue that this element is intentional and funny.

But many of the repetitions have struck editors over the years as things that need to be cut, and probably as leftovers from merged multiple versions of the play. Lindsay in the Oxford text printed a lot of these lines but bracketed them. In order to stick with the Oxford continuous line numbering, and because at least some of the bracketed lines are of interest, I have translated almost all of them here. These lines appear in square brackets; as in the other plays, passages in curved brackets {} are additions I have made.

The Play's Ending

Beyond redundancy lies the problem of the play's ending. *Poenulus,* as now printed in the Oxford text, has a double ending (really more of a shredded set of endings), which attests to the changes to the script that must have taken place over the millennia, possibly going back to an original rehearsal script. If all of them are kept, the result is like Brian Eno's deconstruction of the Pachelbel canon—surreal. Any current director should certainly take whatever seems most useful from the options available here; many previous directors obviously did just that, probably adding improvements of their own.

METER AND MUSIC

Meter is treated more loosely in this translation than in *Iran Man;* the iambic senarii are often translated into iambic pentameter, and the long lines are somewhat flexibly iambic or trochaic. But the translation is still line-for-line, though less strictly word-for-word than in either *Weevil* or *Iran Man.* There are two big songs: the girls' song in act 1 is in bacchiacs in the original, which is the same as the striptease beat—ba BOOM BOOM, ba BOOM BOOM—and it is done here to the tune of "My Heart Belongs to Daddy," which has a similar beat. The girls' song in act 5 is in anapests in the original, known as "marching anapests" from their common use in marching numbers in ancient drama, and the song is here accordingly done to the tune of "When the Saints Go Marching In." I have also put in three other very short songs (255–56, 359–63, 1199–1200), only the first of which is sung in the original; the other two will have to compensate for a few short sung sections here translated as spoken.

READINGS

Highly recommended: Franko 1994 on the use of the word *Poenus* in connection with ethnic slurs; John Henderson 1999 on the social and historical context of the play; Slater 1992 on the prologue. See now in general Baier 2004, especially the essays by Stefan Faller on the Punic aspects of the play, Elaine Fantham on the girls, and Niall Slater on Syncerastus and slave subjectivity. Maurach's commentary (1988), the only full commentary on this long and difficult play, often suffers from literal-mindedness and lack of a sense of humor.

THE SETTING, THE NAMES, AND THE CAST

The setting had to have a double resonance—one of forests and boar hunting and epic poetry, and another of recent and ongoing wars. So I set the play in Sarajevo, thinking of the happy Winter Olympics that preceded the grim siege (see volume introduction under "Location" on the shelf life of this transposition). But again, because this is Plautus, the play is also set *here*—wherever "here" is.

Except for "Hanno" and "Giddenis," all the original names in *Poenulus* are Greek. Since I was transposing Aetolia onto the former Yugoslavia, I also transposed all the Greek names as Slavic names—none specifically Yugoslavian, but then none of the Greek names are specifically Aetolian. This turned out to be a useful exercise, since, come to think of it, there is a rich tradition of comic Slavic names in English. However, just as the plays are in Latin, not Greek, the language of the translation is colloquial English without any Slavicisms, other than in a few Greek-based jokes.

The play constantly repeats the sum of money involved in the plot to trick the pimp, "three hundred gold Philips"; it must be a running joke somehow. The "gold Philip" was a famous coinage of Philip II of Macedon, whose descendant, Philip V, was a serious enemy of Rome during this period. The Aetolians made the bad mistake of siding with him against Rome. I made the coins into "gold rubles," a nonexistent coinage, but one that fits with the Slavic setting and sounds somewhat comic in English, though the king joke is lost.

BORIS, A YOUNG GENTLEMAN

Agorastocles is the leading young man, wealthy, on his own, and endearingly klutzy. His name literally means something like "Pride of the Agora," and sounds upper class; "Basil" or "Cyril" would do as well, or take your pick. Boris's lines are here written for someone with an upper-class English accent; I had Hugh Grant in mind. Agorastocles also has a tendency to speak in quasi-tragic, hifalutin language, hence the occasional Shakespearian or pseudo-Shakespearian line for him here.

IGOR, HIS SLAVE

Milphio is a worrier; his voice sounded good to me as Woody Allen's. "Milphio" seems to mean "one who suffers from falling-out of the eyelashes" (no kidding), so a literal translation would be something like "Scummo" or "Schmutzo." The name is unique to this play; "Igor" here recalls the paradigmatic monster-movie servant. (It's also a bad bilingual pun.)

TCHOTCHKA AND KATYA, (WORKING) GIRLS

"Adelphasium" and "Anterastilis" are the kinds of flowery names that ancient prostitutes sometimes had, though at the end of the play it's clear that they're about to go through some whores' rite de passage where they would get their final whore names. The Latin dramatis personae labels them "girls," not "prostitutes." "Adelphasium" literally means something like "Little Sister," and "Anterastilis" means something like "She Loves Him, Too," or "Boyfriend Stealer." Hence "Tchotchka" ("knickknack") and "Katya" (sounds like "Caught-ya"). The female parts might have been played by *cinaedi,* like drag queens (see volume introduction under "Background on Roman Culture" and "Audience and Venue"); or not. But the girls' first duet reminded me of Marilyn Monroe and Jane Russell in *Gentlemen Prefer Blondes.* Their lines are written for comic-sultry falsetto voices; I was thinking of Ru-Paul for Tchotchka and someone less dignified for Katya—maybe Guy Pearce as in *The Adventures of Priscilla, Queen of the Desert* (1994).

THE WOLF, A PIMP

"Lycus" is a Latin transliteration of the Greek word for "wolf"; compare Mr. Wolf/Lyco the banker in *Weevil.* But this Lycus is somewhat dumb, and all pimps are despicable in Roman ideology. Rick Moranis would be good in the role, or Danny DeVito, but I imagined the Wolf's lines here as spoken by Arnold Schwarzenegger, especially bearing in mind the pimp's threats to take on Venus in his opening speech.

GENERAL POPOFF, A SOLDIER

This is a small exemplar of the "swaggering soldier" stock role, made for John Cleese, and the lines here are written as if spoken with his pukka-sahib English accent. "Antamonides" literally means something like "Son of Defender." Compare Lt. Napoleon Plaza-Toro in *Weevil.*

LAWYERS (CHORUS)

The Lawyers in the play are peculiarly Roman. Roman law is often described as "self-help." If you want to take somebody to court, you go out and get witnesses, and they all go to court with you and participate in your case; it's all over very fast. The witnesses have to be citizens. Boris overdoes it and brings back *advocati,* legal counselors: in general, men who assisted a litigant; here, more like cheap lawyers. The ones in this play are explicitly freed slaves (519), and they complain that Boris thinks they're low class; he certainly shows no signs of paying them, and treats their help as a favor, as if they were his friends (not really). Since they're not so bright, I've imagined Keanu Reeves as their spokesman and written lines thinking of him, as in *Bill and Ted's Excellent Adventure* (1989). But the Lawyers may have taken turns, or spoken together; this is a rare example of a chorus in a Roman comedy. On law in Roman comedy—an issue in all three plays in this volume—see Scafuro 1997.

BLINI, BORIS'S FARM MANAGER

Collybiscus is Agorastocles' *vilicus*—his farm manager and slave overseer. He would be a slave himself, a middleman between the master and the brutalized farm workers who would have had no hope of manumission; the role of the *vilicus* is memorably described by Plautus's contemporary the elder Cato in his *De Agricultura* (see Shaw 2001: 33–40). I have translated *vilicus* throughout as "overseer," to foreground its suggestion of collusion, though it also strongly connotes the country. Collybiscus would usually spend his time on the country estate—that's why nobody knows him. A *vilicus* is responsible and earnest and chosen for loyalty to the master; in the play, Collybiscus gets dressed up as a mercenary, a thrill for him. I imagined Philip Seymour Hoffman as in his role in *The Big Lebowski.* "Collybiscus" literally means something like "Small Change," or else "A Very Small Round Cake" (*blini* are little pancakes). In a non-Slavic translation, it would be hard to choose among many possibilities for his name: Mr. Muffin, Brownie, Macaroon, Nutball, Shortbread, Cupcake, Twinkie, Biscuit (even sounds like "Collybiscus") . . .

VODKA, THE WOLF'S SLAVE

This is a small but hyper part; I imagined it with Jack Black. "Syncerastus" literally means "Mixed-up-in," as in "In Cahoots." Or, probably, "Mixed," as in "Mixed Drink." Slivovitz, Martini, Cocktail, Jello Shot, Shaken . . .

SADDAM, AN ARAB

Eddie Murphy, as in his "African exchange student" bit in *Trading Places,* would make an ideal Saddam, and his lines here are written for the peculiar accent Murphy uses in that film. Saddam has to be a stage Carthaginian, as opposed to an authentic one. Plautine comedy is not the home of realism. For the name Hanno, see the introductory section above.

YASMIN, A NANNY

Terry Jones, one of the members of the Monty Python group, makes a wonderful older lady (cf. *Monty Python's The Meaning of Life*); Yasmin's lines here are written for a cracked Cockney falsetto. Divine, as in *Hairspray,* would have been good, too. The name "Giddenis" is Carthaginian, here rendered as "Yasmin" with thoughts of Jasmine, the heroine of the Disney cartoon *Aladdin.*

BOY

A fifteen-year-old boy suitable for playing Yasmin's long-lost son.

THE MAID

The *ancilla* has only one line, but it's a good one. The role would make a good cameo for a great character actress, like Mary Wickes, who played the comic nurse in *The Man Who Came to Dinner* (1941) and *Now, Voyager* (1942). Again, though, she would originally have been played by a male actor; Divine would be good.

With this play I found it helpful to think of real male actors in all the roles. Gender is performed here, that's the whole point; and so is race, or ethnicity. I imagined the only free and elite citizens in the play, Boris and General Popoff, as played by English actors, and all the slaves and lower-class people as played by Americans.

CAST OF CHARACTERS

Boris, a young gentleman	[Agorastocles, a young man]
Igor, his slave	[Milphio, a slave]
Tchotchka, a girl	[Adelphasium, a girl]
Katya, a girl	[Anterastilis, a girl]
the Wolf, a pimp	[Lycus, a pimp]
General Popoff	[Antamonides, a soldier]
Lawyers	[Advocati]
Blini, a farm overseer	[Collybiscus, a farm overseer]
Vodka, a slave	[Syncerastus, a slave]
Saddam, an Arab	[Hanno, a Carthaginian]
Yasmin, a nanny	[Giddenis, a nanny]
Boy	[Boy]
the Maid	[Slave woman]

A nonspeaking Announcer may be needed in the prologue, but is not in the OCT Cast of Characters.

Scene

Sarajevo [Calydon]
There are two houses side by side. One belongs to Boris, the other to the Wolf, a pimp. Exit stage L leads to the forum; exit stage R, to the harbor.

Songs

There are two long songs and several short ones in *Towelheads;* they appear in the body of the play set up as songs in English. A nonmetrical translation appears after the end of the play.

PROLOGUE

The actor who plays IGOR *is onstage, out of character, and speaks the prologue.* The scene is set for the play. A nonspeaking announcer may be planted in the audience.*

[IGOR:] *Boris Godunov,* by Pushkin*—I'd like to start

      the rehearsal—   iambic senarii

yeah, that's how I'd like to begin, in the words of that great tragedy:

"Silence! Silence! He speaks. Hush, hush! Give ear!

Such is the decree of thy Tsar"—OK, of thy drama nazi,*

thou should sit in thy seats and keep thy chin up,   5

whether you've come here starving or with a full belly.

If you ate, you were a lot smarter;

if you didn't eat, you'll have to fill up on corny jokes.*

And if you could've eaten, and came here instead,

you're full of it altogether, to sit on an empty stomach.   10

(Psst! Announcer!) "In every district send edicts"*—to hear ye!

(ANNOUNCER *begins trying to announce, but is repeatedly cut off by speaker.*)

I've been wondering if you knew how to do your job;

use your voice—you do make your living off your mouth.

Yeah, if you don't open your mouth, you're gonna starve.

—OK, siddown now, and you'll get a bonus. (ANNOUNCER *vanishes.*)   15

By the power vested in me—"Change not procedure!"*

No overage toyboys* sitting on the stage;

no cops walkie-talking—or their rods*—

no ushers wandering in front of people

or showing seats, while there's an actor on stage.   20

People who slept late at home, when they could,

have to stand now—no complaints—or refrain from sleeping.

Slaves, no hogging the seats, make room for the free,

or shell out for your freedom—and if you can't do it,

better go home, and save yourself double trouble: 25

so they don't stripe you with rods here and straps at home

if your master gets home and finds your work ain't done.

And, nursing mothers*—could I ask you to care for your babies at home,

the little munchkins,* and don't bring 'em to watch,

so you don't go dry, and the kids don't die of hunger,   30

or even worse, get hungry and bleat like goats here.

And ladies—could we ask you to watch in SILENCE, laugh in SILENCE,
and refrain from ringing those lovely bell-like voices,
and take your delicious dishy gossip HOME,
and don't be a pain to your husbands here like you are at home.   35
And as for the members of the Academy:*
let no Oscar* be given to any player unfairly;
don't let 'em be shoved out the door because of "who you know,"
so some no-talent bum gets in before somebody really good.
Oh, that reminds me, I almost forgot: 40
while the show is on, limo drivers!*
Now's the time to blitz the bars, OK? Now's your chance,
now, while those nachos* are hot from the oven—charge!
So, OK, these be the commands of the imperial drama nazi,*
by the power damn vested in me, and you better remember it.   45
But it's about time that I deported myself
back to the pitch for the play, so you can get savvy* like me.
I'm gonna map out the state lines, the frontiers, the border zones,
'cause I'm the border patrol man* around here.
But if you don't mind, I'd like to tell you the name   50
of ye olde comedy; hate it? I'm still gonna tell you,
since the guys in the front office* said I could.
This play was called in Greek "The Man from Baghdad,"*
or in Latin "The Uncle," by Plautus de Cornpone-Jones.*
{But the title page says "Poenulus," and our translator
tells us that translates as "Towelheads." Well, we'll see.}
OK, now you got the name! Now here's the rest   55
of my account*—this plot line's gonna get audited here
—which means this stage must be the audit-orium,
and you're the IRS!* Please, pay attention.
There once were two guys from Baghdad. . . . *
Their fathers were brothers, and loaded, a classy family.   60
Of these two, one is living, the other has passed away.
And I happen to know I got my facts straight here
'cause the undertaker told me, the same one who undertook him.
But the old guy who's now dead—this guy's son—
the only one he has, gets snatched away   65
from his stately home, from his dad, and from Baghdad
as a boy of seven, six years before his dad dies.*

Since he sees his only son is lost to him,
the dad gets very sick from so much grief
and he makes his cousin* be his only heir, 70
so he goes to paradise without travelers checks {he left home without 'em}.*
The guy who snatched the kid takes him to Sarajevo,*
and sells him here to a certain rich old man,
who wanted children, and couldn't stand women. {Hmm.}
Little does the old guy know it, but he's bought the son of an old friend! 75
And he adopts him as his son, this boy,
and makes him his heir, when he himself kicks off.
And this young man lives there, in that house. *(Points.)*
OK, meanwhile back in Baghdad, our story continues. . . .
I'm heading back, if you want to send a message; 80
cash only, please, otherwise fageddaboudit.
And if you pay me the cash, also you can fageddaboudit.
But remember the old guy in Baghdad who's still alive?
That's this kid's uncle? He had two little girls,
one five years old, the other only four. 85
With their nanny, they disappear one day from the Casbah.*
The guy who takes *them,* brings them to Belgrade,*
and sells 'em all, the nanny and the young ladies,*
for cash on the barrel, to a man—if a pimp is a man—
the damnedest guy* the world has ever seen. 90
OK, you figure it out yourself, you take a guess,
what kind of a man he is, when he's called "the Wolf."
This pimp then moves from his old place in Belgrade,
and just recently winds up also here in Sarajevo,
on business. And he lives in *that* house *there. (Points.)* 95
The young man is desperately dying for one of the girls,
his own cousin! But he don't know who she is,
in fact he's never touched her, that's how the pimp soaks him,
and he hasn't even now had sex with her,
or ever rented her out—while the pimp won't let her go. 100
He can tell the kid loves her and he wants to jack up the price.*
The younger girl some soldier wants to buy
to be his sex-toy —seems he's crazy about her.
But the Arab*—the girls' dad—after he loses them,
he looks for them everywhere, on land and sea. 105

And whenever he gets into a new town, on the spot
he looks up all the hookers, wherever they hang out;
he pays his money, he rents by the night, he asks 'er then*
where she's from, what country, was she caught or kidnapped,
what's her family, and who her parents were.*   110
And so ingeniously he seeks his daughters.
And he knows every language, but he pretends
he don't. He's an Arab, he's sneaky—what's to tell?*
This guy's ship just docked here yesterday evening,
the father of these two girls; and he's also this young man's uncle.   115
Are you with me on this? If you got it, pull—
but don't break it*—please—let me get through.
Whoops, I almost forgot to tell you the rest.
That guy who adopted this guy as his son,
he was an old friend of this guy's Arab uncle,   120
[who'll come here today and find his daughters,
and this son of his brother, as I happen to know.
OK, gotta go get dressed.* So follow along, you got it.]
This guy who's coming here today will find his daughters
and this son of his brother. OK, bye now, sit tight,   125
I'm going—now I want to turn into somebody else.
What's upcoming, there's folks coming up to show you.
Goodbye, gimme a hand, you should live and be well. . . .
*(Exit [*IGOR*] into Boris's house.)*

ACT 1

SCENE 1: BORIS *and* IGOR
Enter BORIS *and* IGOR *from Boris's house.*

BORIS: I've often entrusted lots of things to you, Igor,   iambic senarii
risky business, losers, pathetic no-hopers,   130
and you always turn 'em around, brilliantly, cleverly,
sensibly, shrewdly, and make 'em prizewinners by your wiles.
And for these good deeds, I confess, should be owed to you
your liberty and many thankful thanks.
IGOR: There's a wise old saying that might be apropos.   135
This sweet-talking you do—like they say, for me

it's phony baloney, a lotta pastafazool.*
Now you're all sweetsy-weetsy*—yesterday you wore out
at least three belts on my back—genuine leather.
BORIS: I'm in love, Igor, and if I did anything for love   140
you have to forgive me, it's only fair. IGOR: Absolutely!
Whoops, now I'm dying of love. Allow me to flog you,
like you did it to me, for no good reason;
and afterwards you can forgive me 'cause I'm in love.
BORIS: If it gives you pleasure, if you feel like it, go ahead—   145
hang me up, chain me, beat me—I authorize you.
IGOR: Yeah, and if you skip out on* your authoring
when you're let loose, I'm the one who's gonna hang.
BORIS: Would I dare to do that, especially to you?
Why, if I see you getting hit, I feel your pain!   150
IGOR: My pain, God, really. BORIS: No, mine. IGOR: OK by me!
All right, whaddaya want? BORIS: Why should I lie to you?
I'm shamelessly in love. IGOR: I can tell by my shoulderblades.
BORIS: But I mean the girl next door, my only Tchotchka,
our pimping neighbor's hooker—the slightly bigger* one.   155
IGOR: I heard you tell me enough times. BORIS: I'm in pieces,
from wanting her. But there's no dirt dirtier
than that pimp, the Wolf, the poor girl's master!
IGOR: Wanna give him something nasty now? BORIS: Oh, yess. IGOR:
          Give him me!
BORIS: Get out of here. IGOR: No, tell me seriously;   160
wanna be bad to him? BORIS: Yes! IGOR: Give him me again;
I'll see to it he'll have something nasty *and* bad.
BORIS: You're joking. IGOR: OK, you want to make her yours*
today, without paying a penny? BORIS: I do, Igor.
IGOR: I'll fix it so you fix it. Don't you have on hand   165
three hundred golden rubles?* BORIS: And another six hundred.
IGOR: Three hundred's plenty. BORIS: What do you want with it? IGOR: Shush.
I'm gonna give you the pimp and his whole *mishpocheh**
today as a gift. BORIS: How'll you do it? IGOR: Wait, you'll see.
That guy Blini's in town now, who runs your country place.*   170
The pimp hasn't met him yet. You get it now?
BORIS: God, I get it, but I don't know where you're going with it.
IGOR: You don't? BORIS: God, no. IGOR: OK, I'll explain it to you.

You're gonna give him the money, and he'll take it to the pimp
and he'll say he's a foreigner in from some other town: 175
he's lookin' for love and a chance to treat himself right
and he wants to find a nice place, no questions asked,*
where he can get nasty and nobody's the wiser.
The pimp, who's crazy for money, will take him right inside:
he'll hide the man and the money. BORIS: I like your plan! 180
IGOR: Then you ask him if your slave is at his house.
He'll think you're looking for me; so naturally he'll
say no; and bam! right there—would you believe it?—
the pimp owes you twice—the money and the cost of the slave.*
And he don't have the dough, either; when he gets to court 185
the judge is gonna make over his whole *mishpocheh* to you*
and that's how we're gonna trap Mr. Wolf the pimp.
BORIS: Your plan—I like it! IGOR: Just wait 'til I gussy it up.
Then you'll like it even more; it's still kinda rough.
BORIS: I'm off to the temple of Venus, if there's nothing you want, Igor. 190
Festival of Love* today. IGOR: I know. BORIS: I want
to feast my eyes on those toothsome little tarts.*
IGOR: Let's get started first on the plan we're working on.
Let's go inside, and find Blini the overseer
and teach him his lines, so he can pull off this caper. 195
BORIS: Though Cupid is doing a job on my heart, still
I'll hearken to you. (*Exit* BORIS *into his house.*) IGOR (*calling after him*): I'll see
            that you don't regret it.
(*To audience.*) This guy has got a stain of love in his heart
that ain't gonna be dry-cleaned without a big bill.*
That's how rotten a guy this pimp the Wolf is; 200
I got my grenade-launcher cocked and aimed right at the fool,
and I'm gonna fire pretty soon now from my bunker* here.
(*Enter* TCHOTCHKA *and* KATYA *from the pimp's house.* THE MAID *is in attendance
            and carries a lot of appurtenances of the toilette—possibly including a
            bathtub, screen for dressing behind, towels, costumes, the whole nine
            yards of the standard getting-dressed-on-stage routine. Equipment might
            also come with a couple of guys with muscles to carry the heavy stuff and
            flex at the appropriate line in Tchotchka's song.*)
—But look, here comes Tchotchka, along with Katya.
It's the first girl who's driving my master crazy.

But I'll call him out.—Hey, come on out, Boris,
if you wanna see some gorgeous spectacles.*
(Enter BORIS *from his house.)*
BORIS: Where's the riot, then, Igor? IGOR: Look, it's your sweetie,
if you want a front-row seat.* BORIS: God shed his grace on thee*
for granting me the sight of so pretty a show!*

SCENE 2: TCHOTCHKA, KATYA, MAID, IGOR, *and* BORIS
The scene opens with a duet by TCHOTCHKA *and* KATYA, *to the tune of* "My Heart Belongs to Daddy," *sung à la Marilyn Monroe, but like* "I Wanna Be Loved by You" *in* Some Like It Hot *rather than like her rendition of* "Daddy" *in* Let's Make Love. *Accompaniment: sax and drum set, striptease beat.*

TCHOTCHKA: A ship at sea,   210
a girl like me—
you better get out on the double!
To rig 'em out
will wear you right out,
'cause a girl like me is trouble.   215

In our boudoir,
with paint and jar,
we work hard at every bubble.
We rub and scrub
for hours in the tub,   220
'cause a girl like me is trouble.

Yes, a girl like me is trouble,
each girl takes two maids just to scrub.
Yes, a girl like me is trouble—
we wore out two guys filling the tub. *(Guys flex.)*
We'll reduce your town to rubble,
from Manhattan to the North Pole,*   227
'cause two girls are double trouble;
we just have no self-control.   230

KATYA *(spoken):* In my opinion, no matter how much she's washed,   232
unless she's well dressed, it's just like she's still a dirty girl!*

(sung) What do I hear,
my sister dear—
though you are so witty and clever?
Our form is art,   235
but it's just a start,
'cause we still can't find a lover.

TCHOTCHKA: Though your advice
may well be nice,
just think and you'll quickly discover
that vile excess
gets you in a mess
when you want to find a lover.

KATYA: And we want to find a lover!
Sister dear, think outside the box—   240
we may want to find a lover,
but we can't if we smell like a lox.*   241
So just let me tell you, brother—
one more word, and then we must dash;
what we need to find a lover
is a rub-a-dub-dub and some cash.

IGOR: That one's a chefette,* Boris, it sounds like: 248
she knows how to soak a herring. BORIS: Must you annoy me?
TCHOTCHKA: Sister dear, give it a rest, puh-leeze; it's bad enough   250
when other folks say it to us, we don't have to give away our dirty secrets
            ourselves.
KATYA: Mum's the word. TCHOTCHKA: Thanks a lot. But now
tell me this: 252a
do we have everything
we should have in order to please the goddess of love? KATYA: I took care of
            everything.
TCHOTCHKA *(sung):* Oh what a beautiful morning, oh what a beautiful day, 255
just right for the goddess of loving, it's Aphrodisia today!
IGOR: Wanna give me a little something 'cause I got you out here?
Something truly fitting as a gift for me, maybe
a case of brandy, perhaps? Promise me? No answer?

(To audience.) Looks like his tongue's too busy hanging out.   260

Why are you standing here like a dummy, you dope? BORIS: Let me love in

       peace, shut up.   trochaic septenarii

IGOR: I'm shutting up. BORIS: If you'd shut up, you couldn't have said, "I'm

       shutting up."

KATYA: Let's go, sister dear. TCHOTCHKA: Whoa, please. Why are you hurrying?

       KATYA: You've gotta ask?

Because our boss awaits at the temple of Venus. TCHOTCHKA: Let him wait then,

       heavens! Wait up.

Now there'll be a crowd at the altar. Or do you want to be pushed around   265

with those streetwalkers? Chain gang girlfriends! Rejects from the

       county farm!*

Poor little dirty groupies of slaves, smeared and stinking with eau de

       camel*—

girls who reek of cheap hotel rooms, and streetcorners, and public toilets!*

Girls no free man ever touched at all, never mind took home with him,

dirty little no-good slave boys' two-dollar cash-on-the-barrel sluts!   270

IGOR: Drop dead, you actually dare to turn up your nose at slaves, you

       shameless thing?

Oh, like she's so beautiful, like millionaires* like to rent her out—

monster woman! She's putting out a lot of big talk for such a piece of nothing,

but I wouldn't give a plugged nickel* for seven nights with her.

BORIS: Great God almighty, what hast Thou to show   275

more fair? and why be you more god than I

who see such graces with my mortal eyes? Venus is not Venus,

for I worship this Venus, oh, may she side with me and love me back.

Igor, hey, Igor, where are you? IGOR: Surely I'm here. BORIS: I see you, and

       don't call me Shirley.*

IGOR: Jokes you're making now, huh, boss. BORIS: You taught me

       everything I know.*   280

IGOR: Oh, like I taught you to love a girl you've never touched? BORIS: Oh,

       that's nothing;

I love God, too, by Jove, and fear him, and I keep my hands off *him*.*

KATYA: Heavens to Betsy, when I look at both our outfits, I'm embarrassed

at how we're dressed.* TCHOTCHKA: No, really and truly, honest to goodness, it's

       good enough.

We're well enough dressed for what we make, and our owner, too,   285

'cause you can't make a living without you got a few expenses, this I know,

though you can't live on nothing if expense is all you got, sister.
So "enough" is more than enough—enough to live on—more than enough
        <for me>.*
BORIS: Igor, God love me, but I would rather have her love me than God.
That woman could make solid rock* fall in love with her.   290
IGOR: Well, you tell no lie, because you're dumber than a rock
for loving her. BORIS: Bear it in mind, I've never blotted my
        escutcheon with her.*
IGOR: Then I'll go right down to the sewage treatment plant* and get
        some schmutz.
BORIS: And the point would be? IGOR: I'll tell you: so I can blot both your
        eschmutcheons.*
BORIS: Bugger off.* IGOR: I already have. BORIS: Loser.* IGOR: No comment.
        BORIS: I wish *that* were true.   295
IGOR: There you go again, being funny, needling me. You're doing my job.*
KATYA: I bet you think you look swell now, sister, all dressed up,
but when you see the other hookers and do a little comparison,
you'll have a heart attack,* if you happen to see a girl who's better dressed.
TCHOTCHKA: I was born without a jealous bone in my body, sister dear.   300
I'd rather that I was decked out in good character than in diamonds,*
'cause diamonds are found by accident but good character comes
        from within.
I'd much rather be talked about for being good than being rich.
A working girl looks much better dressed in modesty than in mink;*
why, a working girl looks better dressed in modesty than in diamonds!   305
Ugly behavior messes up a pretty dress worse than mud;
nice behavior makes up for an ugly dress any day.
BORIS: Hey, you! D'you want to do something pretty splendid? IGOR: Sure I do.
BORIS: Can you hear me? IGOR: Yes I can. BORIS: Go right home and
        hang yourself.
IGOR: What for? BORIS: 'Cause never again will you hear so many
        words so sweet.   310
What do you need to live for? Listen to me, just hang yourself.
IGOR: OK, if you're gonna be there with me hanging like a bunch of bananas.*
BORIS: But I love her. IGOR: But I love to eat and drink. TCHOTCHKA: Hey,
        lookit! KATYA: What do you want?
TCHOTCHKA: Can you see? My eyes were full of schmutz, now am I
        nice and shiny?

KATYA: No, I think there's still a little dirt in the middle of your eye.

    TCHOTCHKA *(to* MAID*):** Gimme a hand. 315

BORIS: *You* handle *her* eyes with your grubby hands? *You* rub them?

KATYA: We've been awfully lazy today. TCHOTCHKA: About what, if I may ask?

KATYA: 'Cause we didn't get down to the temple of Venus long before daylight

to be the first ones there to start the fire. TCHOTCHKA: Uh-uh, we don't need to.

It's girls whose faces won't stand the light* who have to go and pray*

    at night; 320

before Venus is out of bed, they're racing off devotedly

to make their offerings. If they showed up when Venus was awake,

they're so ugly, I think they'd scare Venus herself right out of the temple.

BORIS: Igor. IGOR: God, alas, poor Igor! And what is it that you want now?

BORIS: I ask you—good Lord—her words—they're like shandy!* IGOR: No, like briquettes,* 325

with sugar and spice and everything nice, whole wheat and chopped

    nuts on top.

BORIS: Isn't she something? The girl I love? IGOR: Something expensive, your

    broker won't love it.*

BORIS: But, dammit, it's not right for a lover to love the bottom line.

KATYA: Let's go, dear sibling. TCHOTCHKA: So go, if you want. KATYA: Follow

    me. TCHOTCHKA: I'm following!

IGOR: They're going. BORIS: Should we go up? IGOR: So go. BORIS *(to*

    TCHOTCHKA*):* Big hullo #1 to you, first prize, 330

(to KATYA*)* and a little hullo #2 to you, second prize; *(to* MAID*)* and hullo #3

to you, no prizes. MAID: Goodness! And here I stayed up all night getting ready.*

BORIS: Where're you heading? TCHOTCHKA: I? To the temple of Venus. BORIS:

    Why? TCHOTCHKA: To get Venus on my side.

BORIS: Hey, could she be angry? God, she's on your side.* I'd put money on it.

What do you say . . . TCHOTCHKA: Why are you bothering me, if I may ask?

    BORIS: Mmm-mmm, so ferocious! 335

TCHOTCHKA: Let me go, please. BORIS: What's your hurry? It'll be crowded.

    TCHOTCHKA: I know.

It's full of other girls that I want to look at, and I want them to look at me.

BORIS: But why do you want to look at ugly girls and give them something

    pretty to look at?

TCHOTCHKA: Because today at the temple of Venus they're having a close-out

    sale on sluts,*

and all the buyers will be there, and I want *me* to be on display. 340

BORIS: Hey, you only have to advertise merchandise nobody wants to buy;

good stuff finds a buyer all too soon, even if it's hidden away.
What do you say? When will you be at my place for a little touchy-feely?*
TCHOTCHKA: That would be when hell freezes over and the dead rise again.*
BORIS: Right there in my house, I've got, I dunno how much in cash that's
    going crazy . . . 345
TCHOTCHKA: Give it to me, I'll fix it up right now, I'll really make it
    go crazy.
IGOR: Jesus, she's a beauty. BORIS: Go directly to hell, do not pass go.*
IGOR: The more I look at her, the cheaper she's starting to look. And like
    stormy weather.
TCHOTCHKA: Let's wrap this up. I'm getting bored. BORIS: Oh, let me help you
    with your wrap.
TCHOTCHKA: Please! I'm in a state of grace! Take your hands off me, Boris! 350
BORIS: What should I do now? TCHOTCHKA: If you're smart, you can end your
    cares in a jiffy.
BORIS: What? You think I don't care for you? Help me, Igor! IGOR: (That's
    my ulcer.)
Whaddaya want? BORIS: Why is she angry with me? IGOR: Why is she angry
    with you?
Why should I care? Is caring about this stuff my job or your job?
BORIS: Now you're really dead, by God, unless you make her as sweet to me 355
as ever is the sea, when there the halcyon raises up her chicks.
IGOR: What should I do? BORIS: Beg her, wheedle her, feel her out. IGOR: I'll do
    that with care.
But look, don't wind up killing this messenger,* OK? BORIS: I wouldn't do that.
    (Cue music.)
TCHOTCHKA (song, to the tune of "I Can't Give You Anything but Love, Baby"):*
You don't treat me right, it's all just schemes, baby;
You'll give me the moon, but it's all dreams, baby. 360
You promised me I'd be free a hundred times;
I wait for you, you don't come through, and my other chances go by.
{Gee, I'd like to see me lookin' swell, baby;
Diamond bracelets Wal-Mart doesn't sell, baby;
So 'til you start to pay you know darn well, baby,}
We're through, and I'm still a slave of love.
(Turning.) Go on, sister. (To BORIS.) Just leave me alone. BORIS: I'm dead.
    Why don't you say something, Igor?
IGOR: Oh, my darling, oh, my treasure, oh, my life, oh, my pleasure,* 365
oh, my bunny, oh, my honey, my salvation, oh, my soul kiss,*

oh, my sugar, oh, my sweetheart, oh, my honeybee, oh, my cheesecake*—
BORIS: In my face—can I allow it? I'm in agony— poor me!
—if I don't put him in a taxi and have him torn limb from limb.*
IGOR: Don't, I beg of you, be angry with my boss on my account.   370
Just don't be angry, and I'll see to it that he gives a bejillion dollars* for you
and he'll make you a citizen of the USA,* and also free.
Why don't you let him go up to you? Why don't you like people
          who like you?
If he told some fibs before, he'll be a truthful boy for you from now on.
Let me beg you, let me grab your earlobes, let me give you a nice big
          soul kiss . . .   375
TCHOTCHKA: Get away from me, you're as big a phony as your master! IGOR:
          But do you know why?
Jesus, I'm gonna make him weepy,* if I don't get you on his side,
and I'm very afraid he'll make me punchy,* if I don't get you on his side;
I know what his temper's like when he gets in a grouchy mood.
So that's why; please, darling, let me talk you into this.   380
BORIS: I'm not worth a brass farthing,* if I don't eradicate
this bastard's* eyes and teeth for him. Hey, I'll show you "oh, my darling,"
I'll show you "sugar, sweetheart, honey, salvation, my soul kiss."
IGOR: Shame on you, boss! You're killing the messenger. BORIS: I'll do worse
          than that:
I'll add on "honey" and "bunny." And "tongue." IGOR: Will you get a grip   .
          on yourself?   385
BORIS: Is that the message I asked for? IGOR: What message did you want?
          BORIS: You have to ask?
OK, here's what you should have said, you sinner (to IGOR, and pointing at
          himself): His darling, if you don't mind;
oh, his sugar, oh, his sweetheart, oh, his honey, oh, his tongue,
his soul kiss, his treasure, his sweet salvation, his good time,
oh, his honeybee, oh, his cheese cupcake,* you bastard,*   390
[his sweetheart, his thrill,* his soul kiss, you bastard.]   390a
All those things you said were yours, that's what you should have said
          were mine.
IGOR: OK! Jesus! OK, I beg you, oh, his darling (and my doom),
oh, his boobacious babe (and oh, my bodacious bane),*
oh, his precious (oh, my pinkeye),* oh, his honey (my liverwurst),*
that you should not be angry with him, or, if that's not possible,   395

you should take a rope and hang yourself along with your boss and the
whole *mishpocheh.**
'Cause it looks like I'm gonna be eating through a straw* on account of you,
and I'm walking around with a back that's all bumpy like an oyster with
scabby sores*
because of your love for each other. TCHOTCHKA: Please, you're asking *me*—
I should stop him from flogging you? Can I make him stop lying to me?   400
KATYA: Just say something pleasant to him, please, so he won't be unpleasant
to *us,* OK? Look, he's holding us back from our business.
TCHOTCHKA: You're right. All right, I'll let this one offense go by for you, Boris.
I'm not angry. BORIS: You're not? TCHOTCHKA: I'm not. BORIS: Give me a kiss
so I believe you.
TCHOTCHKA: Later, I will, when I come back from temple. BORIS: Then go, do
please dash!   405
TCHOTCHKA: Follow me, sister. BORIS: And—hullo? Can you hear me?
TCHOTCHKA: Constantly. BORIS: Do give Venus
a great big hullo from me. TCHOTCHKA: I'll tell her. BORIS: And here's another
thing. TCHOTCHKA: Now what?
BORIS: Say your prayers as fast as possible. And—hullo? Give us a look! . . .
She looked at me. *(Calling after* TCHOTCHKA.*)* By George, I'm sure Venus will do
the same for you!
(Exeunt TCHOTCHKA, KATYA *stage L;* THE MAID *and the equipment go into the
pimp's house.)*

SCENE 3: BORIS *and* IGOR

BORIS: Well, Igor, what's the plotline now? IGOR: You flog me   iambic senarii   410
and call a realtor:* you can certainly
sell this house, Jesus, no problem for you.
BORIS: Why's that? IGOR: 'Cause you spend most of your time in my face.
BORIS: Just sit on that. IGOR: Well, what do you want now?
BORIS: I gave three hundred rubles to Blini—the farm overseer?—   415
a while ago, before you called me out here.
Now I beg you, Igor, by this right hand
and by its sister, left, and by your eyes
and by my love and by my beloved Tchotchka,
and by your liberty— IGOR: I.e., by nothing.   420
BORIS: Igorochka,* good, kind Igor, my salvation,

do what you promised you would do for me,
so I can waste this pimp. IGOR: Elementary, really.
Go, bring your witnesses; I'll be inside meanwhile
tricking out* your overseer with my best tricks   425
and training him in the art of the con.* So you get going.
BORIS: I'll run away now. IGOR: That's more my job than yours.*
BORIS: And, I, I, if you just do this for me— IGOR: Just go.
BORIS: If I don't this very day . . . IGOR: Just go! BORIS: . . . set you free . . .
IGOR: Just go. BORIS: I won't deserve . . . IGOR: Oy! BORIS: Hullo!
        IGOR: Just go!   430
BORIS: As much as all the souls in Hell— IGOR: Are you going yet?
BORIS: Nor all the water in the sea— IGOR: Will you go already?
BORIS: Nor all the clouds in the sky— IGOR: You're gonna keep going?
BORIS: Nor the stars in heaven— IGOR: You're gonna keep hurting my ears?
BORIS: Nor this nor that nor—really, I'm serious—   435
no—really, dammit—it hardly needs saying—why not?—
but just one word—you can say whatever you want,
but—no, Christ, I'm really serious, and you know why?
As God is my witness—want me to swear on the Bible?*—
what should be all right between us—so help me God—   440
you see what it looks like? Do you believe what I'm babbling?*
IGOR: If I can't make you leave, I'll leave myself;
Jesus, a speech like that—Sigmund Freud you'd need,
to analyze it—it's worse than the Oedipus complex.*
(Exit IGOR into Boris's house.)
BORIS: Exit Igor, angry. Now I have to be careful   445
not to throw my own spanner in the works of love.
I'll go get witnesses,* since love tells me
to let a slave command me, though I'm free.
(Exit BORIS stage L.)

ACT 2

SCENE 1: THE WOLF and GENERAL POPOFF
Enter THE WOLF from stage L.

WOLF: Goddamn any pimp who after this day   iambic senarii
ever slaughters a victim for Venus anywhere   450

or gives her so much as a grain of incense. Just today,
just my luck, I sacrificed six lambs—
but God* was mad at me, and I couldn't get
Venus on my side whatever I did.
So I can't get the holy OK.* I blew that joint,   455
I was mad at her, and told her, "No guts and no glory"*
[No, I didn't want to offer them, since the soothsayer   456a
said nothing good: the goddess didn't deserve it, I think.],   456b
and I slammed that greedy Venus right on the mat.*
Since she didn't want to be happy with what's enough,
I called it quits. That's just the kind of guy I am.
And I'm gonna fix God almighty,* too,   460
and make him* toe the line* and not be greedy,
when he* hears how the pimp slammed Venus on the mat.
And that two-bit* soothsayer, he was just as bad—
he said that all the guts predict for me
bad stuff, big losses, God* is mad at me.   465
Who made *him* the expert on heaven and earth?
Right after that I got handed a thousand in cash.—
But hey, what happened to that soldier, anyway,
who gave me the money? I told him "Let's do lunch."
Wait, here he comes. (*Enter* GENERAL POPOFF *from stage L.)* POPOFF: As I was
                starting to say,   470
friend pimp, about that battle in Cincostan,*
when I killed 60,000 flying men
in a single day, with my own bare hands . . .
WOLF: Flying men? POPOFF: Yes indeed, that's what I said.
WOLF: You mean to tell me there are men with wings?   475
POPOFF: There *were*. Unfortunately, I killed them all.
WOLF: How could you? POPOFF: I'll tell you.* I equipped my men with glue
and slingshots; they lined them with leaves from the sassafras tree.*
WOLF: What for? POPOFF: Of course, so the glue wouldn't stick to the slingshots.
WOLF: Keep going. (Damn, what a liar!) What happened next?   480
POPOFF: They proceeded to load their slings with major globs
of glue, and I ordered those flying men to be terminated with extreme prejudice.
Long story short—whichever ones they glue-gunned,
that was it: they fell to earth like kumquats.*   484–85
As each one fell, I killed him on the spot,

with a pinfeather through each skull, like killing doves.*

WOLF: Damn, if that ever happened, may God grant

that I always give* and never get the holy OK.

POPOFF: You don't believe me? WOLF: I believe you—the way you

should believe me. 490

Come on, let's go in. POPOFF: While they fire up the grill,*

let me tell you about one more battle. WOLF: I'm not stopping you.

POPOFF: Just listen. WOLF: Listen I won't, by God. POPOFF: Excuse me?

By God, I'll beat your head like a punching bag,*

unless you listen to me or go to the devil.* 495

WOLF: I'd rather go to the devil. POPOFF: Are you really sure?

WOLF: I'm sure. POPOFF: Oh. Then won't you, on this Feast of Love,

make over to me your tart, the slightly smaller one?

WOLF: The way things went for me at the temple today

I'm putting off business until some other day. 500

POPOFF: I'm under orders to treat all days alike.*

WOLF: Let's just go in. This way, follow me. POPOFF: Right-ho.

For today I am your soldier of fortune.*

(*Exeunt into the pimp's house.*)

ACT 3

SCENE 1: BORIS *and* CHORUS OF LAWYERS

Enter BORIS *from stage L;* LAWYERS *follow slowly.* LAWYERS *all have sunglasses in their pockets.*

BORIS: God love me, there's nothing more annoying than a

sluggish friend, trochaic septenarii

especially to a man in love—whatever he does, he's in a hurry. 505

Just like now: I'm bringing my lawyers, why must they slump like slugs,*

slower than garbage scows* on a windless sea.

And I truly went out of my way to avoid the senior partners—

I know they don't move that fast, I was afraid they'd slow me down.

Sad—I wound up anyway with the fondling fathers,* the flopfooted*

slowpokes, 510

—OK, if you're going to come today, let's go! (or go to hell.)*

Is this how a friend ought to go to the aid of a man in love?

This unusual pace of yours is as slow as picking cotton,*

or did you learn to walk this way when you were working on the
        chain gang?
LAWYERS: Hey, you, though we seem to you like poor blue-collar guys,   515
if you don't talk nice to us, Mr. Rich Noble Guy,
we know how to carve up a rich guy, no problemo, no fear.
We're not liable to you for what you like or what you hate;
when we paid for our freedom, we paid with our money, not yours;
we just gotta act like free men. We don't give a damn about you,   520
so don't think we're here as slaves bonded out* to your romance.
Free guys gotta stroll through the city, free guys gotta take it easy,
I think it's a slave-oid thing to run around like some nut {in a play}.*
Specially when the country's at peace and the enemy's terminated,*
there's no point in starting a riot. If you were in such a rush,   525
you should have brought us lawyers over here yesterday.
Don't hold your breath for one of us to go running through the
        streets today,
while people throw rocks at us because we look like looney tunes.*
BORIS: But if I'd said that I was taking you home to lunch,
you'd have run faster than a stag, you'd have a stride like a man on stilts.* 530
Now since I've named you my lawyers, and to serve as witnesses,
suddenly you've got flat feet,* and you're beating the snails in slowness.
LAWYERS: Well, and ain't that a good reason to run full speed ahead,
when you can drink and eat as much as you want, on him, until you're stuffed?
And you'll never have to pay back your host, who's footing the bill?   535
But still, with him or with whomsoever,* though we're just poor
        blue-collar guys,
we do have food at home to eat, so don't grind us down all hoity-toity.
And whatever little bit we have there, it's ours, not yours,
we got no beef with* nobody and nobody got no beef with us.
None of us is about to bust a gut* on account of you.   540
BORIS: I must say you're awfully touchy, I was only having a joke with you.
LAWYERS: OK fine, then please take what we said to you as a joke.
BORIS: Please, then—good Lord!—help me like speedboats, not like
        garbage scows—
at least get a wobble on—I can hardly ask you to get a move on.
LAWYERS: If you want to take it slow and mellow out, we can help you;   545
if you're in such a big rush, you better hire FedEx,* not a lawyer.
BORIS: You know the situation, I told you what I need you to do,

about this pimp? Who's made a mockery of my love for so long?
How we've made a plot against him involving some money and my slave?
LAWYERS: Oh, we know all that stuff already, if these folks in the
        audience know;   550
it's for these guys, after all, that this play is being put on.
You'd better explain it to them, so whenever you do it, they'll know what
        you're doing.
Don't pay any attention to us: we know the whole plot, because
we all learned it with you, so we could say our lines back to you.
BORIS: I can't argue with that. But do go on, so that I know you know it,   555
explain the plot, and tell me what I said to you a while ago.
LAWYERS: Really? Is this a test? You don't think we remember
how you gave three hundred rubles, cash, to Blini the overseer
for him to bring it over here to your nemesis, the pimp,
so he can pretend to be a foreigner from some other town somewhere?   560
And when he's brought it, you'll come here searching for your slave,
and also your money. BORIS: You remember it! Excellent memory! You've
        saved me.
LAWYERS: And he'll deny it, he'll think you're in search of Igor,
and that's good for a double fine.* You'll clean out the pimp.*
And you want us to witness this for you. BORIS: You've got my thing.   565
LAWYERS: Hardly, God, it's so teeny—just with our fingertips.*
BORIS: This has to get done fast, on the fly. Hurry, now, as much as you can.
LAWYERS: OK, then, goodbye. You better hire yourself some speedy lawyers;
slow ones, that's us. BORIS: You go very well, you just talk so damned badly.
Oh, if only your leg* would fall right on your toes—that's what I wish.   570
LAWYERS: But, jeeze, we wish your tongue would fall on your crotch,*
        and your eyes would fall on your shoe.
BORIS: Oy! It's hardly your place to be touchy when I was just having a joke.
LAWYERS: And it's not your place, man, to say mean things to your friends
        as a joke.
BORIS: Never mind all this. You know what I want. LAWYERS: Sure, we're
        righteously hip:*
ruin the pimp as a perjurer, that's what you're hot for. BORIS: You've got
        my thing.   575
Look! By an amazing coincidence here comes Igor with the overseer,
and he's one royally rigged-out hombre,* like a craftsman of the con.*

Enter IGOR *and* BLINI *from Boris's house.* BLINI *is dressed as a mercenary, sporting a lot of weapons and a black trenchcoat. But there might be a few wisps of hay still adhering to him.*

IGOR: Now you got the instructions by heart? BLINI: Absolutely. IGOR:

      Just stay hip.*   trochaic septenarii

BLINI: Don't need to tell me! Nope, hippo hide ain't gonna be hipper than me!*

IGOR: Make sure you got every word well rehearsed for our clever plot.   580

BLINI: Why, golly, I been better rehearsed than a tragic actor. Or a comedian!*

IGOR: You're one righteous dude. BORIS *(to* LAWYERS*):* Come on. *(To* IGOR.*)*

      Here's the witnesses. Look how many.*

IGOR: You couldn't have got men better suited for the job we have in hand.

Court's always in session for them—they're courthouse boys, straight, no chaser,*

they practically live in the courtroom, you could see 'em there more than

      the judge.   585

The guys who write the lawsuits aren't bigger legal finaglers* today

than these guys—if they got nobody they can sue, they're repo men.*

LAWYERS: You'll burn in hell. IGOR: You, too, God knows—with him or with

      whomsoever,

but you're doing a good, kind deed, when you help my boss in love.

But do these dudes all know the score? BORIS: Everything, they

      have it down.   590

IGOR: Then, everyone, please pay attention. I believe you know this pimp,

the Wolf? LAWYERS: For sure. BLINI: But, golly, I don't even know what he

      looks like.

You gotta show the man to me, OK? LAWYERS: We'll take care of it.

We've heard enough. BORIS: He's got the three hundred in gold, all counted out.

LAWYERS: So we really gotta take a look at this money of yours,* Boris,   595

so we'll know what we should say when we testify soon in court.

BLINI: Go on, take a look. LAWYERS: OK, audience, we'd like you to know this is

      definitely money—

funny money: in the decadent West* they soak this stuff and feed it to cows.*

But for the job we have to act like it's rubles—so that's what we're doing.

BLINI: But you also gotta act like I'm a foreigner. LAWYERS: Obviously,   600

and like you just got here today and met us and asked us, for sure,

to point you to a place where you could be free* and enjoy yourself,

where you could make love, and drink, and party like Eurotrash.* BLINI:
          Holy cow! Bad dudes!

BORIS: Well, I taught 'em. IGOR: And who taught you? BLINI: Go on, you guys
          better go in, Mr. Boris,

so the pimp doesn't see you all here with me and our clever plan   605

doesn't get all discombobulated. LAWYERS: Yes, the dude is rightly right,

do what he says. BORIS: OK, let's go. But you— LAWYERS: Nuff said! Get going!

BORIS: I'm going. LAWYERS: Excuse me, jeeze, why don't you go? BORIS: I'm

          going! *(Exit* BORIS *and* IGOR *into Boris's house.)* LAWYERS: Right!

(Creaky door sound.)

BLINI: Shh! Shut up! LAWYERS: What's up? BLINI: The doors of this house just
          did a terrible deed.

LAWYERS: What kind of deed is that? BLINI: They farted,* right out loud.

          LAWYERS: Well, God damn you!   610

Go on, get behind us. BLINI: Yes, sir. LAWYERS: We'll be going in front of you.

BLINI: (Yeah, that's what these city boys like to do: they like to put
          guys behind 'em.)*

LAWYERS: Look, that guy coming out there, he's the pimp. BLINI: Good casting!
          He looks evil.*

And now—that guy who's coming out?—gonna suck his blood by
          remote control.

SCENE 3: THE WOLF, LAWYERS, *and* BLINI
Enter THE WOLF *from his house.*

WOLF: OK, I'll be back soon, soldier: I want to get   iambic senarii   615
some guests to keep us company, good ol' boys;
meanwhile my people will set up the barbecue
and I think the women will be home from services soon.
But why's this crowd coming up the street? Bringing me something?
And this guy in the trenchcoat,* who's he? —Look, back there
          behind them.   620

LAWYERS: We citizens of the former Yugoslavia* wish you well, Mr. Wolf,
though actually good health is the last thing we wish we were bringing you,
and though we're not so pumped up about pimps, normally.   622a

WOLF: And I wish you good luck, though I know for sure,
you're not gonna get lucky, 'cause Lady Luck won't let you.

LAWYERS: Jerks like this keep their bank account in their big mouth,   625 so they collect interest when they trash people better than them.

WOLF: A guy who doesn't know the way to get to the beach
needs to find a storm drain* to go along with him.
I didn't know the best way of trashing you:
now you're my drain—I'm set to follow you: 630
if you talk nice to me, I'll stick to your side—
if you talk trash to me, I'll step on your butt.

LAWYERS: You know, if you do right by a bad guy, it's just the same risk
as if you do bad by a right guy. WOLF: How's that? LAWYERS: Lemme tell ya.
If you do right by a bad guy, you're wasting your time;   635
if you do bad by a right guy, it'll bust your chops.

WOLF: Bravo, that's brilliant. But what's it to me?

LAWYERS: Because we've come to you to pay our respects,
though we're not so pumped up about pimps, normally.*

WOLF: If you're bringing me anything good, I'm grateful.   640

LAWYERS: Any of our goods? To you? Nah, we neither brung 'em nor give 'em
nor promise 'em, and we're not sorry, either.

WOLF: By golly, I believe you; that's you all over.
But now whaddaya want? LAWYERS: This guy in the trenchcoat—see him?
The war god is mad at him. BLINI: Yeah, well, I'm rubber, you're glue!*   645

LAWYERS: And now we're bringing him to you, the Wolf, to get ripped.

BLINI *(points to self, speaks to audience):* This boy's goin' huntin' today and bag
          him a nice trophy,
the dogs are drivin' this Wolf nicely now into the trap.

WOLF: Who's this? LAWYERS: We don't know who he is, honestly;
except we went down to the harbor early this morning,   650
and we saw him getting off a trading ship. Really.
He comes up to us right away as he gets off;
he says hi, we say hi back. BLINI *(to audience):* Bad dudes!
This ain't *their* first time at the rodeo.*

WOLF: What then? LAWYERS: So then he ropes us into conversation.   655
He says he's a foreigner here, he's new in town;
he wants us to show him a free and easy place,*
where he can get nasty. We brought the dude to you.
And you—if God loves you, here's your chance to do business.

WOLF: Oh yeah? LAWYERS: He's asking for it,* and he's got dough.

          WOLF: He's mine.*   660

LAWYERS: He wants a drink and some lovin'. WOLF: I'll show him a nice place.

LAWYERS: But he definitely wants to lie low, so nobody knows
or spies on him. See, he was a hit man* in Kosovo*—
he told us so himself—working for the Israelis;*
and he's running away from there, since the place got captured.   665
BLINI *(to audience):* Hit man—pretty funny—and Kosovo!—awesome!
WOLF: May God be very nice to you, since you've
filled me in nice and flushed me out a nice turkey.*
LAWYERS: And yeah (he told us himself), so you should take care of him better,
he's packing three hundred rubles in cash as backup.   670
WOLF: I'm a king, if I can snag this guy today.
LAWYERS: Hey, he's all yours. WOLF: God, please, encourage him
to stay with me for the finest in hospitality.
LAWYERS: It's not our job to encourage foreign dudes (or not);
you do your own business, if you know what's good for you.   675
We've got the turkey almost into your trap;*
now it's your job to catch him if you want him caught.
BLINI: You taking off? What about what I asked you, pal?
LAWYERS: You better tell your business to this guy, young dude.
He's the right man for the job you're interested in.   680
BLINI *(in stage whisper):* OK, but I want you to see me pay him the money.
LAWYERS *(stage whisper back):* {Don't worry,} we'll be watching from over there.
BLINI: You've really done me a service. WOLF: Here comes money!
BLINI: Yeah, and it's gonna have a kick like a mule.
WOLF: (I'll greet this guy sweetly.) My greetings, from host   685
to guest! I'm glad to see you arrived here safely.
BLINI: God bless you sir, for your concern for my safety.
WOLF: They say you're looking for a place to stay. BLINI: I'm looking.
WOLF: And so they said, those guys who left just now,
you're looking for a little tête-à-tête.* BLINI: No way in the world.   690
WOLF: Excuse me? BLINI: If I wanted the Hotel Rat-a-tat-tat,
I'd go straight to the prison the minute I got here.*
No, I'm looking for a place where I'll be handled sweeter
than the Shah of Iran's* family jewels.*
WOLF: Damn if I'm not gonna set you up to party,   695
if you can handle being in a very nice place
in a very nice cushiony bed with your arms around
a very nice girl to play with. BLINI: Way to go, pimp.
WOLF: Where you can wallow in wine so old it's toothless—   700

Bordeaux, champagne, chablis, and of course Merlot.*   699
And then I'll sprinkle* you with sweet perfume—
long story short—I'll fix it, when you're in the hot tub
the locker room guy's gonna make it just like a perfume store.
But all this stuff I said is just like a hit man.*
BLINI: How so? WOLF: Because it all wants cash on the barrel.   705
BLINI: Golly, you don't wanna get it more'n I wanna give it.
LAWYERS (to audience): Why don't we call Boris outside to us here
so he can be his own best witness of this? (Calling inside.)
Hey you—wanna catch a thief? Get on out here
so you can watch the dough being given to the pimp.   710

SCENE 4: BORIS, LAWYERS, BLINI, and THE WOLF
Enter BORIS from his house.

BORIS: What is it? Can I help you, casual passersby?* LAWYERS: Look to
            your right.   iambic senarii
Your slave will give the dough to the pimp himself.
BLINI: Go on, take it; here we have, counted out, solid gold,
three hundred of the coinage known as rubles.
Use this to set me up good; I want it spent in a hurry.   715
WOLF: Hot damn, you've got yourself a bodacious bartender!
Come on, let's go inside. BLINI: I'm following you.
WOLF: Let's go, pick it up, we can make chit-chat inside.
BLINI: I'll tell you all my adventures fighting in Kosovo.
WOLF: OK, just follow me. BLINI: Take me—you've got yourself a slave.*   720
(Exeunt THE WOLF and BLINI into the pimp's house.)
BORIS: OK, now what's the plotline? LAWYERS: Just do the right thing.
BORIS: And suppose I can't pull it off? LAWYERS: Just make it so.
BORIS: You saw how the pimp took the cash? LAWYERS: Indeed we did.
BORIS: And you know that guy's my slave? LAWYERS: Indeed we do.
BORIS: And that's against the law? LAWYERS: Indeed we know.   725
BORIS: Great! OK, I want you to remember all this
when we go see the judge. LAWYERS: We do remember.
BORIS: What if I beat down his door and catch him redhanded?
            LAWYERS: Approved.
BORIS: . . . and if I beat it and it won't crack? LAWYERS: Break his egg.*
BORIS: . . . and if the pimp comes out, then what? Do I ask him   730

whether my slave is there or not? LAWYERS: Why not?
BORIS: With two hundred golden rubles, cash? LAWYERS: Why not?
BORIS: And that's when the pimp will go wrong. LAWYERS: How so? BORIS:
       You're asking?
Because he'll be told a hundred short! LAWYERS: Good thinking.
BORIS: He'll want the other searched for. LAWYERS: Naturally.   735
BORIS: He'll just deny it at once. LAWYERS: On oath, for sure.
BORIS: The fellow will tie himself up in theft. LAWYERS: Indubitably.
BORIS: What absolutely ever came in, {he stole}. LAWYERS: Why not?
BORIS: May God almighty rot you. LAWYERS: Why not you?
BORIS: I'll go and beat on his front door. LAWYERS: Sure, why not?   740
(Creaky door sound.)
BORIS: It's time to shut up now; the doors have farted.*
I see the pimp, the Wolf, is coming outside.
Stand by me, please. LAWYERS: Why not? If it's all right,
we'll disguise ourselves,* so that the pimp won't know us,
since we were the ones who got him into this mess.   745
(LAWYERS put on sunglasses.)

SCENE 5: THE WOLF, BORIS, and LAWYERS
Enter THE WOLF from his house.

WOLF: The priests can all go hang themselves right now,   iambic senarii
before I believe another thing they say:
why, just a little while ago they predicted
some huge expensive problem was in the stars;
and right away I fill my wallet with money.   750
BORIS: Hullo there, pimp. WOLF: God bless you, Boris. BORIS: {That's funny;}
you're saying a bigger hullo than you usually do.
WOLF: A calm has arisen, like for a ship at sea;
wherever the wind blows, that's where the sails turn.
BORIS: May all at your house be well (excepting you).   755
WOLF: They're quite well, since you ask, but not for you.
BORIS: Send me, please, today, your girl Tchotchka,
on this the glorious festal day of Venus.
WOLF: Did you eat a hot lunch today? Tell me, please.
BORIS: Now what? WOLF: You're just flapping your gums to ask for her.* 760

BORIS: Now, listen up, pimp, I've heard my slave is with you.

WOLF: Is with *me?* You'll never prove I did it.

BORIS: You're lying; he came to you and brought you gold.
That's what was reported to me by reliable sources.

WOLF: You're bad. You've come to catch me out? You and who else?*   765
Nobody of yours is with me, and nothing of yours.

BORIS: Make a note of that, legal dudes. LAWYERS: We do remember.

WOLF *(to audience):* Ha ha ha,* now I got it, I see through it now.
These are the guys who put me together with
the foreign guy from Kosovo, that's what burns their brains—   770
that I'm gonna make a three-hundred-ruble profit.
Now 'cause they know this guy is my old enemy,
they've dragged him in to say that it's his slave
and his gold that's with me; they've cooked up this fraud
to do me out of the dough and divide it among them.   775
They're expecting to steal a lamb from the Wolf. No way!

BORIS: You deny the gold is with you, and my slave?

WOLF: I do; and I'll howl* when I do it, if that helps.

LAWYERS: You're finished, pimp. That guy we said was from Kosovo?
He's this guy's farm overseer, and his slave   780
who gave you three hundred rubles in cash just now.
And that's the very gold—right in that sack.

WOLF: You're dead, assholes.* LAWYERS: No, that's what's ready for *you.*

BORIS: Come on, jailmeat,* drop that sack right now:
I caught you redhanded. *(To* LAWYERS.*)* Good grief, please pay attention,   785
until you see me remove my slave from these premises.

(Exit BORIS *into the pimp's house.)*

WOLF: Damn, now I'm sunk for sure, and no problemo.
This was a setup job, they plotted against me.
But why don't I just boogie out of here—and onto
a cross, before I'm dragged to the judge with my neck in a noose?   790
Damn, I wish I had those priests and soothsayers;
if they promise something good, it comes at a crawl,
if they promise something bad, there it is, right there.
Now I'll go consult my friends, and see what they think
the best way might be for me to hang myself.   795

(Exit THE WOLF *stage L.)*

SCENE 6: BORIS, BLINI, *and* LAWYERS
Enter BORIS *and* BLINI *from the pimp's house.*

BORIS *(to* BLINI*):* Go ahead, so they can see you leaving the house.   iambic senarii
(To LAWYERS.*)* Is this my slave? BLINI: Dang, you know I am, Mr. Boris.
BORIS: How now, foul pimp? LAWYERS: The defendant has disappeared.
BORIS: Soon to be appearing on a cross near you.
LAWYERS: Suits us. BORIS: Tomorrow I'll have this bloke indicted.   800
BLINI: And me? BORIS: You disappear, and put your old costume back on.
BLINI: They didn't make me a soldier for nothing, no, sir.
I got a tad of looting in; while the pimp's crew
is snoozing, I stuff myself with the barbecue. {Just like Rambo!}*
I'll disappear now. BORIS: You've all handled this with style.   805
Lawmen, you've done me good service here today.
Tomorrow morning—please—meet me downtown.*
You, follow me inside. So long, all. *(Exeunt* BORIS *and* BLINI *into Boris's*
        house.) LAWYERS: So long to *you.*
He's got a fine way of bringing damages—
he thinks we should be his slave and buy our own lunch.   810
Well, that's how these rich guys are today, for sure;
if you do 'em a good deed, you get a one-ounce thank-you;
make a mistake, they hand out a two-ton grudge.*
Let's go home right now, if you don't mind;
we've pulled off the scam that we were trying for,   815
and foiled the corrupter of citizens, Wolf the pimp.
(Exeunt LAWYERS *stage L.)*

ACT 4

SCENE 1: IGOR
IGOR *enters from Boris's house.*

IGOR: I'm waiting to see just how nicely my machinations are
        getting along;   iambic octonarii and septenarii
I want to ruin this lowlife pimp, who's soaking my poor miserable boss,
who then beats *me,* and hammers me, not just with his fists but even
        his feet;
it's misery to be a lover's slave, and one who can't have the girl he loves.   820

But, whoa, I see the pimp's own slave, Vodka, he's coming back
   from temple,
I think I'll listen in and see just what he has to say for himself.

SCENE 2: VODKA *and* IGOR
Enter VODKA *from stage L. He is schlepping a bunch of religious paraphernalia, in-*
cluding buckets and various tools such as might be useful in cutting up slaughtered farm
animals.

VODKA: It's plain to see that God and Man don't care at all for a
   guy like me,   trochaic septenarii
a guy who's got a master who's the type like the one that I've got here;
There's no one worse in the universe nor a bigger liar on land or sea,   825
than my boss is—no one so dirty—no one so smeared all over with filth.
As God's my witness, I'd rather drudge in the quarries or in the mill,*
all my life long, dragging my heavy ball and chain along with me,*
than slave like this in this pimp's house and associate with the kind you
   get there.
What a den of iniquity! I'm telling you, so help me God,   830
you could see anybody there—it's just like you went to hell!
Millionaires and regular guys,* freed slaves, thieves and fugitives,
beaten, bound, or debtor slaves; any guy who's got the price,
all kinds are accepted here. And so throughout the house
it's shadows and darkness, food and drink, just like some seedy bar
   and grill.   835
And there you'll see guys writing letters—yeah, letters to Johnny Walker,*
and his pal Jim Beam, with the address written in two-foot neon letters*—
we got a full assortment of booze at our house, you can take your pick.*
IGOR *(to audience):* God, this all sounds very strange, unless the pimp's
   adopted him,
'cause it certainly sounds to me like he's practicing the pimp's eulogy.   840
I'd like to interrupt this guy, but I'm liking listening to him too much.
VODKA: When I see this stuff that happens here, it's torture: high-priced
   houseboys here
are losing their shirts and everything else, and to their own bosses, too.
And in the end there's nothing left: easy come is easy go.
IGOR: Hoo ha, big knocker, you'd think he was Mr. Responsible,*   845
when, God, he could teach La-Z-Boy* to take it easy.

VODKA: And now here I'm lugging the pots from the temple of Venus back to
the house,
the boss couldn't get Venus on his side with a slaughtered ox on her special day.*
IGOR: Venus has got good taste. VODKA: In fact, our working girls, on their
first try,
got the blessing of Venus pronto. IGOR: Yeah, good taste, just like I said.   850
VODKA: Now home I go. IGOR: Hey, Vodka! VODKA: Who's that calling
Vodka here?
IGOR: Your pal. VODKA: Some pal you are, you're blockin' the path of a guy
who's loaded down.
IGOR: OK, payback, I'll return you the favor whenever you want—just say
the word.
And that's a promise. VODKA: If that's for real, I'll do you this favor. IGOR:
Whaddaya mean?
VODKA: I mean next time I'm due to take a beating, you can provide
the skin.   855
Get outta here, whoever you are. IGOR: I'm bad. VODKA: For yourself. IGOR: I
want you.
VODKA: My load's got me down. IGOR: Just put it down and look at me. VODKA:
All right,
though I hardly have the time. IGOR: Hello, Vodka. VODKA: Hey, Igor!
God and all the saints bless— IGOR: Who? VODKA: Not you and me, buddy*—
and not my boss, anyway. IGOR: Then God bless who? VODKA: Some guy who
deserves it.   860
Damn sure none of us does that. IGOR: You're very funny. VODKA:
Bully for me.
IGOR: What's up? VODKA: I'm doing what a guy who's caught with another guy's
wife rarely gets away with.*
IGOR: What's that? VODKA: I'm bringing my tools* home safe. IGOR: Oh, God
damn you and your master too.*
VODKA: No, he won't damn me, but I can see that he damns the pimp, if I
felt like it.
Yup, damn my boss, if I weren't scared for my own skin, Igor. IGOR: What
is it? Tell.   865
VODKA: You bad? IGOR: I'm bad. VODKA: I'm hosed.* IGOR: Come on, ain't that
the way it's supposed to be?
But what's "hosed" for you? You've got in the house all you can eat and all you
can love,

and you never have to pay your girlfriend a nickel. You got her for free!

VODKA: So help me God almighty— IGOR: Jesus, you certainly need the help.

VODKA: I want to destroy this crew. IGOR: Go ahead, knock yourself out, if
      you want. 870

VODKA: It's not easy to fly without wings; my wings got no feathers. (*Lifts arms.*)

IGOR: So stop shaving your damn armpits: I promise you, in two months
you'll have wings just like a goat.* VODKA: Get lost.* IGOR: You and your
      master, too.

VODKA: Yeah . . . to know him is to know him. The guy can be had like *that.*

IGOR: Whaddaya mean? VODKA: Like you could keep your mouth shut about
      anything. IGOR: No, I swear, 875
I'll keep your secret totally quiet, better than a woman with laryngitis.*

VODKA: And I could bring myself to believe you, if I didn't know you so well.

IGOR: Your secret is safe with me, I swear. VODKA: I can hardly believe it, but
      I want to.

IGOR: You know that your boss and mine are deadly enemies? VODKA:
      Sure I know.

IGOR: Because of love— VODKA: You're wastin' time. IGOR: Why so? VODKA:
      Because you're tellin' old news. 880

IGOR: So why would you doubt my boss would gladly do whatever he
      could to yours?
Anything he could do bad. And serve him right. So what *you* do to help us out,
makes *his* job that much easier. VODKA: But, Igor, there's something I'm
      scared of!

IGOR: What? VODKA: That while I'm setting a trap for my boss, I'll ruin
      myself likewise.
If my boss knew that I'd blabbed this thing to anyone, 885
bam! Right there on the spot he'd change my name from Vodka to
      Broken Leg.

IGOR: Jesus, no living soul will ever find out about it from me,
except I might tell just my boss, and I'll make him promise
never to tell it was your idea. VODKA: I can hardly believe it, but I want to.
But you got to keep this to yourself. IGOR: On my honor as a Boy Scout.* 890
Speak out freely—the time is right, the coast is clear; I think we're
      alone now.

VODKA: If your boss wants to do the right thing* he can waste my boss. IGOR:
      How can that be?

VODKA: Easy. IGOR: So fix it so I know this "easy," so he can know it, too.

VODKA: 'Cause Tchotchka, the girl your boss is crazy about, is freeborn. IGOR: How is that?

VODKA: The same way that her sister Katya is, the other one. IGOR: Prove it, then,   895
so I can believe it. VODKA: Because he bought them both in Belgrade as little girls,

from some Taliban thug.* IGOR: What'd he pay? VODKA: Eighteen thousand, coin of the realm,

for the two little girls, and then Yasmin, the nanny, she makes three.

And the guy who was selling them admitted they were stolen goods;

he said they were Iraqi citizens,* from Baghdad.* IGOR: God bless you,   900

a very nice crime you have to tell. See, my boss, Boris,

he was born in the same place, and carried off at the age of six,

and then the guy who kidnapped him took him here and sold him here

to my old boss, who adopted him and made him his heir when he passed away.

VODKA: You're telling what makes it even easier; Boris can get 'em freed from slavery,   905

as fellow citizens; it's the law!* Not a word? IGOR: Shush a minute.

VODKA: He'd definitely checkmate* the pimp if he takes the girls away.

IGOR: I'll see to it that he's ruined before he moves a single pawn.

It's all set. VODKA: God, just let me not be this pimp's slave any more.

IGOR: Damn, I'll see to it that you're freed alongside me,* if God is willing.   910

VODKA: From your lips to God's ear. You gonna hold me up any more, Igor?

IGOR: Goodbye and good luck to you. VODKA: Jesus, it's up to you and your boss.

Goodbye, and remember, it's *our* little secret. IGOR: You never said a thing. Goodbye.

VODKA: But it's useless, unless you do it while it's hot. IGOR: You're cute when you nag me.

Don't worry, it'll happen. VODKA: You got good material here, you just need a good mechanic.   915

IGOR: Could you be quiet? VODKA: I'm quiet, I'm going. *(Exit* VODKA *into the pimp's house.)* IGOR: Please, don't do me any favors!

—OK, he's gone. God in heaven clearly wants my boss to be saved

and the pimp to be annihilated; what a downfall looms for him.

It wasn't enough he had one bombshell* thrown at him, now there's two?

I'll go in, to report to the boss. If I call him out in front of the house,   920

the stuff that you just heard, if I tell him all over again, that's just silly.
Better I should just bore one guy inside than all of you out here.
[Lindsay here brackets a simplistic seven-line summary in verse that seems to be
the work of an ancient editor: 923–29]
(Exit IGOR *into Boris's house.)*

ACT 5

SCENE 1: SADDAM

Enter SADDAM *from stage R, followed by Arab slaves carrying his bags, including the*
BOY. SADDAM *is elaborately dressed as a stage Arab, and wears long black robes;*
amongst his accessories is a hipflask. He also carries a large object to serve as the hospi-
tality token. The porters wear large gold earrings and carry a lot of heavy bags.

[SADDAM: Baruch Atah Adonai Eloheynu melech   iambic senarii   930
ha-olom, asher kid-sha-nu b'mitz-vo-tav
v'tsi-va-nu l'had-lik ner shel yom tov.
Baruch Atah Adonai Eloheynu melech
ha-olam bo-rey p'ree ha-ga-fen.
Lollapalooza Vladimir shish-kebab   935
abracadabra gesundheit ish ka bibble
alakazam Aladdin Ali al-Boris
felafel casbah ooga-booga salam
salami salami baloney open sesame]*

SADDAM: Baruch Atah Adonai Eloheynu melech   940
ha-olom, asher kid-sha-nu b'mitz-vo-tav
v'tsi-va-nu l'had-lik ner shel yom tov.* *(Awaits response "Amen" from all Jews*
in audience.)
Baruch Atah Adonai Eloheynu melech
ha-olam bo-rey p'ree ha-ga-fen.* *(Takes a sip from his hipflask. Awaits*
response "Amen" from all Jews in audience.)
Lollapalooza Vladimir shish-kebab   945
abracadabra gesundheit ish ka bibble
alakazam Aladdin Ali al-Boris
mekka lekka hi mekka hiney ho
salami salami baloney open sesame.
O gods and goddesses who guard this city,   950

I pray that what I have come here to do
I may do well: that you will grant to me
to find my daughters and my brother's son
[who were stolen from me, and my brother's son.]
But long ago my host here was Vladimir;   955
they tell me he has done what we all must do.
They say his son is here, Boris by name;
to him I'll go, and bring this hospitality token,*
{a memento of auld lang syne and happy memories}.
We were told he lived somewhere in this neighborhood.
I'll ask these fellows whom I see exiting the house.   960

SCENE 2: BORIS, IGOR, *and* SADDAM
Enter BORIS *and* IGOR *from Boris's house.*

BORIS: You say Vodka told you, Igor, yourself,   iambic senarii
that the girls are both freeborn, and both were kidnapped
from Baghdad? IGOR: Yes, I do, and if you want to do the right thing,*
you'll claim them both as freeborn right away.
Y'know it's a sin to let your fellow citizens   965
be slaves, right in your face, when they were free at home.*
SADDAM: Lord God almighty, please help me, I pray!
What is this sweet speech my ears are gobbling up?
The speech of these persons is certainly made of chalk;
how they have wiped off all my blackitude!*   970
BORIS: If I had a witness* for this, I'd do what you say.
IGOR: Whaddaya talkin', witness? Why don't you take him like a man?*
Lady Luck will be on your side somehow, you'll see.
BORIS: It's a lot easier to start than it is to go through with it.
IGOR: But what's this bird who's arrived here in the bathrobe?*   975
Think his clothes* were stolen at the gym?*
BORIS: By Jove, his face—he must be an Arab.* IGOR: A wog!*
By Jove, his slaves—they're pretty old and ancient.
BORIS: How do you know? IGOR: Well, they got a lot of baggage.* See 'em?
Looks to me like they were absent the day they handed out fingers.* 980
BORIS: What now? IGOR: Well, look—they go around with their rings
        in their ears.*
SADDAM *(to audience):* I'll go up to them and talk to them in Arabic.*

If they answer, I'll go on speaking Arabic;

if not, then I'll change my tongue to match their customs.

IGOR: What about it—you remember any Arabic?   985

BORIS: No, by Jove. How could I have, you tell me,

when I was lost to Baghdad at the age of six?

SADDAM (*to audience*): Lord God almighty, many freeborn boys

were lost to us in just that way from Baghdad.

IGOR: Well? BORIS: What do you want? IGOR: Want me to greet him

        in Arabic?   990

BORIS: Can you? IGOR: There's no more Arabian Arab than me today.

BORIS: Go up and ask him what he wants, why he's come,

who he is, where he's from, what city: spare no effort.

IGOR: Salami. Where are you from, or from what town?

SADDAM: Saddam bin Muthumbaleh ooga booga akbar.   995

BORIS: What's he say? IGOR: He says his name is Saddam, he's from Baghdad.

He's the son of Muthumbaleh, also from Baghdad.

SADDAM: Salami. IGOR: He says hi. SADDAM: Gimel. IGOR: He wants

        to give you

some kind of gift, I dunno. Did you hear him promise?

BORIS: Greet him in return in Arabic from me.   1000

IGOR: Salami gimel, he says to you, from him.

SADDAM (*points to mouth*): Sheikh, felafel. IGOR: Better you than me.

BORIS: What's he say? IGOR: He says he's got a terrible toothache.

Maybe he thinks we're dentists. BORIS: {Do you think?}

Say no; I don't want to mislead a guest.   1005

IGOR: Hear that? SADDAM (*nods genially*): Allah Mecca Sahara. BORIS: Yes,

        that's right;

I want him to *make sure* about it *all*, that's fine.

Ask him if he needs anything. IGOR: Hey, you with no belt,*

what are you doing in this city? What are you looking for?

SADDAM: Saladin. BORIS: What's he saying? SADDAM: Shwarma. BORIS:

        Why's he here?   1010

IGOR: You didn't hear? He says he's bringing *salad*

for the parade at the *drama* festival*—to give to the sponsors.*

SADDAM: Salaam chador djellabah. BORIS: What's he saying now?

IGOR: He's bringing a *door* with him, and some *jellybeans,*

he wants you to help him *sell* them, if you will.   1015

BORIS: I bet he's a merchant. SADDAM: Kabul. IGOR: He wants to *carpool!*

SADDAM: Chicken Vindaloo! BORIS: Igor, what's he saying now?
IGOR: He wants you to check if his *chick* is in the *loo,**
whoever *she* is,* unless you've got a better translation;
also Gloria was sick on the subway Monday.*　　　　　　　　　　　1020
BORIS: Where do I come in on this? IGOR: He wants you kept informed
so you don't think he's getting any on the sly.
SADDAM: Afghani! Iraqi! IGOR: Whoa, watch out you don't do what he asks you.
BORIS: What's he saying? What's he asking? Tell me!
IGOR: He wants you to have him wrapped in an *afghan** and then　　　1025
put lots of *rocks* on top, so that you'll kill him.
SADDAM: Hummus bin Qaddafi! BORIS: Tell me! What is it now?
What's he say? IGOR: Jesus, I have to admit this time I'm stumped.
SADDAM: Well, I will unstump you; from now on I will speak English.*
A slave must you be, by God, both worthless and also bad,　　　　　　1030
to make mockery of a foreigner and a newcomer.
IGOR: But, Jesus, you must be a con man and a shyster
to come here and make a fool of us, you schmo,*
you speak with forkèd tongue like snake in the grass.
BORIS: No nasty words here, control your mouth now, Igor.　　　　　　1035
You'll keep from insulting this person, if you're wise.
I don't want you to speak improperly to those who share my blood.
I was born at Baghdad, just so you know.
SADDAM: O fellow citizen, greetings! BORIS: Gosh, you too, whoever you are.
And if you need anything, please, do let me know　　　　　　　　　　　1040
for the sake of our homeland. SADDAM: Many thanks to you.
[But actually I have an old friendship here; I seek
Vladimir's son—point him out if you know him—named Boris.]
But do you know any young man here named Boris?
BORIS: If you're looking for the adopted son of Vladimir,　　　　　　　1045
I'm the very man you seek. SADDAM: Oho! What's this I hear?
BORIS: That I am the son of Vladimir. SADDAM: If that is so,
let's compare our tokens of hospitality—I've got mine.
BORIS: Let's have a look.— It's just like the one I have at home!
SADDAM: My host! Many greetings. For your paternal father,　　　　　1050
Vladimir, was then my former host.
This was my token of hospitality with *him.*
BORIS: So you'll enjoy my hospitality.
For I never turn down a guest nor dear old Baghdad,

that's where I come from. SADDAM: Lord bless you, boy,   1055
what *do* you mean? How can this be, that you were born
at Baghdad? Here your father was a citizen of the former Yugoslavia!*
BORIS: I was kidnapped from there. Here your friend Vladimir
bought me, and he adopted me as his son.
SADDAM: And *he* was also adopted. By old Mikhail.*   1060
Enough of that, let's talk about you. Tell me,
do you at all remember your parents' names,
your father and mother? BORIS: I do. SADDAM: So tell me then.
Perhaps I knew them, maybe they're my relations.
BORIS: My mother was Noor, my father was named Dodi.*   1065
SADDAM: I wish your father and mother were living still.
BORIS: Are they dead? SADDAM: It's so indeed, and I could hardly bear it.
For Noor, your mother, was my esteemed cousin;
your father, he was the son of my father's brother,
and he made me his heir, when he passed away,   1070
and how I miss him, now that he is dead.
But if it's really true you're Dodi's son,
there should be a mark right there on your left hand
where a monkey bit you when you were a little boy.
Show me, let's see. BORIS: Voilà. SADDAM: Your hand! Good heavens!   1075
BORIS: My uncle, I greet you. SADDAM: And I greet you, dear Boris.
I seem to be born again, now that I've found you.
IGOR: Gosh, I'm glad this has all worked out so well for you.
But do you mind if I give you some advice? SADDAM: Not at all.
IGOR: You ought to give the kid his father's money.   1080
He ought to have the goods his father had.
SADDAM: I hardly think otherwise; all will be returned;
I'll give it all back to him, if he'll come home with me.
IGOR: You should give it back to him even if he lives here.
SADDAM: Why, I'll even leave him my money, should I pass on.   1085
IGOR: A festive idea just popped into my head.
SADDAM: What's that? IGOR: We need your help. SADDAM: Just name
        your pleasure;
you shall have my help at once, however you like.
What is the deal? IGOR: Can you be, you know, tricky?
SADDAM: To an enemy can I—tricking a friend is silly!   1090
IGOR *(points at* BORIS*)*: God, he's *his* enemy. SADDAM: I'll be glad to hurt him.

IGOR: This guy *(points at* BORIS*)* loves one of the pimp's girls. SADDAM:
    Very wise.

IGOR: The pimp lives right next door. SADDAM: I'll be glad to hurt him.

IGOR: He's got two little slave girls working for him—

sisters; and Boris is dying of love for one of 'em   1095

and he's never besmirched her virtue.* SADDAM: Unripened lovemaking!*

IGOR: The pimp is teasing him. SADDAM: He does have a business to run.

IGOR: Boris wants to give him the business. SADDAM: Good man!—if he does it.

IGOR: Now this is my plan and here's my game:

that we should get you to say these are your daughters   1100

kidnapped from you as little girls from Baghdad,

and that you should claim them both as Iraqi citizens,*

as if they were both your daughters. Understand?

SADDAM: Of course I do. For indeed my own two daughters,

along with their nanny, were kidnapped as little girls.   1105

IGOR: God, you're a good faker. That's what I liked about him, right

    from the start!

SADDAM: I feel it more than I could wish. IGOR: Jeeze, what a guy!

He's clever, he's bad, he's crude, he's hip and tricky!

Look at him crying! So he'll pull it off better that way.

He's even better than me, and I'm the architect here.   1110

SADDAM: But tell me about their {old} nanny—what does she look like?

IGOR: Not tall, kind of what you call swarthy. SADDAM: That is her!

IGOR: She's a good looker, her face is as black as her eyes.

SADDAM: You paint her beauty to me most well in words.

IGOR: You wanna see her? SADDAM: I would rather see my girls.   1115

But go and call her; if these are my daughters,

if she's their old nanny, she'll know me right away.

*(*IGOR *knocks on the pimp's door.)*

IGOR: Hey! Anybody home? Tell Yasmin, please,

she should get out here. There's someone here to see her.

SCENE 3: YASMIN, IGOR, SADDAM, BORIS, *and* BOY

YASMIN *answers the door of the pimp's house.*

YASMIN: Who's knocking? IGOR: Who's next to you? YASMIN:

    What do you want? IGOR: Ahem.   iambic senarii   1120

You know this guy in the bathrobe, who he is?

YASMIN: Why, who's this I see? Oh, dear Lord God almighty,
it's my old master, father of mah little lambs,*
Saddam of Baghdad. IGOR: Hoo, but she is sharp.
This guy from Baghdad is one great magician,*   1125
he hypnotizes* 'em all to think what he wants.
YASMIN: O master, greetings, Saddam, most unhoped-for one,
for me and for your daughters, greetings—oh,
don't stare at me, don't look at me that way.
Don't you know your Yasmin, your handmaiden?   1130
SADDAM: I recognize you. But where are my girls? I must know!
YASMIN: At Venus's temple. SADDAM: What are they doing there?
YASMIN: Today's the Love Festival in honor of Venus:
they've gone to pray to the goddess to be good to them.
IGOR: God, their dream's come true, now that he's here.   1135
BORIS: I say! Those girls are this man's daughters? YASMIN: I'm telling you.
(To SADDAM.) Your family values have saved us, absolutely,
because you've come here today, in the nick of time;
for today your girls would have taken their professional names*
and be earning their bread on their backs* (not nice for ladies).   1140
BOY: Salami, Mama! YASMIN: Salami, Alcatraz omigod
muezzin longlost camel Sahara gevalt!
BORIS: What are they saying between themselves? Tell me!
SADDAM: He's greeting her as his mother, she greets her son.
(To YASMIN.) Be quiet and spare us your womanish furniture!   1145
BORIS: What furniture? SADDAM: Loud yelling. BORIS: Let 'em be.
SADDAM (to IGOR, pointing to his slaves): You take these men inside; and the
        nanny, too,
tell her to go with you. BORIS: Do as he says.
IGOR: But who'll point the girls out to you? BORIS: I will, I'm an expert.
IGOR: I'm off then. BORIS: I'd rather you do it than announce it.   1150
I want you to set up a dinner for my newfound uncle.
IGOR (to the slaves): I'll salami you—I'll put you on the treadmill,
and then off to the mines and a big fat ball and chain.
I'll fix it so you don't give this hotel five stars.*
(Exeunt IGOR, YASMIN, BOY, and slaves into Boris's house.)
BORIS: Did you hear me, Uncle? Please, don't deny what you said;   1155
please promise me your older daughter in marriage.
SADDAM: It's a deal. BORIS: Do you promise me? SADDAM: Indeed I do.

BORIS: My uncle, bless you. Now you're really mine.

Now finally I'll get to chat freely with her.

Now, Uncle, if you want to see your daughters,   1160

follow me. SADDAM: I can hardly wait! I follow you!

BORIS: What if we go to meet them? SADDAM: But I am afraid

we shall miss them on the road. God almighty,

restore my fortunes, bring certainty out of doubt.

BORIS: I'm positive my love will be with me.   1165

But look, I see them. SADDAM: Those are really my daughters?

What big girls they've turned into! They were so little! BORIS: You
    know what it is?

They're glam rockers: of course they wear platform shoes.*

*(Cue music; segués from "Take a Walk on the Wild Side" to "When the Saints Go
    Marching In.")*

[*Enter* IGOR *from Boris's house.*

IGOR: God, it looks like today, what I said as a joke,

it's really coming true, no fooling, it's serious,   1170

that these daughters of his are being found today.

BORIS: Golly, it's certain now. Igor, take these fellows

inside! We'll be heading the girls off here.]

SCENE 4: TCHOTCHKA, KATYA, SADDAM, *and* BORIS

Enter TCHOTCHKA *and* KATYA *from stage L. The scene opens with a song by*
TCHOTCHKA *and* KATYA *to the tune of "When the Saints Go Marching In."* SADDAM
takes over at the end, and the audience is encouraged to join in throughout.

ALL *(with audience):* Oh, when the sluts go marchin' in,

Oh, when the sluts go marchin' in,

oh, well, I want to be in that number,

when the sluts go marchin' in!

TCHOTCHKA: Oh, when the sluts hit Venus's shrine

I must say they all looked divine.   1175

Gee whiz! The outfits all were charming,

and worthy of that Venus mine.

ALL *(with audience):* When every ho shouts hi-de-ho,

When every ho shouts hi-de-ho,

Oh, well, I want to be in that number (hallelujah!)
When the ho's shout hi-de-ho.

TCHOTCHKA: Oh, Venus's shrine looked great today,
a world of charm in every way,
and sweet perfume, it sure smelled purty,
not dirty in our Venus's shrine.

BORIS *(with audience):* Oh, when the tarts are on the march,
oh, when the tarts are on the march,
Oh, well, I want to be in that number,
when the tarts are on the march.

TCHOTCHKA: And all the working girls were there,
yes, hookers came from everywhere,   1180
they all were here in Sarajevo,
to show our Venus that they care.

ALL *(with audience):* Oh, when the strumpet starts to blow,
oh, when that strumpet starts to blow,
oh, well, I want to be in that number,
when the strumpet starts to blow.

KATYA: One thing's for sure, we aced the test,
of all the girls we were the best.
And not one boy yelled out "Yer ugly!"
the way they did to all the rest.

TCHOTCHKA: Why sister dear, that's just not nice,
let *them* praise *us*—take my advice.
KATYA: That's fine with me! TCHOTCHKA: We're just too well-bred *(spoken)*—
        unlike *them!*   1185
(Sings again.) We should be pure and free from vice!

ALL *(with audience):* Oh, when the sluts go marchin' in,
oh, when the sluts go marchin' in,
well, I want to be in that number,
when the sluts go marchin' in.

SADDAM *(with audience):* No, when the saints go marchin' in,
oh, when the saints go marchin' in,
well, I want to be in that number,
when the saints go marchin' in.

SADDAM: Oh, holy God, who made our clay,
who holds our dreams, grant me today,
that I may find my own precious darlins,
and set them free—reward my love, I pray.   1190

ALL *(with audience):* Oh, when the saints [etc.]

BORIS: I'll see to it that God takes care of everything, 'cause he owes me one,
     and he's scared of me. SADDAM: Please, be quiet.
BORIS: Don't cry, Uncle. {TCHOTCHKA: Yeah, don't bag, Dad.}
KATYA: How thrilling for a girl it is, dear sister, if she wins the prize;   1192a
like us, today we beat 'em all for bare-faced beauteosity.
TCHOTCHKA: You're dumber, sister, than I want. Or do you feel
     beautiful—I ask you—
if you don't get your face all smeared* with soot? BORIS: Oh, Uncle, oh,
     Uncle mine.   1195
SADDAM: What is it, son of my brother, what do you want? Do tell.
BORIS: *I* want *you* to do that. SADDAM: But *I'm* doing *this.* BORIS: Oh, Uncle,
     my Unclest Uncle.
SADDAM: What is it? BORIS: She's charming, she's chic. And so brainy.   1197a
SADDAM: The mind of her father has she—so, brainy!
BORIS *(song, reprising "My Heart Belongs to Daddy"):*
It may be true
at least per you
that she got some brains from her daddy,
but that was then—
that's over, amen—
now her brains come from this laddie.   1200
TCHOTCHKA: We didn't come from that kind of family, even if
     we are slaves, sister,   trochaic septenarii
that it's right for us to do anything that any guy could poke fun at.
Women have lots of faults, but this is the biggest one of all,

when they please themselves too much and don't work hard enough on
     pleasing the men.
KATYA: Ooh, it was just too thrilling, the signs we found in our sacred
     guts, sister, 1205
and what the holy soothsayer said about us both. BORIS: About me, I hope.
KATYA: That we'd be free in just a few days and never mind our master, the
     pimp.
But I don't know how to hope for it, short of a miracle, or if our parents
     showed up.
BORIS: Golly, it was thanks to me that soothsayer promised freedom to them,
Uncle, I know; 'cause he knows I love her. TCHOTCHKA: Sister, follow me.
     KATYA: I'm coming. 1210
SADDAM: Before you go away, I want you both, if you don't mind. Please wait.
TCHOTCHKA: Who's calling us back? BORIS: A man who wants to do right by
     you. TCHOTCHKA: Now's a good time.
But who's this guy? BORIS: A friend to you. TCHOTCHKA: Just as long as
     he's no enemy.
BORIS: He's a good guy, darling. TCHOTCHKA: Gee, I like that better than
     a bad guy.
BORIS: If you're gonna be friends, be friends with him. TCHOTCHKA: The answer
     to prayer (not). 1215
BORIS: He wants to do a lot of nice things for you. TCHOTCHKA: A good man is
     hard to find.*
SADDAM: I'll be a source of joy to you. TCHOTCHKA: Gee, we'll be a source of
     pleasure to *you*.
SADDAM: And of freedom. TCHOTCHKA: At that price, you'll easily
     make us yours.
BORIS: Uncle dear, God love me, I swear I would—if I were St. Joseph,
by golly, I'd take her for my wife and kick the Virgin Mary out.* 1220
She's such an old-fashioned girl, she talks so sweetly and prudently,
every word she speaks is like the Girl Scout promise.* SADDAM: She's
     certainly mine.
But note how cleverly I approached them. BORIS: Gosh, it was elegantly done.
SADDAM: Shall I go on testing them? BORIS: Keep it short; they're getting thirsty
     in the audience.
SADDAM: What's all this? Why don't we get down to business? I'm making a
     citizen's arrest! 1225

BORIS: That's the right stuff, Uncle! Shouldn't I grab this one?

SADDAM: Hold onto her. iambic septenarii

TCHOTCHKA: Is this guy really your uncle, Boris? BORIS: I'll see you find out.
Damn, I'll take my revenge on you properly, I'm going to make you my wife.

SADDAM: Let's move along, no delays. I'll back you up; go on, take her.

BORIS: You'll back me up, after I take this girl and love her and
squeeze her. 1230
But no, what I wanted to say was—golly, that's what I wanted to say.

SADDAM: You're hanging back. I'm arresting you, or maybe grabbing
you is better.

TCHOTCHKA: But why are you arresting us? What have we done to you? BORIS:
He'll tell you there.

TCHOTCHKA: Even my own dogs bark at me? BORIS: But, golly, just you
play with them:
give me a kiss instead of a doggy bag, throw in some tongue
instead of a bone. 1235
You'll see, I'll make this dog behave for you—he'll be like butter.*

SADDAM: Go, if you're going. TCHOTCHKA: What have we done to you?

SADDAM: You're thieves, the both of you.

TCHOTCHKA: We stole from you? SADDAM: You, I say. BORIS: And I know all
about it. TCHOTCHKA: What kind of theft? BORIS: Ask him.

SADDAM: For many years the two of you've been keeping my daughters
hidden from me,
and indeed they're freeborn, free, and come from a highly
respectable family. 1240

TCHOTCHKA: Heavens to Betsy, you're never going to hang a crime
like that on us.

BORIS: Wanna bet? The one who loses has to give the winner a great big kiss.

TCHOTCHKA: I'm not talking to you, please leave. BORIS: But, golly, you have to
talk to me.
For this man is my uncle, so I have to speak up* for him;
and I'll explain how it is that you've committed many thefts 1245
and how it is that you keep this man's daughters as your slaves,
though you know they're free girls kidnapped from their fatherland.

TCHOTCHKA: Where are they? And whom, I'd like to know? BORIS: They've
been soaked long enough now.

SADDAM: Should we tell them? BORIS: Gosh, I think so, Uncle. TCHOTCHKA:
Poor me, I'm scared, I don't know

what this is about, dear sister; I'm standing here speechless, I can't think.　　1250
SADDAM: Now pay attention, women. My first wish, if this could be,
would be that God wouldn't let bad things happen to good people;
but now, for what the good Lord is giving to me, to you, and to
　　　　your mother,*
it's only right that we should give eternal thanks to God above,
since God above approves of our family values, and rewards them.　　1255
You are my daughters, both of you, and this is your cousin, too,
the son of that cousin of mine: Boris. TCHOTCHKA: Excuse me, please,
are these guys teasing us? Is this for real? BORIS: No, as God is my witness,
he's your father. Give him your hand. TCHOTCHKA: Why, Daddy! We'd given up
　　　　hoping for you.
Let us hug you? KATYA: Daddy, dearest, we've been wanting you　　1260
and waiting for you. SADDAM: They're both my daughters! KATYA: Let's both
　　　　give him a hug.
BORIS: Who's going to hug me then? SADDAM: Now I'm the lucky one,
now I can cover up the misery of many years with this pleasure.
TCHOTCHKA: We can hardly seem to believe it. SADDAM: I'll give you
　　　　reason to believe:
your old nanny recognized me first. TCHOTCHKA: Where is she, please?　　1265
SADDAM: In his house. BORIS: Excuse me, what's the point of hanging on his
　　　　neck so long?
You—at least you can quit. I don't want him to be strangled
before he's given us his blessing. TCHOTCHKA: I'm stopping. KATYA: It's
　　　　been so long!
Hello there! SADDAM: Let's all have a great big group hug.
It doesn't get better than this anywhere on earth! BORIS: A well-deserved
　　　　happy ending.　　1270
SADDAM: He finally gets what he wanted. BORIS: O Rembrandt, O
　　　　Michelangelo,*
why did you die too soon? You could have painted this tableau!
A tableau like this—I wouldn't let just any painter handle it.
SADDAM: O God, I give to you the many thanks you
　　　　richly deserve,　　　　　　　　　　　　　　trochaic septenarii
you have given me so much happiness, you have given me
　　　　so much joy:　　1275
that my daughters should return to me and my paternal power.
TCHOTCHKA: Daddy, your devotion to family really saved the day for us.

BORIS: Uncle, be sure that you remember that you promised your
           elder daughter
to me in marriage. SADDAM: I do. BORIS: And then about the dowry . . . what
           were you saying?

SCENE 5: GENERAL POPOFF, TCHOTCHKA, KATYA, SADDAM, *and* BORIS
Enter GENERAL POPOFF *from the Wolf's house.*

POPOFF: If I don't jolly well get revenge for that thousand I
           gave the pimp,   *trochaic septenarii*   1280
then the city comedians* can have me for a laughingstock.
That utter lowlife rushed me off, mind you, to "do lunch" with him,
then out he went, and left me there like a butler in the hall,
and neither the pimp nor the girls came back, and I wasn't given a
           thing to eat.
I took hostages* for the balance of my brunch, and out I went;   1285
that's how I showed him; I'll touch Johnny Pimp for the army tax.
He's picked on the right man to swindle out of a thousand in cash!
But I wish my lady friend would show up here now that I'm angry;
now, by God, I'll black her all over with my fists so she looks like a crow,
I'll stuff her so with darkness, that she'll be much darker still   1290
than those Africans who carry the bucket around the ring at the fights.*
TCHOTCHKA *(to* BORIS*)*: Oh, please hold me closer, darling; I'm awfully
           scared of hawks,
they're scary monsters, and one of them might carry off your little chick.
KATYA: Oh, I can never hug you hard enough, Daddy! POPOFF: I'm late.
I should be able to forage myself a bit of lunch now, just about.   1295
But what's this? What's this? What is this? What do I see? How
           can this be?
What's all this doubling over? What's all this twin-twinning up?
Who is this fellow with the long dress like an altar boy?*
Do my eyes deceive me? Isn't that my lady friend, Katya?
Yes it is, by jingo. I knew she wasn't taking me seriously.   1300
Isn't the girl ashamed to embrace a doorman* in the middle of the road?
Dammit, I'll turn him in to the M.P.s* for a first-rate torture job.
These cross-dressers are a bunch of gigolos, the whole lot of them.*
But I'll just have a word with this African queen.*   *iambic senarii*
Here, you, I'm talking to you, girly man,* have you no shame?   1305

What do you think you're doing with a girl like that? Speak up!

SADDAM: Young man, I greet you. POPOFF: No thanks, that's none of your
        business.

How could *you* touch *her* with your finger? SADDAM: 'Cause I feel like it.

POPOFF: You feel like it? SADDAM: Yes, I said so. POPOFF: You shoelace, you
        want to be crucified?

You dare to set up as a lover, you big toe,   1310

or put your filthy hands on what real men love?

You skinned sardine, you seedy Levantine,

you smelly sheepskin, you fishmarket, you smashed olive,

you stink of garlic and onions worse than New York cabdrivers.*

BORIS: Excuse me, young man, do you need some teeth removed?*   1315

Is that why you're bothering him? Or are you looking for trouble?

POPOFF: Why not bring your maracas, Charo,* if you've got
        something to say?

You look to me more like some drag queen* than a man.

BORIS: You want to know what kind of fag I am? Slaves!

Come on out, and bring my cricket bat.* POPOFF: Oh, dear, if I
        said anything   1320

in my joking way, please don't take it seriously.

TCHOTCHKA: What's got into you, I wonder, General Popoff,

to speak so rudely to our cousin and father?

For this man is our father; he found us just now

and *(points to* BORIS*)* this son of his brother. POPOFF: God love me,   1325

well done, {old man}. I'm so glad, the pleasure's all mine,

especially since this will hit the pimp dashed hard,

and since your good luck comes to you due to your own goodness.

TCHOTCHKA: Goodness had everything to do with it.* Believe it, papa.

SADDAM: I do. BORIS: And so do I. And look, here comes the pimp, by an
        amazing coincidence,   1330

I believe. POPOFF: And so do I. BORIS: By George, he's arriving conveniently.

Look, I see the good man, he's on his way home.

[SADDAM: Who is this person? BORIS: Whichever you please—the pimp
        or the Wolf.

He had your daughters here, slaving away,

and stole my gold from me. SADDAM: Nice friends you have!]*   1335

Let's take him to court. SADDAM: Let's not. BORIS: Why not? SADDAM: Because

it's much more pleasing to put him on the chain gang.*

SCENE 6: THE WOLF, BORIS, SADDAM, *and* GENERAL POPOFF
TCHOTCHKA *and* KATYA *are present but do not speak in this scene.*
Enter THE WOLF *from stage L.*

WOLF: No one is led astray, certainly, in my opinion,   iambic senarii
who tells his troubles straight off to his friends;
for one and the same thing was clear to all my friends: 1340
I should hang myself, or lose everything to Boris.
BORIS: Pimp, let's go to court. WOLF: I beg you, Boris,
just let me hang myself. SADDAM: *I* summons you to court.
WOLF: What do *you* want with me? SADDAM: Because I assert these women
are free, and freeborn, both; they are my daughters!   1345
They were kidnapped with their nanny as wee small girls.
WOLF: Why, I've known that for a long time, and I always wondered,
why no one came to manumit them. Imagine!
They're certainly not *mine.* POPOFF: Pimp, you're going to court.
WOLF: You're talking about lunch. I owe you; I'll take care of it.   1350
BORIS: You owe *me* a double penalty for theft. WOLF: Take what you want from
        here. *(Points to pocket.)*
SADDAM: And you owe me heinous punishments. WOLF: Take what you want
        from here. *(Points to pocket again.)*
POPOFF: You owe *me* a thousand in cash. WOLF: Take what you want from here.
        (Points to pocket again.)
I'll pay for everything now with my hip, like a hockey player.*
BORIS: Are you resisting arrest? WOLF: No, not a bit.   1355
BORIS: So go inside, girls. But, Uncle mine,
promise me your daughter in marriage, like you said.
SADDAM: Would I dare do otherwise? POPOFF: Best wishes! BORIS: The
        same to you.
POPOFF: Pimp, I've got this with me as a claim ticket* for my thousand in cash.
        (Brandishes weapon.)
WOLF: Damn, I'm a dead man! BORIS: Well, pretty soon, if you
        go to court.   1360
WOLF: Why don't I just make myself your slave. Who needs a judge?
But, please, let me pay back your three hundred rubles
without the double penalty. I think I can scrape it together;
tomorrow I'll liquidate my assets.* BORIS: Fine—as long
as I can keep you in handcuffs in my basement.*   1365

WOLF: OK, fine. BORIS: Come inside, dear Uncle, to celebrate
this happy day in a jolly way—bad for him, good for us.
Goodbye to all. We've had a lot to say,
but in the end, the pimp was forced to take it.
And now, the final seasoning* to our play: 1370
please do applaud our comedy, as you like it.
FIRST ENDING

SCENE 7: BORIS, THE WOLF, GENERAL POPOFF, SADDAM, TCHOTCHKA, *and*
KATYA
(picks up at line 1322)
Enter THE WOLF *from stage L.*

BORIS: What are you doing, soldier? What's possessed you   iambic senarii
to speak roughly to my uncle? Don't be surprised at the girls
if they follow him: he's just discovered they're his daughters
—yes, both of them. WOLF: Uh-oh, what did I just hear him say?   1375
Now I'm a dead man! POPOFF: Where were they lost from their home?
BORIS: They're from Baghdad. WOLF: But I'm going to hell.
I was always worried that someone would come from there
and recognize them both—and now it's happened. POPOFF *(looks at
          KATYA): Oh, no!*
WOLF: Looks like the end of my eighteen grand in cash   1380
that I paid for them. BORIS: And the end of *you,* Mr. Wolf.
SADDAM: Who is this person? BORIS: Whichever you please—the pimp
          or the Wolf.
He had your daughters here, slaving away,
and stole my gold from me. SADDAM: Nice friends you have!
POPOFF: Pimp, I always believed that you were greedy,*   1385
but those who know you better say you're thievy.*
WOLF: I give in. I'm begging you on my bended knees*—
(to BORIS*)* you, too, and I now know that you're their cousin:
since you're gentlemen, you should also *act* like gentlemen,
and see to it that you take pity on someone who begs you like this.   1390
I've known they were freeborn girls for a long time, really,
and I wondered if anyone would show up to claim them.
They're definitely not *mine.* And also—your rubles—
I'll return what I still have, and I give my oath

that I did nothing with malice aforethought, Boris.   1395
BORIS: What's fair for me to do I'll decide for myself.
Let go of my knees. WOLF: All right, it's your decision.
POPOFF: Hey, pimp. WOLF: Why do you want a pimp? We're
          doing business here.   trochaic septenarii
POPOFF: You owe me a thousand, cash, before you're carried off to the
          chain gang.
WOLF: God forbid. POPOFF: That's it: today you're going to be dining out.   1400
Now you owe my money, his, and your neck, pimp, all three at once.
SADDAM: What is the proper thing for me to do, I am thinking it over with me.
If I want to punish him, I will be going to court in a foreign town,
and I have heard quite a bit about the moral fiber here.
TCHOTCHKA: Daddy, don't have anything to do with this lowlife, I beg you.   1405
KATYA: Listen to my sister. Just leave, don't lower yourself to fight with
          this nasty man.
SADDAM: Very well, pimp. Although I know you have deserved to go under,
I will not mess about with you. BORIS: Nor I. If you'll return my money,
pimp, when you get off the chain gang—you can go straight to Death Row.*
WOLF: What else is new? POPOFF: And I, Mr. Arab—I'd like to clear things up
          with you.   1410
If I said anything while I was upset that might have offended you,
do forgive me, this I beg; and that you've found your daughters—
God love me, I'm delighted. SADDAM: I forgive you and I believe you.
POPOFF: Pimp, you still should get me a lady friend or give me back my
          thousand in cash.
WOLF: Would you like to have my girl saxophone player?* POPOFF: I don't want
          any saxophone player;   1415
it's impossible to tell whether her cheeks or her tits are bigger.
WOLF: I'll find one you'll like. POPOFF: See to it. WOLF: And I'll give you your
          money back tomorrow.
BORIS: See to it that you remember. WOLF: Soldier, follow me. POPOFF: Lead
          on, I follow.
(Exeunt THE WOLF and GENERAL POPOFF into the Wolf's house.)
BORIS: What do you say, Uncle dear? When do you plan to leave for Baghdad?
For I'm sure to go with you. SADDAM: As soon as I can, hey presto!   1420
BORIS: Well, I need to find a realtor,* I would have to stay here a few days . . .
SADDAM: Whatever you say. BORIS: Come on, let's go, let's give ourselves a
          break. ALL (to audience): Applaud!

NONMETRICAL TRANSLATIONS OF SONGS

The Girls' Bathing Song

TCHOTCHKA: If anybody wants to make himself a world of trouble,   210
he should get himself two things—a ship and a woman.
For no two things make more trouble,
especially if you try to rig 'em out,*
and these two things are never rigged out enough,
'cause neither of 'em ever gets filled up full of riggin' out.   215
And when I say these things I'm talkin' about what I learned at home,
'cause the two of us from dawn 'til broad daylight,
[after dawn broke, we never gave up]
never quit but stayed hard at work
bathing and rubbing and washing and primping   220
with powder and paint, polish and padding;
and the two maids who were assigned to each of us,
they helped us in washing and scrubbing,
and we wore out two men, who carried the water.
Get outta here, that's how much work one woman takes.   225
But two women—I know for sure—could be more than enough for
any one city you please, a great big one—
night and day, year in year out, forever
they're primping and bathing and scrubbing and polishing.
'Cause a woman just has no control: 230
we never know how to lay washing and rubbing to rest.*   231–31a
KATYA: 'Cause a girl who's washed, unless she's all dressed up, in my opinion, it's
        just like she's not clean at all.
I'm surprised at you, sister dear, to tell such a story,*
when you're so clever and learned and witty.
For even though we devote ourselves to the principles of good grooming,   235
we can hardly find ourselves a little lover-man or so, try as we may.
TCHOTCHKA: It's true. But still, think about this one thing:
moderation in all things, sister, is the best way to go.
All kinds of excess make excessive trouble for everyone, all by themselves.
KATYA: Sister, think, please, how us girls get a reputation   240
just like pickled fish are judged too salty—
without any charm, without any sweetness,
unless they're soaked in lots of water for a long time—

they're smelly and salty and you wouldn't want to touch 'em.
Women are the same breed—   245
not too tasty and not too pretty
without a beauty regime and considerable expense.

Tchotchka, off to the Festival
What a day—beautiful and festive and full of loveliness,   255
gosh, it's worthy of Venus, whose Aphrodisia it is today.

Tchotchka to Boris
TCHOTCHKA: You don't do right by me, you just dawdle and scheme.
You make promises, lots of 'em; they all turn into dreams.   360
You promised me freedom not once but a hundred times;
while I'm waiting for you, I never got myself another supply.
And one never comes through, and I'm still as much a slave as ever.

The Girls' Festival March
TCHOTCHKA: Today it was well worthwhile for anyone with a real feeling
        for beauty
to feast his eyes—anyone who came to the shrine today to see
        the costumes.   1175
Jeepers, I just loved the working girls' outfits today, they were so nice,
worthy of that oh-so-lovable goddess, Venus; and I didn't turn my nose up
        at her today.
There was such a world of charm there, a place for everything and
        everything in its pretty place.
And Arabian perfume and incense
filled the air; oh, Venus, your holiday   1179a
and your temple didn't seem dirty today, there was such a crowd of girls
        there who work for you,   1180
who'd come to see our Venus of Sarajevo. KATYA: One thing's for sure, at least
        as far as us—
we definitely won the prize for beauty, and conquered all, dear sister,
        yes we did;
and none of the boys there made fun of us, and golly, sister, they did it to all the
        other girls.
TCHOTCHKA: I'd rather hear it from other people, sister, than hear you praise
        yourself like that.

KATYA: Me too. TCHOTCHKA: And, golly, me too, since I'm aware of whence we
        came, and whence these other girls came, too;   1185
we're from a good family, it behooves us to be prim and proper.
SADDAM: Our father, who watchest over and nurturest the human race, through
        whose power we breathe the breath of life,
in whom are all the hopes and dreams of mortal men, grant us this day a lucky
        day, I pray,
for doing my business, that those little girls I lost so long ago, those little girls I
        lost from our fatherland,
return liberty to them, that I may know there is a reward for a love that
        refused to die.   1190

Boris's Reprise

BORIS: Not much! Crikey, she used up the brains she got from you long ago.
Now she's brainy from here, smart from here—however smart she is, it comes
        from my love.   1200

NOTES

This . . . girls: This section translates the acrostic *argumentum,* or brief precis, affixed to
    the beginning of the play; the original one is shorter, since the acrostic is POENU-
    LUS rather than TOWELHEADS. But the sense is roughly the same.

Prologue: The text does not specify which character speaks the prologue; we do hear at
    the end of it that the speaker is playing a part in the play. Bibliography in Mau-
    rach 1988: 44; see esp. Slater 1992.

1   *Boris . . . Pushkin:* The first two words of *Poenulus* are *Achillem Aristarchi,* "the
    Achilles of Aristarchus." Plautus's contemporary Ennius staged a version of this
    Greek play of the mid-fifth century B.C.E. So this is a real play, probably in re-
    cent translation and revival, and focusing on the story of a famous ancient war-
    rior. The first line is set up to be a shock to the audience ("Are we at the right
    play?"). It sets up questions about comedy and tragedy and their relation to war
    that run on into the play. The tag in lines 3–4 may well be a quotation from the
    Ennius translation; here I have used a pastiche of lines from the Alfred Hayes
    translation of *Boris Godunov.* This play by Pushkin was chosen to match the
    transposed setting of the play, but starting with "*Julius Caesar* by William Shake-
    speare" also works well, and it is easy to find lines there to fit this speech (see act
    1, scene 2, as well as the obvious "Friends, Romans . . ."). On the opening lines,
    see Gowers 1993: 91.

4	Tsar . . . drama nazi: An attempt to render a complex pun in the Latin: the quotation ends with *imperator,* "general," "commander" (probably referring to Agamemnon); the line then finishes *histricus.* This is a pun on *histrio,* "actor"; the commander is a histrionic (*histricus*)/Histrian *(Histricus)* one. See *Towelheads* introduction on Histria (a peninsula east of what is now Venice) as a Roman enemy during this period; the Histrians were sea raiders, and ran afoul of Rome before the beginning of the Second Punic War.
8	Fill up on corny jokes: Note repeated theme of hunger in the prologue; see volume introduction on class and the Roman audience (under "Audience and Venue" and "Food"). The word translated here "corny jokes," *fabulis* ("comedy," "play," "stories") may be a pun on *fabulis,* "little beans" (see Gowers 1993: 60, 79, who points out the use of *fabuli* as theater snacks, like popcorn, and the general use in Plautus of junk food as a metaphor for theater). For "fill up" (*saturi fite*), cf. Fat Jack (Saturio) in *Iran Man* and Weevil's joke at *Weevil* 362; is there a running joke here on *saturi* "full" and *satura* "satire"?
11	Psst . . . hear ye: Literally, "Arise, Herald, and obtain from the folk a hearing"; probably another line from the *Achilles.* The quoted half-line in the translation is from *Boris Godunov* again.
16	By . . . "Change . . . procedure": Literally, "Order in the court; respect my authority"; magistrate's formula, followed by (probably) more tragic parody. The line in the translation is more *Boris Godunov.*
17	Overage toyboys: Latin *scortum exoletum;* see note on *Weevil* 473.
18	Cops . . . rods: The Latin talks about the lictors, magistrates' guards who carried rods as symbol of the magistrates' authority, though they were not to be used for hitting. Cf. jokes about slaves being hit with rods, below, line 26; *Iran Man,* notes at 28 and 279; *Weevil,* note at 193.
28	Nursing mothers: Latin *nutrices,* "wet nurses."
29	Munchkins: Latin *minutulos,* "teeny-weenies."
36	Members of the Academy: Latin *ludorum curatores,* "those in charge of the games"—the aediles.
37	Oscar: Literally, "palm." The palm branch in antiquity was given to a winner of the Olympic games. These lines suggest there might have been a drama competition at the Roman games as there was at the Athenian festivals, but we have little other evidence on this.
41	Limo drivers: Latin *pedisequi,* male slaves who went around with their masters; "personal assistants."
43	Nachos: Latin *scribilitae,* "a kind of cheese tart" *(OLD).*

44 Imperial drama nazi: See note on line 4 above. Both Maurach 1988 and Slater 1992 point out that there is one type of person who is not restricted by the speaker's orders; this is what Maurach calls "theater for the privileged free man." But it's also a privilege to be addressed from the stage, and the free man is here excluded from that address.

47 Savvy: Latin *gnarures,* a colloquial and archaizing form of *gnarus,* "knowledgeable."

49 Border patrol man: Latin *finitor,* literally "surveyor"; the metaphor in 48–49 is of the military engineering that established national borders and land redistribution, a Roman specialty.

52 Guys . . . office: "Those who have this in hand," i.e., the magistrates.

53 "The . . . Baghdad": Greek *Karkhedonios,* "The Carthaginian."

54 In . . . Jones: Literally, "in Latin, Plautus Uncle Pultiphagonides." The punctuation and text of this line are uncertain; some think the play is called "Uncle Pultiphagonides," or that Plautus *is* Uncle Pultiphagonides. *Puls* is mush made of grain, esp. barley, and in this period was a staple food of poor Italians; cf. note on *Weevil* line 295. *Pultiphagonides,* "*Puls*-Eater-Son," is a comic name formation; like others in Plautus (see notes on *Iran Man* 120, 702–5), it contains a Greek element (*-phag-*) plus a Greek patronymic (*-ides,* "son of"). Hence "de Cornpone-Jones" as aristocratic in form, using a patronymic, translating Roman "*puls*-eating" into a U.S. equivalent, and dealing with Plautus and class issues. On *puls* and this name, see Gowers 1993: 54–57, 64.

56–58 Account . . . IRS: Just as lame in Latin—a joke on the double meaning of "account."

The IRS: Latin *iuratores,* "tax officials."

59 Baghdad: Carthage; so translated throughout.

67 Note that Boris's date of birth puts him right in the middle of the Second Punic War for any likely production date of this play.

70 His cousin: This family tree is a bit confusing:

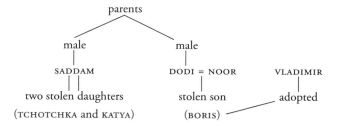

Although in the play Saddam is often described as Boris's paternal uncle, in fact he is Boris's paternal first cousin once removed, and his daughters are Boris's second cousins. Saddam also defines Boris's mother as his *sobrina,* "second cousin."

71   He goes . . . 'em: Literally, "he goes to Acheron without money for the trip."

72   Sarajevo: Calydon. See volume introduction (under "Locations") on the fleeting usefulness of this translation. In this play, "here" is the location of a recent war overshadowed but not forgotten. The siege of Sarajevo is already receding into the mists of history. Readers should substitute as appropriate.

86   Casbah: "The Magara," here used as a place within Carthage, evidently derived from Latin *magalia,* a Roman stereotype-word for African housing. The Casbah is the old quarter of Algiers, not Baghdad, but it does overlook the site of a Carthaginian trading post. It features in the 1938 film *Algiers,* in which Charles Boyer says "Come with me to the Casbah," a classic and much-parodied Orientalizing line.

87   Belgrade: Anactorium; see introduction to *Towelheads,* and note on line 72.

88   Young ladies: Translates Latin *virgines;* cf. Cherry in *Iran Man.* Note that Tchotchka and Katya are listed in the Latin dramatis personae as *puellae,* "girls"; they are supposedly not yet prostitutes. They do seem to have finished some preliminary training, though; see line 1139.

90   Damnedest guy: Latin *sacerrumo. Sacer,* "sacred," can also mean "forfeited to a god due to an offense against divine law."

101   Wants . . . price: Literally, "wants to catch the guy in his *bolo* [haul]"; cf. note on *Iran Man* 658.

104   Arab: Latin *Poenus.* As Franko 1994 emphasizes, *Carthaginiensis* in this period is a neutral technical term for a citizen of Carthage; *Poenus* is a general term for a person of Phoenician descent living in the western Mediterranean, and is commonly associated with pejorative terms.

108   Then: Or "afterwards"! See *Towelheads* introduction on other examples of this plot in antiquity.

109–10   This list of questions is like the ones posed to Cherry by the pimp as prospective buyer in *Iran Man* (lines 630–49).

113   He's . . . tell: See *Towelheads* introduction on *Punica fides.*

117   Don't break it: This joke has exercised the ingenuity of editors but has to be phallic; cf. Boris and the Lawyers, below, 565–66; *Weevil* 44–45.

123   Get dressed: Latin *ornabor,* a play on theatrical costuming; see below at 284, 425, 577; *Weevil* 464; and notes on *Iran Man* 158, 335, 462.

137   Phony . . . pastafazool: Latin and Greek *gerrae germanae, hai de kollurai lurai,* phrases that have the same meaning as the translation and work on the same principle. Maurach thinks Boris's opening speech is like a prayer to a god, and Igor's reply is ironically set up to be an equally serious proverb, which turns out to be the slang of line 137. Both the Latin and Greek phrases in this line are obscure, but the double jingle is definitely not pious in tone. *Gerrae* may = "penis"; *kollurai* is "bread soup" or "pasta" (see *Iran Man* 92, with note), here translated with the Italian-American "pastafazool" (from *pasta e fagiole,* "bean soup"), = "nonsense."

138   Sweetsy-weetsy: Latin *blandidicus.*

147   Skip out on: As slaves proverbially want to do in Roman culture; oddly enough, it is seen as a character flaw. Cf. *Iran Man* 421.

155   Bigger: Latin *maiusculam*—a word ambiguous between "larger" and "older," as "bigger" is in English.

163   Make her yours: Literally, "make her your *liberta,*" your freed slave; see notes on *Iran Man* 474–75, 737, and also on line 168 below.

166   Three hundred golden rubles: Latin *nummi Philippi;* see volume introduction under "Money" on translating money, and *Towelheads* introduction on the repetition of this figure in the play.

168   *Mishpocheh:* (Yiddish), translating Latin *familia,* "household, extended family." The legal goal here is that Boris will, by means of a lawsuit, acquire ownership of all the pimp's slaves plus the pimp himself, as a debt slave.

170   Who . . . place: Blini is the *vilicus* ("overseer," "farm manager") and a slave himself; see *Towelheads* introduction under "The Setting, the Names, and the Cast."

177   Nice place . . . asked: Latin *locum . . . liberum,* "a free place," "a place of freedom"; cf. below, 602, 657.

184   Pimp owes . . . slave: Literally, "the pimp's a double thief." This refers to the penalties for theft in Roman law, which in special circumstances, e.g., concealing stolen goods, involved up to four times the value of the thing stolen .

186   The judge . . . you: Literally, "the praetor will make over to you his whole household"—including slaves.

191   Festival of Love: Aphrodisia; see *Towelheads* introduction on religious festivals in Calydon.

192   Feast . . . tarts: Literally, "delight/snare my eyes in the prostitutes' *munditiae.*" *Munditia* is elegance achieved through the toilette.

199   That ain't . . . bill: Literally, "that can't be washed off without great expense."

201–2   Grenade-launcher . . . bunker: Latin *ballista . . . e ballistario;* cf. *Weevil* 395, 690. Igor has the *ballista* well cranked up *(intenta)* so it's cocked and ready to shoot and will strike hard. The Latin is a more phallic threat than the English.

206, 208–9   Spectacles . . . seat . . . show: Latin *ludos . . . spectare . . . spectaculum;* the vocabulary comes from the games (like the one at which this play was being performed).

208   God . . . thee: Literally, "Oh, may the gods give many good things to you"; Boris tends to wax poetic.

227   We'll . . . Pole: The metaphor "woman = ship," though hardly new in Plautus, resonates with Rome's continual state of war in these years; the First Punic War, in which one famous Hanno figured, was a naval war. A threat to a *populus* (227), "even the biggest one" (= Rome), was only half funny at this time; Hannibal got up to the gates of Rome.

232   This line is attributed to Tchotchka in the text. Editors have felt that the line doesn't match Tchotchka's overall opinions, and some assign it to Katya, as I have here.

241   Like a lox: Literally, "like *salsa muriatica,*" pickled salt fish. See literal translation after the end of the play; the metaphor is extended and surprisingly gross. Women's genitals are said to smell like fish in later Roman satire.

248   Chefette: Latin *coqua,* a coinage from the normal *coquus* (masc.); women were not particularly associated with cooking in Roman culture. Note that in the original, the song continues through line 260.

266–68   Much-discussed lines. Literally, "among the *prosedas* ['prostitutes'], girlfriends of *pistores* [flourmill workers; see *Iran Man* 22 for the mill as slave prison], leftovers [or queens] of things *alica*-related [*alica* is a kind of grain], poor dirty *servilicolas, schoeno delibutas* ['smeared with the aromatic eastern grass called "camel's hay"'], who stink of the *stabulum* ['stable/brothel'] and the *statum* [? 'stance'], the *sella* ['seat,' ? = public toilet, haunt of prostitutes] and pure *sessibulum* [seat]." *Servilicolas* is translated here as *servili-colas,* "slave-followers," rather than following the standard interpretation that takes this word as a diminutive of "slave-girl." As with *prosedas,* all the last four terms relate to the image of the cheap prostitute as one who sits or stands out on display under a placard with her name and price. Tchotchka strongly differentiates herself from these.

272   Millionaires: Literally, "kings"; see volume introduction (under "Topical Jokes") on kings in Plautus.

274   A plugged nickel: Latin *nebulai cyatho,* "a ladle-full of cloud."

279 Shirley: Boris says, "Igor, hey, Igor, where are you?" Igor replies, "I am here *[assum]* with you, look." Boris interprets this to mean "Roasted *[assum]* with you, look," and replies, "but I wish you were boiled." Hence the translation: one bad old joke for another.

280 Jokes . . . making: Latin *facis delicias;* perhaps with a hint of *deliciae* = "toyboy."

282 God . . . him: Literally, "the gods . . . them."

284 Dressed: This scene again makes much use of forms of *orno;* see note on 123.

288 This line is corrupt; the sense is clear.

290 Solid rock: Literally, "a flint stone."

292–94 Boris says "I've never slimed *[limavi]* heads with her"; see Wright 1974: 71, who says this is an expression out of archaic Latin, and that it would have been obscure then, too, but probably sexual. It seems likely. Maurach claims it means "kissed" rather than anything more intimate (cf. the expression "suck face"). Igor replies, "I'll go to the fishpond or the reservoir and get some sludge *[limum]*." Boris says, "What do you need that for?" and Igor replies, "I'll tell you: so that I can slime her head and yours."

295 Bugger off: Literally, "Go to the bad thing." Loser: Literally, "you're ruined."

296 There . . . job: Literally, "You wound me by mocking me and you make *delicias*"; cf. on line 280.

299 Heart attack: Latin *cordolium,* literally "a pain in the heart."

301 In diamonds: "In much gold."

304 Mink: Latin *purpuram,* "purple dye"; purple was extremely expensive to produce, hence = "luxury wear," the prerogative of the upper class.

312 Like a bunch of bananas: Literally, "like a dried grape."

315 TCHOTCHKA *(to* MAID*):* The change of speaker here is a textual variant.

320 Won't . . . light: Literally, "nocturnal faces." Pray: "Sacrifice."

325 Like shandy [i.e., a mixture of beer and lemonade]: Latin *mulsa,* "honeyed" (as in the wine drink called *mulsum*).

Briquettes: Latin *laterculos* literally means "little bricks"; nowhere else in Latin is it used to refer to baked goods—elsewhere it describes building materials and cattle feed. In this joke, Igor replaces Boris's sweet image with one that fits better with his own opinion of Tchotchka, and then in line 326 pretends to make up for it by frosting the bricks with sesame and poppy seeds (which were sweets in Roman cooking, cf. Petronius *Satyricon* 1.3, where they are joined with honey), whole wheat, and chopped nuts. If *laterculi* were baked goods, they sound more like bagels than cookies; see volume introduction under "Food." The tone must be sarcastic.

327   Isn't . . . love it: Literally, Boris says, "Do I seem to love much?" and Igor replies, "Expense, which Mercury doesn't love." Mercury was the god of finance.

332   Maid's speech: Literally, "I lost both my lamp oil and my effort."

334   God . . . side: The OCT assigns this line to Tchotchka.

339   Close-out sale on sluts: Latin *mercatus meretricius,* "prostitute market."

343   When . . . touchy-feely: Latin *quando . . . apud me mecum palpas et lalas,* "when do you stroke and chat with me at my house." A manuscript variant has *mecum caput et corpus copulas,* "link head and body with me."

344   When . . . again: Literally, "on the day the death god lets the dead out of Acheron."

347   Go . . . go: Assignment of this line to Boris is a textual variant.

358   Don't . . . messenger: Literally, "Don't comb out this orator with your fists afterwards."

359–63   (*Song*): This was not a song in the original; see nonmetrical translation after end of play.

365–67   Igor's list of endearments includes many common Latin expressions that can't be translated literally:

366   Bunny: "Little eye." Honey: "Little lip." Soul kiss: Latin *savium* (Latin had three words for "kiss"; this was the sexiest).

367   Sugar: "Honey" (the Romans did not have sugar). Sweetheart: "Heart." Honeybee: "Bee sting." Cheesecake: "Little sweet cheese."

369   If . . . limb: Literally, "if I don't order him to be rushed away at once to the executioner in a four-horse chariot."

371   Bejillion dollars: Latin *ninnium,* "a word of unknown meaning" *(OLD).*

372   A citizen of the USA: "An Athenian citizen"; cf. *Iran Man* lines 474–75. This is especially odd considering that Boris is Aetolian and Carthaginian, but not Athenian: another instance of Athens = here = Rome? A trace of a Greek original?

377, 378   Weepy . . . punchy: Latin *ploratillum, verberetillum*—made-up diminutives based on the words for "weep" and "flog."

381   Worth a brass farthing: Latin/Greek *trioboli,* "worth three obols."

382   Bastard's: Latin *mastigiae,* from Greek *mastix,* "whip"; another slave torture epithet. Cf. *Weevil* 567.

390   Cheese cupcake: Latin *dulciculus caseus,* "little sweet cheese." Bastard: Latin *mastigia* (see on 382).

390a   Thrill: Latin *studium,* "object of focused desire"—so "thrill" as in "You're My Thrill"; "fancy," "love-object," "obsession."

393   Boobacious . . . bane: Latin *amica mammeata . . . inimica et malevola,* "big-titted girlfriend . . . ill-willed she-enemy."

394   Precious, pinkeye: Latin *oculus,* "eye" vs. *lippitudo,* "eye disease" (cf. *Weevil* line 318; *Iran Man* line 11). Honey, liverwurst: *mel,* "honey" vs. *fel,* "bile, gall-bladder, bitterness."

396   *Mishpocheh:* See line 168.

397   Eating . . . straw: Literally, "staying alive in sips."

398   Back . . . sores: Literally, "I'm walking around with a back that's ridged with sores like an oyster has ridges" (not "striped" as in *OLD,* surely).

411   Call . . . realtor: Literally, "hold an auction"—usually indicative of bankruptcy.

421   Igorochka: *Milphidisce;* cf. on the name "Sophoclidisca" in *Iran Man* introduction.

425   Tricking out: Latin *ornamentis . . . exornabo:* cf. lines 123, 284; more theatrical language.

426   Art of the con: Latin/Greek *sycophantiis;* cf. introduction to *Weevil* on parasites, and note to *Weevil* 463 on *sycophantae* as con artists.

427   More . . . yours: Runaway slave joke; cf. *Iran Man* 421.

439   Swear . . . Bible: "Do you want me to say with good faith?"

441   Babbling: Latin *fabuler;* rel. *fabula,* "play," "story."

443–44 Sigmund . . . complex: Literally, "You'd need Oedipus, who solved the riddle of the Sphinx, to figure out that speech."

447   Witnesses: See on "Lawyers" in *Towelheads* introduction. The word for "witnesses," here *testis,* is the source of many jokes in *Weevil* based on its double meaning, "testicles" (which also = "manhood," "courage"), and so there is possibly another joke on Boris here. See note at *Weevil* 30–38.

453–65 God . . . God . . . him . . . he . . . God: Literally, "the gods . . . the other gods and goddesses . . . them . . . they . . . the gods."

455   The holy OK: "I can't *litare,*" = "I can't obtain favorable omens from a sacrifice," "can't please the deity."

456   No guts and no glory: Literally, "I forbade the innards to be cut out."

457   Slammed . . . on the mat: Latin *adii manum,* "I put my hand on her," perhaps a metaphor from wrestling; cf. *Iran Man* 796.

461   Toe the line: Literally, "be more content."

463   Two-bit: See note on line 381.

471   Cincostan: *Pentetronica,* a nonsense place-name made from the Greek word *pente,* "five." Many editors have thought the original said something else, more intelligibly funny; guesses include Ritschl's *Ptenanthropica* ("Bird-man-land") and Leo's *Ptenolatronica* ("Bird-thug-land").

477   I'll tell you: Cf. *Weevil* lines 407–53; this often cues a lie.

478   Sassafrass tree: Latin *farferi.* This sounds like a nonsense word, but was the name for the plant coltsfoot; hence "sassafrass," a real name that sounds silly.

484–85 Kumquats: "Pears" in the original.

487   With . . . doves: This practice is elsewhere unattested for Rome, but Maurach 1988 says this method of killing birds exists today.

489   Give: "Sacrifice."

491   Fire . . . grill: "While the innards are being brought in," here and throughout.

494   Like . . . bag: "With punches."

495   Go . . . devil: "Go to the bad cross."

501   I'm . . . alike: The OCT assigns this cryptic line to the Wolf.

503   For . . . fortune: With this line, cf. line 720, where a similar statement has an important double meaning.

506   Slump like slugs: Latin *spissigradissumos,* "sluggish-steppingest."

507   Garbage scows: Latin *corbitae,* cargo ships; also at 543.

510   Fondling fathers: Latin *procos*—an upper class of citizens in early Roman history; a pun on *procos,* "suitors."

        Flopfooted: Latin *loripedes,* "strapfooted"; occasionally applied to real people, but more commonly, in fantastic geographies, applied to the "snakefooted" people who live in far-off lands (see Evans 1999).

511   Go to hell: "Go to the bad cross."

513   As . . . cotton: Latin *succretust cribro pollinario,* "sifted through a flour sieve"— another mill reference?

521   Bonded out to: Latin *addictos;* this verb is used of debt slavery (also in 186 above). Plautus is said to have written a play called *Addictus;* see volume introduction under "Who Was Plautus?"

523   {In a play}: The Lawyer's joke here is based on the stock joke of having a slave run in a play, seen in *Weevil* in Weevil's entrance, though he's not a slave; cf. the opening sequence of *A Funny Thing Happened on the Way to the Forum*.

524   When . . . terminated: See introduction to *Towelheads;* this line has been used to argue that the play was performed after 197 B.C.E. or after 190/89 B.C.E. For attempts to date the play by internal evidence, see Maurach 1988: 32–33.

528   Like looney tunes: Latin *pro cerritis,* "like people possessed by Ceres."

530   Like a man on stilts: Another reference to the entertainments at the *ludi*.

532   Flat feet: Literally, they are *podagrosi*—gouty; gout was an illness commonly complained of in Roman texts.

536   With . . . whomsoever: Possibly legalese; echoed by Igor in line 588.

539   Got no beef with: Latin *flagitamus;* see notes on *Weevil* line 145; *Iran Man* lines 406–26, 569. *Flagitatio* often involves yelling at someone in public in order to get back misappropriated goods.

540   Bust a gut: Latin *rupturus ramites,* "about to burst our lungs."

546   FedEx: Latin *cursores,* "runners."

564   Good for a double fine: See note on line 184 on Roman law concerning theft. You'll . . . pimp: Latin *addicetur;* see notes on lines 521 and 720.

565–66 You've . . . fingertips: This seems to be a small-penis joke; cf. the similar joke at 116–17, and at *Weevil* 44–45.

570   Leg: Latin *femina.* Literally, "thighs." The interchange of insults here sinks to a low level.

571   On your crotch: Latin *in lumbos,* "onto your hips/buttocks/genital area."

574   Righteously hip: Latin *callemus probe;* cf. *Iran Man* line 305 and note.

577   One . . . hombre: Latin *basilice ornatus;* see notes on 123 and on *Iran Man* 29, 462 (same phrase) and notes.

            Craftsman of the con: Latin *fabre ad fallaciam,* literally "craftily for the con."

578   Stay hip: Latin *vide sis calleas.*

579   Don't . . . me: See volume introduction under "Catchphrases," and note on *Iran Man* 305.

581   Tragic . . . comedian: Same joke at *Iran Man* 465.

582   Look . . . many: OCT attributes Boris's line here to Igor.

584   Courthouse . . . chaser: Latin *comitiales . . . meri,* literally "undiluted *comitium* guys." For the *comitium,* see *Weevil* lines 400–403, 470.

586   Legal finaglers: Latin *iuris coctiores,* a pun on *iuris doctus,* "learned in law," the technical term for a trained lawyer (as in the current J.D. degree). *Coctiores* (for *doctiores*) = "more cooked," tying the Lawyers to a general Plautine connection between cooking and conniving; cf. Gowers 1993: 77.

587   They're repo men: Latin *litis emunt,* "they buy lawsuits." This joke accuses the Lawyers of a practice like what collection agencies do. See Sidonius Apollinaris *Letters* 5.7.2, where this appears in a list of shady practices.

595   Take . . . yours: Cf. *Iran Man,* line 440.

598   In the decadent West: Latin *in barbaria;* see volume introduction (under "Locations") on Plautus's use of *barbarus* to mean "Italian." *Barbaria* is an insulting term for "elsewhere"; in the Balkan perspective of the Lawyers, then, crude agricultural practices are associated with a place they reject as other, which is also the position of the audience.

        They . . . cows: Literally, "after this gold is soaked, cows get fat on it." Some kind of dried vegetation seems to be used here as stage money; commentators advocate lupines, but maybe it was fenugreek (*faenum Graecum,* "Greek hay"), another common ancient cattle feed, which has round gold-colored seeds.

602   Place . . . free: Latin *liberum . . . locum,* literally "a free place." This expression recurs throughout Blini's scenes to describe where he wants to have fun. For Blini it has a double meaning. Cf. 177, 657.

603   Party like Eurotrash: Latin *pergraecere,* literally "act really Greek," a word that supposedly came into Latin on increased contact with the Greeks of southern Italy and Sicily. On the association between Greekness, food, and partying, see Gowers 1993: 61.

610   Farted: Latin *concrepuerunt,* "creaked/farted." See note on *Weevil* line 295. This is the usual door cue; Blini makes it an issue.

612   City boys . . . behind 'em: "City boys" = Latin *scurrae;* see notes on *Weevil* 296–97, 484; Corbett 1986. This joke probably implies that *scurrae* like anal sex with other men; but cf. Maurach 1988, who rejects a sexual meaning and says the joke has to do with the struggle for precedence among various hangers-on, translating "they're always trying to get ahead." But this would surely still be a double entendre.

613   Good . . . evil: A joke about the pimp as evil stereotype in comedy.

620   In the trenchcoat: Latin/Greek *chlamydatus.* On the *chlamys,* see *Weevil* lines 611, 632; *Iran Man* line 155.

621   Citizens . . . Yugoslavia: Latin *Aetoli cives.*

628–32 Storm drain: Latin *amnem,* literally, "river." The Wolf's speech here has puzzled many readers; this is an approximation of its sense.

639   Repeats line 622a.

645   I'm . . . glue: Literally, "On your head be it!"

654   This . . . rodeo: Literally, "How expertly they set off on the con!"

657   Free . . . place: Latin *locum . . . liberum*, as in 177, 602.

660   Asking for it: This line assignment is the result of an emendation. He's mine: Literally, "He's my loot/trophy *[praeda]*"—picks up on Blini's use of *praeda* in the context of hunting in 647.

663   Hit man: Latin *latro*, "brigand," "thug." Kosovo: Literally, "Sparta."

664   For the Israelis: Literally, "for King Attalus"; he was king of Pergamum in Asia Minor, and troops from his country were involved in the war in Sparta (195 B.C.E.), though after his death. See note on *Iran Man* 339.

668   Turkey: Latin *praeda* again; cf. lines 647, 660.

676   The turkey . . . trap: Literally, "the dove into the space for fowlers' nets."

690–92   You're . . . here: Literally, the Wolf says, "You were looking from *muschis*," to which Blini replies, "If I were looking for a lodging free from flies *[muscis]*, I would have gone straight to the *carcer* when I got here." Lindsay argued that the manuscript reading *muscis* in 690 had to be an error for a word that sounded like *muscis*, to enable the heard-wrong joke in 691–92, and chose Greek *muschis*, a rare word = "genitals"; Maurach suggests Greek *amustis*, "deep drinking," but not enthusiastically. Why there should be no flies in the *carcer* is a mystery; editors connect this with Blini's repeated request for privacy (flies = onlookers?). The first word must be unusual and the second more familiar and connected with the *carcer*, so I have just put in a French word and an English mis-hearing. The *carcer*, here translated "the prison," was a building in the Roman Forum where (rare) executions of citizens were carried out (note that Blini, as a slave, would have been ineligible for punishment there—he's trying to sound like a free man). Cf. *Weevil* 692; below, 1409.

694   The Shah of Iran's: "King Antiochus's" (Antiochus III, the Seleucid king of Syria, was involved in the fighting in Greece throughout this period and was famous for luxury).

         Family jewels: *oculi*, "eyes." The term "King's Eye" was used by Greeks to describe important courtiers of the Great King of Persia (cf. Aristophanes *Acharnians* 92ff.); *oculi* is also occasionally used in Latin = "testicles," e.g., Martial 3.92.2.

699   Bordeaux . . . Merlot: "Leucadian, Lesbian, Thracian, Chian wine." Lines 699 and 700 are reversed here only for sense in translation. Cf. *Weevil* 78; Plautus specifies wine by type only here. Chios was later associated with luxury.

701   Sprinkle: Literally, "fill with *geumatis*"—a Greek word meaning "small amount."

704   Like a hit man: Latin *latrocinantur,* "acts like a *latro*"—see line 663.

711   Casual passersby: Boris calls them *testes,* "witnesses."

720   You've . . . slave: Latin *addictum tenes;* see note on line 521 on *addictus;* and line 564.

729   . . . And . . . egg: The Latin has a terrible pun: *si pultem non recludet* means both "If I knock and he won't open" and "If he won't break open the porridge." The Lawyers reply, *panem frangito,* "break his bread."

741   Doors . . . farted: Just *crepuerunt* again. Boris could be picking up on Blini's joke, or not.

743–44   If . . . ourselves: Literally, "If you want (us) to cover our heads"; cf. *Weevil* 288, 293, 389, where having the head covered indicates slyness or having something to hide. This detail perhaps corresponds with a much later observation by the philosopher Seneca (mid-first century C.E.): Maecenas used to appear in public "with his head covered in a *pallium* with his ears sticking out on either side, no differently than the runaway slaves of the rich man do in the mime" (*Ep. Mor.* 114.6). On mime, see volume introduction under "Who Was Plautus?"

760   You're . . . gums: Literally, "You're cooling your mouth now."

765   You . . . else: Latin *cum testibus,* "with witnesses"; perhaps another testicle joke, see *Weevil* lines 30–38, 565, 622, 695.

768   Ha ha ha: Latin *Hahahae.*

778   I'll howl: Latin *aruio.* The *OLD* says this may be a colloquial form of *ravio,* "be hoarse"; surely it is onomatopoeia, reproducing the noise the Wolf would naturally make.

783   You're . . . assholes: Literally, "Woe upon your age!"

784   Jailmeat: Latin *furcifer,* "fork-bearer." The *furca* was a Y-shaped frame used as a slave punishment; for insults like this one, in which slaves are taunted with the punishments inflicted on them, cf. *Weevil* 193; *Iran Man* 11, 21–28, 278–79, 419–26, 795, and H. Parker 1989.

804   {Just like Rambo}: Blini frames his lunch as an epic deed, like the night raid in the *Iliad;* he needs a similar modern context.

807   Downtown: Latin *in comitio;* see above, 584; and notes on *Weevil* 400–403, 470.

812–13   One-ounce: "Lighter than a feather." Two-ton: "leaden."

827   In the quarries or in the mill: See *Iran Man* 22 on the mill as a place of slave punishment; the quarries served the same purpose, as seen esp. in Plautus's *Captivi.*

828   Dragging . . . me: Literally, "with my side weighted down with strong iron."

832   Millionaires and regular guys: Latin *equitem, peditem*, "a knight, a foot soldier"; this expression means "all male citizens," from the old military class divisions of the Roman people.

836–38   Letters . . . pick: Literally, "letters made of clay, / [branded like a runaway slave]/[sealed with pitch], and the names on them are a cubit long; / that's the choice of wine jugs we got at our house." This joke treats wine amphoras as reading matter, like the whiskey signs in the translation. See Niall Slater's essay in Baier 2004.

845   Mr. Responsible: Latin *frugi bonae*, literally, "characterized by good morality"; see note at *Iran Man* 449 on the old-time Roman virtue *frugi*; below, 963.

846   La-Z-Boy: Latin *Ignaviam*, invoking a (female) personification of laziness and cowardice; cf. *Iran Man* line 850, and 890 below. See MacCary and Willcock 1976 on *Casina* 128–29 for a list of similar jokes in Plautus.

848   The boss . . . ox: Literally, "where the master couldn't make Venus favorable to him on her holy day with his sacrifices."

859   Not us, buddy: Same joke at *Iran Man* line 205.

862–63   A guy . . . tools: The reference here is to the traditional punishment for adultery, which included castration by the offended husband; see *Weevil*, lines 30–38. "Tools" literally = *vasa* ("jugs") = "testicles."

        God . . . too: "May the gods ruin you and your master!"

866   I'm hosed: Latin *male mihi est*, "It is ill with me."

873   Like a goat: Romans found armpits disgusting when smelly, and jokes conventionally use "goat" to mean "bad armpit smell"; cf. Catullus 69, 71; Horace *Epodes* 12.5; Ovid *Ars Amatoria* 1.522, 3.193. But plucking armpit hair was associated with women and effeminacy; see Richlin 1995.

        Get lost: "Go to a bad thing."

876   Than a woman with laryngitis: Literally, "than what is said to a mute woman."

890   On . . . Scout: Literally, "Belief isn't better placed in Fides [Good Faith] herself." For the joke, cf. 846.

892   Do . . . thing: Latin *facere frugem*.

897   Some Taliban thug: Latin *praedone Siculo*. Sicily was yet another old battleground of Rome, from the First and Second Punic Wars, and appears in Plautus as the source of wickedness; see volume introduction under "Locations."

900   Iraqi citizens: Latin *ingenuas,* "free-born girls." From Baghdad: "From Carthage."

906   It's the law: The method and rationale of this claim are as in *Iran Man:* a slave could be claimed into freedom from his master by someone who knew him to have been free.

907   Checkmate: Latin *ad incitas rediget;* a technical term from a chess-like game. Line 908 continues the metaphor.

910   I'll see you freed alongside me: In fact, Vodka makes no further appearance, and Igor disappears in act 5 without a reward of any kind. Cf. the disappearance of Fat Jack and Cherry in the *Iran Man* finale. Igor's promise depends on the Wolf's *familia* being adjudged to Boris, at which time Boris will free them together.

919   Bombshell: Literally, "projectile."

930–39   In the manuscripts, lines 930–39 and 940–49 seem to be doublets; Lindsay bracketed 930–39 and accepted 940–49 as closer to the original text. The two speeches are both in a sort of Punic alphabet soup; 940–49 is even more garbled than 930–39. Both include versions of the name of the young man and his adoptive father. See *Towelheads* introduction on the question of how much, if any, of Saddam's opening speech is in genuine Punic in the original, and the politics of such a move.

940–49   The translation here first tries out the theory that the speech is in Punic, might have been recognizable as such, and might have been understood by a few people in the audience; scholars think that the speech is a prayer, matching the Latin of 950–54, hence the translation here into two Hebrew prayers (should be Arabic; see *Towelheads* introduction). The translation of the rest of the speech uses Orientalizing gibberish to try out the alternate theory that the speech is in stage Punic, to give a sense of what effect that might have had in production. Either way, the joke in beginning a scene like this is like the joke of beginning the prologue with the announcement of a different play.

940–42   Baruch . . . shel yom tov: These three lines are the Hebrew prayer for lighting the Sabbath candles.

943–44   Baruch . . . ha-ga-fen: These two lines are the Hebrew prayer for blessing wine.

958   Hospitality token: Latin *tesseram,* a small cube or die with markings; *tesserae* were split and held by host and guest to confirm identity when they met again. The gloss in the translation is aimed at helping an audience understand a custom with no modern equivalent. Or translate "friendship ring"?

963   Do the right thing: Latin *frugi esse;* see note on 845.

965–66 For the sentiments expressed in these lines, see notes on *Weevil* 300, 607, and the scene of Cherry's sale in *Iran Man* act 4, scene 4.

970 Blackitude: Latin *sordituadinem,* a made-up word from *sordes,* which = (1) dirt, filth, (2) dark clothes worn by mourners, (3) squalor, baseness. Saddam is perhaps dressed in black, as befits his bereaved condition. But see below for indications that Carthaginians were portrayed onstage as dark-skinned.

971 Witness: Latin *testis;* another testicle joke? See above, 765, and note on *Weevil* 30–38. "To have testicles" = "to be a real man" in Roman humor, and line 972 indicates Igor thinks Boris isn't, here.

972 Like a man: Latin *fortiter,* "bravely."

975 In the bathrobe: Latin *cum tunicis.* The *tunica* was a unisex undergarment; for its association with foreignness, see *Iran Man* 155.

976 Clothes: Latin/Greek *pallio* (the *pallium* was standard Greek men's outerwear, but also the costume of the comic actor).

At the gym: Literally, "at the baths."

977 Face . . . Arab: Literally, "his face is Punic" (the line indicates that Saddam's mask or makeup would have looked Punic but unfortunately does not specify how).

A wog: *guggast homo.* The meaning of *gugga* is unknown; see Maurach 1988 ad loc. Commentators look for some kind of pun on *Punica* "Punic" and *punicea* "scarlet," and, connecting with "bird" in line 975, tend to think a *gugga* is a red-faced bird, a bittern (Greek *guges*) or a heron (roughly, "His face is Iraq-an" "Must be a robin!" or "His face—he's a pinko!" "He's a flamingo!"). But not all birds are funny, and the *guges* is hardly a household word, thus a difficult choice for a punchline; maybe this is just a nonsense insult like *migdilix* (1033). Hence the translation "wog."

978–79 Old . . . baggage: The Latin has a pun on *sarcinatos,* "loaded with baggage" / "patched and mended."

980 Looks . . . fingers: Literally, "and, if I'm not mistaken, they have no fingers on their hands."

981 Their . . . ears: Some joke. Pierced ears and earrings show up as a suspicious, exotic accessory of male foreigners from the Orient in Petronius *Satyricon* (102.14, associated with Arabs) and in Juvenal *Satire* 1.104–5 (proof of birth near the Euphrates); see Mayor's commentary on Juvenal ad loc. for a list of areas of Africa and Asia associated by Romans with this practice. Plutarch attributes to Cicero a joke about pierced ears at the expense of a man rumored to be of African ancestry (*Cicero* 26).

982 In Arabic: Latin *Punice.*

1008 You . . . belt: Romans used the way a man's tunic was belted as a sign of his character, much as we now diagnose attitude and sexual orientation from clothing. To walk around with no belt at all, so that your tunic hung low, was the sign at best of a dissolute lifestyle, and probably of effeminacy.

1011–12 *Salad* . . . *drama* festival . . . sponsors: "He says he wants to give African mice to the aediles for the parade at the games." The aediles were the officials who paid for Roman public entertainment, including comedy. In the original, the Punic in these and the following lines sounds like the Latin words in Igor's speeches; Igor's assumptions about what the Punic means derive from stereotypes of Africa as exotic and a source of exotic animals for display at Rome, and of Carthaginians as traders.

1014 A *door* . . . *jellybeans:* "He says he's brought spoons, gutters, and nuts."

1016 *Carpool:* The Latin says "lard."

1018 He . . . *loo:* Literally, "He says he's got spades and reaping boards to sell."

1019 Whoever . . . is: Literally, "for the harvest, I guess."

1020 Also . . . Monday: "So he could dig his garden and reap the grain." The line in the translation is an old student joke, a mistranslation of the Latin *sic transit gloria mundi,* "Thus passes the glory of the world." It's the same kind of joke.

1025 Have . . . *afghan:* Literally, "have him put under a basket." This refers to a mode of execution attested elsewhere, e.g., Livy 4.50.4.

1029 English: "Latin."

1033 Schmo: Latin *migdilix,* which the *OLD* calls "a word of unknown meaning, a form of abuse."

1057 Citizen . . . Yugoslavia: Latin *Aetolum,* "an Aetolian."

1060 By old Mikhail: In the original, "by Demarchus."

1065 Noor, Dodi: In the original, Ampsigura, Iahon—Carthaginian-sounding names.

1096 Besmirched her virtue: Latin *incestavit,* "made her unchaste."

Unripened lovemaking: Latin *acerba amatio. Acerba* = "unripened," hence "sour, harsh"; *amatio* is a fancy formation from "love."

1102 Iraqi citizens: See note on line 906 above on the process of claiming a person out of slavery; also *Weevil* 620, *Iran Man* 163, 474–75.

1123 Mah little lambs: Latin *mearum alumnarum,* "of the baby girls I nursed." The translation is a tribute to Hattie McDaniel in *Gone with the Wind;* see Joshel 1986 on relations between ancient wet nurses and their former charges.

1125   Magician: Latin *praestrigiator,* "deceiver," "juggler."

1126   Hypnotizes: Latin *perduxit,* "brings over by persuasion."

1139   Would . . . names: Literally, "would have changed their names"; see the *Towel-heads* introduction on the girls' names.

1140   On . . . backs: Literally, "from their body."

1154   So . . . stars: Literally, "so you praise these accommodations only moderately." Igor threatens Saddam's slaves with the stock list of slave punishments; see line 784 above. "Ball and chain" (1153) = *codex,* a tree stump that served a similar purpose.

1168   They're . . . shoes: This line has caused many headaches. The OCT prints *Thraecae sunt: in celonem sustolli solent,* = "They're Thracian women; they always are mounted on a stallion." Leo suggested: "They're tragic actresses *[tragicae];* they always wear wooden shoes *[calones].*" Tragic actors wore *cothurnoi,* platform boots.

1195   Face all smeared: Cf. *Weevil* 589, with translation there.

1216   A good . . . find: Literally, "You do well to do well by good people"; proverb format.

1219–20 If . . . out: Literally, "If I were Jupiter . . . I'd kick Juno out."

1222   Every . . . promise: Literally, "how modestly she made her speech." The list of virtues Boris attributes to Tchotchka in 1221–22 bears little resemblance to the ideas she expresses in her song.

1236   I'll . . . butter: Literally, "I'll make this dog be more tranquil than oil."

1244   I have to speak up: "I have to be his *patronus*"; see note on *Iran Man* 737.

1253   Your mother: Look fast! This is the only mention of Saddam's wife's existence.

1271   O . . . Michelangelo: "O Apelles, O Zeuxis the painter": the two most famous Greek painters, "classic" in Plautus's time.

1281   City comedians: Latin *scurrae;* see note on 612 above. Taken with line 1280, this line gives a sense of ridicule as part of the game of male jockeying for prestige, which it certainly was.

1285   Hostages: Latin *pignus,* "security," "a pledge"; General Popoff has exacted military justice and taken what he could get.

1291   Than . . . fights: Another cryptic line; literally "than those *Aegyptini* who carry the caldron around the circus at the games." *Aegyptini,* despite appearances, = "Ethiopians," though this is attested only in Festus's dictionary (26L), where it could just be an effort to explain this line.

1298   Like an altar boy: Latin *quasi puer cauponius,* "like a boy who works at an inn." *Puer* here = "slave." Inns were disreputable places to work; waitresses at inns were, in law, the equivalent of prostitutes. So there is a hint here of sexual use.

1301   Doorman: Latin *baiiolum,* "porter."

1302   To the M.P.s: Latin *carnufici,* "to the executioner"; cf. line 369 above, and *Iran Man* 547.

1303   These . . . them: Literally, "Really this tribe with the beltless tunics are woman-izers."

1304   African queen: Latin *amatricem Africam,* "African hussy."

1305   Girly man: Latin *mulier,* "woman"; this line could of course be addressed to Katya.

1314   New York cabdrivers: Literally, "Roman rowers" (galley slaves). A rare mention of Rome in the plays. On garlic as poor people's food, see Gowers 1993: 62.

1315   Do . . . removed: Literally, "Do your cheeks or your teeth itch?"—a slang expression, like "Are you cruisin' for a bruisin'?"

1317   Your maracas, Charo: Literally, "your tympanum." The tympanum was the hand drum played by the eunuch priests of Cybele and always suggests sexual passivity in males.

1318   Drag queen: Latin *cinaedum. Cinaedi* in Plautus seem to be sexy dancers, but this is also an insulting term (cf. the end of *Iran Man*). See volume introduction (under "Background on Roman Culture" and "Audience") on the ancient sex/gender system and on the *cinaedus* in comedy.

1320   Cricket bat: Latin *fustis,* literally "clubs."

1329   Goodness . . . it: Literally, "By Castor, he says what's believable." The translation is a tribute to Mae West.

1333–35 These lines are repeated at 1382–84.

1337   It's . . . gang: This line is corrupt; this is a reconstruction of the sense based on Hanno's claim at 1352 that the pimp owes him "punishments" and on Boris's reference to chains at 1409. For associations between Carthage and torture, see introduction to *Towelheads.*

1354   I'll . . . player: Maybe, like Einstein in *Iran Man,* the Wolf is keeping his money in a wallet tied around his neck. So he has actually been pointing at his neck in 1351–54, and here says, "I'll pay for everything with my neck like a porter." Or this might just continue the joke about hanging.

1359   Claim ticket: Latin *arrabo,* "earnest money," "deposit"; this line must cue a physical threat.

1364   Liquidate . . . assets: "I'll hold an auction"; see note on line 411.

1365   I can . . . basement: Literally, "you're at my house in wooden custody." In early Roman law, debtors could be adjudged to their creditors; as, in Dickens, the imprudent wind up in debtors' prison, so in Plautus they might wind up enslaved and imprisoned at their creditor's house. "Wooden" here perhaps refers to the *codex,* the tree stump acting as ball and chain; cf. above on 1153.

1370   Seasoning: Latin *condimentum.* See Gowers 1993: 65 on this line and Plautus's use of food metaphors for his own writing.

1379   Oh, no: This line is hard to motivate for the General, though at the end it becomes clear that what he wants is a prostitute, rather than Katya in particular. But these words might well just belong to the Wolf.

1385   Greedy: Latin *rapacem.*

1386   Thievy: Latin *furacem.*

1387   On . . . knees: Literally, "by your knees"; see note on *Weevil* 630.

1409   To Death Row: Latin *in carcerem.* See note on 690–92 above.

1415   Girl saxophone player: Latin *tibicinam;* see volume introduction under "Music." *Tibicinae* (usually translated "flute-girls") often appear at drinking parties in company with prostitutes.

1421   Find a realtor: Literally, "hold an auction." Here this act constitutes a moving sale.

NOTES ON NONMETRICAL TRANSLATIONS OF SONGS

213   Rig 'em out: Latin *exornare;* see note on *orno*/costume above, line 123, and other examples at 284, 425, 577; "primping" in 220 = *ornari.*

231a   Lay . . . to rest: Literally, "sing a dirge for."

233   Tell . . . story: Latin *fabulari* also = "make idle talk"; cf. Boris at line 441.

BIBLIOGRAPHY

GENERAL REFERENCES

Items not found among the primary references are listed in the subsections that follow.

Ahl, Frederick. 1984. "The Art of Safe Criticism in Greece and Rome." *American Journal of Philology* 105: 174–208.

Althusser, Louis. 1971. "Ideology and Ideological State Apparatuses (Notes Towards an Investigation)." In his *Lenin and Philosophy and Other Essays,* 127–86. New York: Monthly Review Press.

Anderson, William S. 1993. *Barbarian Play: Plautus' Roman Comedy.* Toronto: University of Toronto Press.

Astin, Alan E. 1978. *Cato the Censor.* Oxford: Clarendon Press.

Barton, Carlin A. 1993. *The Sorrows of the Ancient Romans.* Princeton, N.J.: Princeton University Press.

Beacham, Richard C. 1991. *The Roman Theatre and Its Audience.* Cambridge, Mass.: Harvard University Press.

Beare, W. 1964. *The Roman Stage: A Short History of Latin Drama in the Time of the Republic.* 3rd ed. London: Methuen.

Benchley, Robert. 1925. "'The King of Razbo-Jazbo.'" In his *Pluck and Luck,* 174–85. New York: Holt / Blue Ribbon Books.

Bertelsen, Lance. 1986. *The Nonsense Club: Literature and Popular Culture, 1749–1764.* Oxford: Clarendon Press.

Bieber, Margarete. 1961. *The History of the Greek and Roman Theater.* 2nd ed. Princeton, N.J.: Princeton University Press.

Boyarin, Daniel. 1993. *Carnal Israel: Reading Sex in Talmudic Culture.* Berkeley: University of California Press.

Branham, R. Bracht, and Marie-Odile Goulet-Cazé, eds. 1996. *The Cynics: The Cynic Movement in Antiquity and Its Legacy.* Berkeley: University of California Press.

Brown, Shelby. 1991. *Late Carthaginian Child Sacrifice and Sacrificial Monuments in their Mediterranean Context.* JSOT/ASOR Monograph Series 3. Sheffield: Sheffield Academic Press.

Brunt, P. A. 1971. *Italian Manpower, 225 B.C.–A.D. 14.* Oxford: Oxford University Press.

Chalmers, Walter R. 1965. "Plautus and his Audience." In *Roman Drama,* ed. T. A. Dorey and Donald R. Dudley, 51–86. New York: Basic Books.

Conley, C. H. 1967 [1927]. *The First English Translators of the Classics.* Port Washington, N.Y.: Kennikat Press.

Corbeill, Anthony. 1996. *Controlling Laughter: Political Humor in the Late Roman Republic.* Princeton, N.J.: Princeton University Press.

Corbett, Philip. 1986. *The Scurra.* Edinburgh: Scottish Academic Press.

Delacoste, Frédérique, and Priscilla Alexander, eds. 1987. *Sex Work: Writings by Women in the Sex Industry.* San Francisco: Cleis Press.

Duckworth, George E. 1942. *The Complete Roman Drama.* 2 vols. New York: Random House.

Dunkin, Paul Shaner. 1946. *Post-Aristophanic Comedy: Studies in the Social Outlook of Middle and New Comedy.* Illinois Studies in Language and Literature 31, 3–4. Urbana: University of Illinois Press.

Edwards, Catharine. 1997. "Unspeakable Professions: Public Performance and Prostitution in Ancient Rome." In *Roman Sexualities,* ed. Judith P. Hallett and Marilyn B. Skinner, 66–95. Princeton, N.J.: Princeton University Press.

Errington, R. M. 1972. *The Dawn of Empire.* Ithaca, N.Y.: Cornell University Press.

Evans, Rhiannon. 1999. "Ethnography's Freak Show: The Grotesques at the Edges of the Roman Earth." *Ramus* 28: 54–73.

Fantham, Elaine. 1975. "Sex, Status, and Survival in Hellenistic Athens: A Study of Women in New Comedy." *Phoenix* 29: 44–74.

Farkas, Anna. 2003. *The Oxford Dictionary of Catchphrases.* Oxford: Oxford University Press.

Fitzgerald, William. 2000. *Slavery and Roman Literature.* Cambridge: Cambridge University Press.

Gamel, Mary-Kay. 2002. "From *Thesmophoriazousai* to *The Julie Thesmo Show:* Adaptation, Performance, Reception." *American Journal of Philology* 123: 465–99. This whole issue of *AJP* is edited by Gamel and focuses on *Thesmophoriazousai.*

Garton, Charles. 1972. *Personal Aspects of the Roman Theatre.* Toronto: Hakkert.

Goldberg, Sander M. 1986. *Understanding Terence.* Princeton, N.J.: Princeton University Press.

———. 1998. "Plautus on the Palatine." *Journal of Roman Studies* 88: 1–20.

Gourevitch, Philip. 2002. "Mr. Brown." *New Yorker,* July 29: 46–65.

Gowers, Emily. 1993. *The Loaded Table: Representations of Food in Roman Literature.* Oxford: Clarendon Press.

Gratwick, A. S. 1971. "Hanno's Punic Speech in the *Poenulus* of Plautus." *Hermes* 99: 25–45.

———. 1973. "'Titus Maccius Plautus.'" *Classical Quarterly,* n.s., 23: 78–84.

Gruen, Erich S. 1990. "Plautus and the Public Stage." In his *Studies in Greek Culture and Roman Policy,* 124–57. Leiden: E. J. Brill.

————. 1992. *Culture and National Identity in Republican Rome.* Ithaca, N.Y.: Cornell University Press.

Habinek, Thomas N. 1998. *The Politics of Latin Literature.* Princeton, N.J.: Princeton University Press.

————. 2005. *The World of Roman Song: From Ritualized Speech to Social Order.* Baltimore: Johns Hopkins University Press.

Hallett, Judith P. 1997. "Female Homoeroticism and the Denial of Roman Reality in Latin Literature." In *Roman Sexualities,* ed. Judith P. Hallett and Marilyn B. Skinner, 255–73. Princeton, N.J.: Princeton University Press.

Hansen, William. 1998. *Anthology of Ancient Greek Popular Literature.* Bloomington: Indiana University Press.

Harvey, P. 1986. "Historical Topicality in Plautus." *CW* 79: 297–304.

Henderson, Jeffrey, trans. 2003. *Aristophanes' Acharnians.* 2nd ed. Newburyport, Mass.: Focus.

Henry, Madeleine Mary. 1985. *Menander's Courtesans and the Greek Comic Tradition.* Frankfurt: Peter Lang.

James, Sharon L. 1998. "From Boys to Men: Rape and Developing Masculinity in Terence's *Hecyra* and *Eunuchus.*" *Helios* 25: 31–47.

Joshel, Sandra R. 1986. "Nursing the Master's Child: Slavery and the Roman Child-Nurse." *Signs* 12: 3–22.

————. 1992. *Work, Identity, and Legal Status at Rome.* Norman: University of Oklahoma Press.

Joshel, Sandra R., and Sheila Murnaghan, eds. 1998. *Women and Slaves in Greco-Roman Culture.* London: Routledge.

Kalman, Maira, and Rick Meyerowitz. 2001. "New Yorkistan." *New Yorker,* December 10, cover.

Kipling, Rudyard. 1929. "Regulus." In *The Complete Stalky & Co.* London: Macmillan.

Krahmalkov, Charles R. 1988. "Observations on the Punic Monologues of Hanno in the *Poenulus.*" *Orientalia* 57: 55–66.

————. 2001. *A Phoenician-Punic Grammar.* Leiden: Brill.

Lape, Susan. 2004. *Reproducing Athens: Menander's Comedy, Democratic Culture, and the Hellenistic City.* Princeton, N.J.: Princeton University Press.

Leigh, Matthew. 2004. *Comedy and the Rise of Rome.* Oxford: Oxford University Press.

Lindsay, W. M. 1904. *The Ancient Editions of Plautus.* Oxford: James Parker.

————. 1904–5. *T. Macci Plauti Comoediae.* 2 vols. Oxford: Clarendon Press.

Lintott, Andrew. 1999. *Violence in Republican Rome.* 2nd ed. Oxford: Oxford University Press.

Lodge, Gonzalez. 1962 [1924]. *Lexicon Plautinum.* 2 vols. Hildesheim: Georg Olms.

MacCary, W. Thomas, and M. M. Willcock, eds. 1976. *Plautus* Casina. Cambridge: Cambridge University Press.

Marshall, C. W. 2006. *The Stagecraft and Performance of Roman Comedy.* Cambridge: Cambridge University Press.

Mattingly, H. B. 1957. "The Plautine *Didascaliae.*" *Athenaeum* 35: 78–88.

McCarthy, Kathleen. 2000. *Slaves, Masters, and the Art of Authority in Plautine Comedy.* Princeton, N.J.: Princeton University Press.

McGinn, Thomas A. J. 1998. *Prostitution, Sexuality, and the Law in Ancient Rome.* Oxford: Oxford University Press.

———. 2004. *The Economy of Prostitution in the Roman World.* Ann Arbor: University of Michigan Press.

Mitford, Nancy. 1975 [1931]. *Christmas Pudding.* London: Hamilton.

Moore, Timothy J. 1991. "*Palliata togata:* Plautus, *Curculio* 462–86." *American Journal of Philology* 112: 343–62.

———. 1994. "Seats and Social Status in the Plautine Theatre." *Classical Journal* 90: 113–23.

Moretti, Franco. 1998. *Atlas of the European Novel, 1800–1900.* London: Verso.

Nixon, Paul. 1916–38. *Plautus.* 5 vols. London: Heinemann.

Opelt, Ilona. 1965. *Die lateinischen Schimpfwörter und verwandte sprachliche Erscheinungen: Eine Typologie.* Heidelberg: Carl Winter.

Packman, Zola Marie. 1993. "Call It Rape: A Motif in Roman Comedy and Its Suppression in English-Speaking Publications." *Helios* 20: 42–55.

———. 1999. "Feminine Role Designations in the Comedies of Plautus." *American Journal of Philology* 120: 245–58.

Palmer, L. R. 1954. *The Latin Language.* London: Faber & Faber.

Parker, Douglass, trans. 1969. *The Acharnians.* In *Aristophanes: Four Comedies,* ed. William Arrowsmith. Ann Arbor: University of Michigan Press.

Parker, Holt N. 1989. "Crucially Funny or Tranio on the Couch: The *Servus Callidus* and Jokes about Torture." *Transactions of the American Philological Association* 119: 233–46.

———. 1996. "Plautus vs. Terence: Audience and Popularity Re-examined." *American Journal of Philology* 117: 585–617.

Patterson, Orlando. 1982. *Slavery and Social Death.* Cambridge, Mass.: Harvard University Press.

Pratchett, Terry. 1990. *Eric.* New York: HarperTorch.

Pulgram, Ernst. 1958. *The Tongues of Italy: Prehistory and History.* Cambridge, Mass.: Harvard University Press.

Rawson, Elizabeth. 1985. "Theatrical Life in Republican Rome and Italy." *Publications of the British School in Rome* 53: 97–113.

Rei, Annalisa. 1998. "Villains, Wives, and Slaves in the Comedies of Plautus." In *Women and Slaves in Greco-Roman Culture,* ed. Sandra R. Joshel and Sheila Murnaghan, 92–108. London: Routledge.

Richlin, Amy. 1992a. *The Garden of Priapus: Sexuality and Aggression in Roman Humor.* Rev. ed. New York: Oxford University Press.

———. 1992b. "Sulpicia the Satirist." *Classical World* 86.2: 125–40.

————. 1992c. "Julia's Jokes, Galla Placidia, and the Roman Use of Women as Political Icons." In *Stereotypes of Women in Power: Historical Perspectives and Revisionist Views*, ed. Barbara Garlick, Pauline Allen, and Suzanne Dixon, 65–91. Westport, Conn.: Greenwood Press.

————. 1993. "Not before Homosexuality: The Materiality of the *Cinaedus* and the Roman Law against Love between Men." *Journal of the History of Sexuality* 3.4: 523–73.

————. 1995. "Making Up a Woman: The Face of Roman Gender." In *Off with Her Head!* ed. Howard Eilberg-Schwartz and Wendy Doniger, 185–213. Berkeley: University of California Press.

————. 1997a. "Carrying Water in a Sieve: Class and the Body in Roman Women's Religion." In *Women and Goddess Traditions*, ed. Karen L. King, 330–74. Minneapolis: Fortress.

————. 1997b. "Gender and Rhetoric: Producing Manhood in the Schools." In *Roman Eloquence: Rhetoric in Society and Literature*, ed. William J. Dominik, 90–110. London: Routledge.

Riehle, Wolfgang. 1990. *Shakespeare, Plautus, and the Humanist Tradition.* Cambridge: D. S. Brewer.

Riley, Henry Thomas. 1881 [1852]. *The Comedies of Plautus. Literally Translated into English Prose.* Bohn's Library edition. London: George Bell.

Rosen, Ralph M., and Donald R. Marks. 1999. "Comedies of Transgression in Gangsta Rap and Ancient Classical Poetry." *New Literary History* 30: 897–928.

Said, Edward. 1979. *Orientalism.* New York: Vintage Books.

Salmon, E. T. 1982. *The Making of Roman Italy.* London: Thames & Hudson.

Scafuro, Adele C. 1997. *The Forensic Stage: Settling Disputes in Graeco-Roman New Comedy.* Cambridge: Cambridge University Press.

Shaw, Brent D. 2001. *Spartacus and the Slave Wars: A Brief History with Documents.* Boston: Bedford / St. Martin's.

Shipp, G. B. 1953. "Greek in Plautus." *Wiener Studien* 66: 105–12.

Slater, Niall. 1985. *Plautus in Performance.* Princeton, N.J.: Princeton University Press.

————. 1992. "Plautine Negotiations: The *Poenulus* Prologue Unpacked." *Yale Classical Studies* 29: 131–46.

Smith, Kevin. 2001. *Chasing Dogma.* Orange, Calif.: Image Comics.

Sznycer, Maurice. 1967. *Les Passages puniques en transcription latine dans le "Poenulus" de Plaute.* Paris: Klincksieck.

Tatum, James. 1983. *Plautus: The Darker Comedies.* Baltimore: Johns Hopkins University Press.

Taylor, Deems, ed. 1941. *A Treasury of Gilbert and Sullivan.* New York: Simon & Schuster.

Taylor, Lily Ross. 1937. "The Opportunities for Dramatic Performances in the Time of Plautus and Terence." *Transactions of the American Philological Association* 68: 284–304.

Thalmann, William G. 1996. "Versions of Slavery in the *Captivi* of Plautus." *Ramus* 25: 112–45.

Thomas, Ross. 1978. *Chinaman's Chance.* New York: Mysterious Press.

Thornton, Bonnell. 1769–74. *Comedies of Plautus, Translated into Familiar Blank Verse.* London: T. Becket and P. A. De Hondt. *Persa* and *Poenulus* trans. Richard Warner.

Tylawsky, Elizabeth Ivory. 2002. *Saturio's Inheritance: The Greek Ancestry of the Roman Comic Parasite.* New York: Peter Lang.

Wiles, David. 1991. *The Masks of Menander: Sign and Meaning in Greek and Roman Performance.* Cambridge: Cambridge University Press.

Williams, Craig. 1999. *Homosexuality and the Roman Man.* Oxford: Oxford University Press.

Williams, Gordon. 1968. *Tradition and Originality in Roman Poetry.* Oxford: Oxford University Press.

Woytek, Erich. 1982. *T. Maccius Plautus* Persa: *Einleitung, Text und Kommentar.* Österreichische Akademie der Wissenschaften Philosophisch-Historische Klasse Sitzungsberichte, 385. Vienna: Verlag der Österreichischen Akademie der Wissenschaften.

Wright, John. 1974. *Dancing in Chains: The Stylistic Unity of the Comoedia Palliata.* PMAAR 25. Rome: American Academy in Rome.

Zinn, T. L. 1965. "Five Westminster Latin Plays." In *Roman Drama,* ed. T. A. Dorey and Donald R. Dudley, 193–226. New York: Basic Books.

Zweig, Bella. 1992. "The Mute Nude Female Characters in Aristophanes' Plays." In *Pornography and Representation in Greece and Rome,* ed. Amy Richlin, 73–89. New York: Oxford University Press.

TRANSLATIONS, COMMENTARIES, AND SPECIAL STUDIES OF THE PLAYS IN THIS VOLUME

These represent only the tip of an enormous iceberg and constitute only a short list of items students and teachers might find particularly useful.

Curculio

Marshall, C. W. 1999. "Quis Hic Loquitur? Plautine Delivery and the 'Double Aside.'" *Syllecta Classica* 10: 105–29.

——. www.cnrs.ubc.ca/masc/curculio.html. On a recent production of *Curculio.*

Moore, Timothy J. 1991. "*Palliata togata:* Plautus, *Curculio* 62–86." *American Journal of Philology* 112: 343–62.

Nixon, Paul. 1951 [1917]. *Plautus.* Vol. 2. "Curculio." Pp. 185–269. Loeb Classical Library. Cambridge, Mass.: Harvard University Press.

Taylor, Henry. 1995. "The Weevil *(Curculio).*" In *Plautus: The Comedies,* vol. 4, ed. David R. Slavitt and Palmer Bovie, 321–73. Baltimore: Johns Hopkins University Press.

Wright, John. 1981. *Plautus:* Curculio. *Introduction and Notes.* American Philological Association Textbook Series, no. 6. Chico, Calif.: Scholars Press.

Persa

Bettini, Maurizio, ed. 1981. *Plauto* Mostellaria Persa. Milan: Arnoldo Mondadori.

Bovie, Palmer. 1995. "The Persian *(Persa)*." In *Plautus: The Comedies,* vol. 4, ed. David R. Slavitt and Palmer Bovie, 3–77. Baltimore: Johns Hopkins University Press.

Faller, Stefan, ed. 2001. *Studien zu Plautus'* Persa. Tübingen: Gunter Narr Verlag.

———. 2001. "Persisches im *Persa.*" In Faller 2001, 177–207.

Marshall, C. W. 1997. "Shattered Mirrors and Breaking Class: Saturio's Daughter in Plautus' *Persa.*" *Text & Presentation* 18: 100–109.

Nixon, Paul. 1950 [1924]. *Plautus.* Vol. 3. "The Persian." Pp. 417–523. Loeb Classical Library. Cambridge, Mass.: Harvard University Press.

Slater, Niall. 1985. *Plautus in Performance,* 37–54. Princeton, N.J.: Princeton University Press.

Woytek, Erich. 1982. *T. Maccius Plautus* Persa: *Einleitung, Text und Kommentar.* Österreichische Akademie der Wissenschaften Philosophisch-Historische Klasse Sitzungsberichte, 385. Vienna: Verlag der Österreichischen Akademie der Wissenschaften.

Poenulus

Baier, Thomas, ed. 2004. *Studien zu Plautus'* Poenulus. Tübingen: Gunter Narr Verlag.

Burroway, Janet. 1970. "*Poenulus,* or *The Little Carthaginian.*" In *Five Roman Comedies,* ed. Palmer Bovie, 197–262. New York: Dutton.

Franko, George Fredric. 1994. "The Use of *Poenus* and *Carthaginiensis* in Early Latin Literature." *Classical Philology* 89: 153–58.

Henderson, John. 1999. "Hanno's Punic Heirs: Der *Poenulus*-Neid des Plautus." In his *Writing Down Rome,* 3–37. New York: Oxford University Press.

Maurach, Gregor. 1988. *Der Poenulus des Plautus.* Heidelberg: Carl Winter.

Nixon, Paul. 1951 [1932]. *Plautus.* Vol. 4. "Poenulus, or the Little Carthaginian." Pp. 1–143. Loeb Classical Library. Cambridge, Mass.: Harvard University Press.

Slater, Niall. 1992. "Plautine Negotiations: The *Poenulus* Prologue Unpacked." *Yale Classical Studies* 29: 131–46.

Starks, John H., Jr., et al. 1997. *Latin Laughs: A Production of Plautus'* Poenulus. Wauconda, Ill.: Bolchazy-Carducci.

HISTORICAL BACKGROUND

Primary Sources on Roman Ethnic Attitudes

Most of the writers recommended in the introduction are available either in the Penguin series or in the Loeb series, which carries the translation on a page facing the Greek or Latin text; most research libraries will have a complete set of Loebs. For a useful translation of Mela's geography, see F. E. Romer, *Pomponius Mela's Description of the World* (Ann

Arbor: University of Michigan Press, 1998). The translation of Petronius by J. P. Sullivan in the Penguin series is funny in British English; the translation by William Arrowsmith (New York: New American Library, 1990) is funny in American English, as is, more recently, the translation by Sarah Ruden (Indianapolis: Hackett, 2000). Roman satirists other than Petronius do not translate well; Rolfe Humphries, *The Satires of Juvenal* (Bloomington: Indiana University Press, 1958), is about the best, but out of print.

On the History of Rome in the Mid-Republic

The standard reference work is *The Cambridge Ancient History,* 2nd ed., vol. 8, *Rome and the Mediterranean to 133 B.C.,* edited by A. E. Astin, F. W. Walbank, M. W. Frederiksen, and R. M. Ogilvie (Cambridge: Cambridge University Press, 1989). This volume contains not only narrative histories of wars throughout the Mediterranean during the years in which Plautus's plays were performed, but intellectual histories of the period, including drama. The lengthy section on Greek involvement eastward into India opens up a vast hybrid culture, which Persia dominated. For a shorter version, I highly recommend Errington 1972, listed above.

On Orientalism

The standard work is Edward Said, *Orientalism* (New York: Vintage Books, 1979). An avalanche of work in postcolonial theory accompanied and followed this book; for a useful reader, see Bill Ashcroft, Gareth Griffiths, and Helen Tiffin, eds., *The Post-Colonial Studies Reader* (London: Routledge, 1995), which includes a whole section on hybridity. There is a shortage of work on colonialism and the cultural work of comedy; excellent, if you can find it, is the lavishly illustrated *Nothing but the Same Old Story: The Roots of Anti-Irish Racism,* put out by a group called Information on Ireland in 1984.

On Roman Slavery

On slaves and resistance in the Republic, see Shaw 2001 (listed above), a collection of primary sources; and Keith R. Bradley, *Slavery and Rebellion in the Roman World, 140 B.C.–70 B.C.* (Bloomington: Indiana University Press, 1998). For a slave's-eye view, which starts in the first century C.E., because slaves' inscriptions do not start in bulk until then, see Joshel 1992. On women and slaves, see Joshel and Murnaghan 1998.

On Roman Ideas about Race and Ethnicity

For an introduction to the question of why this issue might matter to American students, see Shelley P. Haley, "Black Feminist Thought and Classics: Re-membering, Re-claiming, Re-empowering," in *Feminist Theory and the Classics,* ed. Nancy Sorkin Rabinowitz and Amy Richlin, 23–43 (New York: Routledge, 1993). The pioneering study of race, Africa, and Rome, with many illustrations, is Frank M. Snowden Jr., *Blacks in Antiquity* (Cambridge, Mass.: Harvard University Press, 1970); it was followed by Lloyd A. Thompson,

Romans and Blacks (Norman: University of Oklahoma Press, 1989), and most recently by Benjamin Isaac, *The Invention of Racism in Classical Antiquity* (Princeton, N.J.: Princeton University Press, 2004), in which see esp. pp. 304–51, 371–405. For a thought-provoking treatment of Roman racism as directed northwards, see A. N. Sherwin-White, *Racial Prejudice in Imperial Rome* (Cambridge: Cambridge University Press, 1967).

INDEX

This index covers the volume introduction and the introductions and notes to the plays.

Greece: as location of Plautus's plays, 21, 39–40, 41; in *Towelheads,* 187; in *Weevil,* 57

Greek(s): associated with partying, 262; attacked in satire, 185; and class in Plautus, 32–33, 107, 111, 161, 162, 170, 255; as effeminate, 41, 118, 120; as exotic, 32–33, 39, 41–42, 44, 59, 100; historical persons in Plautus, 37; names, 21, 41–42, 107, 175, 195; as native tongue, 13, 21, 33, 62

Habinek, Thomas, 25, 32, 51
Hallett, Judith, 16, 30
Hanno, 6, 187, 191, 192–93
Henderson, John, 14, 193, 194, 195
Hercules as popular deity, 102, 160
Histria, 17, 187–88, 252
homosexuality: female, 16, 30; male, 16, 29–30, 34, 98, 102, 104, 105, 119–20, 161, 165, 166, 167, 172, 180, 252, 270
homosociality, 112
Hrotsvitha, 193
hunger, 14, 40, 45, 46, 172, 252
hybridity, 37, 39, 40, 42, 59, 99; in language, 161, 162, 170, 173, 177; in location, 188

immigrants, 24, 25, 34
insult matches, 8, 45, 58, 166, 169, 171–72, 261
interpellation, 3, 30; of slaves, 22, 30, 192
Irwin, Steve, 36, 48
Italy: as "barbaric," 40, 99; changed in Plautus's lifetime, 16–19; and locations, 39, 41

Jerome, 11, 12, 13
jokes: anatomical, 97, 102, 103, 105, 106, 107, 108, 170, 180, 254, 255, 256, 257, 259, 261, 263, 264, 265, 267; books of, 171; about chains, 100, 107, 108, 161, 174, 265, 269, 271; about illicit sex, 97, 265; about love as property, 97; about male homosexuality, 161, 165–66, 170, 172, 262; on names, 43, 103; about personified qualities, 181, 265; shadow, 169; theory of, 3; used by *parasiti,* 101,

171. *See also* excremental humor; eye disease jokes; kings; sexuality; slaves, punishments of

Joshel, Sandra, 29, 268
Juvenal, 53, 185, 267

Kabuki as analogy for Roman comedy, 22
kings, 17, 37–38, 44, 102, 103, 170–71, 188, 196, 256, 263
Kipling, Rudyard, 26, 191–92
Krahmalkov, Charles, 189–90

Latin, 32, 41, 102, 161, 162, 170, 185, 191
law: in Plautus, 27, 105, 106, 173, 197, 255, 261, 262, 266, 268; Roman, 15–16, 26, 197, 255
left hand, 167
legal language, 105, 162, 165, 177, 261
Lehrer, Tom, 36, 50
Leigh, Matthew, 15, 17, 25, 106
Lindsay, W. M., 5, 7, 8, 52, 189, 194
line assignments, 7–8, 117
Livius Andronicus, 10, 13
locations, 39–40, 60, 193–94, 195; and freedom, 161, 255, 262, 263
Lucian, 114
Lucilius, 34
ludi. See festivals

marriage, 16; plot, 31
Marshall, C. W., 9, 21, 48, 61
Marx Brothers, 20, 35
masks, 21, 99, 179, 187, 267
Maurach, Gregor, 195, 255, 257, 261, 262
McCarthy, Kathleen, 30, 31, 45, 111, 167
McGinn, Thomas, 16, 21, 60, 102
men: in the city, 101, 104–5, 262, 269; classes of, 265; names of, 41; old, 27; sexuality of, 29–30, 104, 105, 119, 167, 180, 262; virtues of, 185. *See also* prostitution; slaves, male
mercenaries. *See* soldiers
metatheater: in Kevin Smith, 48, 112; in Plautus, 8, 19, 48, 60, 64, 113, 164, 165, 170, 171, 173, 179, 252, 254, 261
meter, 50–53; in *Iran Man,* 52, 116; in *Towelheads,* 194–95; in *Weevil,* 52, 62

mills as place of slave punishment, 5, 12, 13, 15, 115, 161, 172, 256, 260, 264

mime, 10, 14, 15, 19, 21, 52, 59, 119, 264

Mitford, Nancy, 34

money, 57, 61, 115; associated with Philip of Macedon, 38, 44, 103, 171, 195, 255; and nationality, 44; as source of humor, 97, 172, 173, 176, 195–96, 253, 258; stage, 40, 172, 262; translating, 44. *See also* bankers; trust

monologues of *parasiti,* 58

Monty Python, 20, 35, 48, 63, 198

Moore, Timothy, 16, 60

Moretti, Franco, 17

music, 19, 30, 49–53, 271; in *Iran Man,* 52, 115–16; in *Towelheads,* 52, 194–95, 199; in *Weevil,* 52, 61–62, 65

Myers, Mike, 36

Naevius, 10, 13

names, 40–43; comic formations of, 40, 43, 103, 164, 173, 177, 253, 260; exotic, 42, 118, 175, 177; in *Iran Man,* 118–20; Roman, 37, 41; in *Towelheads,* 196–98; in *Weevil,* 62–64. *See also* class; men; prostitution; slaves; women

Nashe, Thomas, 5

New Comedy, 14, 27, 171

Nixon, Paul, 9, 33–34, 64

obscenity, 24, 34–35, 46–47, 116–17, 181

occentatio, 8, 58, 98, 171, 174, 261

opera as analogy for Roman comedy, 22

orchestration, 51, 52

Orientalism, 1, 6, 17, 26, 39, 41, 43, 44, 57, 63, 101, 103, 113, 114, 117, 118, 164, 177, 181, 186, 191, 254, 266, 267, 268

Oscan, 13, 21

Packman, Zola Marie, 27

palliata, pallium. See costume

"parabasis moments," 38, 61, 105, 112, 162, 174

paraklausithyron, 57, 58, 174

parasitus, 58; as comic, 46; difficulty of translating, 45–46; and flattery, 101; in *Iran Man,* 46, 111, 118; likened to

Cynic philosopher, 31, 59, 164; in *Weevil,* 46, 63, 100. *See also* jokes

Parker, Holt, 11, 23, 45, 99, 160, 264

parody, 35–36, 170, 256. *See also* epic; tragedy, parody of

peculium, 115, 165, 166

percussion, 51, 52

performance: of gender and race, 198; of Plautus's plays, 3, 5, 16, 23–24, 32, 48–53, 61

Persa, meaning of, 4, 7, 9, 117–18

Persia, 40, 103, 113, 177, 191, 263

Petronius, 53, 165, 257, 267

pimps, 16, 46, 102, 196; insulted, 100, 166, 171–72; in *Iran Man,* 120; tied to the Orient, 57, 63; use of stick by, 171; as villains in Plautus, 38, 46, 176, 196; in *Weevil,* 60, 63

Plautus: as actor, 48, 112; canon of, 10; dating of plays of, 11, 188, 261; identity of, 9–14; illustrations of plays of, 5–6; lifespan of, 11; manuscript tradition of, 5, 117, 194; in the mill, 5, 12, 161; name, 9–10, 22, 32, 253; publication in modern Europe, 5; publication of plays in antiquity, 4; topicality of, 17, 37–38, 58, 105, 162, 163, 180

playwrights, 13–14, 23. *See also* Accius; Caecilius Statius; Ennius; Livius Andronicus; Naevius; Plautus; Terence

Polybius, 11, 24, 53, 188, 190

Pompeius Festus, 11, 32

poverty, 15, 16, 29, 253, 270; as popular setting for stories, 45, 111

P.O.W.s, 13, 15, 19, 22, 26, 29; language of, 33, 190; renaming of, 13, 14, 26, 41–42; return of, 15, 106, 191

Pratchett, Terry, 25–26

prison, 107, 108, 263, 271

prologues, 8, 25, 28, 37, 113

Propertius, 58

prostitution, 13, 16, 61, 178, 256, 270; associated with the Orient, 114; associated with theater, 19; and brothels, 192, 256; festival of, 28, 188, 255, 258; as investment, 102; as licit sex, 97; location of in Rome, 104, 256; male, 102, 104, 120, 252, 270; and names, 62, 63, 64,

119, 196; in the Plautine plot, 27, 29, 45, 46, 186, 254; specialized, 167; subject to civil disabilities, 13, 16, 19, 61. *See also* pimps
Pryor, Richard, 45
Public Enemy, 14, 52, 116. *See also* rap music
Punic (language), 32, 42, 185, 188–90, 198, 266
Punic Wars, 10, 16, 17, 23, 24, 39, 185, 187, 189, 190, 191, 193, 253, 256, 265

quiritatio, 107

race: in antiquity, 186; in *Iran Man,* 113; in Kevin Smith, 113; in Renaissance illustrations of Plautus, 6; in *Towelheads,* 186, 187, 192, 198, 267, 269
rape, 24, 27, 29, 169, 180
rap music, 14, 51, 52, 116
refugees, 24, 25, 101, 188
Regulus, 191–92
religion: and augury, 162; jokes about, 47, 170, 269; and swearing, 47; women's, 28; and worship of Jupiter, 47, 100, 115, 163, 168. *See also* Hercules
rhyme, 51, 166
riddles, 52, 170
rituals of reversal, 22
Rome: as location of *Weevil,* 57, 60, 104–5; as venue for performance, 30, 193–94

Said, Edward, 1, 17, 186
Saturday Night Live, 20, 35, 48
Saturnalia, 21
scene headings, 6–7
scurrae, 101, 262, 269
sets, 7–8, 65, 111, 121, 172, 199
settings. *See* locations
sexism, 27
sexuality: of actors, 29–30; of audience, 29–30; of characters, 29; illicit, defined, 97; and insults, 30, 34, 47, 101, 107, 161, 165, 169, 170, 171, 172, 177, 180, 270; Roman norms for, 16
Shakespeare, 5, 40, 49, 51, 196
Shaw, Brent, 19

Sicily, 17, 39, 171, 191, 265
slang, 2, 32, 33–34, 44, 46–47, 64, 111, 113, 170, 255, 261
Slater, Niall, 8, 177, 179, 195, 251
slaves: as actors, 19, 21–22, 30, 114, 192; agricultural, 25, 197; in the audience, 16, 21, 29, 101, 106, 111, 114, 192; background on, 15–16; castrated, 181; and debt (see also *addictus*), 13, 255, 260, 266, 271; difficulty of translating, 44–46; escape fantasies, 117, 192; as exotic, 57, 63; female, 27, 29, 105, 106, 114; freed, 13, 14, 15, 44–45, 105, 115, 173, 178, 181, 197, 255; lack of parentage of, 14, 101, 168, 178; language of, 33, 170; literature of, 1, 22, 114, 192; as main characters, 111; male, 29, 104, 119, 252; manumission of, 106, 165, 173, 266, 268; names of, 14, 22, 41–42; punishments of, 12, 15, 21, 36, 45, 99, 105, 108, 160, 161, 165, 168, 169, 172, 174, 179, 181, 252, 258, 259, 264, 269; rebellions of, 19, 190, 192; Roman playwrights as, 14; as runaways, 59, 101, 172, 255, 259, 264; running, 261; and slang, 111, 113, 170; of slaves, 113; and social death, 175; sold as children by parents, 15, 16, 29, 114; of soldiers, 37; testimony of, 107, 173; as used for sex, 29, 30, 34–35, 97, 102, 104, 119, 120, 165, 166, 167, 169; as war captives, 19, 25, 29; as wet nurses, 29, 252, 268. See also *peculium*
Smith, Kevin, 48, 111–13, 120, 164, 175
sodales, 98, 174
soldiers, 25, 26, 33, 37, 59, 61, 64, 98, 103, 104, 106, 107, 170, 197, 263, 264; connected with the exotic, 40; language of, 178; reported use of literature by, 98. *See also* army; war
Sparta, 39, 188, 263
stage crew, 25
stage directions, 7–8, 25
staging, 61, 167, 172, 176, 189, 194
Starks, John, 9
subversion, 21, 24
supplication, 107, 271
swearing, 46–47

sycophanta, 40, 104, 259
Sznycer, Maurice, 189

Tatum, James, 9, 194
Terence, 10, 11, 14, 22, 23, 24, 27, 34
theater: building, 103; competitions, 252; in Epidaurus, 60; as escape, 113–14, 161; material remains of, 16; snacks, 252; temporary in Plautus's time, 23
Thomas, Ross, 26
Thornton, Bonnell, 5, 9
Three Stooges, 20, 35
topicality. *See* Plautus, topicality of
trade: associated with Carthage, 268; and Plautus's life, 12; as source of audience, 24; as source of Greek loanwords, 33; as source of humor, 25; as source of slaves, 41, 181
tragedy: parody of, 196, 251, 252; war, 251
translation: approaches to, 2–3, 30–47; first into English, of Plautus, 5; other, of plays in this volume, 9; political meaning of in early modern England, 5; and transposition, 31, 39–40, 42, 47, 163, 164, 190, 195, 254
trust, 61, 115, 172, 173, 185

Umbria(n), 11–12, 14, 21, 32, 108

Varro, 10, 12–13

war: and animals, 44; and conditions of production of Roman comedy, 14, 15–19, 29, 37, 103, 160, 188, 192, 253, 256; as source of Greek loanwords, 33. *See also* army; soldiers
wet nurses, 29, 252, 268
Williams, Craig, 20, 29, 120
Williams, Gordon, 102
Wilson, Flip, 36
Wodehouse, P. G., 41, 49
women, 16, 28; as actors, 20–21, 119, 120; in the audience, 16, 27–29, 252; as commodities in Plautus, 27–28, 58; and cooking, 256; and depilation, 265; divided by class, 28; dowry of, 171; favorite swear-word of, 33; genital humor about, 256; as mothers, 16, 29, 269; as musicians, 271; names of, 41–42, 63, 175; old, 27, 28, 58, 62, 167, 186; roles for, 19, 27, 28, 58, 112, 119, 120; sexuality of, 16; as witches, 169; as wives, 16, 27, 28, 46, 178; as writers, 28. *See also* prostitution; slaves, female
Woytek, Erich, 7, 117, 181
Wright, John, 10, 22, 27, 63, 257
writers. *See* playwrights

xenophobia, 3, 101, 113. *See also* Orientalism

Designer:	Barbara Jellow
Text:	10/14 Adobe Garamond
Display:	Akzidenz Grotesk Condensed
Cartographer:	Bill Nelson
Compositor, printer, and binder:	Sheridan Books, Inc.